Leftist Internationalisms

New Approaches to International History

Series Editor: Thomas Zeiler, Professor of American Diplomatic History, University of Colorado Boulder, USA

Series Editorial Board:
Anthony Adamthwaite, University of California at Berkeley (USA)
Kathleen Burk, University College London (UK)
Louis Clerc, University of Turku (Finland)
Petra Goedde, Temple University (USA)
Francine McKenzie, University of Western Ontario (Canada)
Lien-Hang Nguyen, University of Kentucky (USA)
Jason Parker, Texas A&M University (USA)
Glenda Sluga, University of Sydney (Australia)

New Approaches to International History covers international history during the modern period and across the globe. The series incorporates new developments in the field, such as the cultural turn and transnationalism, as well as the classical high politics of state-centric policymaking and diplomatic relations. Written with upper-level undergraduate and postgraduate students in mind, texts in the series provide an accessible overview of international diplomatic and transnational issues, events and actors.

Published:
Decolonization and the Cold War, Leslie James and Elisabeth Leake (2015)
Cold War Summits, Chris Tudda (2015)
The United Nations in International History, Amy Sayward (2017)
Latin American Nationalism, James F. Siekmeier (2017)
The History of United States Cultural Diplomacy, Michael L. Krenn (2017)
International Cooperation in the Early 20th Century, Daniel Gorman (2017)
Women and Gender in International History, Karen Garner (2018)
International Development, Corinna Unger (2018)

The Environment and International History, Scott Kaufman (2018)
Scandinavia and the Great Powers in the First World War, Michael Jonas (2019)
Canada and the World since 1867, Asa McKercher (2019)
The First Age of Industrial Globalization, Maartje Abbenhuis and Gordon Morrell (2019)
Europe's Cold War Relations, Federico Romero, Kiran Klaus Patel, Ulrich Krotz (2019)
United States Relations with China and Iran, Osamah F. Khalil (2019)
Public Opinion and Twentieth-Century Diplomacy, Daniel Hucker (2020)
Globalizing the US Presidency, Cyrus Schayegh (2020)
The International LGBT Rights Movement, Laura Belmonte (2021)
Global War, Global Catastrophe, Maartje Abbenhuis and Ismee Tames (2021)
America's Road to Empire: Foreign Policy from Independence to World War One, Piero Gleijeses (2021)
Militarization and the American Century, (2022)
Leftist Internationalisms: A Transnational Political History, Michele Di Donato and Mathieu Fulla (2022)

Forthcoming:
Reconstructing the Postwar World, Francine McKenzie
China and the United States since 1949, Elizabeth Ingleson

Leftist Internationalisms

A Transnational Political History

Edited by
Michele Di Donato and Mathieu Fulla

BLOOMSBURY ACADEMIC
LONDON • NEW YORK • OXFORD • NEW DELHI • SYDNEY

BLOOMSBURY ACADEMIC
Bloomsbury Publishing Plc
50 Bedford Square, London, WC1B 3DP, UK
1385 Broadway, New York, NY 10018, USA
29 Earlsfort Terrace, Dublin 2, Ireland

BLOOMSBURY, BLOOMSBURY ACADEMIC and the Diana logo
are trademarks of Bloomsbury Publishing Plc

First published in Great Britain 2023
Paperback edition published 2024

Copyright © Michele Di Donato and Mathieu Fulla, 2023

Michele Di Donato and Mathieu Fulla have asserted their right under the Copyright, Designs and Patents Act, 1988, to be identified as Editors of this work.

For legal purposes the Acknowledgements on p. xiv constitute an extension of this copyright page.

Series design by Catherine Wood.
Cover image © Photo 12 / Alamy Stock Photo.

All rights reserved. No part of this publication may be reproduced or transmitted in any form or by any means, electronic or mechanical, including photocopying, recording, or any information storage or retrieval system, without prior permission in writing from the publishers.

Bloomsbury Publishing Plc does not have any control over, or responsibility for, any third-party websites referred to or in this book. All internet addresses given in this book were correct at the time of going to press. The author and publisher regret any inconvenience caused if addresses have changed or sites have ceased to exist, but can accept no responsibility for any such changes.

A catalogue record for this book is available from the British Library.

A catalog record for this book is available from the Library of Congress.

ISBN: HB: 978-1-3502-4791-8
PB: 978-1-3502-4794-9
ePDF: 978-1-3502-4792-5
eBook: 978-1-3502-4793-2

Series: New Approaches to International History

Typeset by Integra Software Services Pvt. Ltd.

To find out more about our authors and books visit www.bloomsbury.com and sign up for our newsletters.

Contents

List of figures ... ix
List of contributors ... x
Acknowledgements ... xiv

Introduction: Leftist internationalisms in the history of the twentieth century *Michele Di Donato and Mathieu Fulla* ... 1

Part One Reinventing left-wing internationalisms in a changing world

1. Transnational socialism entering a nation-state: From Ottoman to Greek socialism, 1912–18 *Kostis Karpozilos* ... 25
2. A transatlantic connector: Bjarne Braatøy in the intersections of intelligence and social democracy, 1923–57 *Nik. Brandal and Eirik Wig Sundvall* ... 39
3. Social democracy and anti-communism in Cold War Asia: The Japan Socialist Party's role in the Asian Socialist Conference in the 1950s *Yutaka Kanda* ... 53
4. Italian communism and the 'rediscovery' of the Third World, 1956–64 *Silvio Pons* ... 67
5. Proletarian internationalism and Third World liberation in the life and politics of South African communist Dr Yusuf M. Dadoo *Arianna Lissoni* ... 81
6. A discreet alternative: The Socialist International's ill-fated battle for 'global Keynesianism' and a New International Economic Order in the 1980s *Mathieu Fulla* ... 97

Part Two When internationalisms meet: Conflicts and cross-fertilizations

7. 'This is the true international of which Moscow only dreams': Contacts, hybridizations and ambiguities in the encounter between socialist and liberal internationalism at the International Labor Office in the 1920s *Adeline Blaszkiewicz* ... 115
8. The Eastern Bloc countries and the question of development at the UN in the 1960s and 1970s *Michel Christian* ... 129

9   Sandinista internationalism: The Nicaraguan revolution and the global
    Cold War *Mateo Jarquín*   143
10 The Socialist International and human rights *Michele Di Donato*   159
11 Solidarity struggles: Transnational feminisms and Cold War lefts in the
    Global South *Jocelyn Olcott*   173

Part Three Grassroots internationalisms, informal networks and new mobilizations

12 The left and the international arena: The Rosenberg case *Phillip Deery* 191
13 The networks of left-wing town planning in Mediterranean Europe
    (1960s–early 1980s) *Céline Vaz*   205
14 An 'Ecological Internationale'? Nuclear energy opponents in Western
    Europe, 1975–80 *Andrew S. Tompkins*   219
15 Analysing informal and indirect participation to transnational
    activist networks: The case of anti-authoritarian feminists in Berlin
    and Montreal *Emeline Fourment*   233

Selected bibliography   248
Index   255

Figures

2.1	Portrait of Foreign Policy Advisor of the SPD Party Board, Bjarne Braatøy. Image courtesy of J.H. Darchinger/Friedrich-Ebert-Stiftung	43
2.2	Bjarne Braatøy, SPD leader Erich Ollenhauer and Minister of Foreign Affairs of Norway Halvard M. Lange in the mid-1950s. Image courtesy of AdsD/FES	50
5.1	Photograph of Dr Yusuf M. Dadoo speaking at the 25th Congress of the CPSU in 1976. Image courtesy of Roshan Dadoo	88
6.1	'The Global Challenge' cover of *Socialist Affairs* no. 4, 1985. Image courtesy of Collection l'OURS/OURS Historical Archives	108
7.1	14 July 1920, Edgar Milhaud on train platform with Albert Thomas, 1st ILO Director. Image courtesy of Archives Historiques de l'OIT/ILO Historical Archives	120
12.1	Demonstration at the Place de la Nation, Paris, to support Julius and Ethel Rosenberg. Photo by Dominique BERRETTY/Gamma-Rapho via Getty Images	199
13.1	A participatory urban planning experience in the Meseta de Orcasitas neighbourhood in Madrid, mid-1970s. Image courtesy of AV de Orcasitas-Archivo FRAVM	211
15.1	Cover of the third issue of RAZZ, an anti-authoritarian newspaper from Hanover, June 1989; courtesy of author's personal archive	239

Contributors

Adeline Blaszkiewicz is Associate Researcher at the Centre d'histoire sociale des mondes contemporains (University Paris 1 Panthéon-Sorbonne). She holds a doctorate in history from the University Paris 1 Panthéon-Sorbonne. Her research focuses on the history of the third French republic, international organizations, French socialism and socialist internationalism. She is the author of *Albert Thomas, le socialisme en guerre (1914-1918)*, Presses Universitaires de Rennes, 2016 and '"Mieux vaudrait après tout se perdre avec Lénine que de se sauver avec Albert Thomas' Construire une voie révolutionnaire face au socialisme réformiste dans les années 1920", *Le Mouvement social*, 2020/1 n°271, juillet-septembre 2020, 41–58.

Nik. Brandal is Associate Professor at Oslo New University College, Department of Political Science and International Relations in Oslo, Norway. Brandal's main research has been on political radicalization, social democracy and the Nordic Model. Among his publications are Social Democracy in the 21st Century (Emerald Publishing 2021, ed. w/ Ö. Bratberg & D.E. Thorsen); 'Between Communitarianism and Individualism: The Nordic Way of Doing Politics' (Routledge 2018, w/ D.E. Thorsen in Witoszek & Midtun, eds., *Sustainable Modernity*); Det norske demokratiet og dets fiender [Norwegian Democracy & It's Enemies] (Dreyer 2018, w/ Ö. Sörensen); 'Small-state Scandinavia: Social Investment or Social Democracy?' (Edward Elgar Publishing 2015, w/ Ö. Bratberg in Baldersheim & Keating, eds., *Small States in the Modern World*); and *The Nordic Model of Social Democracy* (Palgrave Macmillan 2013, w/ Ö. Bratberg & D.E. Thorsen), and Ved utopiens slutt: Den vestlege maoismen [Ending Utopia: Maoism in the Western World] (Dreyer 2013 in Sörensen, Hagtvet & Brandal, eds., *Venstreekstremisme: Ideer og bevegelser*).

Michel Christian is Researcher at the University of Geneva. His researches extensively dealt with the social history of the Communist parties in power in the Eastern Bloc countries (the GDR and Czechoslovakia). He is now doing research on the question of development, early childhood education and care, using international organizations as a field of observation. He recently published *Camarades ou apparatchiks ? Les communistes en RDA et en Tchécoslovaquie (1945–1989)* (2016) and with S. Kott and O. Matejka, *Planning in the Cold War. Competition, Cooperation, Circulations* (2018); 'Un printemps des crèches à l'Est ? Le cas de la RDA', *Annales de démographie historique*, Nr. 1, 2019, S.185–215.

Phillip Deery is Emeritus Professor of History at Victoria University, Melbourne. He has authored more than 100 scholarly publications in the fields of Cold War studies, labour movement history, and intelligence and security studies. He is the author or co-author of six books, including *Red Apple: Communism and McCarthyism in Cold War New York* (New York: Fordham University Press, 2014), *The Age of McCarthyism: A Brief History with Documents*, 3rd edition (Boston: Bedford/St. Martin's, 2016) and *Spies and Sparrows: ASIO and the Cold War* (Melbourne: Melbourne University Press, 2022).

Michele Di Donato is Assistant Professor of Contemporary History at the University of Pisa, Italy. His research and publications focus on the international history of the European Left, the Cold War and late twentieth-century globalization. Among his publications: 'Landslides, Shocks, and New Global Rules: The US and Western Europe in the New International History of the 1970s', *Journal of Contemporary History*, 55:1 (2020), 182–205; 'Reform Communism' (co-authored with Silvio Pons), in Juliane Fürst, Silvio Pons and Mark Selden, eds., *The Cambridge History of Communism*, vol. III (Cambridge: Cambridge University Press, 2017), 178–202; 'The Cold War and Socialist Identity. The Socialist International and the Italian "Communist Question" in the 1970s', *Contemporary European History* 24:2 (2015): 193–211; *I comunisti italiani e la sinistra europea. Il PCI e i rapporti con le socialdemocrazie (1964–1984)* (Rome: Carocci, 2015).

Emeline Fourment is Assistant Professor in Political Science at the Université de Rouen Normandie (France). Her research deals with women's movements, health movements, gender-based violence and critical criminology in comparative perspective (Germany, Québec, France). Her doctoral dissertation examined various appropriations of feminist theories (materialist, queer or intersectional) in anti-authoritarian communities in Berlin and Montreal. She is now working on justice practices that are developed in feminist and antiracist social movements as alternatives to criminal justice. She is also co-coordinator of the international French-speaking research network VisaGe, which focuses on gender-based violence. Among her publications: "Militantismes libertaire et féministe face aux violences sexuelles", *Sociétés Contemporaines* (December 2017); "Une dinosaure chercheuse dans le milieu libertaire allemand", *Bulletins de méthodologie sociologique* (July 2019); "L'Université produit-elle des féministes libertaires? Imbrications et tensions entre socialisation universitaire et socialisation militante", *Revue Française de Science Politique* (September 2022).

Mathieu Fulla is a Research fellow at the Center for History at Sciences Po (Paris). His main research areas are the history of the West European Labour Movement and its relationship with capitalism and the state from 1945 to the present. He has published *Les socialistes français et l'économie (1944–1981),* Paris: Presses de Sciences Po (2016), and co-edited with Marc Lazar *European Socialists and the State in the Twentieth and Twenty-First Centuries*, Palgrave (2020). Additionally, he has written about French socialism in media outlets such as *Le Monde* and *The Conversation*.

Mateo Jarquín is Assistant Professor of History at Chapman University in Southern California. His scholarship asks how twentieth-century revolutions in the so-called Third World have framed global debates about development, democratization and international relations. His forthcoming book examines the rise and fall of Nicaragua's Sandinista Revolution (1979–90) through a global and Latin American lens. Publications arising from this research agenda include articles in *Cold War History* and *The Americas: A Quarterly Review of Latin American History*. Additionally, he has written about contemporary Central American politics in media outlets such as *The New York Times*, *Axios* and *The Washington Post*.

Yutaka Kanda is Professor of Japanese International History at Niigata University in Japan. His research interests include Japan's Cold War diplomacy with the Sino-Soviet bloc and the foreign policy of the moderate left in post-war Japan. He is the author of *Japan's Cold War Policy and China: Two Perceptions of Order, 1960–1972* (Routledge, 2020) and 'The Transformation of a Manchukuo Imperial Bureaucrat to Postwar Supporter of the Yoshida Doctrine: The Case of Shiina Etsusaburō' in Barak Kushner and Sherzod Muminov, eds., *The Dismantling of Japan's Empire in East Asia: Deimperialization, Postwar Legitimation and Imperial Afterlife* (Routledge, 2017).

Kostis Karpozilos is the director of the Contemporary Social History Archives (ASKI-Athens, Greece). His forthcoming book (*Out of Bounds: A Transnational History of Greek Communism*) addresses the interplay of diasporic communities, transnational networks and experiences of displacement in the development of the Greek communist movement. He is the author of *Red America: Greek Communists in the United States, 1920–1950* (Crete University Press, 2017; Berghahn Books, 2023) and (co-authored with Dimitris Christopoulos) *10+1 Questions and Answers on the Macedonian Question*, Rosa Luxemburg Stiftung, 2018. Kostis was a postdoctoral fellow at Columbia University, Princeton University and the Oxford University and currently teaches at Panteion University in Athens. He received his PhD at the University of Crete (2010) and his MA at Sheffield University (2004).

Arianna Lissoni is Researcher at the History Workshop at the University of the Witwatersrand in Johannesburg and part of the 'Global Soldiers in the Cold War: Making Southern African Liberation Armies' project. She has co-edited the books: *One Hundred Years of the ANC: Debating Liberation Histories Today* (2012), *The ANC between Home and Exile: Reflections on the Anti-Apartheid Struggle in Italy and Southern Africa* (2015) and *New Histories of South Africa's Apartheid Era Bantustans* (2017), and co-authored *Khongolose: A Short History of the ANC in the North West Province from 1909* (2016).

Jocelyn Olcott is Professor of History, International Comparative Studies, and Gender, Sexuality, and Feminist Studies at Duke University. She is the author of *Revolutionary Women in Postrevolutionary Mexico* (Duke University Press, 2005) and *International Women's Year: The Greatest Consciousness-Raising Event in History* (Oxford University Press, 2017) as well as co-editor with Mary Kay Vaughan and Gabriela Cano of *Sex in Revolution: Gender, Politics, and Power in Modern Mexico* (Duke University Press, 2006; in translation with Fondo de Cultura Económica, 2009). She has published articles in *Journal of Women's History*, *Journal of Contemporary*

History, *Hispanic American Historical Review*, *Gender & History*, and *International Labor and Working-Class History* and served as a senior editor of the *Hispanic American Historical Review*.

Silvio Pons is Professor of Contemporary History at the Scuola Normale Superiore of Pisa. He is the President of the Gramsci Foundation in Rome. He has extensively written on the Cold War, the Soviet Union, European Communism and the global history of Communism. His main publications include *Stalin and the Inevitable War* (Frank Cass 2002) and *The Global Revolution. A History of International Communism* (Oxford University Press 2014). He is the General Editor of the *Cambridge History of Communism* (Cambridge University Press 2017).

Eirik Wig Sundvall is Senior Lecturer in modern international and transnational history at the University of Oslo. Sundvall has researched labour history from the First World War to the Cold War, with emphasis on transnational ideological influence, network entanglements and propaganda. He defended his doctoral thesis *Border Crossing Socialism: Transnational Studies of the Norwegian Labour Movement, 1920–1955* in January 2020. His publications include "Propaganda 'Worth an Army': The Norwegian Labour Party, Haakon Lie and the transnational dissemination of Cold War propaganda, 1945–55" (*The International History Review*, 2019), and the book *Gerhardsens valg* (Gyldendal, 2016) on the Norwegian Labour Party's relations with Soviet Russia from 1917 to 1949.

Andrew S. Tompkins is the author of *Better Active than Radioactive! Anti-Nuclear Protest in 1970s France and West Germany* (Oxford University Press, 2016). He has worked as Lecturer in Modern European History at the University of Sheffield and as a researcher in Global History at the Universität Erfurt. He lives in Berlin.

Céline Vaz is Associate Professor of Contemporary History at Université Polytechnique Hauts-de-France (UPHF, Valenciennes). She is a specialist in French and Spanish urban history, in urban social movements and the circulation of urban knowledges. Among her publications: 'Villes espagnoles et austérité: une histoire de longue durée', *Annales de géographie* (2019/3); 'Les mobilisations d'associations de quartier à Madrid à la fin du franquisme', in *La ville est à nous! Aménagement urbain et mobilisations sociales depuis le Moyen Age* (Presses uniiversitaires de la Sorbonne, 2018); 'Los arquitectos a finales del franquismo, entre crisis profesional y compromiso político-social', *Segle XX. Revista catalana d'història* (2017).

Acknowledgements

Collective volumes reflect collective efforts, and we believe that this is particularly true of this book. Our first acknowledgement goes to the fantastic team of authors that has made this book possible. Throughout the project, their input and feedback have been crucial to us, and turned our responsibility as editors into an exciting opportunity for intellectual exchange and learning.

We owe special thanks to Bloomsbury. The editor of the *New Approaches to International History* series, Tom Zeiler, enthusiastically supported our project and provided us with precious suggestions for improving and refining it. Maddie Holder and Abigail Lane have been extremely supportive and understanding editors. We are also very grateful to the anonymous reviewers who examined the book proposal and the manuscript for their useful comments.

This book is the outcome of a research endeavour that began in 2017 with the launching of the monthly seminar *Les gauches et l'international/The Left and the International Arena* at the Centre for History at Sciences Po, in Paris. We organized the seminar together with Bruno Settis after discussing the idea with several colleagues and friends, including Massimo Asta, Judith Bonnin and Thomas Maineult. We thank them all for their suggestions and their friendship. The seminar received support from the European Union's Horizon 2020 research and innovation programme under the Marie Skłodowska-Curie grant agreement No 704507, and from the Jean Jaurès Foundation. We would like to extend our warmest thanks to Thierry Merel, the director of the Foundation's History and Archive division, who has been a crucial interlocutor and supporter of the project. At Sciences Po, Mario Del Pero and Marc Lazar have been invaluable sources of inspiration and advice. Years of exchanges with them have decisively contributed to shaping our understanding of international history and of the history of the Left. Most important of all, we would like to thank all the speakers who intervened throughout the two years of the seminar: this book would not exist without them.

We had the opportunity to discuss our ideas and projects for this book during seminars held at the Jean Jaurès Foundation, with Jean Numa Ducange and Elisa Marcobelli, and at the Marc Bloch Centre in Berlin, thanks to an invitation by Silke Mende and Jakob Vogel. Katherine Marino, David Priestland and Stephen Whitefield gave us generous advice as we were preparing the book proposal. Last but not least, very special thanks to Melek Fırat Altay for Nâzım Hikmet.

Introduction: Leftist internationalisms in the history of the twentieth century

Michele Di Donato and Mathieu Fulla

In February 1939, the Turkish poet Nâzım Hikmet had already spent more than a year in prison since his last incarceration. From his detention site in Istanbul, he wrote for his wife, Piraye, poems that mixed, in his characteristic style, romantic and political themes:

> I would have liked to travel the world
> and see the fish, fruits and stars I haven't seen.
> However I
> made my European journey only in writings and pictures.
> In my whole life
> I have never received a single letter
>   with its blue stamp cancelled in Asia.
> Me and our neighbourhood grocer
> We are both mightily unknown in America.
> And yet,
> from China to Spain, from the Cape of Good Hope to Alaska
> in every nautical mile, in every kilometre I have friends and enemies.
> Friends that we have not even met once
> yet we can die for the same bread, the same freedom, the same longing.
> Enemies who thirst for my blood,
>   whose blood I thirst for.
> My strength:
> I am not alone in this big world.
> The world and its people are no secret in my heart
>   no enigma in my science.
> I joined my rank
>   openly and calmly
>   in the great struggle.

And outside of this rank
> you and the earth
>> do not suffice for me.
Even if you are breathtakingly beautiful
> and so is the warm earth.¹

A follower of Mustafa Kemal in his youth, in the early 1920s Hikmet had shifted his ideological allegiances from nationalism to Marxism, like many around the world in the generation that came of age in the aftermath of the First World War.² At the age of twenty, he travelled to the Soviet Union, where he attended the Communist University for the Toilers of the East and got introduced to the local cultural and artistic scene.³ Upon his return to Turkey in 1924, he set out to marry his political activism and poetry. The first writer to introduce the language of modern politics into Turkish verse, he resorted to a new, modernist style that garnered a large number of admirers from within and outside the communist movement. Already in 1925, however, he was sentenced to fifteen years in prison because of his political activities, and fled to the Soviet Union. Amnestied in 1926, in 1928 he was arrested as he was illegally crossing the border to re-enter Turkey. He spent the following ten years under police surveillance and in and out of prison, until, in 1938, he was condemned to twenty-eight years for allegedly inciting the armed forces to revolt. He would remain in jail until 1950.⁴ His liberation had become an international *cause célèbre*, championed by a committee led by Tristan Tzara and supported by the likes of Albert Camus, Jean-Paul Sartre, Simone de Beauvoir and Pablo Picasso. As pressure from the Turkish authorities continued even after he left prison, Hikmet fled the country once again in 1951, seeking refuge in the Soviet bloc. Living in the USSR until his death in 1963, he went through his own ambiguous and tormented reckoning with Soviet power and the crimes of the Stalin era. He also managed to make many of the journeys he was dreaming of in the poem he had written in the Istanbul prison. He travelled Asia, Africa and the Caribbean; became a founding member of the writers' division of the Afro-Asian People's Solidarity Organisation; wrote 'lyric reportages' from Cuba and Tanganyika; and established relations with many anti-colonial activists.⁵

The world depicted in Nâzım Hikmet's poem, and the very life experiences of the author, epitomize internationalist imageries, networks and practices that were quintessential to the political cultures of the Left. Internationalism informed

---

1. Nâzım Hikmet, 'Dünya, Dostlarım, Düşmanlarım, Sen ve Toprak', in *Tüm Eserleri 4 – Şiirler 4* (Istanbul: Cem Yayınevi, 1978), 111–12. Throughout the book, translations into English are by the authors (unless otherwise stated).
2. Erez Manela, *The Wilsonian Moment: Self-Determination and the International Origins of Anticolonial Nationalism* (Oxford and New York: Oxford University Press, 2007).
3. James H. Meyer, 'Children of Trans-Empire: Nâzım Hikmet and the First Generation of Turkish Students at Moscow's Communist University of the East', *Journal of the Ottoman and Turkish Studies Association* 5, no. 2 (2018): 195–218.
4. Saime Göksu and Edward Timms, *Romantic Communist: The Life and Work of Nazım Hikmet* (London: Hurst & Co., 1999), 32–137.
5. Gül Bilge Han, 'Nazım Hikmet's Afro-Asian Solidarities', *Safundi* 19, no. 3 (2018): 284–305.

communist, socialist and left-wing organizations, but also the mindset and biography of many individuals. It created new bonds among people, transcending national borders, but was far from a Panglossian cosmopolitanism: the world it described and inhabited was marked by conflict. Internationalism came in many forms, from grassroots mobilizations to institutionalized structures. And it interacted with nation-states, national interests, international institutions. Starting from the nineteenth century, and all the more so since the Bolshevik revolution, different strands of left-wing political culture created each their own international organizations and transnational networks – most often in competition with one another. And they often chose different sides in the international disputes and struggles of their epoch – the First World War, decolonization, the Cold War. Internationalism was not the exclusive prerogative of the Left, nor was it consistently the dominant aspect of its political cultures. Important as they were, internationalist practices always suffered from serious limitations – from the lack of financial and organizational means to their sometimes difficult reconciliation with the priorities of national politics. Nevertheless, it would be impossible to understand the history of the Left without making reference to internationalism. Likewise, any history of twentieth-century internationalism that chose to disregard the Left would be an incomplete one. The essays in this collection will try to bring together different narratives in order to promote a new understanding of the internationalisms of the Left, and of their significance to the history of the twentieth century.

Scholarship on internationalism has been growing steadily in the last two decades. A long-neglected theme, internationalism has been re-examined in the context of the global and transnational turns in historiography. As students of international history grappled with 'an increasingly global world, in which trans-border flows challenged the dominance of the nation-state both as an empirical phenomenon and as an explanatory framework for scholarship', their interest grew for international organizations and transnational encounters and entanglements.[6] Recent studies have significantly broadened our understanding of late nineteenth- and twentieth-century internationalisms, uncovering the realist and idealist motives, the networks and the different practices of a wide variety of actors that engaged with 'international cooperation and internationalising ambitions'.[7]

---

[6] Kiran Klaus Patel, 'An Emperor without Clothes? The Debate about Transnational History Twenty-five Years On', *Histoire@Politique*, n° 26 (2015): 2. On global and transnational history, see Akira Iriye, *Global and Transnational History: The Past, Present, and Future* (Basingstoke: Palgrave, 2003). Prominent examples of this new history of internationalism are: Mark Mazower, *Governing the World: The History of an Idea, 1815 to the Present* (New York: Penguin, 2013); Glenda Sluga, *Internationalism in the Age of Nationalism* (Philadelphia: University of Pennsylvania Press, 2013); Glenda Sluga and Patricia Clavin (eds.), *Internationalisms: A Twentieth-Century History* (Cambridge: Cambridge University Press, 2017); Sandrine Kott, *Organiser le monde: une autre histoire de la guerre froide* (Paris: Seuil, 2021).
[7] See the presentation of the Bloomsbury book series 'Histories of Internationalism', edited by David Brydan and Jessica Reinisch, https://www.bloomsbury.com/us/series/histories-of-internationalism (last accessed 10 January 2022).

The last wave of historiography on internationalism, however, has had a complicated relationship with socialist, communist and other left-wing organizations. Some authors have preferred to disregard these traditions in order to highlight different strands of internationalist thought and action. In the introduction to their influential collection *Internationalisms*, for instance, Glenda Sluga and Patricia Clavin make explicit their intention to 'counter the reductive definitions of internationalism as only a communist idea, at times still prevalent in the historiography of the twentieth century'.[8] In other cases, socialist, and especially communist internationalism, have been dismissed because of their proximity to state actors. Epitomizing a widespread tendency, Akira Iriye argued in his trail-blazing book on international organizations that the Comintern 'was much more a national than an international body, expressing the interests and objectives of the Soviet Union, and its activities, therefore, were more part of the story of inter-state affairs than of international organizations'.[9] Finally, a broader tendency seems to be at play. As much of the new global and transnational history emerged in direct opposition to 'traditional' political and diplomatic history, some of its practitioners display a sort of engrained mistrust of studies on political parties and organizations, preferring to focus on cultural and social forms of transnational entanglement instead.[10]

As many have pointed out, this focus was sometimes paired with an inclination to depict transnational connections as inherently progressive in nature, as part of a whiggish narrative of globalization as an inexorable and benign process of cosmopolitan unification of the world.[11] This interpretation also entailed, as a frequent by-product, the idea that the increasing relevance of transnational forces made the nation-state less and less important as a historical actor, and hence as an object of study. Such views have been criticized by historians who insist on the continuing relevance of the state, and on the need to appreciate the entanglements of state power and cross-border flows as constitutive elements of the modern era.[12] By the same token, recent research has insisted on the importance of non-liberal traditions of internationalism, and has reminded that the liberal international order has been repeatedly challenged both from the left and from the right.[13] As Jessica Reinisch put it, treating socialist and communist projects as 'not part of the "real" transnationalism family' could lead to sidelining 'important chapters of the history of internationalism'.[14]

---

[8] Sluga, and Clavin, 'Rethinking the History of Internationalism', in *Internationalisms*, 12.
[9] Akira Iriye, *Global Community. The Role of International Organizations in the Making of the Contemporary World* (Berkeley: University of California Press, 2002), 31.
[10] This trend was noted already by Patricia Clavin, 'Defining Transnationalism', *Contemporary European History* 14, no. 4 (2005): 421–39, 422.
[11] See Jeremy Adelman, 'What Is Global History Now?', *Aeon Magazine*, 2 March 2017, https://aeon.co/essays/is-global-history-still-possible-or-has-it-had-its-moment (last accessed 23 May 2022); Frederick Cooper, 'Le concept de mondialisation sert-il à quelque chose? Un point de vue d'historien', *Critique internationale* 10, no. 1 (2001): 101–24.
[12] For a concise presentation of this argument, see David Reynolds, 'Turn, Turn, Turn', *Ricerche di Storia Politica* 19, no. 3 (2016): 265–8.
[13] See the special issues 'Agents of Internationalism', *Contemporary European History* 25, no. 2 (2016), ed. Jessica Reinisch; 'The Dark Side of Transnationalism', *Journal of Contemporary History* 51, no. 1 (2016), eds. Kiran Klaus Patel and Sven Reichardt; 'Liberal and Illiberal Internationalisms', *Journal of World History* 31, no. 1 (2020), eds. Philippa Hetherington and Glenda Sluga.
[14] Jessica Reinisch, 'Introduction: Agents of Internationalism', *Contemporary European History* 25, no. 2 (2016): 195–205, 197.

A rich body of work has thus emerged in recent years that examines the history of left-wing internationalism in light of the global and transnational turns: not to re-affirm some sort of primacy of 'red' internationalism, but to embed the latter in the multifaceted history of the modern international projects and practices. 'Communism is transnational, but we needed the perspective of transnational history to be able to think about it as such', Sabine Dullin and Brigitte Studer eloquently remarked.[15] By embedding left-wing internationalism in this broader context, it is possible to overcome old binaries and foreground the participation of left-wing forces to the processes that shaped the globalization of politics during the twentieth century. If interaction with national realities and state power is considered as a structural condition of modern internationalism, issues such as the centrality of the Soviet Union to international communism, or the nationalization of democratic socialist parties, can be taken into account as aspects that defined the specificities of the international engagement of these political cultures, rather than as factors that should discourage enquiry.[16] This process of historicization, one should add, is also facilitated by the collapse of communism as a global alternative, at least in its twentieth-century form: if one leaves Cold War dichotomies behind, left-wing internationalism can be more easily 'explored in ways that generate less heat and more light'.[17]

A question that may arise is whether taking this comprehensive approach may entail the risk of watering down the distinctiveness of 'red' internationalism. In a recent debate on inter-war democratic socialism, for instance, Talbot Imlay has warned against enfolding socialist internationalism into liberal internationalism, and insisted instead on the exclusive nature of transnational socialist relations: the fact that socialists shared some objectives with liberal internationalists and co-operated with international institutions such as the League of Nations, he argued, did not lessen the particularity of their approach, and should not lead to considering their international activity a 'variant of liberal internationalism'.[18] In putting together this

---

[15] Sabine Dullin and Brigitte Studer, 'Communism + Transnational: The Rediscovered Equation of Internationalism in the Comintern Years', *Twentieth-century Communism*, no. 14 (2018): 66–95.

[16] We shall limit ourselves to mentioning a small number of particularly significant works. On communism, see especially the three-volume *Cambridge History of Communism*, general editor Silvio Pons (Cambridge: Cambridge University Press, 2017). See also David Priestland, *The Red Flag: A History of Communism* (New York: Grove Press, 2009); Silvio Pons, *The Global Revolution: A History of International Communism 1917-1991* (Oxford: Oxford University Press, 2014); Brigitte Studer, *The Transnational World of the Cominternians* (Basingstoke: Palgrave Macmillan, 2015). On democratic socialism: Talbot C. Imlay, *The Practice of Socialist Internationalism: European Socialist and International Politics, 1914-1960* (Oxford: Oxford University Press, 2018); Christian Salm, *Transnational Socialist Networks in the 1970s: European Community Development Aid and Southern Enlargement* (Basingstoke: Palgrave Macmillan, 2016); Ettore Costa, *The Labour Party, Denis Healey and the International Socialist Movement. Rebuilding the Socialist International during the Cold War, 1945-1951* (Basingstoke: Palgrave Macmillan, 2018).

[17] Oleksa Drachewych and Ian McKay, 'Left Transnationalism? The Communist International, the National, Colonial, and Racial Questions, and the Strengths and Limitations of the "Moscow Rules" Paradigm', in *Left Transnationalism: The Communist International and the National, Colonial, and Racial Questions*, ed. Oleksa Drachewych and Ian McKay (Montreal & Kingston: McGill-Queen's University Press, 2019), 4.

[18] Imlay, *The Practice of Socialist Internationalism*, 12–13. The target of Imlay's criticism was Daniel Laqua, 'Democratic Politics and the League of Nations: The Labour and Socialist International as Protagonist of Interwar Internationalism', *Contemporary European History* 24, no. 2 (2015): 175–92.

collection, our approach has been different. We have chosen to lay stress precisely on the interactions and hybridizations with different international projects and forces that contributed to shaping and transforming left-wing internationalist practices over the decades. From the general principle that these practices can only be understood as part of the international history in which they developed, we derive a preference for a broad definition of left-wing internationalism and for an inclusive perspective aimed at embedding the Left in a more comprehensive picture of international entanglements and influences. From Imlay, however, we borrow – and adapt to a wider scope, focusing not only on socialist parties but on a larger variety of left-wing actors – the idea of considering internationalism as a 'practice', that is, a concrete effort at transnational cooperation and engagement, rather than a theory or an abstract set of values. Throughout the book, 'internationalism' is thus used as a functional umbrella definition for a vast array of practices of transnational political organizing, cooperation and solidarity; cross-border circulation of political actors, information, ideas and experiences; engagement with international organizations and internationalizing initiatives. For left-wing actors, it should be noted, these practices also involve a significant symbolic dimension, epitomizing allegiance to specific political cultures and transnational 'imagined communities'.[19]

The definitions of 'Left' and 'left-wing internationalism' are indeed capacious and contested ones, and as such they require to be contextualized. In his monumental study on the Left and democracy, Geoff Eley contended that for most of the last century the Left 'was defined by socialist and communist parties, who, despite their mutual antipathies, also acknowledged a common tradition going back to the late nineteenth century'. If, however, 'socialism was always the core of the Left' (at least from around the 1860s onwards), the Left was also 'always larger than socialism'. Autonomous traditions existed alongside the main socialist organizations, and, especially in the last quarter of the twentieth century, 'a new feminism, and a proliferating ferment of new social movements, identity-based activism, and alternative political scenes' started exerting increasing influence. This ascending trend was in contrast with the decline of the 'Old Lefts', which were hit by the breakdown of the socio-economic structure and system of politics in which they had prospered.[20]

Such a broad definition undoubtedly ends up lumping together under the same label very different actors and phenomena, and, as such, has been subject to multiple criticisms – by those who insist on the irreconcilable distance between communism and democratic socialism, to start with.[21] Laying stress on the importance of common

---

[19] For a discussion, see Soyang Park, 'Internationalisms', in *The Palgrave Dictionary of Transnational History*, ed. Akira Iriye and Pierre-Yves Saunier (Basingstoke: Palgrave, 2009), 586–90.
[20] Geoff Eley, *Forging Democracy. The History of the Left in Europe, 1850–2000* (Oxford: Oxford University Press, 2002), 5–8.
[21] This is for instance a crucial theme in the late works of Tony Judt: see Tony Judt, *Reappraisals: Reflections on the Forgotten 20th Century* (London: Vintage, 2010); Timothy Snyder and Tony Judt, *Thinking the Twentieth Century* (New York: Penguin, 2013).

heritages dating back to the nineteenth century, however, appears particularly appropriate when examining left-wing internationalism.

The Left, in its many currents, was indeed internationalist from its commencements in the tumultuous politics of revolutionary France.[22] Revolution quickly became a central idea of political thought and served 'as a yardstick that for the first time divided Left and Right'.[23] After the Congress of Vienna, solidarity beyond the re-established European borders was a prerogative of several strands of radical thought advocating democracy and the establishment of universal (male) suffrage. Democratic nationalists such as Giuseppe Mazzini were active in the transnational space of exile politics and supported the creation of an international society of independent, democratic nation-states, which was to emerge through popular uprisings against the established conservative and reactionary regimes.[24] Early socialist thinkers also formulated ambitious projects of transnational cooperation. In France, Henri de Saint-Simon proposed broad visions of reform of the international order as a counterpart to his core preoccupation with the needs of a society organized around industry, science and progress. If his project of a 'harmonious international order led by scientists, engineers, and savants' formed an original alternative to the principles of the post-1815 Restoration, his designs were far less unconventional in their stark Eurocentric bias – they incorporated notions of international hierarchy, distinguishing between 'educated' and 'ignorant' nations.[25] The heirs of his tradition, together with radical democrats and followers of socialists such as Etienne Cabet, Charles Fourier, Pierre Leroux and Louis Blanc, developed a body of values and symbols that aimed to marry democracy, equality and international fraternity in the project of a peace-loving 'universal Republic'.[26] Internationalism, together with socialism and feminism, was a key element in the original thinking of Flora Tristan, whose tract calling for a 'Workers' Union' had a significant circulation at the time of its publishing in 1843.[27] Chartism, the first mass movement of the British working class, drew inspiration from strains of

---

[22] On the birth of the concepts of Right and Left in post-revolutionary France see Marcel Gauchet, 'La droite et la gauche', in *Les lieux de mémoire*, vol. 2, ed. Pierre Nora (Paris: Gallimard, 1992), 395–467. For a classic discussion of their enduring relevance see Norberto Bobbio, *Left and Right: The Significance of a Political Distinction* (Cambridge: Polity press, 1996).

[23] Jürgen Osterhammel, *The Transformation of the World: A Global History of the Nineteenth Century* (Princeton: Princeton University Press, 2014), 514.

[24] Christopher Alan Bayly and Eugenio Federico Biagini (eds.), *Giuseppe Mazzini and the Globalisation of Democratic Nationalism, 1830–1920* (Oxford: Oxford University Press for the British Academy, 2008); Stefano Recchia and Nadia Urbinati (eds.), *A Cosmopolitanism of Nations: Giuseppe Mazzini's Writings on Democracy, Nation Building, and International Relations* (Princeton: Princeton University Press, 2009).

[25] Jan Eijking, 'A "Priesthood of Knowledge": The International thought of Henri de Saint-Simon', *International Studies Quarterly* 66, no. 1 (2022): 1–11, 1.

[26] Sudhir Hazareesingh, 'The Utopian Imagination. Radical Republican Traditions in France, from the Enlightenment to the French Communists', in *Radical Republicanism: Recovering the Tradition's Popular Heritage*, ed. Bruno Leipold, Karma Nabulsi and Stuart White (Oxford: Oxford University Press, 2020), 215–37. See also Christophe Prochasson, 'Les premiers socialismes', in *Histoire des gauches en France*, ed. Jean-Jacques Becker and Gilles Candar, vol. 1 (Paris: La Découverte, 2005), 405–25.

[27] Brigitte Krulic, *Flora Tristan* (Paris: Galllimard, 2022); Máire Fedelma Cross, *In the Footsteps of Flora Tristan: A Political Biography* (Liverpool: Liverpool University Press, 2020), 81–8.

radical thought originating in France and in the United States, and, in turn, inspired the strategies and practices of a variety of movements in continental Europe and in the British settler colonies, where many exiled Chartists had forcibly or voluntarily relocated after the repression of the movement in the 1840s.[28]

Marxian internationalism, Mark Mazower has argued, should be analysed in this framework, as 'one variant of the profusion of mid-nineteenth-century visions of world order' that contested the counterrevolutionary system of post-1815 Europe.[29] The 1864 International Working Men's Association (IWMA), in which Marx played a major role, connected with the heritage of the uprisings of 1848–9, with pre-existing revolutionary references, and with different traditions of solidarity among workers. Its establishment, however, marked a turning point in that it heralded the rise of the international demands and practices of working-class-based labour movements whose consolidation was accelerating with the diffusion of industrialization and the ensuing social dislocations. Workers' solidarity in the economic struggle against capitalism was to gradually supersede the battle for democracy and self-determination as the main driver of cross-border activism.

Internationalism, it should be stressed, was constitutive to this phase of socialist organizing. Transnational campaigning supported by the IWMA developed before the formation of the various national socialist parties. The First International was not a federation of political parties but a far more grassroots affairs. It gathered 'trade unions, associations, individual members and activists' and favoured 'various forms of solidarity among workers: from the coordination between unions to prevent the international circulation of strike breakers, to the support of political refugees'.[30] These practices of mutual aid, it has been suggested, delineated an effort at correcting labour's disadvantage in respect to capital in a moment of accelerating globalization.[31] Insisting on the central role of trade unions, Marcel van der Linden has proposed to characterize this as a form of 'sub-national internationalism': 'because no national trade unions as yet existed', he argued, 'international contacts were always between local organizations in different countries'.[32] The brief history of the First International also introduced a fundamental split between socialist and anarchist internationalisms. Although both currents had participated in the creation of the IWMA, anarchist followers of Mikhail Bakunin were expelled from it in 1872. Rejecting political intermediaries and centralized organizations, activists who self-defined as anarchists mostly went on to opt for looser and more flexible forms of transnational cooperation.[33]

---

[28] Fabrice Bensimon, 'Chartism in the British World and Beyond', in *The MacKenzie Moment and Imperial History: Essays in Honour of John MacKenzie*, ed. Stephanie Barczewski and Martin Farr (Cham: Palgrave Macmillan, 2019), 311–35.

[29] Mark Mazower, *Governing the World: The History of an Idea* (New York: Penguin Books, 2012), 55.

[30] Fabrice Bensimon, Quentin Deluermoz and Jeanne Moisand, 'Introduction', in '*Arise Ye Wretched of the Earth': The First International in a Global Perspective*, ed. Fabrice Bensimon, Quentin Deluermoz and Jeanne Moisand (Leiden: Brill, 2018), 4. See also Marcello Musto (ed.), *Workers Unite!: The International 150 Years Later* (New York and London: Bloomsbury Academic, 2014).

[31] Nicolas Delalande, *La lutte et l'entraide. L'âge des solidarités ouvrières* (Paris: Seuil, 2019).

[32] Marcel van der Linden, *Workers of the World: Essays toward a Global Labor History* (Leiden and Boston: Brill, 2008), 270.

[33] See Constance Bantman, 'Internationalism without an International? Cross-Channel Anarchist Networks, 1880–1914', *Revue belge de philologie et d'histoire* 84, no. 4 (2006): 961–81.

Although short-lived and beset by ideological rifts, the 'International' left a crucial symbolic and linguistic legacy. As the epitome of the emancipatory struggles of the working classes, it was feared and respected in equal measure by foes and friends who, incidentally, all grossly overestimated the organization's might and financial resources. All but secondary in propagating the myth was a song, *l'Internationale*. Originally written by Eugène Pottier in 1871, the fateful year of the Paris Commune, it gained a rapid fame after being set to music two decades later. Its tune and lyrics, soon to be translated in many languages, entered the global imagery, together with the Paris Commune's red flag, as a symbol of the revolt of the 'wretched of the Earth'.[34] The image on the cover of this book reproduces a booklet with the music score and the lyrics of the song. In it, the flag of the International is held by a fighting *Marianne* clad in a half-torn red dress – a clear sign of continuity in the revolutionary imagery, but also an unmistakable marker of the Eurocentric mindset that dominated the socialist movement.[35]

These ideas, however, travelled outside Europe, and leftist internationalisms shaped a set of linguistic references that contributed bolstering militants and sympathizers in their allegiance to a cross-border 'imagined community'. Crucial in this dissemination of common linguistic references were radical exile communities of intellectuals and political activists, as well as newspapers and publications reporting on European affairs, whose diffusion exemplified the dynamics of nineteenth-century globalization (and their entanglements with imperial networks). In Egypt, for instance, socialist ideas started to be debated 'thanks to the existence of a group of regular newspapers which started publication in Arabic in the late 1860s'. By the end of the nineteenth century, the word used by Arab intellectuals to refer to revolutionary socialism was 'The Commune' (*al kumun*) or the *internasyonal*, whereas the most direct translation of the term socialism (*ishtirakiyyah*) had been 'emptied of violent, revolutionary connotations'.[36] Typically, this transnational circulation of ideas relied on the key role played by intermediaries adapting concepts and values to local contexts, reshaping some of them while rejecting others.

If the origins of left-wing internationalism lie in the European nineteenth century, this collection focuses on a different phase, beginning with the global upheavals of the First World War, and, not accidentally, takes on a broader geographical scope. The crucial relevance of this turning point to the history of internationalism is widely recognized in the literature, even though interpretations vary as to whether the post-First World War blossoming of internationalist organizations and initiatives (starting with the

---

[34] Patrizia Dogliani, 'The Fate of Socialist Internationalism', in *Internationalisms: A Twentieth-Century History*, ed. Glenda Sluga and Patricia Clavin (Cambridge: Cambridge University Press, 2017), 38–60, 40–1.

[35] See Maurice Agulhon, *Marianne au combat. L'imagerie et la symbolique républicaines de 1789 à 1880* (Paris: Flammarion, 1979); id., *Marianne au pouvoir. L'imagerie et la symbolique républicaines de 1880 à 1914* (Paris: Flammarion, 1979).

[36] Mourad Magdi Wahba, 'The Meaning of Ishtirakiyyah: Arab Perceptions of Socialism in the Nineteenth Century', *Alif: Journal of Comparative Poetics*, no. 10 (1990): 42–55.

League of Nations and its offshoots) should be considered more as a fresh start or, as Iriye suggested, as the 'resumption of an earlier trend that had been momentarily suspended'.[37] For the history of the Left, in any case, the First World War is all the more significant because of its decisive concurrence with the emergence of a new internationalist project born out of the Bolshevik revolution, whose shock waves were to ripple across all left-wing traditions. Conflicts and interactions between different internationalist designs and practices that developed in parallel with the collapse of the pre-1914 European and Eurocentric order loomed large over the twentieth century.

The multiple trajectories explored in this book defy any idea of orderly progress or linear historical evolution. It can be useful, however, to reflect at least on a number of moments and keywords that epitomize different stages, aspects and problems of left-wing internationalist experiences. The first keyword, somewhat paradoxically, is 'nationalization'. Twentieth-century left-wing internationalisms developed in what was increasingly a world of nation-states. This shift was already evident at the end of the previous century in what would become known as the Second International. Differently from its predecessor, the Marxist International born in Paris in 1889 was structured around the nationally based socialist parties that were springing up all around Europe – the German Social Democratic Party (SPD) being both the quintessential example of this trend and the leading force of the International.[38] Internationalism remained a key inspiration for the socialist movement, but its practices readjusted to the reality of the nationalization of the working classes and to the growing acculturation of socialists to the modern state, whose machinery many started to regard as a tool that could be used to promote a transition towards a socialist society.[39] Institutionalization played out not only in the orientations of the socialist movement (as shown, for instance, by the definitive marginalization of anarchist tendencies), but also in the International itself. At the beginning of the new century – 'at a time when international institutions were generally *en vogue*', as Patrizia Dogliani remarked – a permanent 'International Socialist Bureau' was formed, based in Brussels and equipped with an equally permanent secretariat, soon to be accompanied by a number of 'agencies' and parallel organizations.[40] As such, the development of the Second International epitomized the broader dialectics between globalizing trends and processes of nationalization that characterized the emergence of different strands of internationalism 'in the age of nationalism'.[41]

---

[37] Iriye, *Global Community*, 20. See also Susan Pedersen, *The Guardians. The League of Nations and the Crisis of Empire* (Oxford: Oxford University Press, 2015).

[38] See classic studies such as Georges Haupt, *La Deuxième Internationale 1884–1914. Étude critique des sources. Essai bibliographique* (Paris: Mouton, 1964); James Joll, *The Second International, 1889–1914* (London: Weidenfeld and Nicolson, 1968).

[39] Mathieu Fulla and Marc Lazar (eds.), *European Socialists and the State in the Twentieth and Twenty-First Centuries* (Cham: Palgrave Macmillan, 2020). For a history of the Left that masterfully stresses the 'national' dimension of socialist parties, see Donald Sassoon, *One Hundred Years of Socialism: The West European Left in the Twentieth Century* (London and New York: IB Tauris, 1996).

[40] Dogliani, 'The Fate of Socialist Internationalism', 42.

[41] Sluga, *Internationalism in the Age of Nationalism*; Pierre Alayrac, *L'Internationale au milieu du gué. De l'internationalisme socialiste au congrès de Londres (1896)* (Rennes: Presses Universitaires de Rennes, 2018).

With the outbreak of the First World War, the tension between internationalism and nationalization proved to be unsustainable for the socialist movement, as the vast majority of socialist parties rallied behind their own countries' war effort. As recent research has shown, efforts at transnational socialist cooperation were not completely wiped out by the war, but the myth of the workers' International was in tatters.[42] The success of the Bolshevik revolution spelt the rise of a new internationalist project that reflected the impact of the war and of the breakdown of the European imperial order it ushered in. Lenin's intransigent revolutionary call and denunciation of the 'revisionism' and 'betrayal' of pre-war social democracy were linked to a comprehensive rethinking of the internationalist mission. The Bolsheviks saw their revolution as just the first stage of a pan-European upheaval that would bring down the capitalist powers and their colonial empires. Communist revolutionaries should be organized in a centralized 'world party of Revolution', prepared to fight an 'international civil war' against the forces of capitalism and imperialism, which were held responsible for the war. And their appeal, in an epoch of imperial collapse and reconfiguration, was to be a global one, unlike that of social democracy.[43] At the turn of the 1920s, most of the revolutionary leaders in Europe, Latin America and the colonial world in Asia and Africa 'were influenced by Lenin's slogans and strategies', even though their ideas and practices 'differed from and at times clashed with those endorsed by Moscow'.[44]

Pre-war socialism had been an essentially European phenomenon – its global outreaches were comparatively marginal and often linked to the activism of European migrants – and its attitude towards the 'colonial question' was generally reserved at best. Although a wide variety of positions was represented, the most influential socialist currents limited themselves to denouncing the 'excesses' of colonialism, but shied away from advocating full-on independence for the subject territories. Even after the war, the dominant position within the re-established Labour and Socialist International (LSI) was one of support for trusteeship and an ill-defined gradual, internationally supervised transition of colonial territories towards self-government. The Bolshevik revolution, on the contrary, launched a radical anti-imperialist message whose echo resonated among anti-colonial activists. Its impact was magnified by the post-war conjuncture. Anti-colonial sentiments had been first fuelled and then frustrated by Woodrow Wilson's promise of self-determination, which many embraced until it became clear that it was fully compatible with the maintenance of ideas of civilizational hierarchy, and that the post-war order would envisage self-government only for the territories that were deemed to have reached an 'adequate' level of development.[45]

---

[42] Imlay, *The Practice of Socialist Internationalism*.
[43] See Silvio Pons, 'Una globalizzazione alternativa? L'internazionalismo comunista nel Novecento', in *Globalizzazioni rosse. Studi sul comunismo nel mondo del Novecento*, ed. Silvio Pons (Rome: Carocci, 2020), 11–28. For an introduction on the Comintern, see Tim Rees and Andrew Thorpe (eds.), *International Communism and the Communist International, 1919–1943* (Manchester: Manchester University Press, 1998); Serge Wolikow, *L'Internationale communiste (1919–1943): le Komintern ou le rêve déchu du parti mondial de la revolution* (Paris: Editions ouvrières, 2010).
[44] Rachel G. Hoffman, 'The Global Red Revolution', in *Revolutionary World: Global Upheaval in the Modern Age*, ed. David Motadel (Cambridge: Cambridge University Press, 2021), 130–51, 144.
[45] Manela, *The Wilsonian Moment*.

Communist internationalism interacted with anti-colonialism not only through the activities of the communist parties that were founded throughout Asia and Africa and those of the Comintern and its cosmopolitan emissaries, but also through the many initiatives aimed at the formation of international cadres, and the support of formally independent organizations such as the 1927 League Against Imperialism. Even though Europe remained the core preoccupation of the Comintern, and in spite of the frequent doctrinal and political conflicts, the imprint of international communism on anti-colonial liberation was significant.[46]

Communists, Brigitte Studer noted, 'established a presence at every scalar level of political space: the international, with the programme of universal proletarian revolution and a tendentially global network of activity; the transnational, with dense exchanges of persons and information; and finally the national, where the struggle was actually played out, the site of concrete political action'.[47] At the same time, however, they experienced to a dramatic extent the contradictory entanglements of internationalism, nationalization and state power. As the global revolution advocated by the early Bolsheviks failed to materialize, the imperative of the defence of the Soviet Union gained central stage and crystallized in Stalin's theory of socialism in a single country. Moscow's control over the Comintern's activities tightened, cosmopolitan aspiration became suspect, and by the second half of the 1930s the politics of repression and terror that had seized the Soviet Union, culminating in deportations, famine and a staggering surge of state-led violence, also swept through the Communist International and its foreign outposts. A dramatic example of these contradictions was the Spanish civil war, which saw both internationalist mobilization on an exceptional scale, and the export of Stalinist repressive practices that fuelled internecine conflict in the Republican camp.[48]

The enrolment of military volunteers in the International Brigades, the broader internationalist mobilization over the Spanish civil war and the brief season of the 'popular fronts' epitomized the potential of anti-fascism as a transnational political culture of the Left, beyond the socialist-communist divide – but also its ambiguities and limits, which were later to fire heated political and historiographical controversies.[49]

---

[46] See Sobhanlal Datta Gupta, 'Communism and the Crisis of the Colonial System', in *The Cambridge History of Communism*, vol. 1, ed. Silvio Pons and Steven Smith (Cambridge: Cambridge University Press, 2017); Vijay Prashad, *The Darker Nations: A People's History of the Third World* (New York and London: The New Press, 2007); Drachewych and McKay, *Left Transnationalism*; Françoise Blum et al. (eds.), *Socialismes en Afrique/Socialisms in Africa* (Paris: Éditions de la Maison des sciences de l'homme, 2021).

[47] Studer, *The Transnational World of the Comminternians*, 4.

[48] See Stanley Payne, *The Spanish Civil War, the Soviet Union, and Communism* (New Haven: Yale University Press, 2004); Lisa A. Kirschenbaum, *International Communism and the Spanish Civil War* (Cambridge: Cambridge University Press, 2015).

[49] See the classic, opposing narratives of François Furet, *The Passing of an Illusion: The Idea of Communism in the Twentieth Century* (Chicago: University of Chicago Press, 1999), and Eric J. Hobsbawm, *The Age of Extremes: The Short Twentieth Century, 1914–1991* (London: Michael Joseph, 1994). For instances of socialist-communist antifascist cooperation see also Gerd-Rainer Horn, *European Socialists Respond to Fascism: Ideology, Activism and Contingency in the 1930s* (Oxford: Oxford University Press, 1996).

Episodes of cooperation, however, were the exception in a context of estrangement and bitter fight between socialists and communists. Socialists rejected the centralized model of the Comintern and espoused leaner and more flexible forms of transnational cooperation, sometimes also interacting with liberal internationalism and the institutions it inspired – such as the International Labour Organization (ILO) that was set up in 1919 under the Treaty of Versailles. Quite tellingly, the ILO's first secretary was a socialist, the French Albert Thomas, who however had fallen in disgrace within his own party due to his heavy involvement in the war, during which he notably served as Minister of Armaments.[50] A crucial aspect of the socialists' exchange was the dialogue on the experiments with welfare reforms and economic planning that were emerging in various European contexts, which were also to leave their mark on Franklin Roosevelt's New Deal.[51]

Possibilities for cooperation were revived in the course of the Second World War, but only after the Nazi invasion of the Soviet Union reactivated the communist movement, which – in a rather revealing development – had been immobilized by its untenable support of the Moscow line since the 1939 Molotov-Ribbentrop pact. Socialists and (especially) communists were key actors in the European Resistance movements, and thus gained unprecedented legitimation. The same applied, on a far larger scale, to the Soviet Union. In Asia, the anti-Japanese fight was crucial to the rise of communism in China, Vietnam and Korea, while in Indonesia a mass communist party developed out of the anti-colonial struggle. Opportunities for mass legal action emerged for communists also in the Arab world and Iran, especially after Stalin's decision to dissolve the Comintern in 1943, which partly assuaged the fears of authorities that used to equate communists with Moscow agents.

As the dust settled on the ruins of war, however, the decisive framework for the internationalist engagement of the different currents of the Left was to be provided by the emergence of the United States and the Soviet Union as the two 'superpowers' that would shape the new world order. Intersecting with the momentous advance of decolonization, the competition between the superpowers gave rise to an expansive and centripetal bipolar system of international relations which would both promote and regiment internationalist ambitions.[52]

---

[50] See Leonardo Rapone, *La socialdemocrazia europea tra le due guerre: dall'organizzazione della pace alla Resistenza al fascismo, 1923–1936* (Rome: Carocci, 1999); Patrizia Dogliani, 'Progetto per un'internazionale "aclassista": il socialisti nell'organizzazione internazionale del lavoro negli anni venti', in *Esperienze e problemi del movimento socialista fra le due guerre mondiali*, ed. Aldo Agosti (Milan: FrancoAngeli, 1987), 45–68; Laqua, 'Democratic Politics and the League of Nations'; Emmanuel Jousse, *Les hommes révoltés: Les origines intellectuelles du réformisme en France (1871–1917)* (Paris: Fayard, 2017).

[51] See Sheri Berman, *The Social Democratic Moment: Ideas and Politics in the Making of Interwar Europe* (Cambridge, MA and London: Harvard University Press, 1998); Kiran Klaus Patel, *The New Deal: A Global History* (Princeton: Princeton University Press, 2016).

[52] Hyung-Gu Lynn, 'Globalization and the Cold War', in *The Oxford Handbook of the Cold War*, ed. Richard H. Immerman and Petra Goedde (Oxford: Oxford University Press, 2013), 584–601; Kott, *Organiser le monde*.

Social democratic internationalism was revamped after the war, and a new Socialist International was founded in Frankfurt in 1951. Its member parties soon came to epitomize the broadly successful effort at mediating between capitalism and social protection through state intervention in the economy and welfare provisions that marked the post-war Euro-Atlantic 'golden age'. Transnational exchange involving both parties and trade unions contributed defining social democratic attitudes on international affairs and on the adaptation of their political and economic culture to the new post-war realities.[53] These exchanges happened in a context that was strongly influenced by the internationalist designs emanating from the United States, whose decision to 'remain in Europe' after the war crucially affected the environment in which the most important parties of the Socialist International operated. Conceptualizing this as a process of Americanization would probably be misplaced: what emerged was rather a negotiated, if lopsided, system of mutual influence and national adaptation, which was all but immune to shifts and evolutions, as a sequence of 'transatlantic crises' would show.[54] By the same token, social democratic internationalism also interacted with other ventures into international cooperation, such as European integration and its institutions.[55] Although the SI remained an overwhelmingly European organization, efforts at engaging with the emerging post-colonial world also manifested themselves recurrently. By the late 1970s, in particular, a new globalist course of the Socialist International emerged with the leadership of Willy Brandt. In the face of the mounting global interdependence, Brandt was determined to pursue an initiative aimed at strengthening the SI presence in the global South and at articulating a proposal of political restructuring of world economic relations that resonated with Third World demands for a New International Economic Order.[56]

Communist internationalism was transformed by the rise of the Soviet Union to the status of world power, leading to a host of contradictory and ambiguous developments. The Comintern was not reinstated after the war – the 'Communist Information Bureau' (Cominform) that was created in 1947 had a limited geographical

---

[53] Guillaume Devin, *L'Internationale socialiste. Histoire et sociologie du socialisme international (1945–1990)* (Paris: Presses de Sciences Po, 1993); Costa, *The Labour Party, Denis Healey and the International Socialist Movement*. On trade unions, see Robert Anthony Waters, Jr. and Geert van Goethem (eds.), *American Labor's Global Ambassadors: The International History of the AFL-CIO during the Cold War* (Basingstoke: Palgrave Macmillan, 2013); Anthony Carew, *American Labour's Cold War Abroad: From Deep Freeze to Détente, 1945–1970* (Edmonton: Athabasca University Press, 2018).
[54] Two useful literature reviews are Holger Nehring '"Westernization": A New Paradigm for Interpreting West European History in a Cold War Context', *Cold War History* 4, no. 2 (2004): 175–91; Alessandra Bitumi, 'Rethinking the Historiography of Transatlantic Relations in the Cold War Years: The United States, Europe and the Process of European Integration', in *Modern European-American Relations in the Transatlantic Space: Recent Trends in History Writings*, ed. Maurizio Vaudagna (Turin: Otto, 2015), 71–95. For a case study, see Julia Angster, *Konsenskapitalismus und Sozialdemokratie: die Westernisierung von SPD und DGB* (München: Oldenbourg, 2003).
[55] See, among others, Kristian Steinnes, *The British Labour Party, Transnational Influences, and European Community Membership, 1960–1973* (Stuttgart: Franz Steiner, 2014); Salm, *Transnational Socialist Networks in the 1970s*.
[56] See Peter Van Kemseke, *Towards an Era of Development: The Globalization of Socialism and Christian Democracy, 1945–1965* (Leuven: Leuven University Press, 2006); Willy Brandt, *Berliner Ausgabe*, vol. VIII, *Über Europa hinaus: Dritte Welt und Sozialistische Internationale*, ed. B. Rother, and W. Schmidt (Bonn: Dietz, 2006).

reach and was destined to a brief existence.⁵⁷ In the USSR and the Soviet-hegemonized Central and Eastern European countries, 'socialist internationalism' could be invoked to justify military intervention on 'deviant' political leaderships, as in the case of the repression of the Prague Spring in 1968.⁵⁸ The transformation of internationalism into an empty slogan utilized by political authorities is best described by the apologue sketched by Czech dissident Václav Havel, about the greengrocer hanging in his shop window the sign 'Workers of the World, Unite!' – 'simply because it has been done for years, because everyone does it, because it is good that way. ... because you have to do it if you want to get by in life'.⁵⁹ And yet, the 'global Cold War' also became an arena for the diffusion of communism as a conduit for aspirations for emancipation, modernization and development, especially in the decolonizing world. The success of the Chinese revolution entailed both the formation of a massive socialist expanse in Asia and the relaunching of a radical message directed at liberation movements throughout the world. After the death of Stalin, the new Soviet leadership displayed a new disposition to support radical anti-colonial movements and assist with socialist development in Asia and Africa. Communist-oriented liberation movements in Vietnam, first and foremost, but also in Southern Africa and elsewhere, captured the global attention and elicited massive transnational mobilizations. The Cuban revolution heralded a militant internationalism that left its mark both on Latin America and throughout the African continent, while also feeding into the radical imagination in Western Europe.⁶⁰ Reform approaches also emerged, especially in communist parties outside power. The latter also wove internationalist networks of their own, sometimes challenging Cold War binaries – as in the case of the Italian Communist Party and its 'Eurocommunism'.⁶¹ As communist networks expanded, however, they became increasingly fragmented. The Sino-Soviet split signalled the end of any notion of 'world communism' as a single entity and was a harbinger of its decline as a global alternative.⁶²

---

⁵⁷ Giuliano Procacci et al. (eds.), *The Cominform: Minutes of the Three Conferences 1947/1948/1949* (Milan: Feltrinelli, 1994).
⁵⁸ Matthew J. Ouimet, *The Rise and Fall of the Brezhnev Doctrine in Soviet Foreign Policy* (Chapel Hill: University of North Carolina Press, 2003).
⁵⁹ Václav Havel, *Le Pouvoir des sans-pouvoirs* (Paris: Editions Première partie, 2021 [1978]), 28–9.
⁶⁰ Odd Arne Westad, *The Global Cold War: Third World Interventions and the Making of Our Times* (Cambridge: Cambridge University Press, 2007); Tobias Rupprecht, *Soviet Internationalism after Stalin: Interaction and Exchange between the USSR and Latin America during the Cold War* (Cambridge: Cambridge University Press, 2015); Piero Gleijeses, *Conflicting Missions: Havana, Washington, and Africa, 1959–1976* (Chapel Hill: University of North Carolina Press, 2002); Jeremy Friedman, *Shadow Cold War: The Sino-Soviet Competition for the Third World* (Chapel Hill: University of North Carolina Press, 2002); James Mark, Artemy M. Kalinovsky and Steffi Marung (eds.), *Alternative Globalizations: Eastern Europe and the Postcolonial World* (Bloomington: Indiana University Press, 2020); Tanya Harmer and Alberto Martín Álvarez (eds.), *Toward a Global History of Latin America's Revolutionary Left* (Gainesville: University of Florida Press, 2021).
⁶¹ Silvio Pons, *I comunisti italiani e gli altri. Visioni e legami internazionali nel mondo del Novecento* (Turin: Einaudi, 2021).
⁶² See Lorenz M. Lüthi, *The Sino-Soviet Split: Cold War in the Communist World* (Princeton: Princeton University Press, 2008); Sergey Radchenko, *Two Suns in the Heavens: The Sino-Soviet Struggle for Supremacy, 1962–1967* (Stanford: Stanford University Press, 2009).

A compartmentalized picture focusing exclusively on the agency of socialists and communists in the framework of the Cold War, however, would not do justice to the variety of post-1945 left-wing internationalisms. Against the Cold War order, left-oriented Afro-Asian solidarity movements emerged forcefully especially after the 1955 Bandung Conference, which contributed structuring networks marrying anti-colonialism, anti-racism and projects for international non-alignment.[63] Third worldism, Jeffrey James Byrne noted in relation to Algeria, involved both transnational anti-colonial cooperation and state-centred notions of international collaboration among post-colonial authorities.[64] Grassroots activists throughout the world tried to carve out spaces for solidarity campaigns that revived humanitarian, pacifist and anti-racist left-wing traditions that sought to escape the rigidities of the bipolar order.[65] Starting from the 1950s, 'New Lefts' sprung up throughout Europe and beyond, often strongly influenced by anti-colonialism and Third Worldism, and always critical of what they saw as the stalemate reached both by communism and social democracy. Calling for participatory democracy and popular control, these movements rebelled against traditional forms of transnational cooperation structured around national political parties and trade unions. For them, keeping a radical anti-authoritarian leftist project implied the creation of 'nonhierarchical associations based on direct democracy'.[66] The 'global 1968' represented a key moment in their development and gave a major push to the establishment of alternative transnational networks of the radical left which would prove influential, if most often short-lived.[67]

The 1960s were also a crucial moment for what Francisca de Haan labels as the 'global left-feminist' movement, whose contribution to the international codification of women's rights is only starting to be explored.[68] If the transnational nature and internationalist engagement of early twentieth-century feminism are widely recognized, recent research is increasingly focusing on transnational networks that epitomized 'forms of feminism that did not adhere to the frameworks of the West and global north', originating both in the socialist countries and in the global South, especially

---

[63] See the special issue 'Other Bandungs: Afro-Asian Internationalisms in the Early Cold War', ed. Su Lin Lewis and Carolien Stolte, *Journal of World History* 30, nos. 1–2 (2019).

[64] Jeffrey James Byrne, *Mecca of Revolution: Algeria, Decolonization, and the Third World Order* (New York: Oxford University Press, 2016).

[65] For an example, see Petra Goedde, *The Politics of Peace: A Global Cold War History* (Oxford: Oxford University Press, 2019).

[66] Terence Renaud, *New Lefts: The Making of a Radical Tradition* (Princeton and Oxford: Princeton University Press, 2021), 8.

[67] See Carol Fink, Philipp Gassert and Detlef Junker (eds.), *1968: The World Transformed* (Cambridge: Cambridge University Press, 1998); Gerd-Rainer Horn, *The Spirit of '68: Rebellion in Western Europe and North America, 1956–1976* (Oxford: Oxford University Press, 2007); Quinn Slobodian, *Foreign Front: Third World Politics in Sixties West Germany* (Durham and London: Duke University Press, 2012); Richard Wolin, *The Wind from the East: French Intellectuals, the Cultural Revolution and the Legacy of the 1960s* (Princeton: Princeton University Press, 2010).

[68] See Francisca de Haan 'The Global Left-Feminists 1960s: From Copenhagen to Moscow and New York', in *The Routledge Handbook of the Global Sixties: Between Protest and Nation-Building*, ed. Chen Jian et al. (London and New York: Routledge, 2018), 230–42.

Latin America.⁶⁹ Works dealing with the role played by feminist organizations from the Eastern Bloc during the Cold War also show the global influence they had in the promotion of a feminist agenda in international organizations, primarily the UN, while highlighting the consolidation of strong bilateral connections between communist and non-aligned Southern countries through this channel.⁷⁰

Old and new social movements thrived after 1968, in a development that was often representative of new sensibilities linked to the growing awareness of global interdependence. Environmentalism, whose relations with the traditional cultures of the Left were always a complex and rocky one, is a typical example. Intrinsically transnational as they were, the new social movements tended to form networks that were more informal and less structured compared to those of the 'Old Lefts'. Moreover, new forms of international mobilization emerged that eluded leftist traditions, such as the ones linked to human rights activism or the mushrooming network of NGOs.⁷¹ The decline of socialist and communist internationalisms was unmistakable even before the end of the Cold War revolutionized the Left and led to the final demise of international communism.

Late twentieth-century globalization unsettled the intricate equilibria between the national and the international dimension of socialist and communist politics and economics. This decline of left-wing internationalism in an age of accelerating globalization can look paradoxical.⁷² Since their origins, socialist and communist movements captured like no other the global and transnational dimension of contemporary politics, economics and international relations. They built global networks and gave a crucial contribution to the 'making of a transnational world'.⁷³ At

---

⁶⁹ Michelle Chase, '"Hands Off Korea!": Women's Internationalist Solidarity and Peace Activism in Early Cold War Cuba', *Journal of Women's History* 32, no. 3 (2020): 64–88, 66. See also Francisca de Haan, 'Continuing Cold War Paradigms in the Western Historiography of Transnational Women's Organisations: The Case of the Women's International Democratic Federation (WIDF)', *Women's History Review* 19, no. 4 (2010): 547–73; Celia Donert, 'From Communist Internationalism to Human Rights: Gender, Violence, and International Law in the Women's International Democratic Federation Mission to North Korea, 1951', *Contemporary European History* 25, no. 2 (2016): 313–33.

⁷⁰ Zheng Wang, '"State Feminism"? Gender and Socialist State Formation in Maoist China', *Feminist Studies* 31, no. 3 (2005): 519–51; Celia Donert, 'Showcasing the Welfare Dictatorship: International Women's Year and the Weltkongress Der Frauen, East Berlin 1975', in *Sozialistische Staatlichkeit*, ed. Joachin Von Puttkamer and Jana Ostercamp (Munich: Oldenbourg, 2012), 143–60; Maria Raluca Popa, 'Translating Equality between Women and Men across Cold War Divides: Women Activists from Hungary and Romania and the Creation of International Women's Year', in *Gender Politics and Everyday Life in State Socialist Eastern and Central Europe*, ed. Shana Penn and Jill Massino (Basingstoke: Palgrave Macmillan, 2009); Kristen Ghodsee, *Second World, Second Sex: Socialist Women's Activism and Global Solidarity during the Cold War* (Durham: Duke University Press, 2019).

⁷¹ References to left-wing organizations were altogether limited also in the most recent feminist and LGBTI+ mobilisations. See for an example, Selin Çağatay, Miia Liinason and Olga Sasunkevich, *Feminist and LGBTI+ Activism across Russia, Scandinavia and Turkey: Transnationalizing Spaces of Resistance* (Cham: Palgrave Macmillan, 2022).

⁷² See Jean-Numa Ducange and Serge Wolikow, 'Internationale, Internationalisme', in *Histoire globale des socialismes XIXᵉ-XXIᵉ siècle*, ed. Jean-Numa Ducange, Razmig Keucheyan and Stéphanie Roza (Paris: PUF, 2021), 286–96.

⁷³ Akira Iriye, 'The Making of a Transnational World', in *Global Interdependence: The World after 1945*, ed. Akira Iriye (Cambridge, MA and London: Belknap Press, 2014), 681–847.

the same time, however, their internationalism had developed in a symbiotic relation with projects for social transformation that were linked to the age of territoriality and industrialization that came to an end in the last quarter of the twentieth century.[74]

Socialist and communist parties survive nowadays throughout the world, although in a much mutated form and context, but the import of their internationalist initiatives is marginal even in contexts of institutionalized transnationalism such as the European Parliament and the attendant system of 'Europarties'. In a different context, it is possible to see legacies of left-wing internationalist practices in several political experiences of the last decades – from the *altermondialiste* network to 'Fridays for Future' and the broader movement for climate justice. A rich and multifaceted tradition, left-wing internationalism has contributed shaping the twentieth century. Its future is uncertain, but much is still to be learnt by investigating into its past.

This book is divided into three parts, which explore different aspects of the history of left-wing internationalism. The first part focuses on how, throughout the twentieth century, socialist and communist internationalisms dealt with, and adapted to, the changing relationship between party politics, the state and the international system. Foregrounding the dialectical relationship between integration into national politics and society, on the one hand, and internationalism, on the other, the chapters investigate the constant reinvention of left-wing internationalist practices in their encounter with the international system of the twentieth century. The selected case studies allow us to discuss crucial questions such as the end of empire, the structuring of international relations around the East-West axis after the Second World War, the emergence of the North-South divide and the impact of late twentieth-century globalization.

The collection begins with a chapter by Kostis Karpozilos examining the transition of a multi-ethnic socialist organization, the Socialist Workers' Federation of Salonica, from the flexible boundaries of the Ottoman Empire to the narrow field of 'national politics' in Greece. In investigating how this organization transplanted and adapted concepts and visions of internationalist socialism into a national setting, this case study offers an opportunity to revisit the overall transition from imperial to national realities after the First World War. The following chapter, by Eirik Sundvall and Nik. Brandal, focuses on a longer timespan (1920s–50s) to examine one of the trajectories of social democracy after the rise of the communist challenge. Centring on the figure of the Norwegian socialist Bjarne Braatøy, who was active both in transnational socialist networks and in Norwegian and US diplomatic activities, the chapter sheds light on an often-overlooked informal side of international politics, namely the transnational interweaving of connections and interactions between individuals, political parties, international organizations and state agencies. As Yutaka Kanda's chapter shows, these connections were however not always effective. Kanda analyses the failure of social democratic internationalist cooperation in post-war Asia, which

---

[74] Charles S. Maier, 'Consigning the Twentieth Century to History: Alternative Narratives for the Modern Era', *American Historical Review* 105, no. 3 (2000): 807–31.

he attributes to fundamental divergences between Asian and European socialist parties over the legacy of empire and the new reality of the Cold War. With the progress of decolonization throughout the 1950s and 1960s, navigating through the East-West and North-South divide became crucial for left-wing parties. Silvio Pons analyses how these dynamics played out even in a communist party in opposition, namely the Italian Communist Party (PCI). As decolonization progressed, Italian communists established significant relations with movements in the Mediterranean basin and in Africa. The chapter explores how this contributed shaping a new understanding of communist internationalism by the PCI, whose involvement with national liberation movements and 'progressive' governments developed quite independently from the Soviet Union. Arianna Lissoni focuses instead on an instance of South-East cooperation. Her chapter examines the exile experience of the South African communist leader Yusuf M. Dadoo and his engagement in the international communist movement before and after he left South Africa in 1960, following the Sharpeville massacre and the banning of the liberation movement by the apartheid regime. This experience epitomizes both the importance and contradictions of communist internationalism during the Cold War: communist networks of political support went global and entwined with Third World liberation, but, for Dadoo and the South African Communist Party, allegiance to the international communist movement also meant siding with Soviet power politics during crises such as the invasion of Hungary in 1956 or Czechoslovakia in 1968. Finally, Mathieu Fulla's chapter foregrounds the encounter between socialist cultures and late twentieth-century globalization. Adopting the lens of socialist international and regional organizations such as the Socialist International and the Confederation of the Socialist Parties of the European Community, the chapter offers a new perspective on the relationship between democratic socialism and capitalism in the 1980s. Rather than a blind conversion by socialist elites to the gospel of market mechanisms, the uneasy alliance they finally concluded with this economic approach should be understood as a failed attempt to promote 'global Keynesianism' as an alternative to monetarist-inspired capitalism in the first half of the 1980s.

The second part of the book examines the interactions between different internationalisms. This means focusing not only on the relationship between different left-wing traditions, but also, and more distinctively, on their encounters with 'the liberal-inclined internationalisms that were characteristic of the … political landscape [of the 20th century] and evident in the advocacy of the primacy of international law and of the inevitability of international institutions'[75]. These encounters set in motion multiple and sometimes contradictory dynamics, ranging from cross-fertilizations and hybridizations between different international approaches, to conflicts and short-circuits.

Adeline Blaszkiewicz focuses on the International Labour Organization in the interwar years. Led by the French socialist Albert Thomas until his death in 1932, the ILO became a point of encounter and hybridization between the internationalisms of the socialists and of the liberal social reformers, who all aimed at offering a reformist alternative to communism. This, however, wasn't approved of by many in the socialist world itself: both the French socialist party and the LSI kept a rather reserved attitude

---

[75] Sluga and Clavin 'Rethinking the History of Internationalism', 3.

towards the ILO, aiming at safeguarding a distinctive socialist identity and outlook. After the Second World War, a significant communist presence also emerged in international intergovernmental institutions. Michel Christian's chapter explores the activities of the Eastern European delegates in the UN institutions dealing with the question of international development, showing the multiple uses they could make of these forums. International institutions became, among other things, stages the communist countries could use to showcase their approach to development issues and promote it among Third World countries. Mateo Jarquín focuses on another instance of intermingling between more radical internationalist approaches and the role of international institutions. His chapter examines the attempt by Nicaragua's Sandinista National Liberation Front (FSLN) – the first and only armed Marxist movement to take power in Latin America after the Cuban Revolution – to put socialist internationalism at the centre of its revolutionary agenda. Rather than promoting the 'revolution without borders' some Sandinista leaders were advocating, however, the government soon found itself in need of interacting with regional and global diplomacy and intergovernmental institutions – such as the Organisation of American States or the UN – to strengthen its legitimacy and seek shield from hostile external interventions. The international history of the Sandinista Revolution therefore indicates trade-offs facing the Latin American Left more widely in the twilight years of the Cold War. The language and practice of liberal internationalism enabled the rise of the FSLN and its survival in an extraordinarily hostile geopolitical context, but it also constrained their revolutionary agenda. Michele Di Donato's chapter focuses on the encounter of social democracy with a new and very different internationalist approach, that of the human rights activists whose role became increasingly important starting from the 1970s. Centring on the activities of the Socialist International, the chapter reflects on the problems and contradictions highlighted by the organization's attempt to elaborate a specific social democratic approach to human rights – a trans-political criterion that was becoming a fundamental standard of international affairs in the broader context of the transformations linked to the 'shock of the global' and the attendant domestic and international shifts and dislocations. Finally, highlighting the interaction between international organizations and grassroots networks focused on improving the status of women, Jocelyn Olcott's chapter forms an ideal bridge between the second and third sections of the book. Her contribution focuses on civil society organizations and activist networks based in the Global South that developed in the context of the UN Decade for Women (1975–85). The Third World-oriented United Nations of the 1970s and early 1980s provided the structure, legitimacy and occasionally funding that supported networks of activist intellectuals. The latter offered critical assessments of capitalist modernization and emergent neoliberalism, but in some instances also engaged with ideas linked to the rising neoliberal currents, such as the cultivation of a dynamic civil society and decentralized politics. This context fostered exchanges between feminists from the Global North and women from the Global South whose political formation had often come through national liberation movements, Marxist political parties and anti-racism campaigns. Although frequently fractious, these encounters helped advancing a South-based transnational feminism grounded in anti-capitalist, anti-imperialist and anti-racist commitments in solidarity with but explicitly and insistently autonomous from the male-dominated political parties and militant movements.

In the last part of the book, the attention shifts from political leaders, party officials, experts and other 'professionals' of internationalism to activists and politically engaged individuals at large. The chapters explore how internationalism became for them a mobilizing factor, as well as the bottom-up transnational connections they developed.

Phillip Deery's chapter tells a story of grassroots mobilization developing beyond party networks in the early 1950s. The chapter examines the major international campaign waged throughout 1952 and 1953 to save Ethel and Julius Rosenberg from execution. The chapter argues that the various 'Save the Rosenbergs' committees in Australia and elsewhere arose prior to and largely independent from official Communist Party involvement or Moscow's influence. Such international solidarity by the Left failed in its ultimate objectives but revealed the scope and potential of global mobilization outside the Stalinist straitjacket in the early Cold War. Starting from the 1960s, the range of left-wing transnational networking broadened to new domains, with a growing focus on societal issues. Céline Vaz examines town planning as an area in which architects and urbanists, but also engineers, geographers and sociologists, all involved in leftist organizations, built transnational networks that blended professional expertise exchange and political engagement. Often radicalized by their involvement in the protests of the 'global 1968', they had in common the rejection of technocratic and functionalist urbanism, which they perceived as one of the numerous symbols of alienation induced by capitalism. On the contrary, they advocated a more humane urbanism, renewed thanks to the participation of inhabitants in the production of the city. Belonging to all the nuances of the left, they built an international network of critical urbanism and urban reform, sometimes advocating what amounted to a 'urban revolution'. Andrew Tompkins's chapter centres on the crucial question of environmentalism and examines the grassroots internationalism of the anti-nuclear movement in Western Europe during the 1970s, focusing on the tensions and tentative alliances between environmentalists and the Left. Looking particularly at the practices of transnational solidarity deployed by anti-nuclear activists engaged in local citizens' initiatives at and across French-German border, the chapter describes the emphasis on local action and personal concern that dominated within the anti-nuclear movement. The movement as a whole opted not for the internationalism of powerful organizations, international politics and global avant-gardes, but instead for forms of grassroots transnationalism that borrowed selectively from experiences abroad and deployed cross-border connections for their symbolic potency. Finally, Emeline Fourment's chapter brings us back to the issue of left-wing feminism. The chapter focuses on recent years and uses a partly different methodology – especially ethnographic research – to examine the experience of anti-authoritarian (anarchist and anarcho-communist) feminists in Montreal and Berlin and the modalities of their participation to transnational activist's networks. Their 'informal internationalism' bypasses traditional networks of left-wing politics but also highlights certain continuities with the longer-term history that is followed in the volume.

Part One

Reinventing left-wing internationalisms in a changing world

1

Transnational socialism entering a nation-state: From Ottoman to Greek socialism, 1912–18

Kostis Karpozilos

Introduction

The Socialist Workers' Federation of Salonica was founded in 1909 in the intellectual and political fervour following the Young Turk Revolution and the promise for a social and political modernization of the Ottoman Empire. The activities of this pioneering multi-ethnic socialist group have attracted historiographical attention as they demonstrate the rising tide of the social question in the urban centres of the Empire.[1] However, these works rarely follow the trajectory of the group in the novel realities created after the Balkan Wars when Salonica became a Greek city.[2] This paper addresses this transition, arguing that the entrapment of the Federation in the boundaries of the Greek State led to the radical remaking of Greek Socialism. Until that point, the socialist movement was confined to small local circles which had, in most cases, marginal activity and impact. In Athens a May Day celebration would involve a couple of dozen true-believers reciting the master narrative of international socialism.[3] Realities in Ottoman Salonica were different: the Federation would report that 'seven thousand socialist demonstrators on the occasion of First of May send their greetings to the international proletariat'.[4]

---

[1] For instance: H. Sükrü Ilicak, 'Jewish Socialism in Ottoman Salonica', *Journal of Southeast European and Black Sea Studies* 2, no. 3 (2002): 115–46; Paul Dumont, 'La Federation Socialiste Ouvriere de Salonique a l' époque des Guerres Balkaniques', *East European Quarterly* 14, no. 4 (Winter 1980): 383–410.

[2] George B. Leon, *The Greek Socialist Movement and the First World War: The Road to Unity* (Boulder Colorado: Columbia University Press, 1976). See also Nikos Potamianos, 'Internationalism and the Emergence of Communist Politics in Greece', 1912–1924, *Journal of Balkan and Near Eastern Studies* 21, no. 5 (2019): 515–31. Antonis Liakos, I Sosialistiki Ergatiki Omospondia Thessalonikis (Federacion) kai i Sosialistiki Neolaia, Paratiritis, Thessaloniki, 1985 and Kentro Marxistikon Erevnon, I Sosialistiki Organosi Federation Thessalonikis, 1909–1918, Syghroni Epochi (Athens: Athens Benaroya, 1989). A. Benaroya, *I proti Stadiodromia tou Ellinikou Proletariatou* (Olkos, 1975), 92.

[3] *Sosialismos*, 28 April 1919, 3.

[4] Federation to ISB, 1 May 1911, AMSAB-ISG, Archive Camille Huysmans, 0222.

The annexation of Salonica in 1912 brought these two worlds in dialogue: their differences were not just in numbers, but entailed radically distinct political imaginaries of socialism. The Federation was framed within an internationalist outlook as well as transnational connections that were in sharp contrast to the predominance of national politics in the minds of Greek socialists. This clash was intensified by the novel questions posed by the outbreak of the First World War and the Russian Revolution. In these turbulent circumstances, the group in Salonica transplanted and adapted concepts and visions of internationalist socialism into a national setting. The outcome was the foundation of a socialist party (Socialist Workers' Party of Greece) in 1918 that did not speak in the name of the nation. The Federation had succeeded to reshape the world of Greek socialism by introducing an internationalist frame of mind. This paper aims to highlight how an 'exilic' community that came to the Greek nation by accident intervened to sponsor a different understanding of what it meant to be a socialist. We should not imagine this process as one where the 'xenos' enters a carefully painted portrait of socialism and finds his position within its borders. It is exactly this movement in entering the painting that blurs the colours, changes the size of objects and dynamically alters the framework itself.

From the empire to the nation-state

'That was, so to speak, the death of our movement'; this is how local socialists reflected on the novel realities following the entrance of the Greek army in the city of Salonica in October 1912.[5] Their circulars sent to the headquarters of the Socialist International describe the moment of transition as one marked by the imposition of military law, censorship and a prevailing atmosphere of intimidation. The disappointment of socialists was not only related to their perilous condition, but was deeply intertwined with the sudden collapse of the vision that had fuelled their imagination. The Socialist Workers' Federation of Salonica had been founded in 1909 on the belief that the forces of historical development would lead to the modernization of the Ottoman Empire and its transformation into a space of ethnic, religious and linguistic coexistence. In May 1910 Kristian Rakovsky had visited Salonica and propagated the prospect of a Balkan Confederation along those lines.[6] Having established from early on connections to the Socialist International, the Federation expressed its sense of belonging to an international movement, while at the same time promoting a local radical culture that was based on the idea of transnational and trans-ethnic solidarity against the divisive effect of nationalism.

---

[5] Federation to ISB, Verein für die Geschichte der ArbeiterInnenbewegung [VGA] Wien, Bestand Sozialdemokratische Parteistellen, Internationales Bureau, Balkanländer 1908–1919, Karton 127, Mappe 790, 1913.

[6] *La Confederation Balkanique et La Classe Ouvriere: Conference tenue sous les auspices de la Federation Socialiste Ouvriere de Salonique par le Dr. C. Racowsky, member du Bureau Socialiste Internationale*, Imprimerie Progres, Salonique, 1910. See also: Anreja Zivkovic and Dragan Plavsic (eds.), 'The Balkan Socialist Tradition, 1871–1915', *Revolutionary History* 8, no. 3 (2003) and Leften Stavrianos, *Balkan Federation: a History of the Movement toward Balkan Unity in Modern Times*, part 2 (Northampton, MA: Department of History of Smith College, 1944).

The Federation – as implied by its name – aimed to create a space of socialist and working-class unity as a response to the realities of the ethnic and religious diversity in the Ottoman Empire. Therefore, it was by default involved in the theoretical debate on the structure of socialist politics confronted with the multiple divisions of the labouring classes. The leading figures of the Federation were influenced by Otto Bauer and his writings on the preservation of the imperial structure as the ideal way to avoid a descent into national hostilities, as well as the importance of a singular socialist group that would allow room for expressions of working-class diversity. Avraam Benaroya, the unquestionable leading figure of the Federation, had a very clear idea in mind on this issue. A Sephardic Jew born in Bulgaria and active in the Bulgarian socialist movement, he had moved to Salonica right after the Young Turk revolution, believing that the time was ripe for the development of socialism in the Ottoman Empire. Benaroya was instrumental in influencing predominantly Jewish labour associations and small socialist groups of the city to form a novel organization, which after various deliberations eventually became the Socialist Workers' Federation of Salonica.

Benaroya had already argued in Bulgaria against the prospect of separate Jewish socialist and labour organizations (as had been the case in Eastern Europe) and defended the position that the interests of the Jewish working-class could be promoted only to the extent that it participated in trans-ethnic socialist and labour organization.[7] Benaroya transplanted this reasoning in Salonica. Even though the Socialist Workers' Federation was grounded on a secular current within the booming Jewish community, it never presented itself as a solely Jewish labour and socialist group. On the contrary, it promoted an image of a multi-ethnic organization that cultivated spaces of expression for all ethnic and religious communities. In 1909, *Fédération* issued a newspaper in four languages: *Amele Gazetasi, Efimeris tou Ergatou, Rabotniceski Wjestnik* and *Jornal del Laborador* were expressions of a political culture that allowed for linguistic diversity and at the same time operated within the supra-language of socialism. Their publishing practice was intended to prefigure the future Balkan Federation: a space recognizing ethnic difference under a common, unifying rubric of social and political organization. In the words of Benaroya, the Federation had decided for 'ethnic and philological reasons to form an organization to which all the nationalities might adhere without abandoning their own language and culture. Better still. Each and every one of them will be able to develop independently its culture and its individuality while working for the same ideal: the socialist ideal.'[8]

The cornerstone of this theoretical and practical architecture was the preservation of the Ottoman Empire. This position was close to the official stance of the Second International regarding the preservation of the status quo as a prerequisite of socialist

---

[7] Avraam Benaroy, *Evreiskiyat vipros y sotsialnata demokratsiya* (Poldviv, 1908). My thanks to Jonathan Schorsch for sharing this pamphlet. See also, Maria Todorova, *The Lost World of Socialists at Europe's Margins: Imagining Utopia, 1870s–1920s* (London-New York: Bloomsbury Academic, 2020), 63–5.

[8] Benaorya to ISB, July 1910, AMSAB-ISG, Archive Camille Huysmans, 0222. See also Abraam Benaroya, 'Die Turkische Gewerkschaftsbewegung', *Sozialistische Monatshefte* 2 (1910): 1079–81.

transformation, but in 1912 this world came to an end.⁹ The Balkan Wars signified the territorial expansion of nation-states and the defeat of the Ottoman Empire, and Salonika became a Greek city. Initially the Socialist Worker's Federation responded with an effort to turn the clock back by appealing in favour of a post-war settlement in which the city would be internationalized. However, the consolidation of Greek hegemony following the end of the Balkan Wars forced the group into a process of renegotiating its role within the new state. 'We have been trying for a long time to contact the true socialist groups in Greece', wrote J. Hazan to the Second International, 'in order to agree on a common plan of action for the future'.¹⁰ The realization of the irreversible nature of the Balkan Wars' outcome was compounded by the cataclysmic effect that the advent of Greek nationalism would have in the ranks of the Jewish community.

The most obvious effect was the rise of Zionism (which had been only marginal in the Ottoman past) as a response to the policies of the Greek State. 'What should be the response of Jewish socialists to Zionism' was the main question addressed to those experienced on the matter at the headquarters of the General Jewish Labour Bund.¹¹ This exchange underlines the networks of the socialists of Salonica and their readiness to address and adapt to novel realities. In an effort to prove the absurdity of Zionist claims, the Federation was eager to recognize that things had changed: 'Jews here enjoy the rights granted to all citizens.' This was true. The consolidation of borders, and more importantly the bilateral treaty between Greece and the Ottoman Empire in 1913 granting Greek citizenship to the inhabitants of the 'New Lands' (newly acquired from the Ottomans, that is), signified a transition to the politics of nation building in Macedonia.¹² For the Greek state, the Hellenization project was instrumental in fending off potential disputes and claims, especially from Bulgaria. In this context, politics of assimilation and suppression went hand in hand.

In this process, the Socialist Workers' Federation of Salonica responded by organizing and encouraging an *event* that introduced a novel protagonist in the transition process to the policies of the nation-state: the multi-ethnic labour force of the New Lands. In April 1914 thirty thousand tobacco workers – men and women from all ethnic communities – participated in an organized strike that spread across Greek Macedonia and lasted for several weeks. The 1914 strike was one of those historical events whose details are less important than the simple fact of its occurrence: this was the introductory act of mass politics in the recently acquired New Lands, and at the same time represented a novel typology of social action. Up to that point, strike activity in the Greek State had been associated with local incidents that had limited

---

⁹ Georges Haupt, *Socialism and the Great War: The Collapse of the Second International* (Oxford: Oxford University Press, 1972), 57–82.
¹⁰ Dumont, 'La Federation Socialiste Ouvriere de Salonique a l' époque des Guerres Balkaniques', 397.
¹¹ YIVO – Institute for Jewish Research, Bund Foreign Committee, RG 1401, Box 9, File 149.
¹² Katherine Fleming, *Greece: A Jewish History* (Princeton, NJ: Princeton University Press, 2008), 67–88. Devin Naar, *Jewish Salonica: Between the Ottoman Empire and Modern Greece* (Redwood, CA: Stanford University Press, 2016), 46–7.

scope. This strike, by contrast, connected the major urban cities of Greek Macedonia (Salonica, Kavala, Drama) under a detailed plan in which coordination was a crucial element.[13]

The Socialist Workers' Federation of Salonica provided the interweaving thread that made this possible, for the Federation's workplace demands were at the same time political demands. Writing in 1911, Benaroya had described the link between the labour union and the political party: the one was the bullet, the other the gun.[14] This reasoning, formulated in the days of Ottoman Empire, was employed again in the 1914 strike, transforming it from a merely 'economic' dispute into a demand for social and political equality within the Greek state. The Federation was entering the Greek public sphere *through* its ability to mobilize and organize. Where early accounts had highlighted its paralysis during the early months of the Greek occupation of Salonica, the strike action reflected a growing self-confidence and a desire for an integration process that would not be defined exclusively by the desire of the State, making a statement of an alternative model of integration. In essence, the Federation transplanted tactics that had served its growth under Ottoman rule into the Greek context. These included the ability to mobilize and negotiate, to raise political demands through the language of financial demands, and to alter the balance of forces by creating spaces of action in order to enlarge the window of opportunity for further advancement of its strategic aims.

The response of the Greek State confirms the impact of this endeavour. The 1914 strike was fundamental in the construction of an equation that haunted the Greek twentieth century: socialism was a tool in the hands of the enemies of the nation. For the local Greek press, the editor of the socialist publication *Avanti* was an 'anarchosocialistoevraiovoulgaros'.[15] The word might not make sense, but its components do: anarchist, socialist, Jew and Bulgarian. These four components combined to conjure a single spectre of dangerous individuals who were acting within national borders to further alien interests. In a trial against Avraam Benaroya, who was also arrested following the end of the strike, the local representatives of state power testified that he was, since his arrival in the city, an agent of Bulgarian interests and his activities during the strike had proven this; after all, he had tried to transform it to a popular uprising.[16] Benaroya and Samuel Yona were persecuted, labelled 'dangerous for national security', and taken to exile; arriving in Naxos, Benaroya and Yona were the first two Greek forbears of a practice that would become a common experience for thousands of political dissenters exiled in the Aegean as enemies of the nation. Socialism was equated, as Efi Avdela has pointed out, with the 'others' of the Greek nation.[17]

---

[13] Kostas Fountanopoulos, *Ergasia kai Ergatiko Kinima sti Thessaloniki* (Athens: Nefeli, 2005), 183–91.
[14] Avraam Benaorya, 'Politiki kai oikonomiki pali', *Efimeris tou Ergatou* (1909), 1.
[15] *Skrip*, 4 September 1914, 2.
[16] Benaki Museum Historical Archives, Eleftherios Venizelos Archive, Box 98.
[17] Efi Avdela, 'Class, Ethnicity, and Gender in Post-Ottoman Thessaloniki: The Great Tobacco Strike of 1914', in *Borderlines: Genders and Identities in War and Peace, 1870–1930*, ed. Billie Melman (New York: Routledge, 1997), 421–38.

Socialism entering national politics

On 23 April 1915 Athens hosted a small gathering of socialists.[18] This was the first time that socialists from Old Greece were hosting their comrades from the New Lands, and their agenda focused on the prospects of unification and participation in the upcoming national elections. While the elections served as the political and ideological formalization of unification between the Old and New lands of the nation-state, they also promised a testing ground for an expression of a new unified socialist movement. There was an innovation in these deliberations: the senior figures of socialism were not invited, as those meeting in Athens were dedicated to an anti-war platform. This was distinct from the positions taken by senior figures of the movement who had sided with the forces within the Socialist International that supported the war effort. On the contrary, the Socialist Workers' Federation of Salonica had attracted the interest of a diverse group of younger socialists who had disagreed with this position.

In this context, the April 1915 meeting can be seen as the inaugural point of a division within the world of Greek socialism on the question of war. This follows the overall development of the European socialist movement and the crisis of the Second International. In the Greek case, there was an additional layer of complexity: the Great War had engendered a rupture between the government of Eleftherios Venizelos and the royal family. The prime minister and his party (Komma Fileleftheron – Liberal Party) argued in favour of Greece's participation on the side of Entente with an eye to further Greek expansion in a favourable post-war settlement. King Constantine, and the party that supported him (Laiko Komma – Popular Party), insisted that national interests lay in a neutral stance, which, in essence, served the Central Powers. This tension culminated in a political crisis that led Greece to the edge of a civil war, later to be called National Schism.[19] Therefore, the ritual of passage into national politics for Greek socialism took form around the dilemma of war or neutrality.

In Salonica representatives of both the Liberal Party and the Popular Party met the leadership of the Socialist Workers' Federation in order to discuss the potential of incorporating socialist candidates on their lists. This was in part a necessary step as the electoral law encouraged coalitions, and at the same time it was evident that the vote of minority populations would be crucial in northern Greece. The decision of the Federation was to collaborate with the royalist camp, reflecting the accumulated bitter experiences from the Venizelist government: the brutal suppression of the 1914 strike and the imprisonment of leading socialist figures. The determining principle of the monarchist-socialist alliance was their common opposition to war. For the Federation, the preservation of peace at any cost spoke to its ideological core and the desires of its supporters: 'Viva la pace! A basso la guerra' was the Ladino slogan heard at its headquarters. As in the case of the 1914 strike one can see continuities with historical

---

[18] *Skrip*, 19 April 1915, 2.
[19] For a synopsis: Thomas Gallant, *Modern Greece: From the War of Independence to the Present* (London and New York: Bloomsbury, 2016), 180–7.

experiences of the imperial period: the Federation had been involved both in the 1908 and 1912 elections supporting socialist candidates, such as the Bulgarian Dimitar Vlahov, and, in 1912, the Liberal Party, and then later became the main oppositional force to the ruling Young Turks. In other words, the Federation had long been adept at negotiating with oppositional powers with the aim of carving out spaces for political action against dominant and oppressive policies.

This interplay between strategic aims and tactical choices was in dialogue with the voice of the newly integrated populations of Northern Greece. The ethnic minorities had little in common with the irredentist ambitions of the Liberal Party peddling the country's entry into the war as a decisive step towards its territorial expansion. The results confirmed the gap between New and Old Greece. The Liberal Party gained an absolute majority in parliament (186 in 316 seats), but the royalists dominated in northern Greece (66 in 74 regional seats). 'Socialist triumphs' announced the Athenian socialist newspaper *Organosis* when two socialist candidates were elected in parliament.[20] It was a moment saturated with symbolism: socialism was propelled into the national political arena by the nation's internal 'aliens' on a platform that questioned the fundamental understanding of 'national interests' as participation in war. It was a turning point for Greek socialism. The Socialist Workers' Federation was making a statement by being the first Greek socialist group to send elected representatives to parliament – and this thanks to a critical mass of voters on the margins of the nation.

In organizing the 1914 strike or participating in the 1915 elections, the Federation thus expressed a decisive shift in the core understanding of what socialist politics were. These developments underline the importance of mobility and interaction in the reshaping of Greek socialism. Among the thousand soldiers who had fought in the Balkan Wars, a handful were socialists: young men who had read Marxist texts and participated in the small-scale groups of Greek socialism. In Macedonia they had encountered a landscape that was closer to their readings: when meeting the powerful tobacco-workers union in Kavala, a socialist lieutenant from the Peloponnese was ecstatic that 'there one can see what social science argues (...) a huge labor hive that is at the same structurally diverse and unified in life'.[21] Young socialists from the 'Old Lands' were attracted more and more to the policies of the group. Their connection to the Federation was not based on ethnic grounds, but on agreement with the innovative aspects that the group represented within the ambit of Greek socialism. The Federation was quick to recognize and nurture this exchange. Socialist candidates in the 1915 elections reveal an interesting pattern: one Jew, Albert Curiel, who had arrived from Izmir and was fluent in Greek; one Greek lawyer, Aristotelis Sideris, who had fought in the Balkan Wars and had decided to join the Federation; and one Athenian socialist, Panayis Dimitratos, who represented the circle of young radicals who challenged the policies of the traditional figureheads of the movement.

[20] *Organosis*, 14 June 1915, 1.
[21] *Akropolis*, 1 October 1913, 2.

War and nationalism

The division of socialists on the question of war spoke to two contending notions of socialist political geography. The Socialist Workers' Federation of Salonica sponsored a transnational horizon rooted in the imperial connections and debates of the federalist vision. In the summer of 1915, Belgrade hosted a meeting of Balkan socialists that shared an anti-war position.[22] Sideris represented Greek socialism. His presence there marked a significant shift; before the War, Greek socialism had declared its support for the idea of a Balkan Federation, but had never participated in similar meetings or had any actual organizational ties with groups and parties of the region. What is more, earlier ties with Kristian Rakovsky allowed the Federation to connect with the proceedings in Zimmerwald and the quest for an alternative version of socialist internationalism. 'Here, since the European war started we have been going through hard times', reported the group from Salonica before expressing its admiration for the 'noble' voices of those ('Liebknecht, Luxemburg, and Zetkin') who went against the war.[23]

The anti-war platform became the rallying point for a meeting between the two socialist representatives in parliament and young Athenian socialists who questioned the traditional figurehead of the movement. Curiel and Sideris brought to Athens the internationalist political geography that had re-emerged during the early years of the War. Echoing the policies of Zimmerwald, they raised their voice in parliament against the deployment of Entente troops in Macedonia, condemned the war as an imperialist project, and defended the right of the labouring classes to peace and prosperity with a call for a Balkan Federation.[24] For the small global community of anti-war socialists, it was a refreshing reassurance. 'Comrades in Greece', rejoiced Robert Grim, 'are following our manifesto'.[25] By doing so the socialists of the Federation questioned the fundamentals of Greek socialism.

Socialism in the Greek state had expressed itself primarily through the language of national modernization. Class antagonism was seen as a sign of progress that would lead inevitably to the triumph of organized labour and the advent of a just society of equals. In this broad vision, the nation was not absent. On the contrary, it was a point of reference either in contrast to the 'backward' Ottoman Empire or as a meeting point of the common people against the corrupt elites and their political parties. Plato Drakoulis was the most recognizable figure of the movement in international socialist forums thanks to his years in Oxford where he taught Modern Greek.[26] Returning to Greece in 1908, he was briefly elected to parliament in 1910 and founded a group that combined Fabian social reformism with bionomic and theosophical principles

---

[22] Rakovsky to Grimm, 26 July 1915, in Horst Lademacher (ed.), *Die Zimmerwalder Bewegung: Protokolle und Korrespondenz, II* (Paris-The Hague: Mouton, 1967), 86–7.
[23] Federation Socialiste Ouvriere Salonique an Sozialdemokratische Partei der Schweiz, 6 October 1915, in *Die Zimmerwalder Bewegung*, 157–8.
[24] *Praktika Synodou tis Voulis*, 24 September 1915.
[25] Grimm to Rakovsky 3 October 1915, in Horst Lademacher (ed.), *Die Zimmerwalder Bewegung*, 151.
[26] See for instance, J. M. Cossano, *M. Pl. Drakoules et la Question Sociale en Grece* (1912).

(upon entering their offices, Benaroya was astonished to see a portrait of Jesus Christ hanging on the walls, with the familiar bust of Marx nowhere to be found). In the words of Drakoulis, borrowing the central term of Greek nationalism, socialism was the 'Megali Idea' [Great Idea] of the twentieth century.[27] This example highlights the systematic conflation between the social and the national question in the mindset of Greek socialists.

The modernizing policies of the Liberal Party, the Balkan Wars and the triumph over the old Ottoman Empire fuelled an understanding of socialism as a projection of national interests. Socialism appeared as the *social* version of the *national* question, a renewing stream of thought that expressed the necessity and the possibility of reforms that would allow the nation to synchronize with the general pattern of historical evolution. *To Koinoniko mas Zitima* [Our Social Question] was an influential book that introduced the concept of social antagonism; the author Georgios Skliros, a diasporic intellectual, interpreted the social question as the meeting point between class and the nation. In a telling example, he made a crucial amendment to the preamble of the Communist Manifesto (that had not yet been translated in Greek): 'the history of all hitherto existing societies is the history of struggle between classes *and nations*'.[28] The messianic quest for a social *and* national regeneration had led socialists to support the Balkan Wars, and now were greeting the advent of the Great War. Their stance reflected a deep-rooted belief that war was a necessary prerequisite for modernization and emanated from their commitment to the idea of the nation as the horizon of social reform.[29] War was neither good nor bad; it was necessary. This was the logical conclusion of an accumulated perception around the priority of the 'nation'.

In the summer of 1915 Nikolaos Giannios initiated a new socialist journal in Athens. The first article of the first issue of *Sosialistika Fylla* had the title 'Jewish Socialism', in which he expressed his disagreement with the recent activities of Socialist Workers' Federation of Salonica.[30] The prominent position of the article revealed the centrality of a perceived juxtaposition between 'Greek' and 'Jewish' socialism. His argumentation was simple: the group endangered the future of the movement by validating the dominant perception of socialism as an alien concept. In this context, Giannios attacked the Federation for promoting slogans and demands that reflected the interests only of the minority populations of northern Greece, thus further alienating 'Greeks' from the movement. He closed with a call to Hellenize the movement: '[Socialism] will be trusted by the Greek world when its headquarters are in the Greek capital, when its mind and heart will belong to a Greek majority.'

Giannios had fought in the Balkan Wars and then returned to Athens to find that younger members of his group, the Socialist Center, had been drawn to the anti-war platform of the Federation. But his attack spoke to a broader concern. In promoting an agenda for the 'nationalization' of the movement, Giannios echoed broader ideological

---

[27] *Erevna*, 1 May 1912, 1.
[28] Georgios Skliros, *To koinonikon mas zitima* (Athens, 1907).
[29] Augusta Dimou, *Entangled Paths towards Modernity: Contextualizing Socialism and Nationalism in the Balkans* (Budapest: CEU Press, 2009), 340–2.
[30] Nikolaos Giannios, 'Evraikos Sosialismos', *Sosialistika Fylla* 1 (July 1915): 1–3.

concerns regarding the New Lands' integration into the Greek state. This logic suggested that new citizens were 'Greeks' on the condition that they did not voice dissent. In opposing Greece's entry into the Great War on the side of Entente, the Socialist Workers' Federation of Salonica had challenged the cornerstones of Greek socialism: sympathy for national interests, and proximity to the Liberal Party of Eleftherios Venizelos, which was an ardent supporter of the country's participation on the side of Entente. For intellectuals like Giannios, the socialism movement ought to follow the example of the Socialist Parties across Europe aligning itself with the government of Eleftherios Venizelos. In this context, the pages of *Sosialistika Fylla* were increasingly peddling the theory that the military confrontation was a clash between liberalism and autocracy, an interpretation that strengthened their commitment to the policies of Venizelos and the Liberal Party.

In the summer of 1916, Eleftherios Venizelos moved his government to Salonica, bringing the country to the edge of a civil war. Socialist intellectuals followed him there and assumed positions of power: Kostas Hatzopoulos, translator of Marx, was appointed head of censorship and Nikolaos Giannios assumed a minor role in Macedonia. Socialists of the 'national' stripe sensed the imminent fulfilment of their prophecy: socialism was becoming relevant as the modernizing nation recognized their theoretical scaffolding. The Great War had signified a dramatic shift in socialist politics across Europe with socialists entering governments and joining the patriotic consensus, but in Greece this shift was not necessary.[31] Socialists were eager to contribute to national politics even before the Balkan Wars. What had changed was the interest of the Liberal Party, and Eleftherios Venizelos personally, to support 'Greek socialism' and create favourable conditions for its inclusion in national politics. This development was defined by the growing realization that post-war deliberations would involve the voice of the organized labour movement. To this end, Eleftherios Venizelos supported actively, and financially, the presence of socialist intellectuals to international socialist meetings in order to promote national aims.[32] Greek socialism was not only speaking the language of the nation; in certain circumstances it was becoming the language of the nation.

Socialism in the making

In November 1918 around forty men met in a room in Piraeus. This was to be the founding conference of the Socialist Workers' Party of Greece (SEKE).[33] This was no new group founded on a split from an existing party, but rather a coming together of diverse local groups that operated in the New and Old lands of the country. Most of the participants had never met before, they had not read the same newspaper, nor they had

---

[31] Geoff Eley, *Forging Democracy: The History of the Left in Europe, 1850–2000* (Oxford: Oxford University Press, 2002), 123.
[32] Leon, *The Greek Socialist Movement and the First World War*.
[33] *To Proto Synedrio tou SEKE: praktika*, Synchroni Epochi (Athens, 1982).

any shared point of reference that would allow them to belong to the same imagined community. This was a community in the making. Perplexed by the rifts and tensions of the preceding years, socialists were rallying to the widespread optimism following the Russian Revolution that history was creating the new future they sought. The proceedings of the conference reflect this. There were many issues to be decided, and each one resulted in lengthy discussions and acrimonious votes, but what defined this moment was its creative openness: socialism was not a set of predetermined policies, but a code to be written from scratch amid the urgent crises of the present, with only an alphabet of basic principles to aid the exercise of authorship.

SEKE was to a great extent a result of the policies of the Socialist Workers' Federation of Salonica. The Federation was the strongest of all local groups, and more importantly it had altered the conceptual frameworks of the Greek socialist movement. The organization of the 1914 strike, the participation in the elections of 1915 and the organic ties with the international socialist movement were innovative aspects coupled with a secular understanding of socialism that left room for experimentation. This tradition proved to be extremely valuable in the post-1917 setting. The founding conference of SEKE was a process in response not only to the cataclysmic developments in Russia, but also to the end of the Great War. The termination of the military confrontation seemed to promise an exodus from the era of violence that had transformed the Balkans since the first regional war of 1912. In this context, the nation-making process was reaching a terminal point, and one could argue (in the circumstances of the armistice) that Greece would now embark into a new period of stabilization. For the Federation, the effort for a unified socialist party served the purpose of creating a political geography that would reflect the novel realities of the nation-state.

The new party had room for those who were until recently considered to be 'aliens', as its statute allowed members 'regardless of ethnicity, race and religion'.[34] This was the last straw for Nikolaos Giannios who wanted small party cells of educated socialists to train those interested in the ideas of social struggle. More importantly the prospect of a mass party that would appeal to minority populations challenged his belief in a strict understanding of Greekness. Dressed in military uniform – a symbolic gesture that implied dominance over those coming from the New Lands – Giannios left the room with his supporters exclaiming 'there are some issues that can only be resolved by a duel'.[35] His departure signalled the final episode of the efforts to reconcile the old world of Greek socialism with the dynamic alliance between the Federation and the young radicals who had been attracted to socialism during the war. For his part, Benaroya insisted that if this was to be a party operating in a national context, it had to be convincingly 'Greek'. Therefore, he proposed that the party's headquarters should be in Athens, while in its Central Committee there was not a single Jewish name among the six selected ones. As it led the process of creating a single socialist party for the new nation-state, the Federation entered a kind of self-denial.

[34] Ibid., 102.
[35] Ibid., 110.

Despite these efforts, the newfound party was not smoothly accepted into the mainstream of Greek politics. The party's opposition to the Greek military expedition in Asia Minor after 1919, its strong following in the New Lands and association with the Communist International transformed SEKE into an enemy of the nation. The rise of anti-communism in the early 1920s was defined by a violent anti-Semitic rhetoric that insisted on the Jewish origins of socialism and communism. Ties to the global conspiracy of 'Judeo-Bolsheviks' against humanity replaced the traditional accusation that Benaroya was a Bulgarian agent. 'The Greek workers, all decent and innocent Greek workers', wrote the former consul to St. Petersburg, 'should know that the founder of Greek communism is a Jew from Bulgaria'.[36] It was an irony of history that in 1925, when these lines were written, Avraam Benaroya was not a Bolshevik any more – if he ever was.

Following the failed revolutionary upheavals of 1919–21, Benaroya and the founding generation of SEKE reached the conclusion that conditions necessitated a shift to reformism. Their proposal of a transition to a 'protracted legitimate existence,' as it became known within the history of the Left, demonstrated a flexible understanding of political praxis that had as its first concern the survival of the socialist idea and the creation of a space for political activity. This policy went hand in hand with a proposal for a tenuous relationship to the emerging Communist International. In essence Benaroya was proposing a reversal to the world of the Socialist International: a socialist party that would engage in national politics, advance its positions gradually and retain close ties to an international network of similar parties. In the new world of communist politics, there was no room for such versions of socialist internationalism. A young generation of radicals who were shaped by the experiences of the Greek-Turkish War (1919–22) and believed in the immediate prospect of the revolution and adhered to the Communist International expelled Benaroya and his comrades from the very party they had founded.

The young cadres that expressed the policies of bolshevization had something in common with the protagonists of this chapter: in their vast majority they were born outside Greece, and entering Greek communism was their way of reaffirming their integration in a novel social and political setting. In essence, they were refugees: refugees from Istanbul who fled to Moscow in the early years of the Revolution, refugees from Asia Minor who arrived to Greece following the Greek-Turkish agreement on the exchange of populations, and refugees from the Black Sea Soviet Republics who were caught in the perplexities of the Russian Civil War. The transition from Greek socialism to Greek communism was to be defined by a new generation of outcasts entering the nation from afar.

---

[36] Aristidis Andronikos, *Ti esti Bolsevikismos* (Typois Korōneou kai Denaxa, Athens, 1925), 159. Paris Papamichos Chronakis, 'Between Liberalism and Slavophobia: Anti-Zionism, Antisemitism, and the (Re)making of the Interwar Modern Greek State', *Jewish Social Studies* 25, no. 1 (2019): 20–44.

Conclusion

The story of the Socialist Workers' Federation of Salonica reveals the impact of radical minorities in the shaping of the socialist and labour movements within the expanding realm of the nation-state. The socialists of Salonica challenged the predominance of the Greek State in the annexed territories of the Ottoman Empire and negotiated their position in the emerging socialist scene of a country that was, until recently, unknown to them. This process did not only radically reshape Greek socialism; it also defined the ideological premises of anti-socialist politics. In both cases, the main point of confrontation was the relationship between the ideas of class struggle and the dynamics of nationalism. In the history of the socialist and communist movement this pivotal issue was often entangled with the transnational connections and internationalist commitments of exilic communities, immigrant groups and diasporic networks.[37] In this context, the case of the Socialist Workers' Federation of Salonica allows us to rethink the national boundaries of the socialist movement and to address the impact of the 'xenos' in the development of the multiple radical worlds in the epoch of the nation-states.

---

[37] Faith Hillis, *Utopia's Discontents: Russian Émigrés and the Quest for Freedom, 1830s–1930s* (Oxford: Oxford University Press, 2021); Ilham Khuri-Makdisi, *The Eastern Mediterranean and the Making of Global Radicalism, 1860–1914* (Oakland, CA: University of California Press, 2013).

2

A transatlantic connector: Bjarne Braatøy in the intersections of intelligence and social democracy, 1923–57

Nik. Brandal and Eirik Wig Sundvall

The "connectors" in informal transnational networks are "difficult prey for historians", as Pierre-Yves Saunier has pointed out.[1] Bjarne Braatøy is such a 'prey', and few historians have 'hunted' on his political trail. Until his ascend to the position of General Secretary of the Socialist International (SI) in 1956, Braatøy mostly stayed on the fringes, seemingly preferring a supporting cast to playing centre stage. His low-key profile is one of the reasons why he, somewhat contrary to his presence at some of the most defining moments in twentieth-century international politics, has largely escaped the attention of historians. Thus, despite his close contact with prominent academics, politicians and intelligence officers across countries and continents, we have had but scant knowledge of his many roles. Pieces may be put together from research on Norwegian and international socialist politics, as well as studies of US intelligence in the Second World War, where he is sometimes mentioned briefly.[2] The Norwegian historian Per Maurseth researched Braatøy's life trajectory for many years but regrettably his planned biography never saw the light of day.[3] Thus, no thorough overview of Braatøy biographical arc exists, and far less an analysis of his influence in the curious intersections of secret intelligence and Social Democracy.[4]

A further explanation for our scant knowledge of Braatøy's influence can be attributed to historians' tendency of 'methodical nationalism'. In a narrative limited to national contexts, Braatøy will inevitably appear as a political bit-player and an

---

[1] Pierre-Yves Saunier, *Transnational History* (Basingstoke: Palgrave Macmillan, 2013), 23.
[2] For historians of international socialism Braatøy seems to be a largely unknown figure, clearly illustrated by the brief mention of him as a "Swedish socialist" in Talbot C. Imlay, *The Practice of Socialist Internationalism: European Socialist and International Politics, 1914-1960* (Oxford: Oxford University Press, 2018), 260.
[3] Besides our own research, we are drawing heavily on the extensive research done by Maurseth, who, it should be noted, did not leave a manuscript. Per Maurseth's research archive can be found at The Norwegian Labour Movement Archives (ARK 2893).
[4] For the most extensive account, see Tore Pryser, *USAs hemmelige agenter: Den amerikanske etterretningstjenesten OSS i Norden under andre verdenskrig* (Oslo: Universitetsforlaget, 2010), 31–2.

outsider. If, on the other hand, we broaden the perspective from the national, and rather focus on transnational actors, organizations, networks and processes, Bjarne Braatøy's role becomes far more significant. Braatøy's life and career provide an entrance to understanding the informal aspects of how political processes are driven through transnational networks consisting of state, semi-state and non-state actors and organizations. This article provides a first scholarly overview of Bjarne Braatøy's life and career, a "biography that crosses boundaries" following a transnational protagonist and delving into the different geographical, political and linguistic contexts he crossed on his path.[5] Our ambition is to establish a basic biographical outline of Braatøy's political life, connections and shifting affiliations, to provide a resource for scholars working on the many historical contexts into which Bjarne Braatøy was embedded at different stages of his career.

An international socialist

Bjarne Frøyland Braatøy (originally Nielsen[6]) was born in the small town of Milaca, Minnesota, on 20 January 1900. His parents, Halfdan and Bertha, were Norwegian immigrants to the United States. His father was a Lutheran priest and returned to "the old country" with his wife and three children in 1908 to work for the Church of Norway. Thus, Bjarne spent the later years of his childhood and adolescence living in Bergen, Drammen and Kristiania (Oslo). In gymnasium, Bjarne Braatøy distinguished himself as such an extraordinary pupil that after matriculation he worked for two years as head teacher in English at a gymnasium in Sandefjord.[7] He had a talent for languages and during his life he learned French, Italian, German and Spanish in addition to his native English and Norwegian.[8] Early on he also exhibited an appetite for international exploration, and he got to see a bit of the world working on merchant ships sailing on ports in Europe, the United States and South America.[9] From 1921 onwards Braatøy studied law at the University of Kristiania/Oslo, with short stays abroad in Berlin and Paris, receiving his Candidate of Law degree (Candidatis Juris) in 1926. By this time, though, politics rather than law was becoming his main interest.

When Bjarne Braatøy joined the Social Democratic youth movement in Norway (NSU), the Norwegian labour movement was amid an internal strife. Unlike most of its European sister parties, the Norwegian Labour Party had joined the Communist International (Comintern) in 1919, and in 1921 the moderate fraction left the party to

---

[5] John Tosh, *The Pursuit of History: Aims, Methods and New Directions in the Study of History* (London and New York: Routledge, 2015), 55.
[6] ARK 2893/F/8. Bjarne Frøyland Nielsen changed his surname in 1927 but will be referred to as Bjarne Braatøy throughout the article.
[7] *Sandefjords blad* 30 May 1934: "Tidligere overlærer ved Sandefjords Handelsgymnasium tar doktorgraden i London".
[8] ARK 2893/F/4. United States National Archives (NARA)/RG 59/800.20211 BRAATOY, BJARNE (FBI investigation), 1943.
[9] ARK 2893/F/5; The Danish Labour Movement Archives (ABA) 39/25: Braatøy to Hans Hedtoft, 1 May 1946.

form the Norwegian Social Democratic Labour Party (NSA). Braatøy's introduction to socialist politics was in the academic milieu of the city's student society (Kristiania Studentersamfunn), where he fought to roll back the influence of the Marxists.[10] In these years Braatøy forged close friendships with later prominent Labour politicians such as Dag Bryn and Halvard Lange. He shared a small apartment with the latter, who would later become Norway's longest-serving Foreign Minister (from 1946 to 1965).[11] Halvard's father, the General Secretary of the Inter-Parliamentary Union and 1921 Nobel Peace Prize laureate Christian Lous Lange, became a personal mentor for Braatøy.[12] Politically isolated in Norway, the NSU nurtured ties to a network of European social democrats. Braatøy was one of the most internationally oriented among the young Norwegian social democrats and participated at conferences and congresses of the Socialist Youth International in different parts of Europe. Braatøy made intimate friendships with several young European social democrats he met at international forums in the 1920s. He developed a particularly close relationship with the chairman of the Danish Social Democratic Youth, the later Danish Prime Minister Hans Hedtoft and the later SPD chairman Erich Ollenhauer.[13]

In the autumn of 1926, a process of reunification between DNA and the NSA was under way. It was a marriage of electoral convenience, as the ideological differences were still very much present. Bjarne Braatøy was to play an important part when the Secretary General of the Labour and Socialist International (LSI), the Austrian Friedrich Adler, came to Oslo in November to assist and approve of the merging of the two parties. At the central board meeting of the NSA, Bjarne Braatøy translated Adler's contributions to the discussion, and wrote German translations of the Norwegian discussion on scraps of paper for him.[14] The unification process brought Bjarne Braatøy to prominence, as he was elected to the central committee of the reunited labour party's new youth organization *Arbeidernes Ungdomsfylking* (AUF) in January 1927. Fortunes were also smiling on him in his personal life. In the fall of 1927, he married Lillemor Munthe-Kaas Knutsen.[15] This, however, did not seem to make Braatøy more homebound to Norway. As he did at so many crossroads of his life, the internationalist at this point suddenly changed his political venue when attractive possibilities arose from abroad.

Braatøy continued to keep Friedrich Adler informed of the developments in the Labour Party through an extensive correspondence,[16] and in January 1928 Adler asked him to work for at the LSI secretariat in Zürich.[17] Braatøy eagerly accepted, and as Adler's secretary he prepared meetings and conferences and wrote reports. After about a year abroad Braatøy returned to Norway. He did not stay for long.

---

[10] Trygve Bull, *Mot Dag og Erling Falk* (Trondheim: J. W. Cappelens Forlag, 1987), 36, 173.
[11] Gidske Anderson, *Halvard Lange* (Oslo: Gyldendal, 1981), 91.
[12] ARK 2893/F/8; Norwegian National Library (NBB) 384 (Christian Lange's letters).
[13] ABA 39/25; ARK 2893/ F/5; Archiv der sozialen Demokratie der Friedrich-Ebert-Stiftung/SPD-Parteivorstand – Büro Erich Ollenhauer. Also: ARK 2893/F/8.
[14] ARK 2893/F/6: Project description (2001).
[15] They were married in October 1927: ARK 2893/F/8.
[16] ARK 1043 (Braatøy, Bjarne)/F/1.
[17] ARK 2893/F/8; NBB 384: Braatøy to Lange, 22 January 1928.

After the loss of his wife to tuberculosis in October 1929, he decided to move back to Zürich after Adler had offered him the permanent position of office manager at the LSI secretariat. Over the next years, Braatøy would return to Norway only for shorter stays, but corresponded with his Norwegian Social Democratic comrades and wrote articles on European socialism and international matters in Norwegian Labour newspapers and journals. In the years at the turn of the decade Braatøy guested socialist and trade union congresses across Europe lecturing, discussing and reporting as a representative of LSI. At the age of thirty, Bjarne Braatøy was actively engaged in the inner life of the international socialist movement. The political network forged at this time became decisive for his further career. Braatøy left the office in Switzerland after disagreements with Adler in 1931. What the actual differences between them were is unclear,[18] but seem to have played into Braatøy's later decision to challenge Adler for his position. Even so, it most likely played a secondary role in Braatøy's choice to leave Zürich, the main reason rather being an attractive offer from London.

In 1931 Bjarne Braatøy on invitation from one of Britain's leading socialist theorists and political scientists, Professor Harold Laski, moved to the UK for doctoral studies in political science at the London School of Economics (LSE).[19] The following year, he also remarried to Maria "Ria" Sauer, the daughter of the German chemist and entrepreneur Arthur Sauer. Beside his doctoral work, Braatøy earned a living as a correspondent for the LSI office in Zürich and writing for Social Democratic newspapers in Germany and Scandinavia. In 1934 he defended his thesis *Labour and War: The Theory of Labour Action to Prevent War*, which was published as a book the same year with a foreword by Laski.[20] One year after Hitler took power in Germany, Braatøy struck the spirit of the times, and the publication received considerable attention in academic and socialist circles in Britain.

During the 1930s Bjarne Braatøy became a familiar figure in the intellectual circles of the British labour movement, and later claimed that he had attended all Labour Party conferences from 1928 to 1940. When Scandinavian party and trade unionists visited London, he put them in contact with influential British counterparts. Such initiatives were part of what he called a "voluntary information service" that kept Nordic socialists informed about developments in the British labour movement.[21] A case in point is the work he did to make the trade unionist Ernest Bevin, one of "the most forceful and enterprising personality we have in the British labour movement", better known among Scandinavian Social Democrats.[22] In the latter part of the 1930s, Braatøy had become an internationally respected journalist and academic who travelled extensively in Europe, constantly nurturing and expanding his political and

---

[18] ARK 2893/F/6: Project description (2001).
[19] ARK 2893/F/5; ABA 39/25: Braatøy to Hedtoft, 1 May 1946.
[20] Bjarne Braatøy, *Labour and War: The Theory of Labour Action to Prevent War* (London: George Allen & Unwin Ltd, 1934).
[21] ABA 39/25: Braatøy to Hedtoft, 1 May 1946; ARK 2893/ F/5.
[22] Arbeitarrörelsens arkiv och bibliotek, Stockholm (AAB) 395/vol. 18: Braatøy to Gustav Möller, 26 March 1937; ARK 2893/F/5; *Arbeiderbladet* 2 December 1936: "Den engelske fagbevegelses leder"; *Meddelelsesbladet*, November 1937: "Ernest Bevin".

Figure 2.1 Portrait of Foreign Policy Advisor of the SPD Party Board, Bjarne Braatøy. Image courtesy of J.H. Darchinger/Friedrich-Ebert-Stiftung.

academic network. His major project during this time was writing a book in English on Swedish social democracy, published under the title *The New Sweden: A Vindication of Democracy* in 1939.[23]

In the spring of that year, fears of war were growing ever greater among European socialists. LSI had in recent years been dominated by German and Austrian socialists in exile, and both Britons and Scandinavians were dissatisfied with their militant activism. The British were fed up with what they saw as the International's attempts to politically control the member parties and wanted the organization to be transformed into an information agency since it had lost its weight as an international. The Scandinavians, for their part, feared that the LSI would threaten their countries' policy of neutrality, with unnecessary provocations against Nazi Germany.[24] As a consequence, an action was launched in May to replace Friedrich Adler as Secretary General. Bjarne Braatøy was promoted as a candidate by the British and Scandinavians, and also some Germans, most notably the leader of the German SPD-in-exile, Erich Ollenhauer, also strongly supported his candidacy. The process led to an upsetting conflict between member parties and actors. The question was, however, rendered

---

[23] AAB 395/vol. 18; AAB 204/vol. 13: Braatøy to Gustav Möller and Per Albin Hansson; ARK 2893/F/5; Bjarne Braatøy, *The New Sweden: A Vindication of Democracy* (New York: T. Nelson and Son, 1939).

[24] Imlay, *The Practice of Socialist Internationalism*, 258–60.

obsolete as the German occupation of Norway, Denmark and France in the spring and summer of 1940 led to the collapse of the LSI, putting an end to any further discussions on a new Secretary General.[25]

Wartime Atlanticist

In the initial phase of the war, Braatøy continued to do what he had been doing for years: connecting people and facilitating relations between Great Britain and the Nordic countries. In wartime there was a new urgency to this action. In a confidential letter to his friend Hans Hedtoft a few years later, he recounted his activities of this period. He portrays himself as a "spokesman" for the Finnish labour movement and "a recognized connoisseur" of Finnish matters at a large meeting of British MPs during the Winter War. At the same time, he had been a "liaison" for Scandinavian diplomatic envoys in complicated matters related to the war between Great Britain and Nazi-Germany. According to himself, he also arranged and led public meetings of journalists and politicians, one of which was attended by Winston Churchill. After the German attack on Norway and Denmark on 9 April 1940, he brought the first Norwegian military officers and politicians from occupied Norway "in contact with the people in the right circles, such as parliament, broadcasting and the press".[26]

Considering the informal nature of Bjarne Braatøy's activities, it would hardly be possible to confirm all the claims he makes in the letter. However, even if we assume that Braatøy might have overstated his role, there is little reason to believe that he should have provided information that was not basically correct in a letter to an old friend a few years after the events took place. Several other independent accounts of his activities support his general claim to have been an informer, connector and liaison in the chaotic crucible of diplomats, political exiles and foreign military personnel that was London in the winter and spring of 1940. One Norwegian officer even claimed in his memoirs that Braatøy had been among the "main people" organizing resistance against the German occupation of Norway, forging personal connections between Norwegian officers and "the important men in London". As such Braatøy was instrumental in the process that led to the establishment of the Norwegian Independent Company 1 within the Special Operations Executive (SOE).[27]

Bjarne Braatøy's informal role was replaced in the summer of 1940 by employment for the Norwegian government in exile in their newly established Norwegian Shipping and Trade Mission (Nortraship) working for the Allied war effort. In July Braatøy travelled to New York with his wife to work as information manager for the shipping director Øivind Lorentzen with editorial responsibility for its newspaper. In addition,

---

[25] Herbert Obenaus and Hans-Dieter Schmid (eds.), *Der Parteivorstand der SPD im Exil: Protokolle der Sopade 1933–1940* (Bonn: Verlag J.H.M Dietz Nachfolger, 1995), 377; Adolf Sturmthal, *Democracy under Fire – Memoirs of a European Socialist* (London: Duke University Press, 1989), 57–8.

[26] ARK 2893/F/5; ABA 39/25: Braatøy to Hedtoft, 1 May 1946.

[27] Svein Blindheim, *Offiser i krig og fred* (Oslo: Det Norske Samlaget, 1981), 91.

he worked as a *Daily Herald* correspondent to the United States and was engaged as a co-editor of the magazine *New Europe and World Reconstruction*, published by the non-profit organization League for Industrial Democracy (L.I.D.).[28] The same year he was also appointed L.I.D. president, a position that he held until 1944.[29] After stepping down as president he stayed on, first as a board member until 1948 and then as a member of the L.I.D. national council until his death.[30]

His work for the Norwegian government was however to be short-lived, as the Americans became aware of his talents and that he was born in the United States. In July 1942 Bjarne Braatøy therefore ended his work for Nortraship, after being offered the position of regional specialist on Scandinavia in the Office of War Information (OWI), which was responsible for American war propaganda abroad. In October of that year, he was appointed Chief Intelligence Officer of OWI's Department of International Operations, headquartered in New York. As Braatøy entered the world of intelligence much of his activities move into the historical shadows. Even so, we know that he functioned as an informal connector for European socialists in the United States. One notable example is his Norwegian party comrade Haakon Lie who was connected to the "right people" in the American trade union movement and given financial support by the OWI for a tour of the United States.[31] Shortly after Braatøy began his work at the OWI, the Federal Bureau of Investigation (FBI) opened an investigation of him, based on rumours that he was not trusted by the Norwegian exile community in London, who he had left "in the lurch" in a critical time and after that been careless in his mention of sensitive information as a Nortraship employee.[32] A senior State Department official justified the need for an investigation by saying that Braatøy in his OWI capacity was "the bottleneck through which all the most confidential directives and information must pass".[33] The FBI investigated the case but concluded in March 1943 that there was no basis for the allegations. All the agency's informants had emphasized that Braatøy was a "splendid man of high ideals", and Braatøy himself rejected the allegations.[34] The rumours were most likely part of a smear campaign by certain Norwegian government officials who wanted to undermine the OWI's Scandinavian Department, which was regarded as a propaganda challenger to the Norwegian government's own broadcasting efforts.[35] We can only speculate on what this meant for Braatøy's loyalties to Norway.

---

[28] ARK 2893/F/4.
[29] Rose L. Martin *Fabian Freeway. High Road to Socialism in the U.S.A, 1884–1966* (Belmont, MA: Western Islands 1966), 247.
[30] Ibid. See also Mina Weisenberg, *The L.I.D. Fifty Years of Democratic Education, 1905–55* (New York: League for Industrial Democracy 1955), 32.
[31] ABA 39/25: Braatøy to Hedtoft, Mai 1, 1946; ARK 2893/ F/5; Morris Weisz' interview with Haakon Lie, 1 March 1994. Library of Congress, Oral History Project, Labor Series: https://cdn.loc.gov/service/mss/mfdip/2004/2004lie01/2004lie01.pdf
[32] ARK 2893/F/4; NARA/RG 59/800.20211 BRAATOY, BJARNE.
[33] ARK 2893/F/4. Memo by State Department Assistant Director Adolf A. Berle, 30 October 1942; NARA/RG 59/800.20211 BRAATOY, BJARNE.
[34] NARA/RG 59/800.20211 BRAATOY, BJARNE: FBI investigation report, 24 March 1943.
[35] Hans Fredrik Dahl, *Dette er London! NRK i krig, 194045* (Oslo: J.W.Cappelens Forlag, 1999), 173–7; This motive was implied by the US official in London who reported the allegations to the State Department: NARA/RG 59/957.00P/3: A. J. Drexel Biddle to Secretary of State, 7 October 1942; ARK 2893/F/10.

The allegations clearly did not stick to Bjarne Braatøy, and after the investigation he was still trusted by the American authorities.

In September 1944 he transferred to the intelligence agency Office of Strategic Studies (OSS). There he was appointed Deputy Chief of OSS' Foreign Nationalities Branch (FNB), serving directly under the intelligence veteran DeWitt Clinton Poole. In March 1945 Braatøy succeeded Poole as Chief. The FNB's responsibility was to obtain basic overviews of war-relevant activities in political emigrant communities in United States. Braatøy supervised seventy employees who worked in subdivisions in several American cities and the department prepared reports, bulletins, newsletters and the like which were distributed to the White House, the Ministry of Defense, the Ministry of Justice and the Ministry of Foreign Affairs, the Allied High Command in Europe (SHAEF), the FBI and the OWI.[36]

The end of the Second World War in the summer of 1945 led to major budget cuts for war-oriented businesses in the United States. Braatøy's Foreign Nationalities Branch also had to reduce its staff. As a result of the American occupations of Germany and Austria, the branch did not terminate its work but concentrated on German and Austrian groups in the United States until the OSS was finally disbanded by President Truman in September 1945.[37] With his links to the European labour movement, the US intelligence community and the British and Scandinavian labour governments, Braatøy was better positioned to be a connector than ever before.

Back to Europe

In the spring of 1946, following the closing of the Foreign Nationalities Branch, Braatøy spent his accrued vacation time on an extended visit to Scandinavia.[38] The stated purpose of the trip was to write articles on the economic and political situation in Scandinavia for *The Nation* and *Overseas News Agency*,[39] but the reason was as much to re-establish his dormant networks within the social democratic movement in order to propose a new role for himself as a mediator between the European and North American left. Braatøy's lobbying efforts to become a Nordic Labour-attaché to the United States, seeking to transform his informal pre-war efforts into a paid position, however, were mostly unsuccessful, as it came to nothing more than a small stipend from the Swedish Labour Union.

After his return to the United States, Braatøy complained in a letter to Hans Hedtoft that he felt that his efforts on behalf of the Scandinavian labour movement were taken

---

[36] ABA 39/25: Braatøy to Hedtoft, 1 May 1946. ARK 2893/F/5; ARK 2893/F/4: Papers from the FNB, Office of Strategic Studies. Original US National Archives code unknown.

[37] Lorraine M. Lees, "De Witt Clinton Poole, the Foreign Nationalities Branch and Political Intelligence", *Intelligence and National Security* 15, no. 4 (2008): 81–103, https://doi.org/10.1080/02684520008432629.

[38] ABA 39/25: Bjarne Braatøy to Hans Hedtoft 1st May 1946; Siegfried Beer, "Exil Und Emigration als Information", in Jahrbuch 1989, ed. Siewald Ganglmair (Wien: Österreischischer Bundesverlag), 135; "Bjarne Braatøy på snarvisitt" in *Arbeiderbladet*, 14 February 1946, 4.

[39] "Stavangerfjord avgikk lørdag", in *Nordisk Tidende*, 31 January 1946.

for granted.⁴⁰ In the letter, which bears the appearance of a job application as much as a friendly exchange, Braatøy explained how he perceived himself as a "middleman", providing an all-important link between the labour movements in Scandinavia and the United States. Furthermore, he warned that if the Scandinavian social democrats failed to formalize this link – which in practice meant hiring Braatøy on his terms – this important connection could very well be lost.⁴¹ We do not know what Hedtoft's response was, but Braatøy's efforts to formalize his middle-man role were once more unsuccessful.

Braatøy was considered for Trygve Lie's administration at the United Nations, but the introduction of national quotas for the office of the Secretary General made this impossible.⁴² In September 1946 he instead took up a position at Haverford College in Pennsylvania, where he taught as a visiting professor in Government Studies until 1948, teaching international politics and foreign policy.⁴³ Among his courses at the renowned Quaker college were seminars on political and social issues related to atomic development, a topic that he would later revisit as an adviser to Eric Ollenhauer.⁴⁴

Another subject that he took an interest in was the emerging 'red scare'. At a public debate in May 1947 he warned that the "'front' of the Red movement" was on the offensive in Europe, and that unless the United States was willing to recommit to defending democracy, "the American cause was definitely losing [...]".⁴⁵ Perhaps his clear stance on the threat of communism in Europe was one of the reasons why he once more was employed by the US government, to work for the Displaced Persons Commission (US-DPC). The programme had been established to handle the vast number of East European refugees still at large in the western occupation zones of Germany and Austria, and in Italy,⁴⁶ and Braatøy's hiring coincided, as we will argue possibly not wholly coincidentally, with the continent's ascension as a battleground in the emerging Cold War.

The recruitment of Braatøy was most likely also due to his extensive knowledge of German language and culture, as well as his experience from the OSS. It is worth noting that after the closing of the FNB in 1945, some of its personnel had moved to the State Department, and most notably De Witt Clinton Poole had overseen the creation of "another group which maintained supposedly private, though officially sanctioned and supported, contacts with foreign nationalities groups".⁴⁷ The activities

---

⁴⁰ ABA 39/25: Bjarne Braatøy to Hans Hedtoft 1 May 1946.
⁴¹ Ibid.
⁴² ARK 2893/F/6: Project description (2001).
⁴³ Whitman, John T., "Bjarne Braatoy Adresses Collection. Interview Reveals Varied Activities", *Haverford News*, 2 October 1946, 3.
⁴⁴ Sozialdemokratischer Pressedienst, P/XI/54 – 5. März 1956. Der neue Sekretär der Sozialistischen Internationale – Bjarne Braatoy, 3; John T. Whitman, "Bjarne Braatoy Adresses Collection. Interview Reveals Varied Activities, *Haverford News*, 2 October 1946, 5.
⁴⁵ "AVC Works Out Controversy", *Haverford News*, 7 May 1947, 1.
⁴⁶ Cf. Wolfgang Benz (ed.), *Die Vertreibung der Deutschen aus dem Osten: Ursachen, Ereignisse, Folgen* (Frankfurt a.M.: Fischer Taschenbuch, 1995).
⁴⁷ Lorraine M. Lees, "De Witt Clinton Poole, the Foreign Nationalities Branch and Political Intelligence", *Intelligence and National Security*, 15, no. 4 (2000), 99.

of the group were built on Poole's prediction that the United States would remain a focus of "refugee and émigré agitation, much of it generated by eastern Europeans".[48] This later led to the creation of the National Committee for a Free Europe in 1949, a front organization for the Central Intelligence Agency (CIA), of which Poole served as its president until 1951.

Initially Braatøy was sent to Austria, but in 1949 he became Senior Officer for the commission's operations in Bavaria, as head of the office in Augsburg.[49] In 1950 his contract was extended until 1952, in order to write up a report detailing the history of the US-DPC.[50] He moved to the headquarters in Frankfurt, which brought him in close proximity to the Bonn headquarters of the reconstituted SPD, and it was around this time that he reacquainted himself with his old friend Erich Ollenhauer, who had risen to the position of vice chair of the party.[51]

From the available sources it is not clear if Braatøy's mission included clandestine work in addition to his formal position within the US-DPC, but circumstantial evidence certainly points to this as a possibility. The CIA was formed in September 1947, and many of Braatøy's former OSS colleagues, such as Poole, were recruited to the new organization.[52] We also know that in addition to resettling refugees, the Displaced Persons programme was also used to recruit German scientists and intelligence officers to work for the American government against Soviet Russia, including several high-ranking members of the Nazi regime. In fact, the CIA was put in charge of screening applicants to root out war criminals, and thus became integrated in the activities of the US-DCP.[53]

The early 1950s, following the outbreak of war on the Korean peninsula and escalating conflict over Berlin, saw a rapid expansion of US intelligence activities in Europe, both through recruitment of foreign nationals and coordination with other US governmental organizations on the ground. The increased need for information led to an intensified campaign to recruit experts, informers and agents, predominantly among the Soviet experts from the former Nazi regime, refugees from the Eastern Bloc and anti-communist social democrats. It takes but a little stretch of the imagination to see that the US-DPC in Germany and Austria would be fertile ground to identify and recruit such individuals, and among the OSS old guard few would be more suitable to head the operation than Braatøy. Furthermore,

---

[48] Ibid.
[49] ARK 2893/F/5. U.S. DISPLACED PERSONS COMMISSION, Field Operations Chart, 1 April 1949. NARA/RG 278/150.
[50] ARK 2893/F/5. NARA/RG 278: Records of the Displaced Persons Commission.
[51] ARK 2893/F/6/: Braatøy's correspondence with Ollenhauer; Cf. Franz Walter, *Die SPD: Biographie einer Partei* (Hamburg: Rowohlt, 2009), 118–19
[52] Cf. Disciples Douglas Waller, *The World War II Missions of the CIA Directors Who Fought for Wild Bill Donovan* (New York: Simon and Schuster, 2015) and Thomas F. Troy, *Donovan and the CIA: A History of the Establishment of the Central Intelligence Agency* (Langley, VA: Central Intelligence Agency, 1981).
[53] Cf. NARA, Implementation of the Nazi War Crimes Disclosure Act. An Interim Report to Congress by the Nazi War Criminal Records Interagency Working Group, October 1999, https://www.archives.gov/iwg/reports/nazi-war-crimes-interim-report-october-1999 [read 28 August 2020].

the change in his job description meant that his area of operations was expanded to all of Western Europe.

It was at this time that he resumed his contacts with people like Eric Ollenhauer, who was a focal point in the anti-communist fraction of the SPD. It is also noticeable that rumours about Braatøy's connection to US intelligence circulated at the SPD-headquarters in the early 1950s, and according to the party's then foreign policy adviser, Heinz Putzrath, Braatøy's close contacts with the American embassy and military attaché were discussed among the party administration.[54] As long as the operational files in the CIA archives remain closed to researchers, the exact connection between Braatøy and US intelligence remains unclear.[55]

Following the closing of the US-DPC, Braatøy was once more left unemployed. His initial attempts at securing a position at the newly established NATO headquarters in Fontainebleau, France, came to nothing,[56] but his old contacts within the social democratic parties of Austria and Germany soon came to his rescue. In the fall of 1952, he was hired as a technical adviser by Eric Ollenhauer, who had acceded to the position of SPD chairman following the death of Kurt Schumacher. According to Putzrath, it was a temporary position on a monthly basis. Ollenhauer therefore organized for him to find additional work in other parts of the party apparatus, leading to Braatøy being regarded as his representative.[57]

Braatøy would remain in Germany, working for the SPD in various capacities, until 1956.[58] The official reason for not returning to the United States was writing a book on the German party, but as no manuscript, draft or even op-eds exist to bear witness of such work, this was most likely a pretext. Officially, Braatøy's role as an adviser to Ollenhauer was mainly within two areas: the nuclear question, which he had worked on while at Haverford, and the question of Germany's admittance to the Western security alliance and subsequent rearmament. As West Germany's admittance to NATO became the possibly hottest topic in Norwegian foreign policy, it is likely that he became reacquainted with his old friend from the Norwegian NSU, Dag Bryn, who served as Norwegian attaché to Bonn from 1952 to 1954,[59] and he also made several personal visits to Hans Hedtoft, who had risen to the position of Danish Prime Minister. Braatøy also played a third important role for Ollenhauer, of which he was eminently suited. He became an unofficial ambassador for the SPD to argue for the readmittance of the party to the 'polite society' of European socialism. His base of operation was the party headquarters in Bonn, from which he maintained his close personal and political connections to social democrats, especially in Scandinavia but also in Belgium and the Netherlands.

---

[54] ARK 2893/F/9: Maurseth's interview with Heinz Putzrath (audio tape) 16 July 1993.
[55] ARK 2893/F/7: Per Maurseth's correspondence with CIAs Information and Privacy Coordinator, 2001–2.
[56] ARK 2893/F/6: Project description (2001).
[57] ARK 2893/F/9: Maurseth's interview with Heinz Putzrath (audio tape), 16 July 1993.
[58] ARK 2893/F/10. NARA/RG 59/110.4 OIR/8-1054: Report on Bjarne Braatøy from HICOG, Bonn, to State Department, 10 August 1954.
[59] ARK 2893/F/5: Reports from Dag Bryn to Norway's Foreign Office.

Figure 2.2 Bjarne Braatøy, SPD leader Erich Ollenhauer and Minister of Foreign Affairs of Norway Halvard M. Lange in the mid-1950s. Image courtesy of AdsD/FES.

As social democrats from all over Europe gathered for the funeral of Braatøy's old friend Hans Hedtoft in the spring of 1955, the most topical question was choosing a successor to Julius Braunthal as Secretary General of the SI. Braunthal was approaching the age limit, and a few months after Hedtofts funeral, Alsing Andersen in a letter to his Scandinavian comrades Haakon Lie and Kaj Björk claimed that Ollenhauer and the SPD were "unconditionally behind" making Braatøy the new Secretary General.[60] Andersen therefore suggested that the Scandinavians should support his candidacy as well.

An electoral committee was appointed, with Morgan Phillips from the British Labour Party, Fritz Heine from SPD and Haakon Lie from the Norwegian DNA. As Alsing Andersen had suggested, Lie and Heine lined up behind Braatøy, but Phillips

[60] ARK 2893/F/10: Andersen to Lie and Björk, 3 March 1955.

remained hesitant to do the same. According to Kaj Björk, the discussion came to a head at a meeting in Zürich when Guy Mollet from the French Socialist Party put forward warnings they had received from the French intelligence services about Braatøy's connection to US intelligence.[61] From our perspective, it's interesting to note that both the arguments for and against Braatøy's candidacy were in their nature transnational. For the SPD he was seen as an ambassador charged with advocating the party's re-entrance to the West European social democratic movement, and for the Scandinavians he was a trusted ally and a counterweight to the potential influence of the French as well as a bridge to renewing the contact with the Germans, that had been the main influence on social democracy in Scandinavia in the late nineteenth and early twentieth century. For the French, on the other hand, Braatøy's connection to American Intelligence as well as being seen as Ollenhauer's handpicked man, both rose suspicions. The British opposition to Braatøy's candidacy is possibly the most surprising, as they had been the most vocal supporters for Braatøy's ascendance to the same position in 1939. While they shared the hesitancy towards a German candidate, especially as it might signal a new Scandinavian-German power block within the organization, it was as much his connection to the American labour movement that seems to have driven the opposition than his work for the US government.[62] Especially Morgan Phillips had a deep and long-held resistance to any American influence in the SI.

What broke the deadlock was the efforts of the Scandinavians, especially Haakon Lie, on Braatøy's behalf. French fear of Braatøy as a trojan horse for American intelligence was allayed and the British opposition neutralized by emphasizing Braatøy's Scandinavian background and connections. That this pressure must have been considerable is illustrated by a letter from Haakon Lie to Heine after Braatøy's death, where he outlined the reason why he did not want to fight for a new Scandinavian candidate: "I do not want to be involved again in a tug of war in this matter. We did a good thing when we fought for Bjarne – but not again".[63] In hindsight, most of the arguments for and against Braatøy have at least some merit. The L.I.D. certainly saw Braatøy as their man, and as Franz Neuman said at Braatøy's introduction as Secretary General, his "parents were Norwegian, he is born in America, have studied at several European Universities and finished his doctoral thesis in England".[64] Perhaps his background was thus most succinctly put by the SPD newspaper *Vorwärts*, stating that he was a "citizen of the world by destiny and profession".[65]

In the spring of 1956 Braatøy finally moved to London to take up the position. His bedding-in period, however, was to be short-lived as the geopolitical situation took dramatic turns following first the uprisings in Hungary over the summer of 1956 and

---

[61] ARK 2893/F/5. AAB 69 (Kaj Björk)/vol. 27: Kaj Bjørk's report from the SI meeting in Zürich, 2–4 March 1956.
[62] ARK 2893/F/9. Department of State, Incoming Telegram to Secretary of State from London, 8 March 1956.
[63] ARK 2893/F/5. Haakon Lie to Fritz Heine 12 April 1957. Partei-Vorstand, folder 01943. Archiv der sozialen Demokratie der Friedrich-Ebert-Stiftung, Bonn.
[64] Martin, *Fabian Freeway. High Road to Socialism in the U.S.A, 1884–1966*, 178; Neumann quoted in "Dr. Bjarne Braatoy. Der mann der Internationale", *Berliner Stimme*, 23 June 1956. Our translation.
[65] "Weltbürger durch Schicksal und aus Berufung", *Neuer Vorwärts*, 9 March 1956.

subsequent Soviet invasion in the fall, and then the outbreak of the Suez Crisis in late October. Both came to impact the work of the SI, as the development in Hungary threatened to create cleavages within the West European left over how to best confront communism and the Eastern Bloc, where irreconcilable factions took up increasingly hard stances. While Braatøy was undoubtedly on the anti-communist side, he had to strike a fine balance as Secretary General, and perhaps no place more so than in the issue of German re-unification that, following the reunification of Austria in 1955, once more had become an issue. From this, it seems clear that Braatøy's work as Secretary General was weighed down more by politics and putting out fires that threatened the cohesion of the SI than policy work. The areas where he was freer to take initiative were the discussions on whether to expand the SI networks to Asia and Latin America, even if this process was fraught with political problems within a Cold War framework.[66] As such he undoubtedly contributed to what would become the globalization of the SI. His old pet project of strengthening the ties between the European and American left, however, seems to have borne little fruition. His untimely death from a stroke only a year into his term thus meant that he returned to relative obscurity in the annals of the socialist movement.

Conclusion

The obituaries give testament to his vast network and areas of operation, but they also bear evidence of why Bjarne Braatøy has remained somewhat of an unknown figure in the history of the socialist movement. According to the German Jusos-newspaper *Klarer Kurs*, Braatøy was "a cosmopolitan and well-travelled", who had found Germany as "a piece of home",[67] while the main Labour newspaper in Norway declared him "a true international socialist» who came to live most of his life "outside of Norway, always preoccupied with connecting two or more countries and working for international cooperation".[68] The transnational nature of his career meant that he was well suited for the role of SI Secretary General, but also that it was only once he acceded to this role that he became noticeable to the general public, who accesses politics in a national setting. His short tenure thus meant that he was to remain somewhat in the shadows, often mentioned in books by or about more renowned figures, but seldom as an important actor in his own right.

In this chapter we are only able to sketch a brief overview of Bjarne Braatøy's biography, which means that central questions remain unanswered. The most important is the exact nature of his connection to US intelligence and what importance this had for his work within the socialist movement in the early Cold War. But hopefully we have established a platform for further research that can shed greater light on Bjarne Braatøy and thus also on the important events in which he partook.

---

[66] Imlay, *The Practice of Socialist Internationalism*, 434.
[67] Karl Garbe, "Bjarne Braatoy", *Klaren Kurs*, April 1957.
[68] "Bjarne Braatøy", *Arbeiderbladet*, 16 March 1957.

3

Social democracy and anti-communism in Cold War Asia: The Japan Socialist Party's role in the Asian Socialist Conference in the 1950s

Yutaka Kanda

Introduction

Following the beginning of the Cold War in the late 1940s, non-communist socialists, often called democratic socialists or social democrats, constructed their international network not only in Europe but also globally. The Socialist International (SI), which European anti-communist socialists established in 1951, included some non-European members from the beginning, such as socialists of Japan, Israel, the United States, Canada and Argentina. On the other hand, socialists in Asia, led by the Burmese, Indians and Indonesians, separately built their international socialist organization, the Asian Socialist Conference (ASC), in 1953. Throughout the 1950s, efforts were made to unite these two socialist networks; these efforts, however, were not successful. Today, the SI still functions as a forum of social democracy, albeit with much less political influence, but the ASC was virtually dissolved by the end of the 1950s.

Although international non-communist socialist networks such as the SI and the ASC have long been overlooked by the majority of Cold War historians, we have recently seen important advances in the field. Most notably, Talbot C. Imlay and Ettore Costa have provided groundbreaking accounts of the SI in the 1950s and its predecessors.[1] Imlay has also revealed European socialists' involvement in the ASC, focusing on the issue of decolonization.[2] In regard to the ASC, Kyaw Zaw Win,[3]

---

[1] Talbot C. Imlay, *The Practice of Socialist Internationalism: European Socialists and International Politics, 1914–1960* (Oxford: Oxford University Press, 2018). Ettore Costa, *The Labour Party, Denis Healey and the International Socialist Movement: Rebuilding the Socialist International during the Cold War, 1945–1951* (Cham: Palgrave Macmillan, 2018).

[2] Imlay, ibid. Talbot C. Imlay, 'International Socialism and Decolonization during the 1950s: Competing Rights and the Postcolonial Order', *American Historical Review* 118, no. 4 (2013): 1105–32.

[3] Kyaw Zaw Win, 'The 1953 Asian Socialist Conference in Rangoon: Precursor to the Bandung Conference', in *Bandung 1955: little histories*, ed. Antonia Finnane and Derek McDougall (Caulfield: Monash University Press, 2010). Kyaw Zaw Win, A History of the Burma Socialist Party (1930–1964), PhD thesis, School of History and Politics, University of Wollongong, 2008, https://ro.uow.edu.au/theses/106/ (last accessed 27 June 2021). Kyaw Zaw Win, 'The Asian Socialist Conference in 1953 as Precursor to the Bandung Conference in 1955' (Paper presented at the Asian Studies Conference of Australia, Canberra, 2004).

Boris Niclas-Tölle[4] and Su Lin Lewis[5] have published highly insightful studies that primarily discuss the roles of the Burma Socialist Party, Indian socialists, and Indonesian and Burmese socialist intellectuals, respectively.[6] However, whereas these scholars mainly address the ASC from the viewpoint of anti-colonialism, neutralism or non-alignment – which I also consider as important aspects of the organization – no one has paid full attention to another significant aspect of the socialist network in the 1950s: competition against communism. In other words, while previous scholars tended to regard the ASC as the network for the South and discuss the SI-ASC relations in the North-South context, it is also essential to consider the fact that they more proactively committed themselves in the East-West conflict of the Cold War than existing studies imagine. That is, anti-communism was deeply rooted in the ASC as well as in the SI and worked as an important unifying factor for both of them, at least in the early 1950s.[7]

This chapter focuses on the role of the Japan Socialist Party (JSP) in the SI and the ASC, as it was one of only two parties to maintain official membership in both. I argue that the JSP has been overlooked as an important bridge between European and Asian socialists, as well as in their leading role in the ideological debate in the ASC. Particularly regarding the latter, I will demonstrate that the JSP and the ASC almost concurrently shifted their ideological position in the middle of the 1950s, from anti-communism and pro-SI stance to neutralism and indifference to cooperation with Europeans. Ultimately, by highlighting the historical role of the JSP, I aim to demonstrate why the SI and the ASC could not succeed in establishing close relationships and why the international non-communist socialist network took root in Europe but not in Asia.

The Socialist International and dissatisfied Asian socialists

Contrary to the period before the Second World War,[8] the post-war European socialists were keen to expand their international network outside Europe. As early as in July 1947, Edith Loeb, Secretary of the Socialist Information and Liaison Office, contacted a Japanese journalist in order to exchange information on socialist parties in Europe and Japan.[9] European socialists showed more enthusiasm for approaching Asian socialists

---

[4] Boris Niclas-Tölle, *The Socialist Opposition in Nehruvian India, 1947–1964* (Frankfurt am Main: Peter Lang GmbH, 2015).
[5] Su Lin Lewis, 'Asian Socialism and the Forgotten Architects of Post-Colonial Freedom, 1952–1956', *Journal of World History* 30, nos. 1–2 (2019): 55–88.
[6] Also, Imlay has recently published his work about the ASC: Talbot C. Imlay, 'Defining Asian Socialism: The Asian Socialist Conference, Asian Socialists, and the Limits of a Global Socialist Movement in 1953', *International Review of Social History* 66, no. 3 (2021).
[7] Older but important studies about the SI and the ASC are: Pradip Bose, *Social Democracy in Practice: Socialist International, 1951–2001* (Delhi: Authorspress, 2005), Julius Braunthal, *History of the International, vol. 3, World Socialism, 1943–1968* (London: Victor Gollancz, 1980), and Saul Rose, *Socialism in Southern Asia* (New York: Octagon Books, 1975).
[8] Braunthal, *History of the International*, 213.
[9] Letter from Edith B. Loeb to 'Dr. Ryu', 16 July 1947, Socialist International Archives [hereafter SIA], 687, Internationaal Instituut voor Sociale Geschiedenis (International Institute of Social History), Amsterdam, the Netherlands [IISG].

after the Committee of the International Socialist Conference (Comisco) was formed in rivalry with the foundation of Cominform in October 1947. In a December 1949 meeting, Comisco unanimously agreed to admit the JSP as a full member.[10]

This decision reflected European socialists' desire to overcome Eurocentrism and pursue racial diversity in their movements. In this sense, the Japanese socialists were a convenient non-European partner because socialist movements in Japan had a decades-long history and the JSP proved popular enough in Japan to take power in government when socialist Katayama Tetsu[11] formed his cabinet in 1947-8. In addition, Europeans' motivation for approaching Asians was strengthened by the fact that communists emerged victorious in the Chinese Civil War in October 1949 and established the People's Republic of China just two months before the unanimous approval of the JSP to Comisco. About half a year after the Japanese participation, Julius Braunthal as Administrative Secretary of Comisco wrote to Sone Eki, a Japanese socialist, that 'European Socialism attributes the greatest importance to the social and ideological trends in Eastern Asia' and 'only Democratic Socialism offers peace, freedom, and security'.[12] In short, Comisco – formed to compete with communists – needed to counteract the success of the communists in expanding their influence in Asia.

For Japanese socialists, connections with European socialists were significant to obtain legitimacy as an internationally recognized socialist movement. The JSP was formed in 1945 by three independent socialist movements, commonly called the rightists, centrists and leftists. At the time of its founding, the rightists controlled the party, but the leftists still maintained a great appeal to the public because they were the only ones who opposed the war. Each faction in the JSP attempted to utilize their relationships with European socialists to consolidate their power, differentiating themselves from other left-wing movements. When the administration of Katayama, a rightist leader, suffered a crushing defeat in the general election in 1949, he was forced to step down, and the leftists in turn took over leadership of the party. Thus, Katayama attempted to restore the influence of rightists by making close ties with anti-communist European socialists.

The JSP leftists also respected European socialists as their ideological model until the formation of the SI in 1951,[13] when the SI's first Frankfurt congress disappointed them. The JSP mission to participate in the Frankfurt congress was headed by a leftist leader, Suzuki Mosaburo. The Japanese socialists were warmly welcomed by Europeans. In this congress, the JSP was elected as the only non-European permanent member of the SI Bureau.[14] The JSP also played a role for bridging European and Asian socialists.

---

[10] Minutes of COMISCO, Paris, 10-11 December 1949, SIA, 265, IISG.
[11] This chapter puts family name first and given name second when writing Japanese names.
[12] Letter from Julius Braunthal to Eki Sone, 8 July 1950, SIA, 687, IISG.
[13] For example, a month before the SI Frankfurt Congress, an article apparently written by a leftist appeared on the official newsletter of the JSP. It particularly praised the peace policy of the Scandinavian social democrats and also argued that none of the British Labour Party's policies was contradictory with JSP's. *Shakai Shimbun*, 15 May 1951.
[14] The Socialist International Circular No. S.C.211/51, 16 August 1951, Gaibun (Foreign Documents) 44, Papers of the Japan Socialist Party[PJSP], the Waseda University Archives, Tokyo, Japan[WUA].

In the SI statute adopted in this congress, the article on 'regional conferences', which aimed at aligning Asian non-communist socialists with the SI, was added 'as a result of the Japanese suggestion'.[15]

However, the Frankfurt congress was to a large extent unsatisfactory for Suzuki and his leftist colleagues. Suzuki did not necessarily reject the anti-communism of European participants – for example, the Frankfurt Declaration was filled with harsh anti-communist statements, such as 'International Communism is the instrument of a new imperialism'.[16] He later reported that one of his purposes joining in this congress was to 'fight against Cominform'.[17] The JSP leftists, however, could not support US military actions against the communist camp as European socialists did. The Frankfurt Congress adopted a resolution entitled 'Socialist World Action in the Struggle for Peace', stating, 'the war in Korea [...] has also shown that collective action by the free democracies can halt aggressions'.[18] This resolution clearly supported the action of UN troops, led by the United States, in the ongoing Korean War. In the discussion for this resolution, Morgan Phillips, Secretary of the British Labour Party, said, 'I hope no-one here takes the view that a realistic attitude towards problems of military defense is incompatible with major reforms in the domestic field or with a left wing attitude to politics in general.'[19] The draft was adopted with no objections but one abstention from the JSP, which insisted, 'we as socialists cannot admit to prioritize the military affairs'.[20] Anti-militarism was the core identity of the JSP leftists.

In addition, an Indian socialist Rammanohar Lohia, who was an observer in this debate, declared 'I am opposed' to this resolution because 'there is not a specific Socialist idea in it'. Although he stated, 'this does not mean to say that we adopt an attitude of neutrality or refuse to meet aggression', it was obvious that he felt sympathy with the idea of neutralism: 'The Socialist parties of Western Europe may have no alternative but to belong to the Atlantic world. But the Socialist parties elsewhere do not feel the same compulsion. They wish to remain outside the system of competing big power alliances.'[21]

There was another issue that the Japanese and Indian socialists differed from the Europeans: anti-colonialism. The Frankfurt Declaration attached importance to tackling against poverty and to aiding economic development to the underdeveloped

---

[15] 'Draft Statute [of the Frankfurt Congress]', no date, 344-13, Papers of Wada Hiroo, Modern Japanese Political History Materials Room, the National Diet Library, Tokyo, Japan [NDL]. 'Dai 8 Kai Komisuko Sokai Narabini Dai 1 Kai Shakaishugi Intanashonaru Taikai ni Kansuru Hokokusho (Report of the eighth Comisco meeting and the first congress of the Socialist International)', no date, 1-079-01, Suzuki Bunko (Suzuki Papers), the Ohara Institute for Social Research, Hosei University, Tokyo, Japan.
[16] 'Aims and Tasks of Democratic Socialism: Declaration of the Socialist International adopted at its First Congress held in Frankfort-on-Main on 30 June–3 July 1951', Official Website of the Socialist International, https://www.socialistinternational.org/congresses/i-frankfurt/ (last accessed 27 June 2021).
[17] 'Dai 8 Kai Komisuko Sokai.'
[18] *Socialist International Information* [hereafter *SII*], 1(27–8), 1951, 11. Collections of *SII* are accessible at the IISG.
[19] Ibid., 14.
[20] 'Dai 8 Kai Komisuko Sokai.'
[21] *SII*, 1(31–2), 1951, 23–6.

regions, insisting that 'Democratic Socialism must inspire the economic, social and cultural development of these areas'.[22] However, it did not clearly defend the *political* independence of colonies. Believing in socialist internationalism, European socialists were not necessarily sympathetic with nationalism of peoples under empire.[23] Wada Hiroo, a participant from the JSP, highlighted the importance of colonial issues: 'we call upon the First Congress of the Socialist International to forge the closest possible links with Asia and to help in securing the liberty and independence of that great Continent.'[24] Lohia also suggested to make 'international Socialism a force which can abolish the international caste system', revealing his belief that socialists must support the independence of all peoples.[25]

Thus, frustrated Japanese and Indian socialists realized the significance of constructing their own network. In Frankfurt, Suzuki frequently met Lohia and another Indian socialist leader, Asoka Mehta, to discuss the detailed plan for the ASC.[26]

Anti-colonialism and anti-communism in the first Asian Socialist Conference

Japanese socialists were not a part of the original members who initiated the plan for establishing a network of Asian non-communist socialists. It began through frequent contacts from 1947 to 1949 among the socialists of Burma, India and Indonesia.[27] Independence of India was accomplished in August 1947, Burma in January 1948 and the war of independence of Indonesia was over in December 1949. Socialists were an important part of political forces fighting for decolonization in their respective countries. Nevertheless, to Asian socialists, European socialists seemed too reluctant in advocating anti-colonialism. Although Indian socialists dispatched their representatives to the Frankfurt Congress as observers, the Burmese and Indonesians refused to participate in the SI because of their distrust of Europeans.

However, the reason that they still needed the international non-communist socialist network was not only for anti-colonial solidarity but also to compete against communism, much like the European socialists forming Comisco and the SI in rivalry with Cominform. The communist offensive was even more aggressive in Asia than in Europe. Under the influence of Moscow, the Communist Parties in India, Burma and Indonesia implemented a policy of armed struggle. In 1948 leaders of the communist parties in Southeast Asia met at a conference in Calcutta to discuss Stalin's new policy presented at the founding conference of Cominform in the previous year. Following this, there were violent uprisings by Communist Parties in Burma and India and a failed

---

[22] 'Aims and Tasks of Democratic Socialism.'
[23] See Imlay's works in particular.
[24] *SII*, 1(31–2), 1951, 14.
[25] Ibid., 26.
[26] 'Dai 8 Kai Komisuko Sokai.' Minshato Kokusaikyoku, 'Shakaishugi Intanashonaru to Minshato (The Socialist International and the Democratic Socialist Party)', *Kakushin* 64, no. 7 (1975): 92.
[27] Kyaw Zaw Win, 'The Asian Socialist Conference in 1953', 2.

attempt of coup d'état by the Indonesian Communist Party.[28] In addition, contrary to Europe, the Cold War did not remain 'cold' in Asia, as evidenced by the wars in Korea and Indochina, which strengthened the anti-communism of socialists. For instance, the Burmese government, led by the national front coalition including the Socialist Party, declared its support for the UN Security Council regarding the Korean War, changing its previous position of neutrality in the Cold War. This decision led to the departure of Marxist leftists from the party, which was initially a serious blow to the socialists, but they soon recovered as the strongest individual party in the election of May 1951.[29] As a result, the right-wing socialists, who supported pro-US policies in the Korean War, gained great influence in the party. In any case, in the late 1940s and the early 1950s, there was a strong motive among the socialists not only in Europe but also in Asia to seek out international connections so as to compete against the communist offensive. As discussed later, the ASC at its birth declared anti-communism as strongly as the SI.

In the case of the JSP, another significant motive for pursuing an international socialist network was the competition among socialists, between the leftists and the rightists. In October 1951, the JSP was split into two parties with the same name (rightist/leftist JSP) as a result of their disagreement over the San Francisco Peace Treaty, which enabled Japan's post-war peace only with the American bloc, and the US-Japan Security Treaty, which permitted US military forces to be stationed in Japan. The rightist JSP basically accepted the pro-US policy of Japanese conservative government, whereas the leftists advocated neutralism and anti-militarism, known as the 'unarmed neutrality' policy.[30] With regard to the international socialist network, the rightists welcomed the anti-communist stance of the Frankfurt Declaration as a proof of their legitimacy as democratic socialists, while the frustrated leftists shifted their attention from Europe to Asia, putting all their energies into constructing the ASC as a network for neutralism. The leftist leader Suzuki returned from Frankfurt via India, discussing the plan about the ASC with Mehta again. In December 1951, another leftist Katsumata Seiichi travelled to India, Burma and Indonesia to discuss the specific details of the first congress of ASC.[31]

The rightist JSP also attached importance to networking with Asian socialists. However, while the leftists wished that the ASC would become independent from the SI, the rightists attempted to combine the SI and the ASC closely in both organization and ideology. As for ideology, the rightists tried to make Europeans more anti-colonialist and Asians more pro-US and anti-communist.

Yet bridging the socialists in two continents was not an easy task. In February 1952, a special committee of SI for 'the Socialist Policy toward the Underdeveloped Areas' met

---

[28] Braunthal, *History of the International*, 231, 262, 293–4. Kyaw Zaw Win, A history of the Burma Socialist Party, 194.

[29] Braunthal, *History of the International*, 265–7. Kyaw Zaw Win, A History of the Burma Socialist Party, 223–5.

[30] See J.A.A. Stockwin, *The Japanese Socialist Party and Neutralism* (Melbourne: Melbourne University Press, 1968).

[31] Shakai Bunko (ed.), *Nihon Shakaitoshi Shiryo (Documents on the History of Japan Socialist Party)* (Tokyo: Kashiwa Shobo, 1965), 249. 'Dai 8 Kai Komisuko Sokai.'

in London, and the members of the rightist JSP attended this meeting. The European socialists at that time were not so interested in promoting national independence of colonies. In this meeting, a Belgian participant, for example, criticized the Japanese, saying that 'destroying the colonial organization is a dangerous idea'. In discussing the committee statement, the Japanese participants and Julius Braunthal, Secretary-General of the SI, insisted on expressing support for the demand of nationalism, but it was rejected by all other European members. The Japanese socialists were successful in inserting the following sentence: 'The Socialist International acknowledges the development of national consciousness as a step for the emancipation of nations.' But as a compromise, the statement also said: 'Socialists condemn the fanatic nationalism that denies the spirit of international cooperation.' On the other hand, the Europeans supported the rightist JSP's proposal to combine Asian socialists with the SI because they also hoped to expand their organization beyond Europe.[32]

It was also hard for the rightist JSP to make Asian socialists friendly to Europeans. In March 1952, members of three socialist parties of Burma, India and Indonesia gathered in the preparatory meeting of the ASC in Rangoon. The Burmese and Indonesians initially planned to meet only among these three parties, but as a result of 'a little more aggressive' attitude of JSP leftists to be allowed to participate, the two JSPs were invited as observers.[33] Reaching agreement about anti-communism was not difficult. The statement published after this meeting was as harshly anti-communist as the Frankfurt Declaration, asserting that 'Cominform Communism denies in practice dignity and equality of man'. But in contrast to the SI, they declared support for anti-colonialism, aiming for 'the complete emancipation of the broad masses of Asia'.[34] On the question of cooperation with the SI, the rightist JSP explained their position, asserting that 'we, as a progressive pacifist force within the Western bloc, are aligned with the Socialist International'. The Burmese and Indonesians were strongly opposed to this remark, boldly stating: 'Europeans cannot understand Asian affairs. Socialist parties of European states, which maintain colonies, cannot be trusted.'[35]

In January 1953, the first congress of the ASC met in Rangoon. It was co-sponsored by the socialist parties of Burma, India and Indonesia, and invited socialists from Japan (two parties: rightist and leftist), Malaya, Lebanon, Pakistan (East and West), Israel and Egypt. The SI dispatched Clement Attlee, former British Prime Minister from the Labour Party, to this congress. Sending the British leader who granted independence of India and Burma implied the SI's enthusiasm for alignment with the ASC.

---

[32] Sone Eki, Matsuzawa Kenjin, and Yamashita Eiji, *Shakaishugi Intanashonaru Shusai 'Mikaihatsu Chiiki ni Taisuru Shakaishugi Seisaku' Kiso Iinkai Hokoku (Report of special committee of the Socialist International for 'the Socialist Policy toward the Underdeveloped Areas')* (Tokyo: Nihon Shakaito Honbu Shuppanbu, 1952), 9.

[33] 'Preliminary meeting for Asian Socialist Conference', no date, No. 1, Subject Files, Papers of Shri Prem Bhasin [PSPB], Manuscripts Division, Nehru Memorial Museum and Library, New Delhi, India [NMML].

[34] Preparatory Committee, Asian Socialist Conference, 'Report of the Preliminary Meeting for the Asian Socialist Conference held at Rangoon (25 to 29 March 1952)', 160–2.

[35] Sone Eki, Matsuzawa Kenjin, and Yamashita Eiji, *Ajia Shakaito Jumbi Kaigi Hokoku (Report of the Preliminary Meeting for the Asian Socialist Conference)* (Tokyo: Nihon Shakaito Honbu Shuppanbu, 1952), 10.

The Rangoon congress revealed three types of positions among Asian socialists on the question of the ASC's relation with the SI: (1) the rightist JSP and the Israeli socialists suggested that the ASC should be an official regional organization of the SI, (2) the leftist JSP wanted the ASC to be an independent organization while maintaining 'close relations' with the SI and (3) Egyptian and Pakistani socialists insisted that the ASC should have no connections with the SI and Asian parties should not even individually be affiliated with the SI. As a result of this discussion, a consensus was reached that the ASC as an independent organization would 'establish a liaison' with the SI.[36] This agreement was satisfactory for the rightist JSP. Sone, who represented it, praised the agreement as 'a great progress', considering the distrust for Europeans by the Burmese and Indonesians at the preliminary meeting.[37]

The Rangoon congress also published the ASC's official demand that the SI accelerate the struggle against colonialism. It 'urge[d] the Socialist International [...] to take a very firm and courageous stand in relation to the question of colonialism'.[38] In contrast to the above-mentioned European socialists' position to 'condemn the fanatic nationalism', the ASC explicitly declared that their socialism was to be integrated with nationalism. One of the most significant statements of this Rangoon congress – 'the principles and objectives of socialism' – emphasized that 'socialists and nationalists are the comrades in arms'.[39]

The Asian socialists differed from Europeans in several points, but it must be noted that the majority of participants did not only support anti-communism but also dismissed neutralism. In 'the principles and objectives of socialism', they harshly denounced that 'Communism [...] stands for the negation of all concepts of freedom, individual self-expression and genuine mass responsibility' and they 'declare[d] [their] rejection of Communism'.[40]

Another important resolution was 'Asia and the world peace'. At the beginning of the discussion for this resolution, the leftist JSP proposed that the Asian socialists should not be 'involved in the struggles between two [Western and Soviet] blocs' but 'adhere to the attitude of neutrality'. They also suggested that the 'Asian socialists should keep out of war and resist any attempt to violate Asia with war' and that 'all foreign troops stationed in Asia must be withdrawn'.[41] The rightist JSP and Israelis particularly opposed to this, and their position prevailed. The conclusion of the debate was a sort that a JSP rightist Sone triumphantly called 'just the same as our party's fundamental policy'.[42] The resolution stated that the ASC's independent position and freedom of

[36] 'Asian Socialist Conference, Report of a Meeting of the Plenary Session Held on 12th January 1953 at 3 p.m.', No. 6, Subject Files, PSPB, NMML.
[37] Nihon Shakaito Kokusaikyoku (ed.), *Ajia no Doko to Sekai Heiwa: Dai 1 Kai Ajia Shakaito Kaigi no Shinso (Asian situation and the world peace: facts of the first Asian Socialist Conference)* (Tokyo: Nihon Shakaito Shuppankyoku, 1953), 21.
[38] *Resolutions of the First Asian Socialist Conference, Rangoon 1953*, Box 4, Accession No. 62, Asian Socialist Conference, National Archives of Myanmar, Yangon, Myanmar, 23.
[39] Ibid., 5.
[40] Ibid., 4–5.
[41] M.S. Gokhale, 'Asian Socialist Conference, Committee "A", Report', Gaibun 228, PJSP, WUA.
[42] Nihon Shakaito Kokusaikyoku (ed.), *Ajia no Doko to Sekai Heiwa*, 29.

movements 'do not mean ideological neutralism', and even implied accepting a military alliance with the United States, by not precluding Asian countries from 'joining any military security system'.[43]

The ASC's anti-communism, even implying approval of pro-US stance in the Cold War, stirred up a strong response from the Soviet Union. Though it was apparently exaggerated, the USSR and its satellites launched a propaganda attack on this congress, condemning that 'the conference is dominated by the Japanese' and that 'the US is using the Japanese Socialists [...] as tools in an effort to re-create the Japanese Greater East Asia Co-Prosperity Sphere under US "imperialist" control'.[44]

The thaw of the Cold War and the destabilization of Asian Socialist solidarity

The SI took the ASC's critique of colonialism seriously,[45] beginning to change their reluctant attitude. At the third SI congress in Stockholm in July 1953, the two JSPs, in particular the rightist Sone, demanded the participants to pass a resolution against colonialism.[46] The Stockholm congress published a statement on colonialism, declaring that the SI 'welcomes the upsurge of national consciousness among the peoples in colonial and dependent territories', and dismissing scepticism of nationalism. It then pledged that the SI 'will give all the aid in its power to assist them to achieve independence and democratic self-government'.[47]

On the other hand, the ASC accelerated its anti-colonial activities after the Rangoon congress. The Bureau Meeting of the ASC began to meet twice a year, first at the time of the Rangoon congress, second in Hyderabad in August 1953, third in Kalaw in May 1954 and then fourth in Tokyo in November 1954. Except for the third meeting, the representative from the SI joined as a fraternal delegate. Cooperation between European and Asian socialists on anti-colonialism was not easy, but there was steady progress.

The second Bureau Meeting in Hyderabad established the 'Anti-Colonial Bureau' as an organization under the ASC, joined not only by Asian socialists but also by members of African liberation movements. It apparently meant that the ASC aimed to become not only a regional organization but also a universal network for the sake of anti-colonialism. The SI was not comfortable with this plan. Morgan Phillips, the president of the SI, implicitly criticized the African involvement, which aroused antipathy of Asian socialists.[48] The Hyderabad meeting also decided to celebrate the

---

[43] Ibid., 27. *Resolutions of the First Asian Socialist Conference*, 18–19.
[44] W. C. Hamilton, 'The Asian Socialist Conference', 7 January 1953, Box 1, Entry A1 5518, General Records of the Department of State, Record Group 59, National Archives at College Park, Maryland, United States.
[45] See also Imlay's works.
[46] *SII*, 3(35), 1953, 616.
[47] *SII*, 3(30–1), 1953, 519.
[48] Minshato Kokusaikyoku, 'Shakaishugi Intanashonaru to Minshato', *Kakushin* 66, no. 9 (1976): 182.

'Dependent People's Freedom Day' once a year in each country. Phillips expressed his willingness to cooperate with this event.[49] Wijono, the ASC's General Secretary from Indonesia, showed his scepticism of Europeans' enthusiasm, but Sone attempted to assuage his doubts.[50]

In the fourth Tokyo meeting, Braunthal, representing the SI, made the official proposal to organize the single Socialist International by combining with the ASC.[51] However, the participants did not even discuss the subject, disappointing him.[52] Nevertheless, the SI continued their effort to be aligned with the ASC, stressing their sincere support for the ASC's anti-colonialism. The fourth SI congress in London in July 1955 successfully issued the joint SI-ASC statement to oppose colonialism, declaring that 'the continuation of colonialism and imperialism [...] is one of the main sources of international unrest and serves as a constant threat to the peace of the world'.[53]

Yet, Asian socialists began to be divided over another important issue: their attitude towards communism. At the time of the Rangoon congress in January 1953, the Cold War in Asia was 'hot'. But it started to 'thaw' especially after the death of Joseph Stalin in March 1953, bringing about armistices in Korea in July 1953 and Indochina in July 1954. In Japan, the rightist JSP had more parliamentary seats than the leftists at the time of their split in 1951, but the latter gained six more seats than the former in the 1953 election, then twenty-two more in 1955. Japanese voters preferred the anti-militarism and neutralism of the leftists in the relatively stable international environment.

The ASC started to waver in its previously agreed stance of anti-communism. In the Kalaw Bureau Meeting in 1954, participants were impressed by the heated debate between U Kyaw Nyein of Burma and Lohia of India over the question of whether 'capitalist imperialism' or 'Soviet imperialism' was more dangerous. U Kyaw Nyein insisted 'the Soviet type of imperialism is, perhaps, even more degrading and even more dangerous, because it is more ruthless, more systematic and more blatantly justified in the name of world communist revolution'. On the other hand, Lohia, defending his faith in neutralism, rejected U Kyaw Nyein's idea as it was 'the choice of the lesser evil'. He emphasized that 'only to the extent that they intensify their struggle against capitalism will it be possible for them to combat communism'.[54]

The less united ASC failed to hold its second congress two years after 1953 as planned,[55] and its last congress was held in Bombay in November 1956. The Japanese socialists participated in this congress as the single JSP due to the 1955 merger of the leftists and rightists. In this new party, the leftists were more powerful than the

---

[49] Morgan Phillips, 'Dependent People's Freedom Day', 30 October 1954, Gaibun 165, PJSP, WUA.
[50] 'Report of the Bureau Meeting of the Asian Socialist Conference held at Hyderabad', 10–13 August 1953, No. 12, Subject Files, PSPB, NMML.
[51] Julius Braunthal, 'Fraternal Address, Bureau Meeting of the Asian Socialist Conference, Tokyo, 19–21 November 1954', SIA, 513, IISG.
[52] Letter from Julius Braunthal to Wijono, 16 January 1955, SIA, 513, IISG.
[53] SII, 5(30–2), 1955, 540. 'The Second Congress of the Asian Socialist Conference.'
[54] Rammanohar Lohia and U Kyaw Nyein, 'Third Force – Two Attitudes?' Socialist Asia 3, no. 2 (1954): 8–9. Collections of Socialist Asia are accessible at IISG. Minshato Kokusaikyoku, 'Shakaishugi Intanashonaru to Minshato', Kakushin 65, no. 8 (1975): 185–6.
[55] Asian Socialist Conference, Three Years of Asian Socialist Conference (Bombay: The Preparatory Committee, Second Congress of the Asian Socialist Conference, 1956), 5.

rightists. The leader of the new JSP was Suzuki, a leftist, and the party declared to seek a 'cancellation' of the US-Japan Security Treaty. The rightists, who wished to promote the ASC's cooperation with the SI and supported a pro-US, anti-communist position, did not have as much influence to lead the discussion as they did in the Rangoon congress.

It was as if the Bombay congress were demanded to give a single answer to the question that U Kyaw Nyein and Lohia discussed, that is, whether Asian socialists should oppose Western colonialism and Soviet communism to the same degree, or should emphasize anti-communism. Significantly, just a month before the Bombay congress, the Soviet army repressed the uprising in Hungary, and the British, French and Israeli military attack of Egypt caused the Suez Crisis. Particularly in the latter case, French socialist leader Guy Mollet was the premier of France leading the war, whereas the British Labour Party condemned the Conservative government's Suez policy. The statements of the Bombay congress about these incidents were expected to be a litmus test for the ASC's ideological position.

The result of the test was that the Asian socialists gathering in Bombay were less anti-communist and more neutralist than they were in the former Rangoon congress. In the discussion, U Kyaw Nyein clearly withdrew his former remarks, saying, 'There was a time when we thought one was better than the other. Today we are convinced that two great countries viz., France and England and also the great power Soviet Russia belong to the same category of imperialists.' Mehta even argued, 'If the Governments of France and Britain had not put this beyond the pales of civilized behaviour, I do not think Soviets would have dared to take this today's step. The Governments of Britain and France have the double guilt not only for the invasion of Egypt but for the murder of freedom forces in Hungary.' Sone was in the drafting members for the resolution on Eastern Europe, but he confessed that he could not take active initiative 'because of the necessity for us to compose our own differences within our delegation'.[56] The Japanese rightists, restrained by their leftist colleagues, could not take this opportunity to advocate anti-communism.

In the published resolutions, the ASC condemned both the Soviet intervention in Hungary and the British-French attack in the Suez. Regarding the latter, while they passed the resolution to note appreciation for the British Labour Party's effort against the war,[57] they were severely critical of French socialists. In addition, it became apparent that the ASC was more distanced from the SI than it was at the Rangoon congress. Attlee's successor as the Labour leader, Hugh Gaitskell, was invited to Bombay, but he did not attend the congress.[58] On the other hand, even the Chilean socialist representatives attended the congress in Bombay, showing the ASC's enthusiasm to become a universal organization for the South, which was not welcomed by European socialists.

---

[56] S.R. Mohan Das, 'Report on the Second Congress of the Asian Socialist Conference, Held in Bombay from 1st of November to the 11th of November', 23 November 1956, No. 23, Subject Files, PSPB, NMML.
[57] Urano Tatsuo, *Shiryo Taikei Ajia Afurika Kokusai Kankei Seiji Shakai Shi(Document series: international, social and political history in Asia and Africa)*, 5(IIa) (Tokyo: Papirusu Shuppan, 1982), 10.
[58] Letter from Hugh Gaitskell to Bjarne Braatoy, 22 August 1956, SIA, 513, IISG.

In the resolutions published at the Bombay congress, whereas they condemned the 'Soviet Union' for their action in Hungary, they never expressed its opposition to 'communism' as they did at the Rangoon congress.[59] Their shift from the Rangoon congress was particularly revealed in the resolution on 'Peace in Asia', which was drafted by the JSP, declaring their positions of neutralism and anti-colonialism. It reads: '[the ASC] demands the abandonment of all systems of military alliances, the withdrawal of foreign armed forces from the territories of all countries, and the repudiation of colonialism in all its forms.'[60] At the Rangoon congress, the Japanese rightists could dismiss this sort of suggestion. However, the leftists prevailed at the Bombay congress. After returning to Japan, the leftist-led JSP proudly published its statement about this resolution: 'it is our pleasure that we could make a constructive contribution to this congress.'[61]

Conclusion

Even after the Bombay congress, European socialists continued to show interest in connecting with the ASC.[62] However, no ASC congress was held after Bombay, and the fifth Bureau Meeting in Kathmandu in 1957 was the last meeting in the history of ASC. Sone persisted on his goal of reconstructing the ASC and combining it with the SI even in the 1960s. In 1963, he visited Burma and India to see former ASC members, and then flew to Amsterdam to participate in the SI congress. He reported to the Europeans that the Asian socialists 'were all in high spirits'.[63]

It is difficult to point to one single reason for the demise of the ASC. One of the decisive factors was the retreat of Socialist Parties in the domestic politics of Asian countries, often suppressed by authoritarian governments. In Burma, for example, Ne Win's repressive regime, established in 1962, arrested members of the Socialist Party and forced the ASC headquarters in Rangoon to close. In Indonesia, Sukarno dissolved the Socialist Party in 1958. The Praja Socialist Party of India largely lost its influence in Indian politics by the end of the 1950s. In Japan, the JSP split again. Some of the rightists, including Sone, left the JSP and formed the new Democratic Socialist Party in 1960. Neither of these two parties could take power in government until the 1990s.

Yet, as we have seen, stagnation of the ASC had already begun in the middle of the 1950s. And what was particularly different between the early and the mid-1950s was the situation of East-West relations in Asia. That is, the communist offensive was intensified throughout Asia in the early 1950s, while the period following the

---

[59] Urano, *Shiryo Taikei*, 5(IIa), 78–86. Although less in quantity, for English, *Asian Socialist Conference Information Bulletin* [*ASCIB*], 1(4), 1956, which is accessible at IISG.
[60] ASCIB, 1(4), 1956, 5–6. 'Peace in Asia', no date, SIA, 513, IISG.
[61] 'Ajia Shakaito Kaigi Dai 2 Kai Taikai karano Kikoku ni Saishite no Nihon Daihyo Dancho no Danwa (Statement by the head of Japanese mission on his return from the second Asian Socialist Conference)', 14 November 1956, in Urano, *Shiryo Taikei*, 5(IIa), 89.
[62] Imlay, *The Practice of Socialist Internationalism*, 447.
[63] SII, 14(16–17), 1964, 185–6. Minshato Kokusaikyoku, 'Shakaishugi Intanashonaru to Minshato', *Kakushin* 69, no. 11 (1976), 173–4.

mid-1950s marked the thawing of the Cold War. Socialists in Asia could be united under the name of anti-communism, but their solidarity became weaker when the communist threat waned.

Distrust among Asian socialists with Europeans over the issue of decolonization was an important factor for the failure to unify the SI and the ASC. However, even though the SI stood closer to the Asians' position regarding decolonization in the mid-1950s, it did not help to strengthen their ties. Their attitudes toward communism diverged after the mid-1950s. The SI repeated its strong anti-communist stance in the Oslo Declaration in 1962.[64] As Asians leaned more to neutralism, European democratic socialism, deeply embedded with anti-communism, lost its attraction.

In the middle of the 1960s, there was an attempt by Lee Kuan Yew of Singapore and the Australian Labor Party to revive the ASC.[65] Since the beginning of the 1970s, the SI took the initiative to hold the conference of socialists in the Asia-Pacific region several times,[66] but none of them continued for long. Social democracy was powerless in promoting international solidarity in Asia, primarily because it was excessively involved in the Cold War.

Acknowledgement

This work was supported by JSPS KAKENHI Grant Number 20K01522.

---

[64] *SII*, 12(24–5), 1962, 354–61.
[65] Singapore Ministry of Culture, *Socialist Solution for Asia: A Report on the 1965 Asian Socialists' Conference in Bombay* (Singapore: Ministry of Culture, 1965).
[66] One of them was the Asia-Pacific Socialist Conference held by the initiative of the Asia-Pacific Bureau of the SI in 1972, joined by the JSP, the Democratic Socialist Party of Japan, and socialists from Malaysia, Singapore, Australia and New Zealand.

4

Italian communism and the 'rediscovery' of the Third World, 1956–64

Silvio Pons

Destalinization and decolonization

Historians have usually seen the relationship between Communism and decolonization in terms of a 'rediscovery' of the Third World after the death of Stalin. In light of Stalin's uncompromising bipolar view on the world, such notion sounds appropriate, even though continuities with the Comintern era should not be overlooked. By the late 1950s, Communist internationalism redefined its own mission because of post-colonial perspectives. However, we still lack empirical evidence and further conceptualization of what the 'rediscovery' of the Third World meant in different areas and to different subjects, besides the Soviet Union and its global effort. The focus on Stalin's successors has provided evidence about Soviet Cold War entanglements, discourses of identification between Socialist models and post-colonial subjects, ideologies and practices of development, and warfare. Analyses of the Sino-Soviet conflict have shown how the concept itself of decolonization implied conflict, as 'peaceful coexistence' and anti-imperialism were likely to clash against each other. Still, multiple visions and interactions in post-imperial spaces, mutual influences between international and local communist and anti-imperialist actors, and the agencies represented by non-state communist parties have yet to be researched and understood on a wider scale.

This chapter analyses the experience of the Italian Communist Party as a case study of European communism's connections with the Third World in the period 1956–64. The PCI was a significant actor on the scene of post-Stalin international communism, as the main Western mass party. The notion of 'polycentrism' coined by the PCI secretary Palmiro Togliatti provided a vision of change in the aftermath of destalinization and decolonization. Its main implication was that the binary worldview of the Cold War could not work any longer in the context of the end of European empires. Italian communists established significant relations in the Mediterranean and in Africa by the late 1950s, as they benefited from the limits of the national colonial heritage, which instead profoundly affected the French communists. However, the role played by the PCI in such framework is poorly studied. The chapter explores how Italian communism contributed shaping a new understanding of Communist internationalism and built political relations with national liberation movements, while acting quite independently from the Soviet Union[1].

After Stalin's death, the Soviet and European communists approached the world outside Europe, reformulating their own visions in the light of the processes of decolonization, which went back to the 1920s, and seemed now to offer formidable perspectives for the expansion of socialism in the world.[2] The alliance between the Soviet Union and China appeared as a vector of new forces of motion generated by the encounter between socialist experiences and the birth of new subjects and anti-imperialist sovereignties. The communists established the vision of a necessary convergence between social progress, the expansion of the socialist camp and the anti-colonial liberation struggles, which would have put the capitalist West on the ropes. In the scenarios opened by the interaction between the 'socialist camp', the liberation movements and the post-colonial states, the Western communists were in most cases considered to be on the margins, with the partial exception of the French who found themselves coming to terms with the end of an empire. In spite of this, they faced up to the repercussions of the phenomenon and redirected a considerable part of their energies and networks of transnational linkages, albeit not seeking to basically update their conceptual tools.

The notion of polycentrism coined by Togliatti in 1956, some months after Khrushchev's demolition of Stalin's myth, revealed a partial rethinking of the strictly Eurocentric vision that had characterized the Italian communists in the Stalin era. The Cominformist thesis of the 'two camps' had placed the Old Continent at the centre of the new bipolar challenge for forging the world order. Togliatti, too, adopted a hierarchical view, indicating the colonial liberation movements as a force auxiliary to the 'socialist camp' and the great countries of the Third World as new subjects on the path to socialism. His polycentric vision seemed however to imply a less rigid version of the Eurocentric tradition and to reflect a growing awareness of the global import of decolonization. While belonging to a country that was marginal to the European colonialist tradition and even more secondary in post-war post-colonial dynamics, the Italian communists felt themselves involved in a role in the Mediterranean. As was in their mentality, they turned to the Soviets to coordinate orientations after the Suez crisis, but provided their own responses by putting themselves forward as a link between the 'socialist camp' and the movements of nationalist, socialist and

---

[1] See S. Pons, *I comunisti italian e gli altri. Visioni e legami internazionali nel mondo del Novecento* (Torino: Einaudi, 2021), chapter 4.

[2] O.A. Westad, *The Global Cold War. Third World Interventions and the Making of Our Times* (Cambridge: Cambridge University Press, 2005), 66 et seq. A. Hilger, 'Communism, Decolonization and the Third World', in *The Cambridge History of Communism, Vol. 2. The Socialist Camp and World Power 1941–1960s*, edited by N. Naimark, S. Pons and S. Quinn-Judge (Cambridge: Cambridge University Press, 2017), 322–31. A. Hilger, 'Mondi diversi, storie intrecciate. Gli stati socialisti e il Terzo Mondo durante la guerra fredda', in *Globalizzazioni rosse. Studi sul comunismo nel Novecento*, a cura di S. Pons (Carocci: Roma, 2020), 133–54.

anti-imperialist inspiration, above all in North Africa. The nexus between Budapest and Suez, evoked by Khrushchev at the moment of the fatal decision to invade Hungary, was used instrumentally in the political polemic. However, it then took on a symbolic and political nature, since it linked the decline of the European empires with the Cold War in Europe.[3]

The sceneries of decolonization offered the possibility of considering a change in the minority and marginalized position that the communists had undergone in Europe after the geopolitical division of the continent, the shift of the axis of the movement towards Asia brought about, by the Chinese Revolution, and the multiple shocks of 1956. Central to them was the perception of a state of relative movement which, while not shedding doubt on the European bipolar order, opened up new chances in terms of relations and strategies. The Soviet Union's openings to the world, symbolized by the various trips abroad of its leaders, especially to the newly independent countries, allowed a broadening of internationalist practices and the possibility of thinking them in a scenario of multiple interactions. Under this aspect post-Stalin internationalism could be configured as a complex of ideas and political practices aimed at mutual integration and at competing on a global scale, much more than had been the case in the Stalinist Cold War.[4]

What hits the eye, however, is not the interaction between the European communists around internationalist themes and practices aroused by decolonization but, on the contrary, the absence of any authentic political coordination. The economic interventions agreed in the Comecon between the states of the Soviet bloc expressed an ideological discourse on non-capitalist development but were only very slightly integrated by forms of political synergy.[5] The European communists presented themselves in scattered order on the decolonization scene, even if all spoke modernizing and progressive languages to connote post-colonial sovereignty.[6] Among the Western communists and the party-states of East Europe the 'rediscovery' of the Third World opened up processes of learning and scenarios of intervention that to a great extent went along in parallel and only communicated sporadically. This was probably the consequence of a perspective that remained centred for everyone on the categories and priorities of the Eurocentric Cold War, but which meant a much lower degree of discipline than in the past, and a broader margin of manoeuvre for autonomous initiative.

---

[3] S. Radchenko, *Il 1956 globale. Gli effetti internazionali della destalinizzazione*, in *Globalizzazioni rosse*, 109–30.

[4] T. Rupprecht, *Soviet Internationalism after Stalin. Interaction and Exchange between the USSR and Latin America during the Cold War* (Cambridge: Cambridge University Press, 2015).

[5] S. Lorenzini, The Socialist Camp and Economic Modernization in the Third World, in *The Cambridge History of Communism*, vol. 2, 343–51. S. Lorenzini, *Una strana guerra fredda. Lo sviluppo e le relazioni Nord-Sud (A Strange Cold War. Development and North-South Relations)* (Bologna: Il Mulino, 2017), 81–4. Ph. Muehlenbeck, *Czechoslovakia in Africa, 1945–1968* (London: Palgrave Macmillan, 2016).

[6] J. Friedman, *Shadow Cold War. The Sino-Soviet Competition for the Third World* (Chapel Hill: University of North Carolina Press, 2015), 71–3.

The Italian communists and Africa

In January 1957, Luigi Longo and Velio Spano met with Khrushchev, Suslov and Ponomarev to discuss the project of installing a 'system of encounters for the exchange of opinions and experiences' and creating an international 'press organ' of the communist parties. Their request, made in the name of Togliatti, for there to be a discussion of 'the causes of the Hungarian events' and 'how these had been possible after twelve years of the existence of system of popular democracy' remained however a dead letter. At the same time, they raised with Khrushchev the question of the role of the Italian communists in the decolonization process. Longo declared that 'for our party an important meaning is attached to the situation in the Arab world and North Africa' and that the communists of these countries, the Egyptians in particular, were turning to the PCI for advice. 'What should we do?' Longo asked, 'Who should deal with them, us or the French? Is it possible to meet and discuss their questions in agreement with the French comrades?' As well as the Egyptians, he mentioned the Moroccan and Tunisian communists, but avoided any direct reference to Algeria, probably because the subject was far too delicate in relations with the French. In essence, the Italian delegates posed concrete problems that had emerged from decolonization in the Mediterranean and involved the role of the European communists. They also made reference to Latin America, albeit generically. Their interrogatives remained however in suspension. Khrushchev limited himself to observing that in the year that had passed since the Twentieth Congress nothing had been done despite the agreement reached then between the PCI and the PCF.[7] In spite of this, the Foreign Section of the PCI established a working agenda for the Mediterranean and Africa under the impetus coming from leaders such as Velio Spano, Giuliano Pajetta and Maurizio Valenzi. Attention focused mostly on Egypt and the figure of Nasser, who had acquired a notable prestige with the Suez crisis and who was a privileged interlocutor for the Soviets.[8]

The main question was however represented by the war of liberation in Algeria. The Algerian National Liberation Front occupied a central position in the constellation of anti-imperialist and post-colonial subjects, with the goal of forming the notion itself of the Third World as a political project. At the World Conference of communist parties held Moscow in November 1957, the voices of the Third World were above all those of the Asian delegates, the Indians and Indonesians in particular, but the question of Algeria also emerged and revealed itself as problematic. The French communists, represented by Duclos, in fact defended the link between Algeria and France, albeit from a socialist perspective, thereby arousing the dissent of the Moroccan leader Ali Yata, who invoked a greater international solidarity for the Algerian anti-imperialist struggle, alluding to the scant involvement of the PCF.[9] At the conference, Togliatti

---

[7] RGANI, f. 81, op. 1, d. 306.
[8] M. Galeazzi, *Il PCI e il movimento dei paesi non allineati (1955–1975)* (Milano: Franco Angeli, 2011), 41–9.
[9] N. G. Tomilina (ed.), *Nasledniki Kominterna. Mezhdunarodnye soveshchaniya predstavitelei kommunisticeskikh i rabochikh partii v Moskve. Dokumenty (noyabr' 1957g.)* (Moskva: Rosspen, 2013), 450.

spoke as a leader of the communist movement and enhanced the perspective of 'peaceful coexistence' as the international condition for developing mass legal parties, on the pattern provided by the PCI. He avoided to quote the term of polycentrism, which both the Soviet and the Chinese disliked, but was the basic notion followed by the Italian Communists. Togliatti proposed avoiding a head-on collision with the PCF on the Algerian subject, but alluding to the Popular Front era brought out the inability to carry forward 'its great policy of 1934', aggravated by the coming to power of De Gaulle. The nationalist ambiguities of the French communists were indefensible, even less so from the viewpoint of a new wave of decolonization on the African continent.[10]

At the end of the decade, the Cuban revolution confirmed to all communists a revolutionary and anti-imperialist season was taking place on a world scale, able to influence the entire Latin American subcontinent and weaken the global power of the United States. The Italian communists constructed their own role without any real coordination of initiative with the 'socialist camp', despite the fact that it had been they who had requested it. In January 1960 Longo informed Suslov that the PCI had direct links with the communists in Egypt and with the 'left democrats' in Somalia, Cameroon, Ghana, Nigeria and other African countries and posed the question of the role to be played in terms of help and assistance. Suslov's reply was very generic. He was 'positive' in his opinion that the PCI should cultivate these relations and offered Moscow's assistance for cadre formation.[11] In other words, the internationalist relation between Moscow and Rome on such a crucial question as African decolonization appeared very vague, at the time when the PCI was weaving its own transnational connections. And this is without taking account of the fact, as emerges from Longo's words, that the Italian communists' outlook and links were not directed solely to North Africa but also to other colonial and post-colonial realities of the African continent. Attention to western sub-Saharan Africa had been developing for about a year after the independence of Guinea had given an impetus to the decolonization of the continent. So it was even more surprising that Suslov gave an evasive reply. It may be asked whether this depended on Moscow's diffidence regarding the theses of the Italian communists on the relation between democracy, nation and socialism, considered too inclusive and unorthodox. In any case the episode is eloquent in demonstrating how labile the coordination of international communism had become since the first phase of decolonization.

The Italian communists adopted a syncretic pedagogy aimed at reconciling nationalism and socialism in the African Arab world as much as in western sub-Saharan Africa. This was the approach to the Republic of Guinea led by Sékou Touré, seen by some as Africa's revolutionary equivalent to Cuba, with the difference that it was following a 'peaceful path' and thus represented an example in line with the Italian tradition.[12] In the case of Egypt, the PCI's judgement on the Nasser regime was expressed

---

[10] FG APC, Executive Committee, Minutes, mf. 22, 3 October 1958.
[11] RGANI, f. 81, op. 1, d. 306, ll. 47–50.
[12] G. Siracusano, *Il PCI e il processo d'indipendenza dell'Africa nera francese (1958-1961)*, in 'Studi storici', 1, 2016, 189–218. G. Siracusano, *La fine di un miraggio politico: lo sguardo del PCI e del PCF sull'Africa subsahariana francofona indipendente (1960-1984). Nuove visioni e prospettive africane dei comunisti occidentali*, Research Doctorate in History e Philosophical and Social Sciences, XXXII cycle, University of Rome 'Tor Vergata', 2019, 127–30, 140–1.

in terms of social progress despite the harsh repression against the communists. At the same time, the PCI sought to aid a weak and fragmented communist movement to develop its own 'national' profile. The possibility of exercising an influence in the country was limited. Egypt did however constitute a crossroad of passages and connections that were useful for playing a role in the anti-imperialist movements in North Africa and even far into the depth of the continent.[13] Between 1960 and 1961 the Congo tragedy and the murder of Lumumba were interpreted as a sign of the aggression of the West, but also as a demonstration of the vulnerability of its power and a confirmation of the necessity to consolidate the autonomous development of the new nation-states.[14]

The Italian communists were aware that the most influential models of state building in Africa – such as the authoritarianism of a Nasserist socialist type or the 'mass democracy' of Touré – presented serious problems of coherence with their political discourse focused on the idea of socialist democracy. This type of contradiction could have its repercussions above all on their credibility as a national force.[15] Considered in this light, the encounter with decolonization sharpened a constitutive and introjected aporia, namely the identification with a single-party system in Europe, which had shown its oppressive face even after the death of Stalin. The incongruences between the ideas of a 'democratic path' to socialism and the reality of the authoritarian regimes in a great part of the post-colonial countries were set aside in the name of internationalism. The interpretation of this notion, even more than in the past, began to assume particular connotations.

The positioning of the Italian communists emerged with clarity as they appreciated the first Conference of Non-Aligned Countries held in Belgrade in September 1961. Togliatti's vision remained centred on bipolar détente and the idea of a socialist path of the emerging countries, but he recognized the legitimacy of Tito's politics and his choice to stay outside the blocs.[16] Above all, it was from this moment on that the notions of the Third World and of Western 'neo-colonialism', understood as economic domination maintained after the end of the empires, entered the lexis of the Italian communists in a stable fashion. The vision of the Third World as an anti-imperialist subject was however adopted sparingly and subordinated to the languages of gradual modernization, centred on agrarian reforms, state-led industrialization and mass democracy. It was in this optic that the Italian communists looked favourably on initiatives such as the Cairo Conference of July 1962 which brought the non-aligned countries into contact with the more radical African leaders and also registered the presence of Latin America, thereby promoting the theme of alternatives to dependence on the capitalist markets and contesting the European Economic Community.[17] They did not present

---

[13] FG APC, Esteri, Mf. 468, meeting of 1 March 1960 to discuss the policy of the PCI towards the Arab countries, 2295, 2299, 2301.

[14] S. Mazov, *A Distant Front in the Cold War. The USSR in West Africa and the Congo 1956–1964* (Stanford California: Stanford University Press, 2010). R. Ledda, *Unità dell'Africa e lotta anticoloniale*, 'Rinascita', December 1960. G. C. Pajetta, *L'assassinio di Lumumba*, 'Rinascita', February 1961.

[15] FG APC, Esteri, Mf. 468, 1 March 1960.

[16] Togliatti, *Discorsi parlamentari*, II, Camera dei Deputati, Roma 1984, 27 September 1961, 1216.

[17] R. Ledda, *Posta al Cairo l'esigenza di riassestare l'economia mondiale*, 'Rinascita', 28 luglio 1962. Id., *I sottosviluppati rifiutano la vocazione 'agricola'*, 'Rinascita', 4 agosto 1962.

themselves in the guise of ambassadors of the Soviet model of development, even if they believed in its potentialities, and showed greater understanding than others for the hybrid solutions adopted by the post-colonial ruling classes, which combined statist approaches and access to the world markets.

At the same time, the Italian communists drew advantage from their national identity. They represented a country that after the war had freed itself of its colonial past and was going headlong through a vigorous modernization process and thereby this presented opportunities and resources that were unavailable or lacking in other countries of southern Europe, Yugoslavia included. They could rightly claim lasting coherence in their anti-colonial struggles, going back to the time of the denunciation of Mussolini's imperialism in Ethiopia. The struggle against fascist colonialism and the analysis of it as an essential trait of the regime was a part and parcel of Italian antifascism itself. This legacy was recognized internationally, most of all in Africa, and helped by the 'decolonization without decolonization' that came about in Italy after the Second World War – that is the end of colonial domination without the traumas and conflicts that characterized the French and British empires.[18]

The French communists' inability to assume consistent positions on Algeria created a void that the Italians filled, establishing a relation with the National Liberation Front and with the Algerian communists which reconnected European anti-fascism with anti-colonialism.[19] The Italian communists knew that the national identity of the French communists was producing an ambiguous position on Algerian independence, recognized as a principle but at the political level put off to a vague future. They maintained that the French were having a negative influence on the Algerian communists, pushing them into preferring the fragile urban proletariat in their social alliances, according to a narrowly Eurocentric schema which dated back to the Stalin era.[20] At the moment of independence, the Italian communists were perceived in FLN circles as an important and autonomous interlocutor, the protagonist of an authentic 'national road' as compared to the constrictions imposed by the Cold War.[21] All this gave their transnational role substantial importance, even in the competition between the Soviets and the Chinese, since to a certain extent it balanced the tendency of the Algerian revolutionaries to look to Beijing rather than to Moscow as a reference point in the light of the problems of backwardness and national construction.[22] Togliatti hailed the end of the war in Algeria, claiming to represent one of the most consistent forces in the defence of the cause of independence from French colonialism, which had touched the sensitivities of vast sectors of public opinion and culture in Europe.[23]

---

[18] G. Calchi Novati, *L'Africa d'Italia. Una storia coloniale e postcoloniale* (Roma: Carocci, 2011), 355–69.

[19] On the positions of the French and Algerian communists in the war in Algeria, cf. A. Ruscio, *Les communistes et l'Algérie. Des origines à la guerre d'indépendance* (Paris: La decouvérte, 2019). A. Drew, *We Are No Longer in France. Communists in Colonial Algeria* (Manchester: Manchester University Press, 2014).

[20] FG APC, Estero, Algeria, 1961, mf. 483, Sul Fln e sul Pca. Appunti sui precedenti storici, 2387–8, 2391.

[21] P. Borruso, *Il PCI e l'Africa indipendente. Apogeo e crisi di un'utopia socialista (1956–1989)* (Firenze: Le Monnier, 2009), 70.

[22] Friedman, *Shadow Cold War*, 134–8.

[23] P. Togliatti, *Algeria indipendente*, 'Rinascita', 7 July 1962.

A new kind of internationalism?

The coincidence between the Cuban missile crisis and the birth of independent Algeria created the preconditions for a qualitative leap. In both cases, the Cold War was intertwined even more closely than before with decolonization. In the missile crisis, the Italian communists were aligned with the Soviet positions, with particular emphasis on the need for détente, at odds with the anti-imperialist internationalism of the Cubans. The relaunch of revolutionary vanguards represented by figures such as Fidel Castro and Che Guevara, but also by Ben Bella, exerted its symbolic attraction and coincided with the loss of momentum of the European peace movement, already in evidence at the start of the decade. The prevalent approach in the PCI was to defend the link between the new subjects of the Third World and the scenarios of 'peaceful coexistence', and to take on board its symbolic impact without yielding to the temptation of contraposing the 'peaceful road' to the more militant variants of anti-imperialism. The PCI however found itself competing with the first intellectual and political expressions of a 'new left', the bearer of a clear Third Worldist and anti-Eurocentric critique which launched a challenge on the global space opened up after the Conference of Bandung and the Suez crisis of 1956.[24] The communist vision, founded on the European political nation, was contested as a form of cultural conservatism, by using arguments of a cosmopolitan origin which were not unfamiliar to the heritage of the communists themselves and were included in the construction of the mythology of the Resistance, rejecting the narration of a 'second Risorgimento' in order to lay stress on that of the incomplete revolution.[25] This Third Worldism re-proposed the legitimacy of violence against colonial oppression, openly invoked by Frantz Fanon's celebrated *The Wretched of the Earth*, which redefined discourses and practices of decolonization in light of the war of Algeria, and found ample intellectual consensus even in the West. The languages used by the Western left became pluralized and expressed different meanings with the birth of a 'new left' critique of the Soviet Union.[26]

Under this pressure, the propaganda and strategies of the leading group in the PCI demonstrated a double register. *Rinascita* hosted authoritative voices of Marxist Third Worldism, such as Jean Paul Sartre, who invited his audience to see the overriding impact made by the Third World as a subject.[27] More in general there was a tendency to broaden the field of vision of its own public on the plurality of anti-imperialist subjects, from the birth of the new post-colonial state in Algeria to the liberation struggles in Africa, linked to figures such as Kwame Nkrumah and Nelson Mandela.[28] At the level of strategies and practices, more evident attention was however paid

---

[24] Ch. Kalter, *The Discovery of the Third World. Decolonization and the Rise of the New Left in France, 1950–1976* (Cambridge: Cambridge University Press, 2016), 90–9.
[25] N. Srivastava, *Italian Colonialism and Resistances to Empire, 1930–1970* (London: Palgrave Macmillan, 2018), 213 et seq.
[26] P. Goedde, *The Politics of Peace. A Global Cold War History* (Oxford and New York: Oxford University Press, 2019), 60, 162–7.
[27] J. P. Sartre, *La guerra fredda e l'unità della cultura*, 'Rinascita', 13 ottobre 1962.
[28] R. Rossanda, *Problemi e prospettive dell'Algeria indipendente*, 'Rinascita', 13 July 1963. N. Mandela, *J'accuse*, 'Rinascita', 29 June 1963. K. N'Krumah, *La ricchezza dell'Africa*, 'Rinascita', 10 August 1963.

to the topics of development and geopolitical pacification, which meant a different approach from Third Worldist thinking. The PCI aimed at putting the question of the Mediterranean and Africa on the political agenda of Italy and of Europe, and supported the 'Casablanca group' constituted by the countries that were operating clear breaks with the colonial past.[29] It was not simply a question of diversified approaches between public and reserved spaces. The impact of the revolutionary Third World also defined a divergence in the party as the vision of 'peaceful coexistence' possessed far less consensus than a few years previously. At the directorate of October 1962, immediately after the end of the Cuban missile crisis, Togliatti spelled this out explicitly: 'Among comrades, there are two conflicting and paralyzing positions: nothing will be done, the USSR will not risk a war. Against this, the USSR will make the Americans see what they do not expect to see. It is not understood that we shall arrive at peaceful coexistence through struggles that are even bitter ones on single concrete objectives.'[30] Togliatti did not assign to himself the role of mediator but relaunched his own vision of 'peaceful coexistence', the authentic centre of gravity of his politics after the death of Stalin. In his speech to the Tenth Party Congress, on 2 December 1962, he asserted that 'peaceful coexistence' was not one option among various others but a necessity for everyone and not exclusively for the 'socialist camp'. 'This is the alternative', he declared, 'either peaceful coexistence or atomic destruction and therefore the end of our civilization or the greater part of it'. He foresaw a new détente stage in international relations after the Cuban crisis and after the end of border hostilities between China and India.[31]

The conflict between Moscow and Beijing, however, underwent an escalation that prevented such vision from being adopted globally by the communists. The growing divergence between the Soviets and the Chinese laid bare many aporiae in the structure and government of the 'socialist camp', in the visions of anti-imperialism, and in Cold War strategies. But most of all they showed how the encounter between communism and decolonization could provide as much a vector of world politics as a space for new conflicts and antinomies, which could not be resolved in the socialism-capitalism dichotomy. At the Party directorate Togliatti said he had 'little enthusiasm' for the conduct of the Soviets, who had been too cautious on Cuba, only then to show their 'exasperation'. The PCI was one of the 'strongest' parties, but if the conflict was to go on, it would have its difficulties.[32] His preoccupation was that the head-on conflict policy fuelled by both sides would have compromised the bases of international communism. In his view the polemic in favour of or against détente did not really go to the heart of the political problem, which was instead 'how must we develop the policy of détente?'.[33]

He then defined the contours of a vision that linked more precisely the role of the communists in the West to the post-colonial world. His idea was that the post-imperial era registered the crisis of all the European ruling classes, most of all the social

---

[29] APC, Foreign series, 1963, mf. 489, Notes by Maurizio Valenzi for a discussion on Italy's policies towards the Third World, 2766–9.
[30] APC, Executive Committee, Minutes, 31 October 1962.
[31] *X Congresso del partito comunista italiano. Atti e risoluzioni* (Rome: Editori Riuniti, 1963), 38–45.
[32] FG APC, Executive Committee, Minutes, 12 September 1963.
[33] FG APC, Executive Committee, Minutes, 11 October 1963.

democratic ones, and that this could open the road to a socialist and anti-Atlanticist way forward. The influence of the communists seemed practicable to him as long as they did not limit themselves to the 'simple and not always fruitful wait for a different future'. Togliatti sought to outline a political perspective, as he had at other crucial moments in the past. His vision contained several approximations and was schematic, above all in its placing of De Gaulle's 'authoritarian power' and Adenauer's *Westpolitik* on a par with Franco's Spain, without even mentioning the subject of European integration. The mentality of the Cold War had thrown a veil over the differentiated analysis of capitalist Europe, which Togliatti had frequently invoked in years past and which he now practised in his approach to the Third World. The strongpoint of his vision was the nexus implied between the role of the Western communists and the diversities of the post-colonial world, which were likely to modify the very notion of socialism.

It was difficult for such a vision to be acceptable in Moscow. The main spectre haunting the Soviets in that moment was the Chinese attempt to gain influence and control over the communist parties in Asia and Africa. The no-holds-barred competition between the Soviets and the Chinese in the Third World was by now a definite fact and was compromising the unity of the communist movement. At a Central Committee meeting in October 1963, Enrico Berlinguer drew attention to the expansion of Chinese influence among communist parties and groups in Asia and Africa. His preoccupation was not however just the containment of Chinese influence but the fact that the conflict between Moscow and Beijing would be an obstacle to confronting 'in their real importance' the problems of the Third World. He praised 'peaceful coexistence', rejecting its contraposition to anti-imperialist struggles, but used words of uncustomary criticism for the 'wholly inadequate' Soviet responses to these problems, which were not made public.[34] In other words, the Italian communists were not limiting themselves to dissent against the option of an excommunication of the Chinese, but were making objections of a political nature to Moscow, regarding the very conception of internationalism and the South of the world. It is not clear whether the whole of the leading group was in agreement with Berlinguer's positions. It was however within this optic that the Italian communists intensified their initiatives in the Mediterranean and in Latin America, in parallel with Zhou Enlai's long diplomatic trip at the end of 1963 and beginning of 1964, which confirmed China's entry into competition for the Third World not only in ideological terms but at the level of developmental aid.[35]

The pivotal moment of PCI's engagement was Togliatti's visit to Belgrade in January 1964. His talks with Tito were based on the common conviction that the 'physiognomy of today's world' had to a large part been modified and that a policy of 'active peaceful coexistence' was by now a necessity. In this context, socialism represented a 'a unitary social and economic process' albeit destined to develop 'in quite varied forms'.[36] The

---

[34] FG APC, Central Committee, 24 October 1963, tape recording. 'L'Unità', 26 October 1963. *Il Partito comunista italiano e il movimento operaio internazionale 1956-1968* (Roma: Editori Riuniti, 1968), 168-98.
[35] Pons, *I comunisti italiani*, Friedman, *Shadow Cold War*, 117-18.
[36] FG APC, Foreign Affairs, 1964, Jugoslavia, mf. 520, 15-21 January 1964, 1393-401.

terrain for the main understanding between the two leaders was however constituted by the Arab countries of North Africa. They shared the opening towards Ben Bella and Nasser, including their vague socialist ideas. They also found common cause in their highly critical assessment of China's policies, albeit with different nuances. Tito was of the opinion that the conflict between Moscow and Beijing was 'in essence one between states' and foresaw that the Chinese would not turn back. Togliatti made the point, in a comment more consonant with the political culture of the Italians, that Chinese pressure was making 'the process of democratization more difficult' in the socialist countries. He foresaw the scenario of an understanding 'between the communist parties of the West and the liberation movements of Africa, Asia and Latin America' and imagined a meeting of the progressive parties and movements of the Mediterranean as a way of challenging Chinese positions at the political level. These words reflected Togliatti's ideas of creating a sphere of intermediate relations between the Soviet Union and the non-alignment represented by Yugoslavia, by opening up a perspective to the communists of the 'capitalist West'.[37]

The commonality of views between Tito and Togliatti outlined a non-indifferent change in the system of relations of the Italian communists, even though they remained loyal to the 'socialist camp'. The convergence on the notion of 'active coexistence' in particular allowed a detachment of this topic from mere identification with Soviet policy and transferred it to the level of the United Nations. Of no less importance was the opening for the Italian communists of the possibility to acquire judgements and information on international politics through the leading group of an influential state, which represented an outlook different from Moscow's or from those of the other socialist countries. Among other things, the Yugoslavs shared with Togliatti their ideas of a change in 'global economic relations' elaborated by the non-aligned states, and their criticisms of the Comecon, inadequate as it was for confronting these type of problems and even for integrating the socialist countries. On his side, Togliatti appeared to outline an inclusive and not solely bilateral strategy, whose aim was to formulate an idea of a community of socialists and of the 'socialist world' much more nuanced and enlarged as compared with that conceived by the Soviets. The PCI's action did not therefore appear as a support for the policies of containment of China then in operation in the 'socialist camp' loyal to Moscow, but as the attempt to construct political alliances and a new sense of internationalism.

Conclusion

In August 1964, Togliatti wrote a 'memorandum' in Yalta, while waiting to meet the Soviet leaders to discuss the Chinese problem. Then he suddenly died. His 'Yalta memorandum' was then published by the Italian communists, despite the

---

[37] FG APC, Palmiro Togliatti, Marisa Malagoli Papers, Journey to Yugoslavia (14 January–1 February 1964), 7–15 e 16–25. FG APC, Foreign Affairs, 1964, Yugoslavia, mf. 520, 15–21 January 1964, 1402–14. For the Yugoslav account of affairs, cf. Galeazzi, *Il PCI e il movimento dei paesi non allineati*, 102–3.

negative opinion of Moscow, and became his political testament[38]. He famously criticized the Soviets for their 'ideological and propagandistic polemic' which placed them on the same level as the Chinese, and appealed to avoid a 'general and consolidated schism'. The document contained few, but important, references to the relations between the Western communist parties and the anti-colonial liberation movements. Togliatti imagined a conference convened by the Western parties with a 'broad area of representation from the democratic countries of the "Third World" and their progressive movements', devoted 'exclusively' to the problem of the 'ways of development of the ex-colonial countries' in order to understand 'what the aim of socialism means for them'. In this way the Chinese would be fought 'with facts, not just with words'. The reference to the fight against the Chinese constituted a persuasive argument when put to the Soviets, but Togliatti's interrogatives were more general and involved the very meaning of socialism throughout the world, which represented also a consequence of his recent rapprochement with Tito. While the break-up of the 'socialist camp' was compromising the vision of an irresistible growth of socialism as a vector of the unification of the world, the sense itself of socialism could not be limited to the 'socialist camp'. In this way, Togliatti took on the task of expressing a critical conscience that was lacking in the Soviet and Chinese leaders. Under this profile, the 'memorandum' took on the aspect of a prophecy destined to remain unheard.

The death of Togliatti coincided with an international conjuncture that would spoil the scenario set out in the Yalta 'memorandum'. In a short space of time, any hopes of avoiding a split between Moscow and Beijing, the socialist orientations among the new Third World States and the prospects for a more credible and incisive destalinization were all lost or significantly diluted. Khrushchev's removal was an unexpected, disconcerting event which did not remedy the dispute with Beijing and reversed the course of political liberalization in favour of technocratic reforms of the planned economy. A coup d'état deposed Ben Bella in June 1965, thus scaling back the project of a revolutionary Algeria in the Mediterranean. A few months later Sukarno, a highly symbolic figure in the Third World, was deposed, while the Indonesian communist party was destroyed by ferocious military repression. Cuba's Third World internationalism maintained its vitality but also challenged Yugoslavian non-alignment and the 'peaceful road' of the Italians. The global mobilization provoked by American intervention in Vietnam took place in a context of profound fractures in the anti-imperialist front, and of the Third World as an imagined subject.

By the end of 1965, Longo acknowledged the disorientation of the leading group, when at the Direction he spoke of a 'vacuum' in the PCI's international relations; and referring to the other Italian parties, he even claimed that they all had international connections, but 'we no longer do'. This claim might have appeared paradoxical, given its long-lasting ideological and practical ties with the Soviet Union and the 'socialist camp', but it revealed a lucid despondency linked to the Chinese schism. Berlinguer went even further, wondering whether the presuppositions of the Yalta 'memorandum'

---

[38] P. Togliatti, 'The Yalta Memorandum' in id., *On Gramsci and Other Writings*, Lawrence and Wishart, ed. and introduced D. Sassoon, London 1979, 285–97.

still existed[39]. These words may suggest that PCI leaders were wondering about the 'memorandum' in light of the significant changes affecting the world scenario. Clearly Longo and Berlinguer were referring not so much to the web of transnational relations woven in previous years, as to the crisis of meaning of the internationalist tradition after the end of communist unity. The unitary appeal of Togliatti's 'memorandum' and the exhortation to the Soviet leadership to take an initiative that could deal adequately with global questions had fallen on deaf ears. Unlike the traditional anti-communist vision, the PCI's problem, already evident for some time, was not the control exerted by Moscow, but the absence of any real exchange, and the consequent inefficacy of the partnership. The very rituality of the encounters between communist parties, especially bilateral ones, was experienced as a straight jacket, but the expansion of relations to other progressive forces in and beyond Europe could not come into being solely via unilateral initiatives. Thus, the prospect of a new kind of internationalism connected to the 'rediscovery' of the Third World proved to be much more difficult and less promising than the Italian Communists had believed. They would find new ways to define their own internationalist political culture only in the aftermath of 1968, the Prague Spring, and the making of a Europeanist vision of global agendas.

---

[39] FG, Apci, Direzione, Verbali, 23 December 1965.

5

Proletarian internationalism and Third World liberation in the life and politics of South African communist Dr Yusuf M. Dadoo

Arianna Lissoni

On 21 March 1960, apartheid police opened fire on a crowd of peaceful protestors in the South African township of Sharpeville, killing sixty-nine people. In the aftermath of the massacre, the regime imposed a state of emergency and declared illegal the main Black political organizations, the African National Congress (ANC) and its breakaway, the Pan Africanist Congress. In this context, ANC Deputy President Oliver Tambo secretly slipped out of South Africa with the task of representing the organization abroad and rallying international support for the anti-apartheid struggle. The South African Communist Party (SACP), in consultation with the South African Indian Congress (SAIC), similarly instructed Dr Yusuf Mohamed Dadoo, a member of its Central Committee and SAIC president, to leave so that he could 'assist with the organisation of solidarity work and consolidate the external apparatus of the Party'.[1]

Founded in 1921 as the Communist Party of South Africa (CPSA), the SACP was reconstituted as a clandestine organization three years after the dissolution and prohibition of its predecessor in 1950. The new 'secret party', to use Tom Lodge's formulation,[2] operated both illegally and covertly throughout the 1950s, with its members active in legal political formations and participating in the mass campaigns of this decade under the banner of the Congress Movement, an anti-apartheid umbrella body led by the ANC. During the 1960 state of emergency, the SACP publicly announced its underground existence, thus breaking the secrecy and relative isolation of the previous decade. In this period, the lines between the ANC and the SACP became increasingly blurred, and leaders from both organizations formed Umkhonto we Sizwe (MK), launched in 1961 and signalling a shift in strategy from non-violence to armed struggle.

---

[1] Brian Bunting, *Moses Kotane: South African Revolutionary*, 3rd ed. (Cape Town: Mayibuye Centre, 1998), 262.
[2] Tom Lodge, *Red Road to Freedom: A History of the South African Communist Party, 1921–2021* (Auckland Park: Jacana Media, 2021).

Born in Krugersdorp, a small mining town west of Johannesburg, in 1909 into a family of Indian Muslim traders, Dr Dadoo had been educated in South Africa, India and Scotland, where he obtained his medical degree. He joined the CPSA in 1939 and soon became a central figure in South African Black opposition politics, particularly devoting himself to building African-Indian unity, and was variously arrested. Although a succession of banning orders prohibited Dadoo from public political activity for much of the 1950s, he was involved in the SACP underground reconstitution. In 1955 the ANC awarded him (in absentia as he was banned at the time) the Isitwalandwe-Seaparonkoe medal, its highest honour. Because of his political stature and international connections, Dadoo was thus chosen to help set up the liberation movement's mission abroad after Sharpeville.

Although the expectation had been that he would soon be able to return to South Africa to continue the struggle, this was the beginning of a life in exile, not just for Dadoo, but for an entire generation of South African political activists. By 1965, repression by the apartheid state had smashed the internal resistance network, with scores of activists being arrested and serving long prison terms, including leading figures such as Nelson Mandela, Walter Sisulu and Govan Mbeki. Those who evaded capture were forced into exile, with the UK and Tanzania initially emerging as the main centres of external political activity. The ANC established its first external headquarters in Dar es Salaam, where the SACP's two top office holders, Moses Kotane (general secretary) and JB Marks (chairman), worked as full-time ANC officials. But in the 1960s independent African states were, with few exceptions, unwilling to host as long-term residents white and Indian communists, who mostly settled in the UK. A small office at 40 Goodge Street, London, became the SACP's main operational base, with Dadoo appointed deputy general secretary 'with the authority to negotiate help from fraternal parties'.[3] In his memoir, Ronnie Kasrils offers a vivid description of the one-roomed office:

> Three old desks, a couple of odd chairs, nondescript carpeting, book shelves and a battered filing cabinet were the furnishings. Photographs of Mandela, Sisulu, JB Marks and Kotane hung imperfectly on the walls under a ceiling that sagged. A bust of Lenin and piles of 'Party' journals from Australia, Cuba, Czechoslovakia, the USA, Nigeria, Vietnam and the like testified to our international links. The pleasant aroma of Dadoo's pipe pervaded the otherwise unremarkable setting.[4]

Across the road at number 38, another office, rented under the name of Inkululeko Publications, housed the editorial board and was in charge of the production and distribution of the *African Communist*, the party's quarterly journal. From this London base, South African communists in exile tirelessly worked to reorganize the party and rebuild the internal resistance movement over the next decades.

---

[3] Lodge, *Red Road to Freedom*, 344.
[4] Ronnie Kasrils, *Armed and Dangerous: My Undercover Struggle against Apartheid*, 1st ed. (London: Heinemann 1993), 100.

Arguably one of the consequences of exile, as Tom Lodge notes, is that the party became entirely reliant on external sources for its survival, with the Soviet Union and other socialist countries providing the bulk of subventions.[5] This assistance has been used as evidence of a Soviet strategy to control southern African liberation movements and by inference to explain the SACP's pro-Moscow positions, with the party siding with the Soviet Union during all the major crises of socialism of the Cold War era, from the 1956 Hungarian crisis to the Sino-Soviet split and the 1968 military intervention in Czechoslovakia.[6] Contrary to this rather functionalist view of socialist solidarity, Vladimir Shubin and Marina Traikova argue that there was 'no threat from the Eastern Bloc', and that support for southern African liberation movements was based on relations of cooperation, friendship, mutual respect and trust.[7] Moreover, the Soviet Union was not just as a source of financial, material and diplomatic support, but also a major inspiration and political model for anti-colonial and liberation struggles across Africa, Asia and Latin America.[8]

This chapter focuses on the SACP's relations of international solidarity, generally referred to as proletarian internationalism in socialist discourse, during its exile years, a period characterized by the twin processes of decolonization and the global Cold War. I attempt to unravel and analyse some of its links with the Soviet Union and the world communist movement through a biographical approach based on Yusuf Dadoo, whose exile experience roughly coincides with the first two decades of that of the party. As one of the party's leading figures and, from 1972 until his death in 1983, its national chairman, Dadoo inhabited a transnational political landscape that gravitated both 'east', towards the Soviet Union, and 'south', towards what was then known as the Third World. The chapter uses individual biography to make visible alternative histories, networks and geographies of solidarity that have been obscured by mainstream post-Cold War politics and narrow nationalist approaches to liberation histories in post-colonial times.

In the absence of an official SACP archive, Dadoo's personal papers at the Robben Island Mayibuye Archives at the University of the Western Cape (UWC) contain rich footprints of his – and the party's – links with a global anti-colonial and internationalist political community that was tri-continental in scope, and was also connected to the working class of capitalist countries through their communist parties. As well as drawing on official statements and other published writings by Dadoo, the chapter relies on the unpublished transcripts of interviews with Dadoo conducted by Essop Pahad in the late 1970s, which include discussions of the SACP's relations with the Soviet Union and socialist countries.

Christopher Lee argues that '[d]iplomatic history is not solely comprised by states. In the case of liberation struggles, it depended on the commitment of individuals'.[9]

---

[5] Lodge, *Red Road to Freedom*, 341.
[6] See Stephen Ellis, *External Mission: The ANC in Exile, 1960–1990* (Johannesburg: Jonathan Ball, 2012).
[7] Vladimir Shubin, and Marina Traikova, 'There Is No Threat from the Eastern Bloc', in *The Road to Democracy in South Africa*, ed. South African Democracy Education Trust, vol. 3, part 2 (Pretoria: Unisa Press, 2008), 985–1066.
[8] See Christopher J. Lee, 'Introduction', in Alex La Guma, *A Soviet Journey, A Critical Annotated Edition* (London: Lexington Books, 2017), 1–60.
[9] Lee, 'Introduction', 25.

As his archive reveals, Dadoo played a central role in the internationalization of the anti-apartheid struggle on a global scale and in the exile diplomacy of the South African liberation movement. This diplomatic work could be very demanding: it involved representing the party at national congresses of fraternal parties as well as international events such as the International Meetings of Communist and Workers' Parties (which Dadoo attended in 1960 and 1969); delivering official messages on behalf of the SACP's Central Committee; entertaining relations with other communist parties (including in the West), liberation movements and post-colonial governments; issuing 'fraternal' messages and other statements of solidarity; and leading official delegations to various countries. The chapter does not attempt to provide a comprehensive account of this expansive network of relationships, but rather to show how Dadoo's political consciousness and vision helped to shape some of these, with particular reference to the Soviet Union, Bulgaria and the movement for world peace.

Proletarian internationalism and Third World liberation

Recent scholarship on southern African liberation movements has drawn attention to their complex entanglements with Eastern Europe during the Cold War and to the role played by individual actors in shaping these networks of solidarity.[10] Within this literature, transnationalism has emerged as an important concept that seeks to understand the international connections of liberation movements and the movements of individual actors across geographical, social and ideological borders beyond the confines of 'nation'. In some cases, this has led to a critique of the very notion of 'national liberation' and the framework of the nation-state which has dominated writings on southern African liberation struggles. Several scholars have adopted the term 'un-national' 'to underscore how much of national liberation took place in and from spaces that were categorically different from the national frame'.[11]

Transnationalism thus offers an important new lens to analyse the dynamics of liberation movements, their leaders, members and international supporters. At the same time, the concept does not necessarily reflect how actors within these movements experienced and interpreted their individual circumstances and the wider environment. Key to understanding what drove this complex set of relationships, as well as Dadoo's own political thinking and activism, is proletarian internationalism, understood as a theory and praxis of solidarity among workers of all countries.

---

[10] See Lena Dallywater, Christopher Saunders, and Helder Adegar Fonseca (eds.), *Southern African Liberation Movements and the Global Cold War 'East', Transnational Activism 1960–1990* (Munich; Vienna: De Gruyter Oldenburg, 2019); and Lee, 'Introduction'.

[11] Louise White and Miles Larmer, 'Introduction: Mobile Soldiers and "Un-national" Liberation of Southern Africa', *Journal of Southern African Studies* 40, no. 6 (2014): 1272. See also 'Special Issue: Liberation beyond the Nation', *Journal of Southern African Studies* 46, no. 5 (2020).

Proletarian internationalism was not only essential for building socialism in any country but, according to Lenin's formulation, it was also inseparable from the question of national and colonial liberation.[12] In Marxist-Leninist terms, national liberation struggles were about the right to national self-determination as a way of resolving the national question, that is, the oppression of one group by another. National liberation was seen as different from narrow bourgeois nationalism, which emphasized national exclusiveness and could descend into (reactionary) chauvinism.

Because of the coexistence of the national with the class struggle in the South African context, in 1928, the 6th Comintern adopted a resolution known as the 'Native Republic' or 'two stage' thesis, which called on the CPSA to work for the creation of 'an independent native South African republic as a stage towards a workers' and peasants' republic, with full equal rights for all races, black, coloured and white'.[13] According to Irina Filatova, 'the slogan of the independent native republic was to have a profound and lasting effect on theoretical thinking and debate within the Party and the ANC.'[14] While the Comintern's role in the native republic resolution is undeniable, it was also the product, as Robin D.G. Kelley argues, of 'the real aspirations of the African people– the return of the land and self-determination'.[15]

In the 1950s, the theory of the national democratic revolution, leading to the overthrow of colonial oppression paving the way to the transition to socialism, was developed by the Communist Party of the Soviet Union (CPSU) in response to the process of decolonization that was then gaining speed.[16] The relationship between the national question and class struggle was further theorized by the SACP in terms of 'colonialism of a special type', that is, a unique type of colonialism, where an independent 'oppressing White nation occupied the same territory as the oppressed people themselves and lived side by side with them'. The party's 1962 programme, *The Road to South African Freedom*, advocated the establishment of a 'national democratic state', whose main content would be the national liberation of the African people.[17] These theories provided the 'ideological glue' for the unfolding alliance between the SACP and the ANC, while crucially shaping the liberation movement's strategy and tactics.[18]

---

[12] For an analysis of internationalism and national liberation in Lenin's writings see Robert Bozinovski, *The Communist Party of Australia and Proletarian Internationalism, 1928–1945* (PhD thesis, Victoria University, 2008), esp. 34–8. See also Vijay Prashad, 'The Internationalist Lenin: Self-determination and Anti-colonialism', *Monthly Review Online*, 10 August 2020, https://mronline.org/2020/08/10/the-internationalist-lenin-self-determination-and-anti-colonialism/ (last accessed 24 May 2022).

[13] Resolution on 'the South African question' adopted by the Executive Committee of the Communist International following the sixth Comintern congress, https://omalley.nelsonmandela.org/omalley/index.php/site/q/03lv01538/04lv01600/05lv01603/06lv01605.htm (last accessed 28 December 2021).

[14] Irina Filatova, 'The Lasting Legacy: The Soviet Theory of the National-Democratic Revolution and South Africa', *South African Historical Journal* 64, no. 3 (2012): 6.

[15] Robin D.G. Kelley, 'The Third International and the Struggle for National Liberation in South Africa', *Ufahamu: A Journal of African Studies* 38, no. 1 (2014): 262.

[16] See ibid.

[17] SACP, *The Road to South African Freedom* (London: Inkululeko Publications, [n.d.]).

[18] David Everatt, 'Alliance Politics of a Special Type: The Roots of the ANC/SACP Alliance, 1950–1954', *Journal of Southern African Studies* 18, no. 1 (1992): 19–39.

Moreover, rather than viewing the national as separate from the international, for communists like Dadoo, proletarian internationalism connected revolutionary struggles in different countries to revolutionary struggle worldwide. It epitomized the 'highest concrete expression of class solidarity both between national groups within a single country, and between different national contingents of the working class of different countries'.[19] In an article in the *African Communist* paying tribute to Georgi Dimitrov on what would have been his 90th birthday, Dadoo quoted the Bulgarian communist and anti-fascist fighter:

> Proletarian internationalism, far from contradicting the struggle of the working people of individual countries for national, social and cultural freedom provides, thanks to international proletarian solidarity and unity in struggle, the support needed for victory in this struggle.[20]

Dimitrov's conclusion, which Dadoo agreed with, was that allegiance to the CPSU and Soviet Union was the principal criterion of proletarian internationalism. As the first workers' state, the Soviet Union, and together with it the socialist countries, constituted for Dadoo the main bulwark 'against imperialism, against capitalist exploitation, against colonialism, for social progress, ... [and] on the vital question of peace'. As such, the CPSU represented the 'sheet-anchor' of the international communist movement. This meant that 'for the communist parties in whatever part of the world they may be, the closest collaboration, cooperation and friendship with the CPSU is an absolute prerequisite'.[21]

As Eddy Maloka notes, 'internationalism is a core component of the activities of any communist party, and, accordingly, the SACP established fraternal relations with like-minded parties all over the world, particularly in Africa and the socialist bloc'.[22] The chapter now turns to some of the party's 'fraternal relations' that Dadoo helped build and nurtured. In his lifetime Dadoo collected a string of honours and awards for his service and contribution to socialism: the Order of Georgi Dimitrov of Bulgaria, the Order of Karl Marx by the GDR, the Order of the Friendship of the Peoples by the Soviet Union, the Gold Medal of Afro-Asian People's Solidarity Organisation, the Scroll of Honour of the World Peace Council (WPC), the Decoration of the Hungarian Peace Movement and Poland's Wielki Proletariat. These awards are evidence of the respect and high esteem Dadoo was held with as a leading figure in the international communist movement.

---

[19] Yusuf Dadoo quoted in Essop Pahad, 'A People's Leader: A Political Biography of Dr Yusuf M. Dadoo', unpublished manuscript, 1990, 80.
[20] Georgi Dimitrov quoted in Yusuf M. Dadoo, 'Tribute to Dimitrov', *African Communist*, no. 50, third quarter (1972): 60.
[21] Yusuf M. Dadoo interviewed by Essop Pahad [London, c. 1978].
[22] Eddy Maloka, *The South African Communist Party: Exile and after Apartheid* (Auckland Park: Jacana Media, 2013), 83.

From London to Moscow

When Dadoo arrived in London in 1960, he joined a small SACP group that had been organizing around Vella Pillay, a fellow party member who had left South Africa with his wife Patsy in 1949 to escape the prohibition of inter-racial marriages. In the 1950s, this London cell served as the main conduit for the party's external relations, depending in turn on the Communist Party of Great Britain (CPGB) for its international contacts and financial support.

In July 1960, shortly after coming out of South Africa and as the SACP announced its underground existence, Dadoo made his first official visit to the Soviet Union. Pillay accompanied him on this trip, which was arranged through the General Secretary of the CPGB, John Gollan. Gollan also wrote a letter of recommendation to the Central Committee of the CPSU, as no prior direct relations existed between the SACP and the CPSU.[23] This reliance on the British party had its origins in the CPSU's practice of devolving its relations with communist parties in the British colonies to the CPGB. As Shubin explains, '[i]t was only in late 1960 that a special Section of African Countries was formed in the International Department of the CPSUCC'.[24]

Although London remained his base for the remainder of his life and political exile, Dadoo frequently travelled to the Soviet Union and other socialist countries. His July 1960 visit to Moscow (followed by a second visit in late 1960, a third in 1961 and countless more in the years to come) marked the beginning of SACP-CPSU bilateral relations and of Soviet financial assistance.[25]

While Dadoo's papers contain little evidence of these early ties, the Soviet Union looms large in the archive and his political life in exile. From 1961, Dadoo attended all the congresses of the CPSU, an experience which he described as 'awe-inspiring'. Hundreds of workers from all over the Soviet Union, including a significant proportion of women, were represented at the congresses, along with fraternal delegates representing the working class and national liberation movement from countries all over the world. The congresses dealt 'with every aspect of life in the Soviet Union', from the planning of the economy, to agricultural production, to industrial development and 'the position of the youth, education, culture and sports'.[26] They also discussed reports on the international political situation, which included analyses of Africa and southern Africa.

---

[23] In his official message of condolences to the Central Committee of the CPGB for the death of Gollan in 1977, Dadoo remembered him as 'great champion of the national liberation movement' who 'always found time to be in the forefront of solidarity actions against the inhuman system of Apartheid'. University of the Western Cape, Mayibuye Centre, Yusuf Dadoo Collection (hereafter MCH05), 1.3.27, Yusuf M. Dadoo to Central Committee, CPGB, 8 September 1977.

[24] Shubin and Traikova, 'There Is No Threat', 991.

[25] Direct contact was established between Moscow and the ANC in late 1962, leading to the first official meeting between the CPSU and the ANC in April 1963. According to Shubin, this was not mediated by the SACP and happened on its own accord, making the ANC the first African liberation movement to have direct links with the CPSU. For a comprehensive review of the military and diplomatic support given to the ANC, SACP and MK in the following decades, see Vladimir Shubin, *ANC: A View from Moscow*, 2nd ed. (Auckland Park: Jacana Media, 2017).

[26] Yusuf M. Dadoo interviewed by Essop Pahad [London, c. 1978].

For example, a statement on 'Freedom for the prisoners of imperialism and reaction' adopted at the CPSU's 25th congress in 1976 condemned 'the racist regime rule over the peoples of the South African Republic, Namibia and Zimbabwe', which represented 'a challenge to the conscience of all mankind'. The statement also referred to the 'inhuman treatment from jailers [that] caused the death of Bram Fisher'[27], and called for the release of all political prisoners.[28] In turn, the SACP's fraternal message to this congress, which Dadoo personally delivered for the first time as SACP chairman, celebrated the Soviet Union as a source of 'moral inspiration and material backing for those still living under the tyranny of capitalism, imperialism, neo-colonialism and racialism'.[29] His reports on the 25th and 26th (1981) CPSU congresses published in

Figure 5.1 Photograph of Dr Yusuf M. Dadoo speaking at the 25th Congress of the CPSU in 1976. Image courtesy of Roshan Dadoo.

---

[27] The South African communist lawyer and political prisoner had died a year earlier after the apartheid government ignored concerns about Fischer's health and calls for his release.
[28] MCH05, 2.1.20, 'Freedom for the prisoners of imperialism and reaction: Statement of the 25th Congress of the Communist Party of the Soviet Union [1976].'
[29] MCH05, 2.1.20, Message of the SACP to the 25th Congress of the CPSU by Chairman Dr Yusuf Dadoo, 24 February 1976.

the *African Communist* spoke of the 'privilege and source of inspiration'[30] to be among those in attendance as 'a deep personal and political experience'.[31]

Georgi Dimitrov and Bulgaria

While the Soviet Union occupied a central place in Dadoo's life and politics, his first visit to a socialist country had actually been to Poland and Bulgaria, and took place much earlier, in 1948. In October of that year Dadoo had left South Africa without a passport to attend to a meeting of the United Nations in Paris. Although he made it to the UK, he was barred from travelling to France and remained stranded for several months in London, where he was hosted by the India League, attended meetings and gave lectures, and interacted with British communists at the CPGB's headquarters in King Street.

At the end of 1948 Dadoo was invited to travel with the then General Secretary of the CPGB Harry Pollitt to attend the congresses of the Polish and Bulgarian parties, where the establishment of people's democracies in Eastern Europe was at the forefront of the discussions. The important question facing both congresses, in Dadoo's mind, was the characterization, role and function of people's democracies – as creating the basis for the transition to socialism. One of the interesting features that Dadoo observed was that power was passing into the hands of the working people as the main driving force in the creation of people's democracies in Eastern Europe. Related to this, it was seen as imperative for people's democracies to have the 'closest collaboration and friendship with the Soviet Union' against US imperialist subversion, which sought to 'turn back the path of these countries from socialism'.[32]

In Warsaw, Dadoo witnessed the devastation and destruction caused by Nazi-fascism in the Second World War, from which the country was striving to emerge. At the same time, this was where the power of fascism had been destroyed, mainly thanks to the Soviet Union and the Red Army. In this there was also a factor of elation for Dadoo, who thought about the rise to power of the 'fascist' National Party back in South Africa just as fascism had been defeated in Europe: 'What was growing out of the ruins and rubble and destruction, a new country, a new Poland, gave one the confidence that these fascists in our own country cannot last long, that they can be defeated.'[33]

In Sofia, Dadoo attended the Fifth Congress of the Bulgarian Communist Party (BCP) and met Georgi Dimitrov, who had become the country's prime minister. The encounter with Dimitrov made a profound impression on Dadoo, who considered it a 'rare privilege' and 'a memorable experience for one to cherish and treasure', as he

---

[30] Yusuf Dadoo, 'An Impressive Demonstration of Communist Unity', *African Communist*, no. 66, third quarter (1976): 48.
[31] Yusuf Dadoo and Moses Mahbida, '26th Congress of the CPSU: The Voice of Reason, Peace, Freedom and Socialism', *African Communist*, no. 86, third quarter: 54.
[32] Ibid.
[33] Yusuf M. Dadoo interviewed by Essop Pahad [London, c. 1978].

later remembered.[34] Dadoo's admiration for Dimitrov dated back to his conduct at the Reichstag fire trial of 1933, where he had turned the accusation of arson back on his Nazi accusers, putting them in the dock. At the time of the South African Treason Trial of 1956–61, Rusty Bernstein, a communist party member who was amongst the accused, wrote a series of articles on the Reichstag trial as 'Dimitrov's defence and conduct in that trial [was seen] as a brilliant model of revolutionary conduct before a fascist court', which in some ways prefigured South Africa's political trials of the 1960s. After Bram Fisher delivered his statement from the dock at his trial in 1966, the BCP wrote in a message of solidarity to the SACP: 'we, Bulgarian Communists, were reminded of the heroic defence by Georgi Dimitrov.'[35]

Dimitrov's role in the Comintern, particularly with regards to the policy of 'popular anti-fascist fronts', also importantly shaped Dadoo's own thinking. Dimitrov's contribution to the defeat of fascism, outlined in his report to the 7th Comintern in 1935, was the idea of the creation of popular anti-fascist fronts that would unite all progressive democratic forces in the struggle against fascism. This was to have a lasting influence on the strategy and tactics of communist parties worldwide, including the CPSA, which turned 'its attention to the work and activities of its members in the trade union and liberation movements' and to the formation of broad alliances against fascism at home and abroad.[36] In 1939, Dadoo was a founder and chairperson of the Non-European United Front (NEUF), an alliance of Black political organizations that provided an important platform for anti-war campaigning until the Nazi invasion of the Soviet Union in 1941 led the CPSA and NEUF to abandon their opposition to the war. In 1947, Dadoo was one of the signatories of the Joint Declaration between the ANC and the Indian Congresses in South Africa which ushered in a new era of African-Indian cooperation. Writing in the centenary year of Dimitrov's birthday in 1982, Dadoo argued that his call for a united front against war was still valid, and that the SACP had remained loyal to Dimitrov's teachings by 'building a united front of liberation in South Africa, based on fraternal cooperation with the African National Congress'.[37]

During his personal interview with Dimitrov in 1948, Dadoo also learned of his esteem for the CPSA and interest in international affairs, including in South Africa. As he later wrote:

> Comrade Dimitrov showed a keen interest in the developments and struggles of the South African people, and a rare appreciation of the intricate problems of our country. On learning that I originated in a Moslem community in South Africa he proposed, and I gladly agreed, that I visit a region in Bulgaria inhabited by the Turkish minority, to see for myself the manner in which the people's government set about solving minority problems. I also took advantage of this visit to explain

---

[34] Dadoo, 'Tribute to Dimitrov', 58.
[35] Ibid., 55.
[36] Ibid., 57.
[37] MCH05, 3, 6.421, 'Message of the SACP on the Occasion of the Centenary of the Birth of Georgi Dimitrov' delivered by Yusuf Dadoo [1982].

to these people the hardships and indignities suffered by the oppressed majority in South Africa.[38]

Dadoo's links with Bulgaria and Dimitrov were renewed in the 1970s, after he became party chairman and as Bulgaria's support for southern African liberation movements and their armed efforts increased. In the first decade of exile, besides the Soviet Union and the GDR, Czechoslovakia had been the most active Eastern European country in terms of this support.[39] According to Shubin and Traikova, in the 1970s and 1980s, Bulgaria started taking on this role. In 1972 an ANC delegation led by Secretary General Alfred Nzo visited 'Czechoslovakia, GDR, Hungary, Romania and Bulgaria and contact between the ANC and Eastern Europe resulted "in a tremendous increase of assistance"'.[40] The following year an SACP delegation consisting of Dadoo, Chris Hani, Moses Mabhida, Joe Slovo and Michael Harmel also went to Bulgaria. In October 1978 the country's leader Todor Zhivkov toured southern Africa and met with various African liberation movements after adopting a five-year plan to deliver arms to Frelimo and MPLA.[41]

The SACP and the ANC were regularly invited to participate in Congresses of the BCP, which Dadoo attended as its official representative, along with delegates from other fraternal parties and organizations.[42] In the fraternal message to the BCP's 11th Congress in 1976 by the SACP's Central Committee, Dadoo spoke of the 'indivisible link between our struggle for liberation and your efforts as part of the world community of socialist nations to consolidate the strength and gains of socialist achievements and march forward to communism'.[43] Regarding the struggle in southern Africa, he commended the BCP and the Bulgarian people for having 'demonstrated time and again that in the fire of struggle you stand unselfishly on the side of freedom and independence'.[44]

As part of official visits to socialist states delegates were taken around to see some of their achievements in terms of industrial development, housing and living conditions, education and healthcare. For example, the invitation to participate in the BCP's 11th Congress in 1976 also included the 'opportunity of becoming acquainted with

---

[38] Dadoo, 'Tribute to Dimitrov', 58.
[39] For East German solidarity, which is not analysed in this chapter, see Hans-Georg Schleischer, 'GDR Solidarity: The German Democratic Republic and the South African Liberation Struggle' in SADET, *The Road to Democracy in South Africa*, vol. 3, part 2. For Czechoslovak involvement in Africa, which, according to Muehlenbeck, happened significantly more autonomously from Moscow than previously assumed, see Philip Muehlenbeck, *Czechoslovakia in Africa, 1945–1968* (New York: Palgrave Macmillan, 2015).
[40] Shubin and Traikova, 'There Is No Threat'.
[41] See Wilson Center Digital Archive, 'Secret Bulgarian Politburo Resolution for Military Aid Supply to Certain National Liberation Movement and Communist Parties', 16 July 1976, https://digitalarchive.wilsoncenter.org/document/112234.
[42] See for example MCH05, 3.5.9, Letter from the Central Committee of the BCP to the CC of the SACP, 1976.
[43] MCH05, The Message of the Central Committee of the South African Communist Party to the 11th Congress of the Bulgarian Communist Party, 1976. Emphasis original.
[44] MCH05, The Message of the Central Committee of the South African Communist Party to the 11th Congress of the Bulgarian Communist Party, 1976.

the successes registered by the Bulgarian people in the construction of socialism'.[45] In January 1980 Dadoo led another official delegation to Bulgaria after being awarded on his 70th birthday the order of Georgi Dimitrov. During the visit the SACP and the BCP held talks on the tasks facing the respective parties and exchanged views on the international situation, which resulted in a joint communique expressing support for the struggle in southern Africa, amongst other issues. The SACP delegation also laid a wreath at Dimitrov's mausoleum in Sofia's central square and visited Vitosha factory, a garment factory producing military uniforms on the outskirts of the city, where a solidarity rally was held.[46]

Receiving the order of Dimitrov, whom Dadoo regarded as 'one of the greatest revolutionaries of the 20th century', was one of the highest points of Dadoo's life.[47] The decoration was in recognition by the CC of the BCP and the Bulgarian State Council of Dadoo's 'great merits for the strengthening of the unity of the international communist movement on the unshakable principles of Marxism-Leninism and proletarian internationalism' as well as his 'personal contribution to the promotion of the friendship and cooperation' between the SACP and the BCP. In bestowing the honour, Zhikov recalled Dadoo making an 'ardent speech' when he had participated in the BCP's Fifth Congress back in 1948 and met Dimitrov.[48]

Dadoo accepted the medal on behalf of the SACP and South Africa's 'struggling people'. In his acceptance speech, he emphasized adherence to proletarian internationalism as 'vital and indispensable in the struggle against imperialism, fascism and reaction and for peace, national independence, socialism and social progress'. Proletarian internationalism, together with the 'maximum unity of progressive forces' and close relations with the CPSU, represented for Dadoo the key principles of Dimitrov that were necessary to counter contemporary 'cold war psychosis'.[49]

Fighting for peace and national liberation

In 1980, Bulgaria was the host country of the World Parliament of Peoples for Peace organized by the WPC. This followed the First World Congress of Peace in Moscow in 1973, and was attended by more than 2000 peace fighters from over 134 countries around the world. Dadoo participated in his capacity as SACP chairman as well as Vice-chair of the ANC's Revolutionary Council. In his message of solidarity to the parliament, he spoke of its 'utmost historic importance for the whole of humankind in the struggle for peace, detente, national independence and social progress'. He emphasized the dangers posed by the recent military alliance, which also included

[45] MCH05, 3.5.9, Letter from the Central Committee of the BCP to the CC of the SACP, 1976.
[46] MCH05, 3.5.4, Joint Communique on the results of the Talks between the Delegations of the BCP and SACP, January 1980.
[47] MCH05, 3.5.2, YMD acceptance speech of the Order of Georgi Dimitrov, 24 January 1980.
[48] MCH05, 3.5.2, Speech by Todor Zhikov at YMD's award of the Order of Georgi Dimitrov [1980].
[49] MCH05, 3.5.2, YMD acceptance speech of the Order of Georgi Dimitrov, 24 January 1980.

nuclear collaboration,[50] between 'fascist South Africa and zionist Israel ... not only to the oppressed people of South Africa and Palestine, the African and Arab countries, but to world peace as a whole'. Identifying US imperialism as 'responsible for the present arms race and the consequent danger of thermonuclear war', Dadoo placed the Soviet Union and socialist countries as standing 'in the frontline of the struggle for world peace, national independence and social progress'.[51]

Preserving world peace, limiting the arms race and implementing disarmament were key concerns for political activists who lived through the death and destruction of the Second World War and the atomic bombing of Hiroshima and Nagasaki by the United States, and the nuclear arms race of the Cold War. The epitaph on Dadoo's tombstone in Highgate cemetery in London, located opposite Karl Marx's grave, is an important reminder of the movement for world peace of this era and of the contribution of the WPC, of which Dadoo was an active member, to the liberation of southern Africa, which has been erased from public memory. It reads: 'He dedicated his life to the cause of national liberation, socialism and world peace.'

The WPC, a body campaigning for peace and disarmament with local committees around the world that still exists today, was originally formed in 1949. As the Cold War developed and its close ties to the Soviet Union revealed, the WPC was dismissed as a Soviet front and an instrument of Soviet foreign policy by the West. A South African Peace Council (SAPC) with regional branches was also formed in South Africa and peace activism was integrated into the campaigns of the Congress Movement in the 1950s. Launched in 1953, the SAPC was formed as 'an independent, non-party, non-sectarian body [which aimed] to promote activities for peace by all possible means among all sectors of the people of South Africa'.[52] The SAPC also supported the WPC's work for peace and disarmament internationally, for example, by sending messages and delegations to WPC meetings. Many of those active in the SAPC, for example, Hilda Bernstein, Ahmed Kathrada and Bram Fischer, were communists, but it also included non-communists like Molvi Cachalia (a leader of the Indian Congress and close associate of Dadoo's) and ANC president and 1961 Nobel peace prize winner Chief Albert Lutuli. The Marxist Reverend Douglas Chadwick Thompson served as its chairman, as well as being a member of the WPC.[53]

South African peace fighters understood the question of national liberation as going hand in hand with that of peace. In a message of solidarity to the 1955 Bandung Conference, which he saw as a decisive step forward in the fight for world peace, Dadoo proclaimed that 'A free Africa and a free Asia are the handmaidens of world peace, progress and human happiness'.[54] In this period the SAPC campaigned against the

---

[50] See Sasha Polakow-Suransky, *The Unspoken Alliance: Israel's Secret Relationship with Apartheid South Africa* (Auckland Park: Jacana Media, 2010).
[51] MCH05, 6.4.82, Contribution by Dr YM Dadoo [1980].
[52] University of the Witwatersrand, Historical Papers Research Archive (HPRA), End Conscription Campaign Papers, AG1977, A5.41, 'There Shall Be Peace and Friendship': The South African Peace Council in the 1950s [n.d.].
[53] See HPRA, Reverend Douglas Chadwick Thompson Papers, A1906.
[54] Yusuf M. Dadoo, 'Greetings to the Asian-African Conference in Bandung', *New Age*, 7 April 1955.

militarization of the apartheid state and indeed the continent, where former colonial powers sought to retain a military presence through military bases and agreements, and to use African territory as a testing ground for nuclear weapons. It called for an end of the sale of arms to South Africa by the major Western powers as it directly enabled the violence of the apartheid state, which in turn by the early 1960s had blocked all possibilities for peaceful protest, forcing the liberation movement to take up arms. Although it was never formally banned, the SAPC effectively ceased to function in 1963 after most of its members, also active in other anti-apartheid organizations, were banned, exiled or imprisoned.[55]

In her study of the politics of peace during the Cold War, Petra Goedde argues that 'decolonization … threw into disarray the neat binaries between war/aggression and peace/nonviolence' and 'unleashed a heated debate among [peace] activists about the legitimacy of violence when confronted with state-sanctioned violence and oppression'.[56] From the 1960s, the WPC began to openly support national liberation struggles in the Third World. As Essop Pahad notes in his unpublished biography of Dadoo, in the early 1960s, 'influential sections of the WPC had not yet fully understood that the struggle against colonialism, imperialism and racism was a vital part of the struggle for world peace'.[57] Under the leadership of Ramesh Chandra, who became the WPC's general Secretary in 1966 and its president in 1977, Dadoo was part of the campaigning within the WPC that led to a new understanding of the role of national liberation struggles in the fight for world peace that included advocacy of armed struggle, serving as a member of the WPC's presidential council until his death.[58]

In 1973, the Commission on National Liberation of the World Congress of Peace, which included an ANC delegation, issued a document titled 'National Liberation: The Struggle against Colonialism and Racism' condemning 'colonialism, racism, apartheid, national oppression and neo-colonialism' as 'major source[s] of international tension and conflict'. It further proclaimed that '[t]he attainment of world peace and security requires the total elimination of all these aspects of imperialism'. National liberation struggles were thus not only just and legitimate, but 'valuable contributions to the promotion of international peace and security and the development of international cooperation'. Finally, the commission called for a total boycott of the apartheid regime, for rendering support to the ANC, and the release of all political prisoners in southern Africa.[59]

---

[55] The South African Peace Council produced a bulletin called *South Africans for Peace*, a few copies of which are available in HPRA, Hilda and Rusty Bernstein Papers, A 3299, G1.4.1.

[56] Petra Goedde, *The Politics of Peace: A Global Cold War History* (New York: Oxford University Press, 2019).

[57] Pahad, 'A People's Leader', 84.

[58] Chandra had been a leading member of the Communist Party of India from the 1940s to the 1960s. Dadoo's appreciation of his work and their comradeship is captured in a birthday message he wrote for Chandra's 60th birthday in 1979, which greeted his 'most valuable dedicated services to peoples' struggles against imperialism, colonialism, racism, Zionism and despotism'. MCH05, 1.3.57, Yusuf M. Dadoo to Romesh Chadra, WPC, Helsinki, 7 April 1979.

[59] 'Mighty Assembly for World Peace', *Sechaba* 8, no. 2 (February 1982): 5–6.

Siphamandla Zondi shows how the idea of peaceful coexistence was adopted by liberation movements such as the ANC as a form of resistance against colonial and apartheid's violence and war, viewing the WPC as a 'movement for decolonial peace'.[60] After going into exile Dadoo became involved in the international work of the WPC to reduce armaments and control nuclear weapons for the peaceful coexistence of different countries and systems – which, as a communist, he understood as laying the necessary foundation for the construction of socialism and later communism.[61] Détente, as the period in the Cold War characterized by the easing of hostility between the two superpowers in the 1970s became known, was seen as of fundamental importance to the struggles of liberation movements in Africa, Asia and Latin America.[62] In a message delivered to the Central Committee of the CPSU on occasion of the 60th anniversary of the October Revolution, Dadoo explained:

> Détente creates conditions most favourable for the advance of the revolutionary forces, inhibiting the aggressor and preventing intervention by imperialism in support of counter-revolution and neo-colonialism. Détente is not yet everywhere operative nor is it irreversible unless we make it so. It has to be fought for, day and night, ceaselessly.[63]

The reference to detente as being 'not yet everywhere operative' points to its different meaning seen from the Third World, where imperialist aggression continued. While the Soviet invasion of Afghanistan in 1979 is conventionally viewed as marking the end of détente, by the end of 1975, the same year that the Helsinki Accords were signed, the 'hot Cold War' was already intensifying in southern Africa with the invasion of newly independent Angola by apartheid South Africa and covert US involvement.[64]

Conclusion

Dadoo died in 1983, before the confrontation between East and West started to come to an end, including in the southern tip of Africa, where Namibia's independence followed by South Africa's transition to democracy happened parallelly with the collapse of the Soviet Union. Therefore, he did not live through the period of reappraisal of socialism and denunciations of Stalin that came with the downfall of Eastern Europe and the USSR, including from within the leadership of the SACP at the time.[65] As Lee has argued in relation to the writings of South African communist Alex La Guma about the Soviet Union, it is not my aim here to absolve or condemn him for what

---

[60] Siphamandla Zondi, 'The World Peace Council and the ANC's International Relations', SADET, *The Road to Democracy in South Africa* 3, part 3, 1485–1518.
[61] Yusuf M. Dadoo interviewed by Essop Pahad [London, c. 1978].
[62] Ibid.
[63] MCH05, 1.3.31, Message to the CC of the CPSU, YMD, 1 November 1977.
[64] See Vladimir Shubin, *The Hot 'Cold War': The USSR in Southern Africa* (London: Scottsville, South Africa: Pluto Press; University of KwaZulu-Natal Press, 2008).
[65] See Joe Slovo, *Has Socialism Failed?* (London: Inkululeko Publications 1990).

in hindsight may appear as errors of judgement.⁶⁶ Rather, the chapter is an attempt to understand and explain the place of the Soviet Union and the socialist bloc in the political imaginary and consciousness of South African revolutionaries of Dadoo's generation in the historical context of the Cold War and Third World liberation.

As Dadoo's personal archive shows, proletarian internationalism played a vital role in the history of the SACP in exile. Although based in London, where the CPGB provided initial contacts and support for the exiled SACP, Dadoo regularly traversed the so-called iron curtain to build and expand the SACP's relations of international solidarity. This wide network of support reflects the political imagination of a different era, when the struggle for national liberation in South Africa – and other countries in the Third World – intersected with the internationalist politics of the world communist movement, at the centre of which was the Soviet Union. As a man of his times, Dadoo strongly believed that the existence of the Soviet Union and its internationalist policy is what made the freedom of the countries of the Third World from colonial and imperialist oppression possible. This was not just some utopian belief, but rooted in his awareness that the balance of forces in international relations was turning in favour of national liberation movements.

---

⁶⁶ Lee, 'Introduction'.

6

A discreet alternative: The Socialist International's ill-fated battle for 'global Keynesianism' and a New International Economic Order in the 1980s

Mathieu Fulla

In June 1984, Willy Brandt, president of the Socialist International (SI), and Michael Manley, the leader of the People's National Party of Jamaica (PNP) who had chaired the recently formed Socialist International Committee on Economic Policy (SICEP),[1] issued a joint statement on the eve of the G7 Summit in London. They argued that the monetarist-inspired policies implemented in the United States by the Reagan administration had aggravated mass unemployment in OECD countries and impeded development in Southern countries.[2] The following year, the Manley committee published a voluminous report entitled *Global Challenge*, proposing an international alternative to monetarism and the economic order embodied by so-called 'adjustment policies' imposed on Southern countries in exchange for loans by the International Monetary Fund (IMF).[3] The authors of *Global Challenge* urged the Reagan administration to break with these monetary policies, which were based on an overvalued dollar and high interest rates induced by the Volcker Shock in 1979. The scope of the report extended beyond economic issues and examined the intersection between common security, North-South dialogue and human rights – three important elements of the SI agenda since Willy Brandt had become its leader in 1976.[4] Reviewing

---

I would like to thank Michele Di Donato and Marc Lazar for their comments on earlier versions of this chapter.

[1] Penti Vaanen (the general secretary of the SI) to Bureau members, Bureau circular No. B9/83, 1 July 1983, 'Work of the Socialist International Committee on Economic Policies', 3 p., Centre of Socialist Archives at the Fondation Jean Jaurès in Paris (below CAS-FJJ), Archives of the Socialist International, 60 RI (WB) 220.

[2] Willy Brandt and Michael Manley, 'Socialist International press release n°5/84', 4 June 1984, CAS-FJJ, Archives of the Socialist International, 60 RI (WB) 220.

[3] *Global Challenge from Crisis to Cooperation: Breaking the North-South Stalemate*, Report of the Socialist International Committee on Economic Policy chaired by Michael Manley.

[4] Michael Manley and Willy Brandt, 'Breaking the North-South Stalemate', *Socialist Affairs*, n°4/85: 7–10, 9.

the financial and structural weaknesses of the organization, which have been analysed by Guillaume Devin,[5] this chapter also argues that under Brandt's leadership (1976–92), the SI briefly succeeded in uniting a variety of politicians and experts from different geographical areas (mainly Western Europe, Latin America and the Caribbean islands), as well as organizations such as the UN, the Confederation of the Socialist Parties of the European Community (CSPEC) and informal socialist-friendly groups of economists. In the mid-1980s, the gap between the economic principles promoted by international socialists and the policies of Western European socialist governments was particularly pronounced.

A year before the Manley-Brandt declaration, the French Socialist Party had organized a series of meetings of Western European socialist leaders. Confidential records from these meetings reveal attendees' growing doubts about the possibility of developing a socialist alternative to the new capitalist order, which was founded in financialization, the primacy of market mechanisms and harsh criticism of the Western European welfare state model.[6] The concerns expressed by the French Prime Minister Pierre Mauroy and his Swedish and Greek counterparts, Olof Palme and Andreas Papandreou, resoundingly echoed the Portuguese President Mario Soares's blunt diagnosis of his own country:

> In Portugal, we had a revolution, but it veered in the direction of a popular democratic type of regime. The Socialist Party opposed it. [We] reintroduced market-based elements into a quasi-collectivised economy. As a result, we were unable to either conduct a social policy or satisfy the capitalists. We retook power because the conservatives failed! We are going to defend the mechanisms that we denounce (such as the IMF). How can this contradiction be untied?[7]

Western European socialists in office were not alone in implementing policies that were at odds with their own ideology. In Australia, the Labour Party headed by Bob Hawke initiated financial deregulation and a floating national currency, prompting the economists Elizabeth Humphrys and Damien Cahill to emphasize its 'active role in constructing neoliberalism in the country'.[8] At the same time, the New Zealand Labour Party, which also came to power in 1983, ushered in 'a period of radical deregulation known as Rogernomics – named for treasury minister Roger Douglas'.[9] These moves have led numerous scholars to conclude that socialism had entered an era

---

[5] Guillaume Devin, *L'Internationale socialiste: Histoire et sociologie du socialisme international* (Paris: Presses de Sciences Po, 1990).
[6] Greta R. Krippner, *Capitalizing on Crisis: The Political Origins of the Rise of Finance* (Cambridge, MA: Harvard University Press, 2011).
[7] Mario Soares, Meeting of the Socialist Heads of state and government, '*Les acteurs du changement*', handwritten report, 18 May 1983, 3 (3 pages), CAS-FJJ, Archives of Lionel Jospin, First Secretary of the French Socialist Party, 2 PS 455.
[8] Elizabeth Humphrys and Damien Cahill, 'How Labour Made Neoliberalism', *Critical Sociology* 43, nos. 4–5 (2017): 669–84, 669.
[9] John S. Ahlquist, 'Navigating Institutional Change: The Accord, Rogernomics, and the Politics of Adjustment in Australia and New Zealand', *Comparative Political Studies* 44, no. 2 (2011): 127–55, 129.

of widespread neoliberal influence, particularly in Western Europe. In his authoritative text on the long-term history of the Left, Geoff Eley argued that Mitterrand's France and Gonzalez's Spain rivalled the neoliberal economics of Thatcher's Britain after 1982.[10] A few years later, a volume compiled by historians and political scientists described the 1980s as the beginning of a new ideological revisionism in Western social democracy through 'an accommodation of neo-liberalism'.[11] More recently, the sociologist Stephanie Mudge has noted the emergence of 'neo-liberalised leftism' in the American Democratic Party, the German Social Democratic Party (SPD), the Swedish Social Democratic Party (SAP) and the British Labour Party. Mudge argues that 'transnational, finance-oriented economists' have exerted increasing influence on partisan socialist elites.[12] While other scholars have rejected 'neoliberalism' as a useful concept for characterizing the transformation of social democracy in the 1980s, they contend that 'globalisation and the market-driven "negative integration"' of the European Union' forced socialism to renounce its principal economic and social pillars, which were based on 'a high degree of social security, to offset cyclical fluctuations in the economy and to prevent economic inequality'.[13]

Historiographical debates over the use of the term 'neoliberalism' to describe these developments are beyond the scope of this chapter. These bodies of work, however, share a common methodological approach: they focus primarily on socialism at a national level by analysing in detail the socialist and social democratic parties in office at the time. Adopting the lens of socialist supranational organizations such as the Socialist International and the Confederation of the Socialist Parties of the European Community (CSPEC), this chapter offers a different perspective on the relationship between democratic socialism and capitalism in the 1980s. Rather than a blind conversion to the gospel of market mechanisms, this uneasy alliance should be understood as a failed attempt to promote 'global Keynesianism' as an alternative to monetarist-inspired capitalism. The Manley working group appointed by the Socialist International pleaded for a multilateral solution to the North-South problem by radically reshaping the economic international system. This call for 'a new Bretton Woods' implied that international organizations such as the IMF should forestall deflationary domestic policies in major countries, write off the debt of the least developed countries, create a 'symmetrical balance-of-payments adjustment process' and fairly represent Western, Eastern and Southern countries. The Manley group also supported a radical change in the dominant macroeconomic framework in the administrations of the Northern countries; it called for the recognition of government intervention, 'both in international finance and in trade in goods and services' as well as the rise of 'international liquidity, relating global credit arrangements [...] to global development

---

[10] Geoff Eley, *Forging Democracy: The History of the Left in Europe, 1850–2000* (Oxford: Oxford University Press, 2002), 427.
[11] John Callaghan, et al. (eds), 'Introduction', in *In Search of Social Democracy: Responses to Crisis and Modernisation*, eds. John Callaghan, et al. (Manchester: Manchester University Press, 2009), 1–6, 3.
[12] Stephanie L. Mudge, *Leftism Reinvented: Western Parties from Socialism to Neoliberalism* (Cambridge, MA and London: Harvard University Press, 2018), 1–42.
[13] Wolfgang Merkel et al., *Social Democracy in Power: The Capacity to Reform* (London and New York: Routledge, 2008), 2.

capacity rather than to short-term balance-of-payments adjustment'. In other words, the experts supported a more stable financial and macroeconomic international framework in the name of North-South solidarity.[14] They thus challenged the US supremacy on the international system by calling for a 'central international reserve currency, the value of which cannot be decisively influenced by the economic policy of one country alone, such as the United States'.[15] Moreover, these socialist experts of the SI assessed that the solution to the rise in inequalities between Southern and Northern countries implied additional spending of some $100 billion a year in order to achieve an expansion of income and trade, in both North and South: 'We are not suggesting a naïve formula by which the world would decrease its arms spending each year [...]. But we are stressing that the target for a global budget to recover income and trade, and restructure and redistribute resources, should, over ten years, be at least equivalent to current global arms spending.'[16] The set of policies endorsed by key figures in international socialism were closely aligned with the 'Eurokeynesian' approach promoted by the CSPEC at the time.[17] The SI's alternative proposal called for aggressive reflation policies in Northern countries and the creation of a New International Economic Order (NIEO).[18] This second recommendation was nonetheless more subdued than the 1974 United Nations declaration issued by the G77, which sought to transform 'the governance of the global economy to redirect more of the benefits of transnational integration toward "the developing nations"'.[19]

Research for this chapter is based on the archives of the Socialist International and the CSPEC at the Jean-Jaurès Foundation, a French Socialist think tank in Paris, and on the vast body of grey literature produced by the supranational organizations. The chapter's first two sections present the principal pillars of the SI's economic alternative programme, respectively a 'tamer' version of the NIEO and 'global Keynesianism'. The third section examines why this project gradually faded in the second half of the 1980s and how this failure intersected with the conversion of socialist organizations to the prevailing market-oriented approach to capitalism.

---

[14] *Global Challenge*, 201.
[15] Ibid., 202.
[16] Ibid., 198.
[17] Andreas Aust, 'From "Eurokeynesianism" to the "Third Way": The Party of European Socialists (PES) and European employment policies', in *Social Democratic Party Policies in Contemporary Europe*, ed. Giuliano Bonolli and Martin Powell (London and New York: Routledge, 2005), 180–96.
[18] A significant body of literature is devoted to the NIEO. See Mark Mazower, *Governing the World: The History of an Idea* (New York: Penguin Books, 2013 [2012]); Giuliano Garavini, *After Empires: European Integration, Decolonization, and the Challenge from the Global South 1957–1986* (Oxford: Oxford University Press, 2012), 215–30; Vanessa Ogle, 'State Rights against Private Capital: The "New International Economic Order" and the Struggle over Aid, Trade, and Foreign Investment, 1962–1981', *Humanity. An International Journal of Human Rights, Humanitarianism, and Development* 5, no. 2 (Summer 2014): 211–34; and the special issue of *Humanity. An International Journal of Human Rights, Humanitarianism, and Development* coordinated by Nils Gilman (vol. 6, n°1, Spring 2015).
[19] Nils Gilman, 'The New Economic Order: A Reintroduction', *Humanity. An International Journal of Human Rights, Humanitarianism, and Development* 6, no. 1 (Spring 2015): 1–16, 1.

Promoting a 'Tamer' NIEO and a 'Eurokeynesian' approach to economic crisis

At the turn of the 1970s, a radical transformation of the capitalist order was far from being the SI's most important priority. Despite the addition of new member parties from Asia, Africa and notably Latin America, the organization's structure remained markedly Eurocentric and prioritized relaunching European integration.[20] The SI's financial and organizational weaknesses, however, hindered its ability to influence European policy, let alone global policies. In the first half of the 1970s, 'reports and drafts for political activities were not written and meetings of study groups or the bureau not organized'.[21] The SI's renaissance occurred later in the decade after Willy Brandt took leadership in November 1976. While acknowledging that the former German Chancellor and his friends, Bruno Kreisky and Olof Palme, formed a highly influential socialist triumvirate in international politics, the historian Talbot Imlay has also concluded that the renewal initiated by Brandt was largely superficial and failed to halt the SI's decline.[22] Recent studies of the Brandt presidency have challenged this assertion, Imlay's study of international socialism notably neglecting the 1970s and 1980s.[23] As Wolfgang Schmidt noted, Brandt's commitment to rebalancing North-South relations from the late 1970s onwards was significant enough that he 'and three different US administrations became increasingly alienated from each other'.[24] Moreover, at the time when Brandt assumed the SI leadership, it was a substantial political force 'composed of thirty-six member parties from across thirty-one nations, counting some eight million militant members and representing an electorate of tens of millions, almost all of them from within the developed world'.[25]

In his inaugural address at the 1976 Congress in Geneva, Willy Brandt named global disarmament, the promotion of human rights across the globe and the establishment of new relations between the North and South as the SI's key priorities.[26] Brandt was not an unconditional proponent of the NIEO, however. Like most Western European socialist leaders, he considered certain aspects of the project too radical. For example, he did not share the idea, promoted by Southern leaders, that each state should be entitled to exercise control over its natural resources and economic activities, 'including the right to nationalization or transfer of ownership to its nationals' in

---

[20] Christian Salm, *Transnational Socialist Networks in the 1970s: European Community Development Aid and Southern Enlargement* (London: Palgrave Macmillan, 2016), 17.
[21] Ibid., 14.
[22] Talbot Imlay, 'Socialist Internationalism after 1914', in *Internationalisms: A Twentieth-Century History*, ed. Glenda Sluga and Patricia Clavin (Cambridge: Cambridge University Press, 2016), 213–42, 237–8.
[23] Talbot Imlay, *The Practice of International Socialism: European Socialists and International Politics, 1914–1960* (Oxford: Oxford University Press, 2017).
[24] Wolfgang Schmidt, 'A Prophet Unheard: Willy Brandt's North-South Policy and Its Reception in the United States', in *Willy Brandt and International Relations: Europe, the USA, and Latin America, 1974–1992*, ed. Bernd Rother and Klaus Larres (London: Bloomsbury, 2019), 67–83, 67.
[25] Garavini, *After Empires*, 231.
[26] Willy Brandt, 'Future Tasks of the International', *Socialist Affairs* 27, no. 1 (January/February 1977).

the name of full economic sovereignty.²⁷ Accordingly, the meeting in Caracas in 1976, which was intended to foster a closer relationship between European and Latin American socialists, revealed deep disagreements between SI members. Although the final declaration (and Brandt's address) publicly endorsed the 1974 'Declaration on the Establishment of a New International Economic Order', Bernd Rother recalled that during the meeting, the Mexican president Carlos Andrés Pérez fiercely 'attacked the European countries for having rejected the idea of a NIEO'.²⁸

Willy Brandt responded to the conflict by applying the core social democratic concept of 'compromise'. A year later, when he chaired the UN's Independent Commission on International Development Issues – at the suggestion of the World Bank President Robert McNamara – Brandt relentlessly strove to forge a middle ground between the NIEO's principles and the economic interests of Western industrialized countries.²⁹ The recommendations of the Commission regarding the economic exploitation of natural resources in developing countries offer a clear example of this standpoint:

> Permanent sovereignty over natural resources is the right of all countries. It is necessary, however, that nationalization be accompanied by appropriate and effective compensation, under internationally comparable principles which should be embodied in national laws. Increasing use should also be made of international mechanisms for settling disputes [between states and transnational corporations].³⁰

Some scholars have suggested that the Brandt Commission 'neutralized the more ambitious facets of the NIEO' by prioritizing 'reform rather than revolution' at the expense of Southern countries.³¹ In the first half of the 1980s, the SI was nevertheless among the few international organizations championing the NIEO as a legitimate framework for North-South relations. Even before the publication of the Brandt Report, the global political climate had become inhospitable to this approach to international relations. In 1979, the Soviet invasion of Afghanistan, the second Oil Shock and the Iranian Revolution had revived the tensions of the Cold War, which illustrates why the industrialized countries – especially the United States – ignored

---

²⁷ General Assembly of the United Nations, 'Declaration on the establishment of a new international economic order', Resolutions adopted on the report of the *ad hoc* committee of the Sixth Special Session, 1 May 1974, 3–5, 4. This document has been republished in *Humanity. An International Journal of Human Rights, Humanitarianism, and Development* 6, no. 1 (Spring 2015).

²⁸ Bernd Rother, 'Cooperation between the European and Latin American Moderate Left in the 1970s and 1980s', in Bernd Rother and Klaus Larres (eds.), *Willy Brandt and International Relations: Europe, the USA and Latin America, 1974–1992*. (London: Bloomsbury, 2018), 195–210, 199.

²⁹ See Brandt's introduction to the report of the commission. Willy Brandt, 'A Plea for Change: Peace, Justice, Jobs', in *North-South: A Program for Survival. The Report of the Independent Commission on the International Development Issues under the Chairmanship of Willy Brandt* (Cambridge, MA: MIT Press, 1980), 7–29, 10.

³⁰ *North-South: A Program for Survival*, 200.

³¹ Umut Özsu, 'Neoliberalism and Human Rights: The Brandt Commission and the Struggle for a New World', *Law and Contemporary Problems* 81, no. 4 (2018): 139–66, 150.

the recommendations of the Brandt Commission. Although the failure of the Cancun summit in 1981 signalled the demise of the NIEO as conceived by its architects – 'the Third World's moment had passed'[32] – a number of politicians and experts in the SI continued to advocate for the project.

Their aspiration to create a new international economic order as outlined by the Brandt Report dovetailed with increasing criticism of the monetarist policies implemented by Ronald Reagan and Margaret Thatcher. At the time, the SI was perhaps the most receptive audience for the underlying call for 'global Keynesianism' put forth by the Brandt Commission. The SICEP determined that a return to full employment and global prosperity would require Northern governments to implement voluntarist economic policies based on new spending to offset what the working group perceived as a global deflationary gap: additional spending of some $100 billion a year would be necessary to inaugurate a decade of genuinely new development.[33]

The development of a supranational Keynesian approach to economic issues had begun to percolate inside Western European socialist organizations in the mid-1970s. The British politician and academic economist Stuart Holland – one of the principal architects of the Alternative Economic Strategy (AES) of the left wing of the British Labour Party in the early 1970s[34] – organized the Initiative for Political and Social Economy (ISPE), an informal working group of left-leaning politicians and economic experts (most of whom were advisers of the former), which met regularly throughout the decade.[35] In the late 1970s, the group launched the 'Out of Crisis project', which promoted an economic alternative founded on the '3R's' – reflate, restructure, redistribute – to counter the trend towards 'beggar-thy-neighbour' deflation.[36] In his introduction to the report Stuart Holland summarized the main lines of the alternative promoted by the working group. Getting out of what he described as the 'vicious circle of deflation in international production and trade', he argued that the main European and OECD countries should increase spending and import demand. This Keynesian-inspired coordinated policy should be implemented at least at a regional level. For the proponents of the Out of Crisis project, such a policy would be effective only if it paired with a vast structural, social and spatial redistribution policy, namely between the competitive sectors and those in trouble, between wealthier and poorer social groups, and between Northern developed countries and Southern developing countries.[37] In other words, this project designed for West European states was a part of a more ambitious project aiming at reshaping the economic international

---

[32] Ogle, 'State Rights against Private Capital', 225.
[33] *Global Challenge from Crisis to Cooperation*, 68.
[34] For more information on the AES, see Mark Wickham-Jones, *Economic Strategy and the Labour Party* (London: Macmillan Press, 1996).
[35] For more on the history of IPSE, see Stuart Holland, 'Not an Intellectual Abdication of the Left. A Response to Dani Rodrik', Polanyi Centre Publications, Advanced Research on the Global Economy, I.2017/WP01, 7–8, https://iask.hu/wp-content/uploads/2017/09/stuart-holland-response-to-dani-rodrik.pdf?x35998 (last accessed 26 October 2021).
[36] Stuart Holland, *Out of Crisis. A Project for European Recovery* (Nottingham: Spokesman, 1983), 13.
[37] Ibid., 14.

system. The design of the '3R' strategy suggested a recourse to econometric models, particularly the model developed by the Cambridge Economic Policy Group (CEPG).[38] These scholars, who worked closely with the leftist experts of the British Labour Party, supported the architecture of the AES, whose neo-protectionist philosophy was inspired by Nicholas Kaldor's work.[39] Like Stuart Holland and Kaldor, some of the scholars themselves (such as Wynne Godley and Francis Cripps) were committed to the left wing of the Labour Party. After the stinging electoral defeat in 1983,[40] the British economists, primarily Stuart Holland, responded to their marginalization in the Party by moving towards more receptive European socialist circles. The left-leaning academic economists at Cambridge thus provided technical support to economic projects prepared by the working groups of the CSPEC and the SI. The recovery plan outlined by the Belgian economist Ludo Cuyvers, one of the most active experts in the CSPEC's working group on economic and social issues, used 'a neo-Keynesian (Kaldorian) model originally developed by the Cambridge Economy Policy Group (Department of Applied Economics, University of Cambridge), which encompasses the world economy as a closed system and in which real income and spending in the nine world blocs of countries are linked to each other via changes in the international trade flows'.[41] Similarly, during a meeting in preparation for the first draft of *Global Challenge*, Oscar Debunne, the secretary of the SICEP, reported that 'the Cambridge Group of economists, who had assisted the "Out of Crisis" group in preparing the technical aspects of their report, had agreed to be of service to the committee in testing certain economic recommendations'.[42]

An epistemic socialist community emerged from the collective research conducted by the New Cambridge School, the 'Out of Crisis Project', the Manley group of the SI and the Claes group created by the CSPEC in 1983. Politicians and experts circulated easily from one group to another, conveying a set of economic and social ideas based on the '3R' approach. During an SI conference in Vienna in 1982, Ulf Sand, a senior member of the Norwegian Trades Union Congress (LO) and the former Minister of Finance, and Frank Vandenbroucke, an economic expert at the Emile Vandervelde Institute in Brussels, both spoke about the problem of reflation in the absence of international co-operation, the broader social implications of unemployment, and the ties between fiscal, employment, social and development policies. Incidentally, both experts belonged to the IPSE forum and Vandenbroucke was also involved in the

---

[38] Francis Cripps and Wynne Godley, 'A Formal Analysis of the Cambridge Policy Group Model', *Economica*, New Series, 43, no. 172 (November 1976): 335–48.

[39] For more on Kaldor's critical analysis of the economic mechanisms of EEC, see Michael A. Landesmann, 'Nicholas Kaldor and Kazimierz Laski on the pitfalls of the European integration process', *European Journal of Economics and Economic Policies: Intervention* 16, no. 3 (2019): 344–69.

[40] Among the extensive literature regarding the major organisational and intellectual reforms initiated by the new Party leader Neil Kinnock, see Christopher Massey, *The Modernisation of the Labour Party, 1979–97* (Manchester: Manchester University Press, 2020), 52–88.

[41] Ludo Cuyvers, 'Macroeconomic Effects of Expansionist Economic Policies: The Case for a Coordinated, Selected and Diversified Reflation in the EEC', July 1986 (revised and updated version), 28 July 1986, 4 (18 p.), CAS-FJJ, Archives of the CSPEC, 50 RI UPSCE 1986–1987.

[42] Minutes of the Meeting of the Socialist International Committee on Economic Policy – Rio de Janeiro, Brazil – 30 September 1984, 3 (4 p.), CAS-FJJ, Archives of the SI, 60 RI (WB) 218.

research led by the Claes group. This fluid circulation of ideas and experts in socialist circles facilitated the drafting process of *Global Challenge*, which aimed to synthesize the mass of documents produced by the supranational organizations and the work of key Western European social democratic leaders in international liberal spheres such as the United Nations.

An international alternative to austerity: The failed mission of *Global Challenge*

At the 1982 SI Conference in Vienna, the Austrian Chancellor Bruno Kreisky called for 'a Marshall Plan for the South' in his opening speech, and Willy Brandt stressed the need for an emergency programme to address the developing crises in North-South relations. The Vienna conference was not an isolated event. The appointment of Michael Manley as head of the SICEP a few months later carried great significance. In 1978, he had received the United Nations Gold Medal for decades of opposition to apartheid and played an important role in promoting the NIEO.[43] Surprisingly, recent studies have not mentioned Manley, although Darrell Levi, his biographer, claims that he defended the NIEO project, alongside the Algerian President Houari Boumediene and the Tanzanian President Julius Nyerere.[44] Manley's elevated profile within the SI tends to support Levi's assertion.

SI officers entertained ambitious goals for the Manley Committee. The primary objective was to 'prepare common guidelines for the implementation, at national and international levels, of economic policies agreed by the Bureau and the Congress of the SI'.[45] It would also provide technical assistance and materials for publication, 'especially on the occasions of high-level economic conferences, e.g. Economic Summits, UNCTAD, IMF/World Bank'.[46] Remarkably, committee members' primary mission was not to produce original research, but to provide an audience for the vast body of existing literature on North-South dialogue about the NIEO, the debt problem, protectionist barriers to trade, deflationary fiscal and monetary policies in the industrial countries, and the dislocation of the global economy. Shortly after the inaugural meeting of the SICEP in November 1983, two sub-committees were formed, both chaired by Western European socialists. Thorvald Stoltenberg, the former Norwegian Minister of Defence in Gro Harlem Brundtland's first administration (1979–81), chaired the group responsible for updating the NIEO project, and the Belgian Socialist Michel Vanden Abeele, a senior adviser in the European Commission's Directorate-General of Development, led the group tasked with designing 'a Socialist

---

[43] Darrell E. Levi, *Michael Manley: The Making of a Leader* (Athens: The University of Georgia Press, 1989), 266–7.
[44] Ibid., 146.
[45] Penti Vaanen to Bureau members, Bureau circular No. B9/83, 1 July 1983, 'Work of the Socialist International Committee on Economic Policies', doc. cit.
[46] 'Socialist International Economic Committee: Review of Work and Proposals for Future Action', Sheffield, 20 June 1984, 2 (6 p.), CAS-FJJ, Archives of the Socialist International, 60 RI (WB) 220.

International programme to stimulate recovery in the world economy by proposing practical measures to resolve the most pressing manifestations of the crisis'. Vanden Abeele exemplified the porosity between supranational organizations: he was also involved in the Claes group of the CSPEC when he chaired the sub-committee of the SI.⁴⁷ Although they represented a less active minority, Latin American, Caribbean and African socialists were represented in both sub-committees by the Socialist Party of Senegal, the Accion Democratica of Venezuela, the National Revolutionary Movement of El Salvador and the People's National Party of Jamaica.

Records of SICEP meetings highlight significant ideological cross-pollination between the SI and United Nations agencies and *ad hoc* working groups, primarily the United Nations Conference for Trade and Development (UNCTAD) and the Brandt Commission. The primary sources of inspiration of the SICEP's experts included the Brandt Report, the Palme Report on common security, the 1974 Declaration on the Establishment of a NIEO and the December 1974 UN Charter of Economic Rights and Duties of States, which legitimized the right of Southern countries to nationalize their natural resources.⁴⁸ Manley Committee activities reached their peak in 1984 and 1985. Within socialist circles, the group successfully facilitated a meaningful dialogue on the growing inequalities between the industrialized and developing countries. A few weeks prior to the Manley-Brandt declaration, the CSPEC and the Dutch Labour Party (PvdA) had published an updated version of the 'Out of Crisis' project signed by several Asian, African and Latin American socialists. Known as the 'Amsterdam Appeal', its signatories called for Europe 'to embark on a renewed special relationship with the countries of the Third World, opening a postcolonial era based on equity, mutual respect, and genuine independence'.⁴⁹

Notable among the signatories of the document were the two leading experts of the Manley Committee, Stuart Holland and Jan Pronk. Pronk's professional trajectory epitomized the circulation of ideas between liberal and socialist international organizations, as well as the supranational circles. In the 1960s, he was a research assistant of Jan Tinbergen, who was the first recipient of the Sveriges Riksbank Prize in Economic Sciences in memory of Alfred Nobel in 1969 for his pioneering work in econometric model building and long-term economic planning. Like Stuart Holland, Jan Pronk decided to become more politically engaged and rapidly rose to become a senior figure in the Dutch Labour Party (PvdA). In May 1973, he was appointed Minister of Development in the coalition government led by the socialist Joop den Uyl (1973–7). Shortly thereafter, Pronk delivered a famous speech to the fifty-fifth meeting of the Economic and Social Council (ECOSOC) in Geneva on July 5 in which he stated that his 'government identifies itself with the underprivileged'.⁵⁰ In 1975,

---

⁴⁷ Interview with Vanden Abeele, Michel from the European Commission 1973–1986, by Christian Van de Velde, recorded on 30 November 2010, Historical Archives of the European Union, 34, https://archives.eui.eu/en/oral_history/INT294 (last accessed 19 October 2021).
⁴⁸ 'Socialist International Economic Committee: Review of Work and Proposals for Future Action', doc. cit., 5.
⁴⁹ PvdA and CSPEC, 'The Appeal of Amsterdam. Out of Crisis, Out of Poverty: A Global Challenge for Europe', 19 May 1984, 6 (7 p.), CAS-FJJ, Archives of the CSPEC, 50 RI UPSCE 1983–1984.
⁵⁰ Jan Pronk and Altaf Gauhar, 'Jan Pronk', *Third World Quarterly* 3, no. 2 (April 1981): 189–209, 192.

Pronk was elected Chairman of the Ad Hoc Committee of the General Assembly's Seventh Special Session on development and international economic cooperation. After his appointment as honorary treasurer of the Brandt Commission, he occupied the position of Deputy Secretary General of the UNCTAD.[51]

This prestigious background gave Pronk substantial authority on the issue of development, and his involvement in the activities of the SICEP bolstered the group's audience within the SI. He was charged with drafting the background and discussion papers addressing the international economic crisis and the position of the developing countries in global trade. Unsurprisingly, Pronk castigated the architects of the Bretton Woods order and their adherents (without explicitly naming the United States) for exacerbating inequalities between the North and South, squandering limited resources and under-utilizing their workforce. His lengthy report called for a socialist economic alternative based on 'global Keynesianism' and a 'tamer' NIEO.[52] Like the Brandt Report and a number of other documents issued by the UN, he underscored the inextricable links between mass poverty in Southern countries and mass unemployment in OECD countries. Accordingly, Pronk called for the Western European socialists in office to promote a concerted global economic relaunch: 'This is a plea for a recovery policy beyond Keynes. [...] More Keynesian than the Keynesian policies after the Second World War because of the global dimension of demand [...]. Beyond Keynes because of the fact that not only the level but also the distribution of global demand is at stake.'[53] Pronk also pleaded for significant reforms of the international economic order in favour of Southern countries. Within the Brandt Commission, however, he was less vocal in supporting the nationalization of natural resources without compensation.

Amended by Stuart Holland and other prominent socialists such as Thorvald Stoltenberg, Luis Ayala, the Chilean Secretary for Latin America and the Caribbean in the SI Bureau, Michael Harrington of the Democratic Socialists of America, and Celso Furtado, an important Brazilian scholar of economic development, this preliminary document inspired the final draft of *Global Challenge*. In early 1985, the members of the SICEP held a two-day meeting in Kingston to refine Pronk's paper. Perhaps due to the meeting's location, a large contingency of Latin American members was in attendance. Their proximity enabled them to include the conclusions of Latin American experts at a recent international conference on debt in Cartagena into the final version of the report. Consequently, the SI document endorsed the proposal for the conversion into grants of the debts of the poorest countries combined with grant conversion of part of the debts of other developing countries, as well as the call for rescheduling the remaining debt of Third World countries, through extension of the time period for repayment principal and 'a ceiling on interest payments not higher than twenty per cent of the export earnings of debtor countries'.[54]

---

[51] Ibid., 189.
[52] Jan Pronk, 'Breaking through the Stalemate in International Economic Development', background paper for the SICEP, 10 August 1984, 7–8 (56 p.), CAS-FJJ, Archives of the Socialist International, 60 RI (WB) 220.
[53] Ibid., 13.
[54] *Global Challenge from Crisis to Cooperation*, 103.

Figure 6.1 'The Global Challenge' cover of *Socialist Affairs* no. 4, 1985. Image courtesy of Collection l'OURS/OURS Historical Archives.

Within the SICEP, however, members were concerned about their ability to influence Western European policymakers. A prevailing mood of distrust was illustrated by Michael Manley's opening address at the Kingston meeting, which candidly acknowledged their disappointing record.[55] These concerns were warranted – *Global Challenge* failed to elicit the interest of Western Europe's socialist elites. Tellingly, the French newspaper *Le Monde* ignored the report, despite the fact that the French Socialist Party was in power.[56] Three years after the report's publication in an essay collection in honour of Olof Palme (who had been assassinated one year earlier), Julius Nyerere bluntly observed that 'for the last six years, very little – indeed almost nothing – which could be called a North-South dialogue has been taking place'. Needless to say, the former Tanzanian president did not mention *Global Challenge* or the activities of the SI.[57] The hegemonic vision of world governance promoted by American neoconservatives, who claimed that the eradication of mass poverty was possible only through 'economic freedom, private investment, and the liberalization of world trade',[58] coupled with the SI's structural weaknesses, are the prevailing explanations for the rejection of *Global Challenge*, but they do not adequately explain its failure.

Internal conflicts inside the SICEP also played a significant role in this ideological defeat. The working group was deeply divided in its approach to international economic issues. The same year that the group published the updated version of *Global Challenge*, Michael Manley called attention to persistent disparities between Western European social democrats and socialists from developing countries in their attitudes towards capitalism in an essay outlining the major obstacles that had kept Jamaica 'taking up the down escalator' towards economic development:

> The Socialist International pulls together under one umbrella all the major political organizations of Europe and the Americas who claim to be either socially democratic or democratic socialists. The democratic socialists are in the main convinced that the present world economic system is in need of radical overhaul. The social democrats, who are more reformist in outlook, are far less clear on the subject of structural change, although they agree that the effects of the system need to be ameliorated.[59]

---

[55] 'Minutes of the meeting of the Socialist International Committee on Economic Policy, SICEP, Kingston, Jamaica – January 31–February 1, 1985', 8 March 1985, 4 (22 p.), CAS-FJJ, Archives of the Socialist International, 60 RI (WB) 220.

[56] An investigation of the archives of *Le Monde* yielded no results, www.lemonde.fr (last accessed 15 October 2021).

[57] Julius K. Nyerere, 'At the Receiving End of the North-South Dialogue', in *New Perspectives in North-South Dialogue: Essays in Honour of Olof Palme*, ed. Kofi Buenor Hadjor (London: I.B. Tauris, 1988), 197–213, 197.

[58] Mazower, *Governing the World*, 360.

[59] Michael Manley, *Up the Down Escalator: Development and the International Economy – A Jamaican Case Study* (London: André Deutsch, 1987), 231–2.

As he had expressed earlier in several meetings of the SICEP, Manley lamented that the Western socialist approach to development focused exclusively on North-South relations, thereby disregarding the benefits of South-South co-operation, including partnerships with the countries of the Soviet bloc, a proposal which was omitted from *Global Challenge*.

These external and internal divisions precipitated the erosion of the consensus around 'global Keynesianism' and a 'tamer' NIEO in the international socialist circles in the second half of the 1980s. The approach to global economic issues promoted by *Socialist Affairs*, the official quarterly journal of the SI, clearly reveals the shift towards centrism that occurred shortly after the publication of *Global Challenge* in 1985. Two years later, a special issue featured an updated version of the document, but it also included an interview with Kjell Olof Feldt, one of the key proponents of the conversion to a so-called 'Third Way', which 'subordinated "security" to growth and the need to create economic efficiency by reducing social expenditure'.[60] Moreover, the editors of *Socialist Affairs* presented this new version of *Global Challenge* in lukewarm terms. They did not attempt to conceal their increasing scepticism about the possibility of improving relations between developed and developing countries: 'This is clearly a daunting task. [...] production, distribution, and exchange have all become highly internationalized and the formulation of an alternative economic strategy has become correspondingly more difficult.'[61] By 1988, *Socialist Affairs* had increasingly become a platform for the promotion of 'Third Way' policies. The journal published numerous articles by Western European party leaders justifying the implementation of economic and social policies founded on a strong currency, supply-side policies, increased flexibility in the labour market and the 'modernization' of the post-war welfare state.[62]

Conclusion

Exploring the socio-economic landscape of the 1980s through the lens of supranational socialist organizations offers new insight into the relationship between democratic socialism and capitalism. Although socialist leaders had become increasingly reliant on economic experts who praised the virtues of austerity and supply-side policies, the genesis of *Global Challenge* confirms that there was also an 'epistemic community' that continued to believe in the prospect of a new international economic order based on 'global Keynesian' policies.[63]

This story is unquestionably a tale of defeat, however. Coupled with the tense international political climate of the time, the SI's structural weaknesses contributed

---

[60] Jenny Andersson, *Between Growth and Security: Swedish Social Democracy from a Strong Society to a Third Way* (Manchester: Manchester University Press, 2006), 121.
[61] 'Focus on the World Economy', *Socialist Affairs*, no. 3/87: 4.
[62] Mathieu Fulla and Marc Lazar, 'European Socialists and the State: A Comparative and Transnational Approach', in *European Socialists and the State in the Twentieth and Twenty-First Centuries*, ed. Mathieu Fulla and Marc Lazar (London: Palgrave Macmillan, 2020), 1–26, 19.
[63] Peter Haas, 'Introduction: Epistemic Communities and International Policy Coordination', *International Organization* 46, no. 1 (1992): 1–35.

to its inability to bring about meaningful change in the early 1980s. Most critically, the SI failed to establish relationships with the leading politicians and experts of its member parties, most of whom were unwilling to engage in an ideological debate to begin with. The disconnect between these two circles helps explain why their economic philosophies took such divergent paths – 'global neo-Keynesian relaunch' for the former and 'austerity with a human face' for the latter. Despite the revitalization launched by Willy Brandt's presidency, the SI also critically lacked adequate representation and financial resources. On the EEC level, the CSPEC had encountered similar difficulties and therefore remained what the political scientist Knut Heidar called a 'second-order party'.[64] In 1985, the organization's political priorities had also shifted from the issues that Brandt had outlined when he assumed leadership. His agenda increasingly prioritized common security and human rights issues over the improvement of North-South relations, as some scholars have recently demonstrated.[65] Lastly, the ideological consensus between the representatives of member parties, particularly those seated on the Manley Committee, was more fragile than it seemed. As Guillaume Devin noted, Willy Brandt (and the Bureau of the SI) had probably overestimated the power of 'moral voluntarism' in the campaign to alleviate mass poverty in the South.[66]

Consequently, the leaders of the supranational socialist organizations emulated their national counterparts in the second half of the 1980s, as in the case of Michael Manley, whose abrupt conversion sowed profound disillusionment among socialists about the capacity of public institutions to offset the detrimental effects of 'capitalism unleashed'.[67] After his re-election as prime minister in 1989, the leader of the PNP promptly abandoned his former ideological convictions and began promoting a pro-market approach to the economy. Shortly after proclaiming himself a 'pro-American' socialist,[68] Manley met with his old French Socialist comrades Pierre Mauroy and Michel Rocard in Paris in June 1989. In an interview with a journalist from *Le Monde*, he openly admitted that the time for a mixed economy was over and that his vision for the economic development of Jamaica would henceforth rely on private enterprise and on using the country's modest resources to create a pro-business environment. Following the lead of several Latin American governments, Manley determined that the best option for the Jamaican economy was to 'play the game of international institutions responsible for administering Third World debt, the IMF, for example'.[69]

Manley's case was not unique. Although the end of the Cold War had opened new possibilities globally, democratic socialism had entered an era during which 'Third

---

[64] Knut Heidar, 'Parties and Cleavages in the European Political Space', ARENA working papers, WP 03/7, 2003, 3, https://www.sv.uio.no/arena/english/research/publications/arena-working-papers/2001-2010/2003/wp03_7.pdf (last accessed 28 July 2021).
[65] Oliver Bange, 'Conceptualizing "Common Security": Willy Brandt's Vision of Trans-bloc Security and Its International perception, 1981–1990', in Bernd Rother and Klaus Larres (eds.), Willy Brandt …, op. cit., 143–60, 149.
[66] Devin, *L'Internationale socialiste*, 337.
[67] Andrew Glyn, *Capitalism Unleashed: Finance, Globalization, and Welfare* (Oxford: Oxford University Press, 2007).
[68] 'Jamaïque Michael Manley: "un socialiste pro-américain"', *Le Monde*, 11 February 1989.
[69] 'Jamaïque: la visite à Paris de M. Michael Manley. La conversion d'un Premier ministre socialiste aux lois du marché international', *Le Monde*, 14 June 1989.

Way' proponents would monopolize local and global political arenas. Instead of proposing alternatives, most Northern socialist leaders and experts suggested political projects that were aligned with the new framework of capitalism, which endorsed financialization, 'market fundamentalism', the imposition of austerity reforms on indebted Southern countries by organizations such as the IMF and World Bank, and 'a pervasive culture of commodified selves and commodified social imaginations'.[70] The conversion of (or resignation to) socialists to this model, which took on it its most radical forms under the reign of the 'Washington consensus', exemplifies the cultural hegemony attained by this vision of capitalism and democracy by the end of the 1980s.

---

[70] Daniel Rodgers, 'The Uses and Abuses of "Neoliberalism"', *Dissent* (Winter 2018), https://www.dissentmagazine.org/article/uses-and-abuses-neoliberalism-debate (last accessed 25 July 2021). The author highlights the analytical shortcomings of 'neoliberalism' to illustrate the significant transformation of global capitalism in the 1970s and 1980s.

Part Two

When internationalisms meet: Conflicts and cross-fertilizations

7

'This is the true international of which Moscow only dreams': Contacts, hybridizations and ambiguities in the encounter between socialist and liberal internationalism at the International Labor Office in the 1920s

Adeline Blaszkiewicz
Translated by Victoria Grace

'This is the true International of which Moscow only dreams.'[1] This enthusiastic statement made by British socialist George Bernard Shaw after his visit to the International Labor Organization (ILO) in 1928 brings to light how some socialists were interested in achieving true internationalism within this international organization created in 1919 for the realization of social justice. At the time, its permanent secretariat, the International Labor Office, was headed by French socialist Albert Thomas, who was a controversial figure in the Second International following his participation in the Sacred Union in France during the First World War as Minister of Armaments from 1916 onwards. From the networks of Thomas, the International Labor Office recruited into its ranks numerous socialists who had taken part in the municipal movement in the late nineteenth century[2] and gained experience in public policy following their participation or support of the economic management of France during the Sacred Union.[3] Some were even Durkheimian sociologists, eager to combine science and

---

I would like to warmly thank Michele Di Donato and Mathieu Fulla for their remarks and suggestions.

[1] International Labor Organization Archive (ILO Archive), CAT 10-34, note from Edgard Milhaud to Albert Thomas (between 1928 and 1930) on 'Quelques points concernant les rapports entre l'Organisation internationale du travail et le socialisme.'
[2] This movement, which promoted the municipal scale as a laboratory for socialist reforms, became internationalized in the interwar period. See Aude Chamouard, *Une autre histoire du socialisme: les politiques à l'épreuve du terrain (1919–2010)* (Paris: CNRS éd., 2013); Patrizia Dogliani, *Le socialisme municipal: en France et en Europe, de la Commune à la Grande guerre* (Nancy: Éditions Arbre bleu, Nancy, 2018); Patrizia Dogliani, 'European Municipalism in the Half of the Twentieth Century: The Socialist Network', *Contemporary European History* 2, no. 4 (2002): 573–96.
[3] John N. Horne, *Labour at War: France and Britain, 1914–1918* (Oxford: Clarendon Press, 1991); Patrizia Dogliani, 'Progetto per un'internazionale "aclassista": il socilisti nell'organizzazione internazionale del lavoro negli anni venti', in *Esperienze e problemi del movimento socialista fra le due guerre mondiali*, ed. Aldo Agosti (Milan: F. Angeli, 1987): 45-68.

action through their involvement in this new centre of international social expertise.[4] For these socialists, following Thomas to the International Labor Office was a means to circumvent their relative marginalization on the French socialist scene.

In their official positions, the socialists proclaimed their independence from the League of Nations and the ILO, which was viewed as the outcome of imperialist power relations at the Paris Peace Conference. Indeed, Patrizia Dogliani showed that the socialists' involvement in the ILO was not encouraged by the Labor and Socialist International (LSI). Officially, the LSI even expressed hostility towards the ILO before agreeing to establish a seemingly instrumental and one-sided relationship.[5] In 1921, the French Section of the Workers' International (FSWI) refused to allow Thomas to combine the mandates of deputy and international official at the ILO, which, for Talbot Imlay, illustrates this culture of independence specific to socialist internationalism.[6] Yet behind the apparent independence of socialist and liberal internationalism, this chapter shows how reciprocal forms of cooperation were implemented from within the International Labor Office. Indeed, the adoption of the first convention on the reduction of the working day to eight hours at the International Labor Conference in Washington in 1919 marked the convergence of liberal internationalism with the socialist and labour movements, which had long campaigned for this reform.

Drawing on the research of Sandrine Kott,[7] this chapter investigates the International Labor Office not as a self-sufficient actor but as a space of expression and encounters with different internationalisms: on the one hand, liberal internationalism partly stemming from the reform movement initiated in the late nineteenth century, and on the other, socialist internationalism in the midst of renewal in the early 1920s. These two internationalist movements coexisted in a sort of complementarity or even interdependence.

In this arrangement, the International Labor Office's director played a pivotal role in shaping these networks, which remained informal, because, from a statutory perspective, political parties cannot be officially represented at the ILO. The socialist officials at the International Labor Office were thus important mediators between these two internationalist movements whose boundaries were more permeable than previously thought.[8] In its functioning, the ILO required the involvement of various political organizations to promote the ratification of international conventions

---

[4] Marine Dhermy-Mairal, *Les sciences sociales et l'action au Bureau international du travail (1920–1939)* (PhD dissertation, EHESS, Paris, 2015).
[5] Dogliani, 'Progetto per un'internazionale "aclassista"'.
[6] Talbot Imlay, 'Socialist Internationalism after 1914', in *Internationalisms: A Twentieth-Century History*, ed. Glenda Sluga and Patricia Calvin (Cambridge: Cambridge University Press, 2017), 213–41. He affirms that socialist internationalism in the 1920s remained 'a matter of socialists'. See Talbot C. Imlay, *The Practice of Socialist Internationalism: European Socialists and International Politics, 1914–1960* (Oxford: Oxford University Press, 2018), 5.
[7] Sandrine Kott, 'Cold War Internationalism', in *Internationalisms: A Twentieth-Century History*, ed. Glenda Sluga and Patricia Calvin (Cambridge: Cambridge University Press, 2017), 340–62.
[8] Glenda Sluga and Patricia Calvin, 'Rethinking the History of Internationalism', in *Internationalisms: A Twentieth-Century History*, ed. Glenda Sluga and Patricia Calvin (Cambridge: Cambridge University Press, 2017), 3–14.

by member states. In this context, moderate socialists were *a priori* the preferred intermediaries, and their support was actively sought by the International Labor Office.

This cooperation emerges from a comparative study of the archives of the office of Albert Thomas, the personal files of socialist officials at the International Labor Office,[9] as well as the LSI archives, which are held at the International Institute of Social History in Amsterdam.[10] This chapter first shows how the International Labor Office played a key role in building connections between liberal internationalism and socialist internationalism. Through the figure of Thomas, it then traces the contours of the socialist-reformist network gravitating around the International Labor Office. Finally, it is shown how this network developed in both competition and complementarity with liberal internationalism, thus providing an alternative to communist internationalism.

International Labor Office: An institution at the crossroads of internationalist traditions

Established in Part XIII of the Treaty of Versailles on Labor, the ILO lies at the intersection of several social reform movements. The ILO's most direct and oldest influence is liberal internationalism, which began to take form in the late nineteenth century in response to the so-called 'social question'. A myriad of social reformers thus created private organizations and met at congresses, thus becoming part of the 'internationalist turning point'[11] at the close of the century. In the wake of the congresses on worker's protections held in Zurich and Brussels in 1897, which gathered parliamentarians, social reformers, Christian socialists and liberals, the common project for the 'international harmonization of social politics'[12] was launched. This movement entered a new phase with the creation of the International Association for Labor Legislation (IALL) in 1900 during the international exhibition in Paris. The aim was to centralize documentation on social legislation in each country from the comparative perspective of international statistics.[13] This ambitious endeavour nevertheless encountered several setbacks and remained in the hands of a small circle of elites (i.e. academics, jurists, doctors, high-ranking officials). The IALL secretariat, set up in Basel in 1901, was later used as the model for the International Labor Office by

---

[9] International Labour Organization Archive (ILO Archive).
[10] International Institute of Social History Archive (IISH Archive); Labour and Socialist International Archive (LSI Archive).
[11] Anne Rasmussen, 'Le travail en congrès: élaboration d'un milieu international', in *Histoire de l'Office du travail: 1890–1914*, ed. Jean Luciani (Paris: Syros, 1992), 119–34.
[12] Isabelle Lespinet-Moret, *Projet global, politique internationale: L'Organisation Internationale et la santé des travailleurs* (Unpublished habilitation thesis, University Évry Val d'Essonne, 2016), 31.
[13] On the origins of the OIT and IALL, see Jasmien Van Daele, 'Engineering Social Peace: Networks, Ideas, and the Founding of the International Labour Organization', *International Review of Social History* 50, no. 3 (2005): 435–66; Sandrine Kott, 'From Transnational Reformist Network to International Organization: The International Association for Labour Legislation and the International Labour Organization 1900–1930', in *Shaping the Transnational Sphere. The Transnational Networks of Experts (1840–1930)*, ed. Davide Rodogno, Bernhard Struck and Jakob Vogel (New York: Berghahn, 2015), 239–59.

the drafters of the Treaty of Versailles.[14] From its creation, the ILO benefited from the growing support of other movements such as Christian socialism through Christian trade unions[15] or even the cooperative movement within the International Cooperative Alliance.[16] The International Labor Office therefore stood at the confluence of diverse strands of internationalisms that came together within this new structure despite their divergences. As the first director of the International Labor Office, Thomas delivered a historic speech to mark the opening of the ILO: 'It is the war that made labor legislation of primary importance. It is the war that forced governments to commit to ending the "misery, injustice, and deprivation" of workers. It is once again the war that made organized workers understand that legal protection, taking full force in the international arena, was necessary in order to realize their aspirations.'[17]

It is therefore not surprising that this reformist socialist, who had been a minister in the Sacred Union and was favourable to the development of strong reformist trade unionism based on the labour model, valued the contribution and support of the international reformist labour movement during the creation of the ILO.[18] At the allied trade union conference held in Leeds in 1916, reformist trade union leaders spoke out in favour of including a Labor Charter in the Peace Treaty in view of forming a world labour parliament. Though in the midst of breaking up, the Socialist International met in Bern in February 1919 to take up these union issues, passing a resolution for the creation of an organization in charge of international labour legislation in the framework of the Paris Peace Conference. Elected director of the International Labor Office at the first International Labor Conference held in Washington in November 1919, Thomas brought with him not only his background as an internationalist socialist but also his entire socialist network, especially (but not only) French socialists, who represented a non-negligible proportion of the first officials at the International Labor Office. Nevertheless, this encounter between socialist internationalism and liberal internationalism was not straightforward. At the start of the twentieth century, the majority of European socialists shunned these private social reform organizations, deeming them too 'bourgeois' and distracting workers from the real struggle for emancipation. Yet certain individuals acted as intermediaries between these two movements, thus forming a 'reformist nebula'[19] or a transnational reformist network[20] that brought together experts, high-ranking officials and politicians of diverse persuasions who were concerned about the issues of housing, social protection and

---

[14] Jean-Michel Bonvin, *L'Organisation internationale du travail: étude sur une agence productrice de normes* (Paris: Presses universitaires de France, 1998), 167.

[15] Aurélien Zaragori, *L'Organisation Internationale du Travail et les milieux chrétiens, 1919-1969* (PhD dissertation, University of Lyon, 2018).

[16] Marine Dhermy-Mairal, 'L'unification du mouvement coopératif au Bureau international du travail: la "révolution silencieuse" d'Albert Thomas', *Le Mouvement Social* 263, no. 2 (2018): 15-29.

[17] Albert Thomas, 'L'Organisation internationale du travail, Origine, développement, avenir', *Revue internationale du travail* 1, no. 1 (1921): 5-22.

[18] Reiner Tosstorff, 'The International Trade-Union Movement and the Founding of the International Labour Organization', *International Review of Social History* 50, no. 3 (2005): 399-433.

[19] Christian Topalov (ed.), *Laboratoires du nouveau siècle: la nébuleuse réformatrice et ses réseaux en France, 1880-1914* (Paris: Éd. de l'EHESS, 1999).

[20] Kott, 'From Transnational Reformist Network to International Organization'.

labour organization. In the framework of the ILO, their meeting was made possible for a variety of reasons: the permanence of these private social reform organizations at the start of the century, the evolutions triggered by the participation of socialists and trade unionists in the economic management of France during the Sacred Union, and the mobilization of specific networks around Thomas.

A reformist socialist network around Albert Thomas

The ILO was created at a particular political moment in the history of left-wing internationalisms, which had been plunged into crisis in the aftermath of the First World War. From an ideological perspective, the ILO was a direct response to the world revolution advocated by Soviet Russia and the creation of the Communist International in March 1919.[21] As the first international organization with a tripartite structure, the ILO promoted a reformist vision of social relations.[22] Its decision-making bodies, including government representatives, employers and workers, drafted international labour conventions and recommendations on the basis of compromise. This tripartite functioning was inspired by the ideas of liberal social reform but heavily criticized by the international communist movement, which denounced it as a form of class collaboration. The socialists had a more ambiguous view of the ILO. Officially, the LSI founded in Hamburg in 1923 oscillated between hostility and indifference towards the ILO, which was still viewed as a body of the League of Nations and thus the outcome of the imperialist balance of power established by the Treaty of Versailles. Numerous socialists from diverse countries nevertheless provided direct or indirect support to the newly formed organization.

An inner circle of close collaborators can be identified at the International Labor Office, recruited from the socialist networks of Thomas. In 1921, five of the nine section chiefs were socialists: Luigi Carozzi from Italy; Jan de Roode from the Netherlands; and Adrien Tixier, Georges Fauquet and Edgard Milhaud from France. Two of the three chiefs of staff who worked for Thomas were French socialists: Camille Lemercier (1920–2) and Marius Viple (1923–32). At the crossroads of the socialist and intellectual circles developed by Thomas before the war, Milhaud was notably tasked with undertaking a broad study on production.[23] Already in the pre-war period, the director of *Annales de la régie directe* promoted municipal socialism, public services and nationalizations[24] in a reformist movement in which Thomas gradually emerged

---

[21] James T. Shotwell, 'The International Labor Organization as an Alternative to Violent Revolution', *The Annals of the American Academy of Political and Social Science* 166 (1933): 18–25.

[22] Sandrine Kott, 'La justice sociale dans un monde global. L'Organisation internationale du travail (1919–2019)', *Le Mouvement social* 263, no. 2 (2018): 3–14; Isabelle Lespinet-Moret and Vincent Viet (ed.), *L'Organisation internationale du travail: origine, développement, avenir* (Rennes: Presses universitaires de Rennes, 2011).

[23] Marine Dhermy-Mairal, 'Edgard Milhaud, un économiste au Bureau international du travail. Faire science en économie sociale, ou la quête d'autonomie d'un savant', *Revue d'histoire des sciences humaines* 31 (2017): 93–112.

[24] Patrizia Dogliani, *Edgar Milhaud e la rivista internazionale 'Annales de la régie directe' (1908–1924)* (Torino: Fondazione Luigi Einaudi, 1985).

Figure 7.1 14 July 1920, Edgar Milhaud on train platform with Albert Thomas, 1st ILO Director. Image courtesy of Archives Historiques de l'OIT/ILO Historical Archives.

as the leader.[25] Yet Milhaud's background was not the only one to lend credence to the hypothesis of a reformist 'Geneva Dream'[26] for socialists whose openly reformist agenda had become marginalized in the national political arena. In 1919, the programme of the FSWI, weakened after the experience of the Sacred Union, reaffirmed its revolutionary character and hostility towards any form of reformism.

The desire of these socialists to move away from the path taken by the French Socialist Party is also reflected in the career of Tixier, a schoolteacher wounded at the front during the war who was recruited by Thomas to take charge of issues relating to the war-wounded and later promoted to head of the Social Security Section. After the war, Tixier distanced himself from the internal debates of the French Socialist Party, including the growing number of militants seduced by the Russian Revolution. His involvement in the International Labor Office may thus be interpreted as the logical consequence of his opposition to Bolshevism and his reformist socialist convictions consistent with the ideal of social justice.[27] Finally, Frenchwoman Marguerite Thibert,

---

[25] Emmanuel Jousse, *Les hommes révoltés: les origines intellectuelles du réformisme en France, 1871–1917* (Paris: Fayard, 2017).

[26] Borrowing the expression of Zara Steiner regarding the – often thwarted – hopes for internationalism among the first members of the Society of Nations. Zara Shakow Steiner, *The Lights that Failed: European International History, 1919–1933* (Oxford: Oxford University Press, 2005).

[27] Gilles Morin and Pascal Plas (ed.), *Adrien Tixier 1893–1946: l'héritage méconnu d'un reconstructeur de l'État en France* (La Geneytouse: Lucien Souny, 2012), 311.

who joined the ILO in 1926 to take charge of women's labour issues, also defended the coherence of her political background, moving from pacifist, socialist and feminist activism to the ILO to work for the improvement of women's working conditions: 'What is socialism if not the pursuit of social justice: this is the primary objective of the ILO. There is no contradiction. I too was a socialist, I joined the Socialist Party at the time of Jaurès in 1912. I also shared the pacifism of Jaurès, so I was troubled when France entered the war in 1914.'[28]

Both political and personal reasons explain the composition of this inner socialist circle around Thomas in Geneva. In the early years of the International Labor Office, its director had considerable freedom in the recruitment of staff. As the leader of a reformist movement within the French Socialist Party, Thomas was surrounded by moderate French socialists, attracted by the aura of the former minister. Yet they also sought to circumvent the marginalization of their movement within their political family after the war. Their attachment to internationalism – which lies at the heart of the socialist project – explained their involvement in Geneva, while their hostility to Bolshevism shaped their actions at the ILO as a response to communist internationalism.

From these elective affinities between reformist socialism and the International Labor Office stemmed a functional imperative for these officials to establish and cultivate networks with socialists from the Socialist Party and the Socialist International. Historiography has shown that at the national level, German Social Democrats or even British Labor were 'national allies' of the ILO, serving as mediators between the international and national levels.[29] However, this connection also manifested within the ranks of the LSI. From 1920, the International Labor Office systematically sent an observer to the International Socialist Congress to report the discussions to the director and forge relations with these potential allies.

These more informal networks formed the contours of a second circle of collaborators and mediators that linked the ILO to the international socialist milieu. For example, the liaison offices of the International Labor Office were headed by Fabra Ribas in Madrid and Alexander Schlicke and later Willy Donau in Berlin.[30] The head of the Paris office, Mario Roques, an intellectual close to socialist circles, acted as a bridge between the International Labor Office and the leaders of the French Socialist Party in the hope that they would support the ratification of conventions in their role as members of the socialist parliamentary group.[31]

---

[28] ILO Archive. Interview with Marguerite Thibert in 1932, republished in *L'Union* 121 (1982). On the life of Marguerite Thibert, see Françoise Thébaud, *Une traversée du siècle: Marguerite Thibert, femme engagée et fonctionnaire internationale* (Paris: Belin, 2017).

[29] On the German case, see Sandrine Kott, 'Germany Globalized? German Social Policy and the International Labor Organization, 1900–1950', in *German Zeitgeschichte. Konturen eines Forschungsfeldes*, ed. Thomas Lindenberger and Martin Sabrow (Göttingen: Wallstein, 2016), 58–79. On the British case, see Olga Hidalgo-Weber, *Dimensions transnationales des politiques sociales britanniques: le rôle de la Grande-Bretagne au sein de l'OIT, 1919-1946* (Geneva: University of Geneva, 2015).

[30] Kott, 'Dynamiques de l'internationalisation'.

[31] On the role of the head of the Paris office, see ILO Archive, CAT 5-35-5 (A) and (B).

During his mandate as the director of the International Labor Office until his death in 1932, Thomas actively sought the support of socialists from ILO member countries that he visited in the context of labour diplomacy prior to the ratification of international conventions by member states. During these trips, he always took the opportunity to organize meetings with local socialist groups to establish more durable links. In his exchanges with socialist or social democrat leaders in power such as Karl Branting in Sweden, Ramsay MacDonald in the UK or even Hermann Müller in Germany, Thomas called for the cooperation of the world's socialist forces to support the action of the ILO, which was regularly portrayed as the outcome of workers' ambitions.[32]

Thomas' chief of staff, the French socialist Viple, was asked by the former to be the intermediary between Geneva and the LSI, a pertinent role for this former Guesdist with Marxist tendencies who had switched to reformism. He thus promoted the activities of the International Labor Office among the authorities of the LSI, which was established in Hamburg in 1923. As an indirect consequence of the Second International, it brought together socialists and social democrats from around the world following a troublesome development period after the war.[33] Viple's multiple meetings with the LSI members made him Thomas' unofficial ambassador of labour diplomacy at the LSI.[34] He represented the director at the International Workers' Olympiads and the LSI congress, both held in Vienna in 1931. There he met the Austrian socialist Otto Bauer whose writings influenced the socialist officials at the International Labor Office. Viple hoped to become a strong advocate of the ILO within the ranks of the LSI. After this meeting, he confided to Thomas:

> It is Bauer who leads the Austrian government. He has a strong position in the International and a growing influence in the milieu of workers and socialists ... In the near future, he will play a leading role. I believe that he is now committed to the Office. He has a better understanding your efforts and speaks of you with the obvious sympathy of one man of action for another man of action. I promised that you would visit him this year. I am sure that it will be a useful meeting.[35]

This array of meetings highlights not only the extent of the International Labor Office's networks but also the permeability between internationalisms, which were more complementary than competitive, and given the economic and social crises of the interwar period, they were especially encouraged to work in collaboration. This connection between international social reform and socialist internationalism is

---

[32] See, for example, the correspondence between Thomas and Karl Branting, leader of the Swedish Social Democratic Party and prime minister of Sweden in the early 1920s; ILO Archive, CAT 7-213. See also the correspondence between the BIT and the British Labour Party; ILO-Archive, CAT 5-64-1-2. On these meetings with members of the Social Democratic Party of Germany, see Sandrine Kott and Dorothea Hoethker (ed.), À la rencontre de l'Europe au travail: récits de voyages d'Albert Thomas (1920–1932) (Paris/Genève, Publications de la Sorbonne/Bureau international du travail, 2015).
[33] Alain Bergounioux, 'L'Internationale Ouvrière Socialiste entre les deux guerres', in L'Internationale Socialiste, ed. Hugues Portelli (Paris: Éditions de l'Atelier, 1983), 23–42.
[34] ILO Archive, P.288, personal file of Marius Viple.
[35] ILO Archive, CAT 4-42, note from Marius Viple to Albert Thomas regarding his trip to Vienna in 1931.

supported by the research conducted by the ILO officials themselves. In the late 1920s, Milhaud and Viple penned a series of notes to summarize the material and intellectual links between the ILO's actions as they conceived them and the ideas of the worker and socialist movements since the nineteenth century: for example, the reduction in the working day or the creation of a new economic and social organization for the emancipation of workers. At the end of the 1920s, Milhaud wrote, 'Some points on the relations between the International Labor Organization and socialism'.[36] Developed around twelve points, he articulates his view of the ideological and political links between the socialist project and the action of the tripartite international organization tasked with implementing social legislation on a global scale. Referring to the ideas of Robert Owen and Karl Marx, the resolutions of the 1925 LSI congress and even the ILO statutes, Milhaud concluded that 'the institution is fully oriented ... toward a socialist economy'. The professor of social economics at the University of Geneva even borrowed a phrase from George Bernard Shaw to affirm, in a voluntarily provocative tone, that the ILO 'is the true International of which Moscow only dreams'. The economic discussions that took place at the International Labor Office in the late 1920s under the aegis of its economists and socialist politicians gave pride of place to the notion of a national and international economic organization, popularized notably within Austrian socialism by Otto Bauer.[37] Even though these reflections coexist with those of classical economists, their very expression at the International Labor Office shows the extent to which the institution lay at the crossroads of diverse influences of thought, with the advent of socialist ideas via Thomas and his socialist colleagues. The theme of the organized economy on an international scale emerges in the projects that Thomas began to formulate in the late 1920s, imagined as a third path between liberal capitalism and state collectivism in response to the global economic crisis.[38] These projects are the consequence of hybridizing liberal and socialist internationalisms in the orbit of the International Labor Office. Behind the seeming independence of socialist internationalism, there was an exchange of ideas and practices, which turned the International Labor Office into the backstage for the revitalization of socialist and labour internationalism. The means of action and universal character of the ILO, which had by then spread to every continent, made it a valuable resource for socialists and trade unionists wishing to promote their actions, which were often limited to Europe.

Converging and diverging internationalisms

The official position of the LSI with regard to the ILO evolved throughout the 1920s. Often equated with the League of Nations, it was initially the object of antagonism before a progressive normalization of relations in the 1920s following a change in

---

[36] ILO Archive, CAT 8-34, note of Edgar Milhaud, 'Quelques points concernant les rapports entre l'OIT et le socialisme'.
[37] Alain Bergounioux and Bernard Manin, *Le Régime social-démocrate* (Paris: Presses Universitaires de France, 1989), 18–37.
[38] Albert Thomas, 'Pour une politique de la coopération internationale', *Revue des études coopératives* 37 (1930): 18–37.

the LSI's political doctrine as well as the interactions facilitated by the international mediators. Thus, at the convening of the constituent congress of the LSI in Hamburg in 1923, a resolution on 'the eight-hour working day and international social reform' was adopted, condemning the governments of member countries for blocking the ratification of the first convention in Washington and encouraging 'workers to combat the attacks against the action of the International Labor Office by diverse capitalist interests, which are always opposed to improving the social conditions of the working class'.[39]

The approach towards the International Labor Office was still vague at this stage, although the LSI recognized the key role of the socialists as allies rallied in support of the ratification of international labour conventions. Not until the congress of Brussels in 1928 did the LSI adopt a clearer position. The memorandum, soberly entitled 'The International Labor Office and the LSI', first outlined the respective tasks of the International Labor Office, the LSI and the International Federation of Trade Unions (IFTU), established in Amsterdam in 1919 and regrouping reformist trade unions. Represented at international labour conferences, the IFTU was responsible for cultivating relationships with the International Labor Office, whereas the socialist parties in member countries were responsible for supporting the ratification of conventions.

The memorandum focused on the exchange of practices and experiences, which began from the early months of the ILO's existence during the International Workers Congress in Geneva in July 1920 which led to the creation of the International Working Union of Socialist Parties.[40] Often disparaged as the 'Two-and-a-Half International', this newly formed group brought together socialist parties, which, like the FSWI and Independent Social Democratic Party of Germany, had quit the Second International but refused to join the Communist International, founded in Moscow in March 1919. The congress organized to mark its creation benefitted, through Thomas' intervention, from the material help of the International Labor Office, which made available typewriters as well as officials with stenographic and translation skills to ensure the smooth running of the sessions.[41] It must be said that the International Labor Office was a babel of languages: English and French were the two official languages – before the addition of Spanish – and the staff were often multilingual.[42] As truly international arenas, these international labour conferences served as the support, if not the model, for the LSI. In 1926, Viple gave Friedrich Adler, the LSI secretary, a report from the technical division of the International Labor Office charged with translating the conference debates into several languages.[43] The memorandum adopted by the LSI in 1928 affirmed that 'international conferences offer an excellent opportunity to enter

---

[39] LSI Secretariat, *Textes des résolutions prises au congrès ouvrier socialiste international de Hambourg, 21-25 mai 1923* (Vienna: LSI Secretariat, 1923), 15.
[40] André Donneur, *Histoire de l'Union des partis socialistes pour l'action internationale (1920–1923)* (Sudbury: Librairie de l'Université Laurentienne, 1967).
[41] ILO Archive, CAT 8-1-1, letter from Camille Huysmans to Albert Thomas dated July 29, 1920.
[42] Julie Lupo, *Le problème de la diversité des langues et la recherche de la langue universelle dans les organisations internationales, 1919–1923* (PhD diss., Université Pierre Mendès France, 2003).
[43] IISH Archive; LSI Archive, file 3097, letter from Viple to Adler dated October 6, 1926.

into contact with representatives of workers from overseas'.[44] The universal vocation of the ILO was thus perceived as a useful means to rebuild the socialist international. In 1929, Thomas' trip to Japan – a founding member of the ILO – and then the International Labor Conference allowed Adler to meet with representatives of the Japanese trade union movement, in particular with K. Matsuoka, the labour delegate at the conference and also a member of the Japanese social-democrat party.[45]

The LSI's competition with the Communist International, which had been spreading intense anti-capitalist and anti-colonial propaganda in colonized countries since the mid-1920s, aroused its interest in the ILO's tools. Building relations with socialist groups in Asia thus needed to respond to the propaganda of the Communist International, which portrayed the LSI as 'the ally of European and American imperialism'.[46]

However, the memorandum stated that 'even for the European labor movement, these conferences as well as the executive board sessions of the International Labor Office provide the opportunity for international contact, which is only feasible because of the considerable financial means at the disposal of the International Labor Office'. The text continued by stating that 'the representatives of the International Labor Office have taken advantage of these opportunities as often as possible to forge international relations'.[47]

The relations between the ILO and LSI cannot be reduced to an instrumental and one-sided exchange, as previously suggested by Patrizia Dogliani.[48] The ILO's liberal internationalism also called on the resources of the LSI to defend its actions, as embodied by the socialist mediators of the ILO. The LSI did not simply exploit the ILO's resources, as forums for dialogue were set up with an exchange of practices and ideas. Thomas knew precisely how to mobilize his socialist networks to obtain useful information when preparing his overseas trips or the ILO's actions. For example, during his visit to the Far East in 1928–9, thanks to Adler's help, he succeeded in meeting Chinese socialist activists.[49]

A comparative study of the LSI and ILO archives reveals the technical cooperation between the two bodies, which had become almost routine by the late 1920s. By cooperating with the LSI, the International Labor Office sought to impose its areas of expertise in the international public debate and support the joint initiatives of the IFTU and LSI. From the early 1920s, these two organizations undertook common actions for the ratification of the first international labour convention on the eight-hour working day. In 1924, Thomas hailed 'the manifesto issued to workers in all countries

---

[44] LSI Secretariat, *Troisième congrès de l'Internationale ouvrière socialiste, Bruxelles du 5 au 11 août 1928* (Zurich: LSI Secretariat, 1928), 76–8.

[45] LSI Secretariat, *Quatrième Congrès de l'Internationale Ouvrière Socialiste, Vienne, du 25 juillet au 1ᵉʳ août 1931. Rapports et comptes rendus* (Zurich: LSI Secretariat, 1932), 107.

[46] LSI Secretariat, *Quatrième Congrès de l'Internationale Ouvrière Socialiste, Vienne. Rapports et comptes rendus*, 107.

[47] IISH Archive; LSI Secretariat, *Troisième congrès de l'Internationale ouvrière socialiste*, 76–8. On the development of socialist internationalism in contrast with communist internationalism, see Imlay, *The Practice of Socialist Internationalism*.

[48] Dogliani, 'Progetto per un'internazionale "aclassista"'.

[49] IISH Archive; LSI Archive, file 398, Topalovic file.

to mark May Day, which rightly stresses the pressing need to internationalize the eight-hour day'.[50] The May Day rallies to defend the eight-hour working day took up this long-standing cause of the labour movement. However, the fact that the very first convention adopted in Washington related to the eight-hour day was as much the result of trade union petitioning as a sign of the potential convergence of the international socialist and labour movements and liberal internationalism. Despite the failure to ratify the convention, notably in the industrialized countries of Western Europe,[51] it led to joint discussions and cooperation between the LSI and IFTU during the 1920s, partly impelled by the actions of the International Labor Office.[52] During the 1920s, the ILO became one of the depoliticized arenas for cooperation between the LSI and IFTU, particularly on the issue of the eight-hour working day, with the ILO's actions supporting the re-internationalization of this historical leitmotiv of the labour movement.

The International Labor Office put its technical competencies at the disposal of these joint political initiatives in the domains of migration, unemployment and social security. In return, the proposals of these two international labour and socialist organizations were integrated into the ILO's discussions. In 1926, the IFTU and LSI organized an international congress on migration. This subject was subsequently included in the work agenda of the International Labor Conference in 1928. The International Labor Office invited a delegation from the LSI to present the decisions of its congress to the Permanent Migration Committee that convened before the conference.[53] Thomas wanted to make the International Labor Office and its Permanent Migration Committee, created at his request, the world's leading expertise on this issue. Thus, by inviting labour representatives, he aimed to counteract divergent opinions by turning the committee into the arbiter of proposals from differing sides.[54] By giving a technical framework to these social and political issues, the International Labor Office became the meeting place of socialist and trade union representatives as well as international social reform experts from the ILO, which could impose its analytical categories on activist discussions.

Several years later, the Unemployment Commission, jointly created by the LSI and IFTU and meeting in Zurich on 21–22 January 1931, partly drew on the expertise of the International Labor Office. Belgian socialist Henri Fuss, secretary of the International Association on Unemployment and director of the Unemployment, Employment, and Migration Section of the International Labor Office since 1924, was tasked with drafting a report on the demographic aspects of the unemployment crisis.[55] This collaboration

---

[50] IISH Archive; LSI Archive, file 3097, letter from Thomas to Adler dated May 24, 1924. In the following year, the May Day slogan was the internationalization of the eight-hour day. LSI Secretariat, *Deuxième congrès de l'Internationale Ouvrière Socialiste, à Marseille du 22 au 27 août 1925* (Brussels: Imprimerie coopérative Lucifer), 63.

[51] Nabjib Souamaa, 'La loi des huit heures : un projet d'Europe sociale ? (1918–1932)', *Travail et Emploi* 110 (2007): 27–36.

[52] IISH Archive; LSI Archive, file 397, correspondence between Albert Thomas and Friedrich Adler.

[53] IISH Archive; LSI Archive, file 902, Weltwanderungskongress, 1926.

[54] Paul-André Rosental, 'Géopolitique et État-providence', *Annales. Histoire, Sciences Sociales* 1 (2006): 99–134.

[55] IISH Archive; LSI Archive, file 781, correspondence between Henri Fuss and Adler from 1930 onwards.

was initiated at the request of Thomas for whom the International Labor Office was 'at the disposal of any labor, trade union, or even political organization requiring its assistance ... and our comrades to help, to the best of our knowledge and strength, find solutions against the terrible evil from which the international proletariat suffers'.[56] This led to the adoption of a resolution at the LSI congress in Vienna in 1931 in support of the ILO's action for unemployment benefits in all countries affected by the economic crisis.[57] In return, the ILO's expertise in this domain served to support the grievances of socialists for the development or improvement of social security at the national level. For example, Tixier, the head of the Social Security Section at the International Labor Office, provided the French labour movement with the entire body of technical literature that he had summarized and simplified. Léon Jouhaux, secretary general of the French General Confederation of Labor (CGT), and Paul Faure, secretary general of the FSWI, both used the texts drafted by the International Labor Office to raise public awareness about this technical and less inspiring issue in *Le Peuple* and *Le Populaire*.[58] This may partly explain the similar language used by the FSWI and CGT in favour of social security systems, contrary to the French Communist Party and United General Confederation of Labor that opposed what they viewed as an instrument of social pacification that served the interests of the bourgeoisie.[59] This example illustrates the exchange of analytical categories and ideas, with the International Labor Office acting as both the support and the pivot.

Conclusion

The 'Thomas years' at the International Labor Office corresponded to a double internationalist moment, as the internationalization of social issues instigated in the late nineteenth century took on a new dimension with the creation of the ILO, which drew on a variety of influences. Socialist internationalism, which was in the midst of renewal in the first half of the 1920s, is one of them. For Thomas' French socialist allies who followed him to Geneva, this meant committing to the international structures in this global centre of social reform in order to counter the revolutionary offensive in Russia that had begun to spread around the world. For the socialists of the second circle who mediated between socialist internationalism and liberal internationalism, this involved supporting the demands of the international labour movement at a time when defining these relations was not always straightforward. The International Labor Office thus became one of the arenas for the rapprochement of the IFTU and LSI. Even if these two internationalisms remained distinct – some socialists denied that Thomas belonged to the socialist family given his participation in the Sacred Union

---

[56] IISH Archive; LSI Archive, file 781, letter from Thomas to Adler dated November 8, 1930.
[57] LSI Secretariat, *Quatrième Congrès de l'Internationale Ouvrière Socialiste, Vienne. Rapports et comptes rendus*, 33.
[58] ILO Archive, CAT 6-C10, social security. The file includes important correspondence between Adrien Tixier, Léon Jouhaux, and Paul Faure.
[59] Michel Dreyfus, Michèle Ruffat, Vincent Viet, Danièle Voldman, and Bruno Valat, *Se protéger, être protégé: une histoire des assurances sociales en France* (Rennes: Presses universitaires de Rennes, 2006), 187–206.

and his ambiguous attitude towards fascist governments[60] – there were nevertheless exchanges of ideas and practices between them. The socialist officials based in Geneva who strived for the convergence of diverse international arenas sought to incorporate the expertise and analytical categories of the International Labor Office into the actions of socialists and trade unionists. This demonstrates the growing legitimacy of scientific knowledge at the International Labor Office in the late 1920s as well as the permeability of analytical categories.[61] The adoption of the theme of the organized economy by the International Labor Office and even the inclusion of social security demands in the activist arsenal of the LSI after the 1929 crisis shed light on these exchanges. Although the 1920s marked the zenith of this dynamic, the sudden death of Thomas in 1932 and the failed bid of the Belgian socialist planner Henri de Man to succeed him marked the end of this internationalist cooperation. The mandate of the British high-ranking official Harold Butler as director of the International Labor Office (1932–8) heralded a re-centring towards more traditional networks of liberal social reform and the distancing of international trade unionist and socialist networks from the ILO.

---

[60] Stefano Gallo, 'Dictatorship and International Organizations: The ILO as a "Test Ground" for Fascism', in *Globalizing Social Rights: The International Labour Organization and Beyond*, ed. Sandrine Kott and Joelle Droux (Palgrave Macmillan: ILO Century Series, 2013), 153–71.

[61] Dhermy-Mairal, *Les sciences sociales et l'action au Bureau international du travail (1920–1939)*.

8

The Eastern Bloc countries and the question of development at the UN in the 1960s and 1970s

Michel Christian

Communism was originally a universalist and as such a non-national movement. In some countries, communist parties have succeeded in taking power and founding lasting political regimes. In these countries – first in the Soviet Union, then in the countries of Central Europe that constituted the 'Eastern Bloc' – parties in power made the achievement of socialism coincide with the national horizon, giving rise to regimes that used both nationalist and internationalist discourses. It is most of the time agreed that these 'lefts of government under communist rule' experienced a kind of internationalization. At the same time, 'internationalism' is also considered as a mere subordination to the Soviet Union, mainly directed against the states of the opposite bloc, with which diplomatic, economic and human relations were subject to close control.

This contribution intends to revisit the history of communist states from a renewed international perspective. It brings in actors – international organizations – and issues – development – that the dominant Cold War narrative has traditionally left aside because of its focus on the East-West conflict[1]. This reassessment requires an effort to think out of the categories that the Cold War has produced, of which Akira Iryie has identified two main effects[2]. The first is a focus on states as the exclusive actors in international relations, which tends to overlook the significant expansion international organizations since 1945 and to reduce them to mere arenas where states and blocs confronted each other[3]. This vision is in line with an interpretation of international relations known as 'realist', which makes sovereign states the only relevant international actors. The second effect of these categories of thought is the

---

This chapter is one of the outputs of the research project *Shared Modernities or Competing Modernities? Europe between West and East (1920s–1970s)* funded by the Swiss National Science Foundation (project 100011_152600/1) and involving Sandrine Kott, Michel Christian and Ondřej Matějka.

[1] For a comprehensive reassessment of the Cold War narrative in development history, see Sandrine Kott, *Organiser le monde* (Paris: Editions du Seuil, 2021).
[2] Akira Iryie, *Global Community: The Role of International Organizations in the Making of the Contemporary World* (Berkeley: University of California Press, 2002), 61–4.
[3] Marie-Claude Smouts, *Les Organisations internationales* (Paris: Armand Colin, 1995).

application of a Cold War logic to historical phenomena that were in fact autonomous. Akira Iriye mentions here globalization and decolonization. One could add the issue of development. Development was not a simple by-product of the competition between East and West[4], firstly because it implies a vision in terms of North-South rather than East-West divide, and secondly because this question pre-existed the Cold War and has continued to be raised up to the present day despite the questioning of the 1980s, which had less to do with the fall of the communist regimes than with the rise of neoliberal conceptions[5].

In order to reinterpret the internationalization of the Eastern Bloc countries during the Cold War, the question of development should not be considered only as a propaganda tool in the hands of the Eastern Bloc state. First, development was as a real domestic issue for those countries that had recently emerged or were emerging from what began to be referred to 'underdevelopment' in the 1950s. Second, international organizations were actors in their own right. Without going so far as to make them autonomous institutions, as did the 'neo-functionalist' approach, these organizations have nevertheless succeeded in advocating development, and have been able to impose agendas, time frames as well as discursive and moral norms to which state actors have had to learn to conform, even when they were seeking to use this or that organization to pursue their own ends.

The 'belief' in development reached its peak during the 1960s and the 1970s.[6] The idea that measurable gaps in wealth and living standards between countries could be filled by appropriate measures at the global level was a consensus, and only the nature of these measures was debated.[7] These two decades logically corresponded to the heyday of Third Worldism on the international scene, in particular in international organizations. But it was also during this period that the Eastern Bloc states were the most active on the issue of development.[8] This contribution seeks to shed light on their activity in the two organizations that were once central but have been marginalized by the neoliberal turn since the 1980s: the United Nations Conference on Trade and Development (UNCTAD), created in 1964, and the United Nations Industrial Development Organization (UNIDO), created in 1967.

Eastern Bloc countries had three main types of relationship with UNCTAD and UNIDO. First of all, they used them as forums to demonstrate the superiority of the socialist model, adapting their Marxist discourse to the developmentalist perspective that prevailed in international organizations. Secondly, UNCTAD and UNIDO were

[4] As this was commonly contended at the time, see Alvin Z. Rubinstein and George Ginsburgs (ed.), *Soviet and American Policies in the United Nations: A Twenty-Five-Year Perspective* (New York: New York University Press, 1971).
[5] As already observed in Heinz W. Arndt, *Economic Development. The History of an Idea* (Chicago: University of Chicago Press, 1989).
[6] Gilbert Rist, *Le Développement: Histoire d'une croyance occidentale* (Paris: Presses de la Fondation nationale des sciences politiques, 1996), 169–74.
[7] Ibid., 195–218.
[8] For a more state-centred approach, see Sara Lorenzini, 'Comecon and the South in the Years of Détente: A Study on East–South Economic Relations', *European Review of History: Revue européenne d'histoire* 21, no. 2 (2014). For an approach that takes the international organizations into account, see Sandrine, *Organiser le monde*, 79–112 and 169–78.

places where Eastern Bloc countries tried to defend their own economic interests, tactically identifying them with those of developing countries. Thirdly, Eastern Bloc countries made noteworthy efforts to have nationals employed in those two international organizations, thus participating in their activities from the inside.

International organizations as forums

The international organizations, especially in the field of development, were an important forum for the Eastern Bloc countries. This is even their most commonly accepted function: they could stage the conflict and rivalry between East and West and thus make a 'socialist' alternative to the capitalist model exist. However, this use as a forum was not immediate. It was the result of a learning process that gradually allowed Eastern Bloc states to produce a discourse adapted to the context of international organizations. At the beginning of the 1950s, Eastern Bloc states opposed the very notions of 'underdevelopment' and 'development' that began to spread widely in the international organizations, seeing them as nothing more than a cover for a new form of exploitation by the capitalist powers, led by the United States. It was true that President Truman himself popularized the term 'underdevelopment' in a famous speech held in January 1949 and equated 'development' with the liberal economic model embodied by the United States[9]. It was also true that the United States was then at the height of their influence in international organizations, while the countries of the Eastern Bloc, on the other hand, had suspended their participation since 1948 and concentrated on their domestic economic transformation.

The issue of development became central in the 1960s with the creation of UNCTAD. Drawing on demands already made within the United Nations Economic Commission for Latin America (ECLAC) since the 1940s,[10] the decolonization movement of the early 1960s raised again the question of international trade in 1962 at the UN General Assembly, which decided to convene a 'United Nations Conference on Trade and Development' (UNCTAD). This resolution led not only to a conference held in 1964 (known as 'UNCTAD I'), but also to its institutionalization as a new international organization, which convened a conference every four years since then. With a General Secretariat headed by the charismatic South American economist Raul Prebisch, UNCTAD aimed at providing a forum for countries of the North and the South to promote the 'structural adjustment' necessary for balanced international trade, not only by defining new trade rules but also by providing developing countries with new infrastructures in the areas of transport, banking and insurance.[11] In UNCTAD's wake, the United Nations Industrial Development Organization (UNIDO) was created three

---

[9] David Ekbladh, *The Great American Mission: Modernization and the Construction of an American World Order* (Princeton: Princeton University Press, 2010).
[10] Eric Helleiner, 'The Development Mandate of International Institutions: Where Did It Come From?' *Studies in Comparative International Development* 44, no. 3 (2009).
[11] Johanna Bockman, 'Socialist Globalization against Capitalist Neocolonialism: The Economic Ideas behind the New International Economic Order', *Humanity: An International Journal of Human Rights, Humanitarianism, and Development* 6, no. 1 (2015).

years later with the aim, complementary to that of UNCTAD, of providing technical assistance to the countries of the South in the development of their national industries.

The rise of 'development' as a global issue took the Eastern Bloc states somewhat by surprise. Certainly, since the Suez affair and the Soviet offer of assistance to Egypt in 1956, or since the assistance offered by the Eastern Bloc countries to Sékou Touré's Guinea in 1958,[12] non-European countries became present on the horizon of Eastern Bloc states' diplomacy. Similarly, there was a number of trade relations between Eastern Bloc countries and countries of the Middle East since the early 1950s.[13] However, Eastern Bloc states do not seem to have been immediately aware or to recognize the significance of the North-South divide. In the archives of the Foreign Ministry of the German Democratic Republic (GDR), the term 'developing countries' was even not used until 1963.[14] This shows that it was in the last moments, when the interests of the 'Group of 77' were being institutionalized within UNCTAD, that East German diplomats adjusted their categories to the new context.

Once the issue of development was understood and accepted by the Eastern Bloc countries, they consistently supported the demands of the developing countries when they were addressed to the 'capitalist' countries, while often describing them, behind the scenes, as 'unjustified and exaggerated' when they were addressed to themselves.[15] In return for this public support, Eastern Bloc countries gained a specific status in UNCTAD, sitting there as a specific group of the so-called 'socialist countries'. To understand the content of this privilege, it should be recalled that the terminology in force at UNCTAD referred to Western countries (NATO and OECD member states) as 'developed market economy countries' (despite the protests of Turkey, Spain and Portugal). By comparison, the designation of Eastern European countries as 'socialist' avoided mentioning them as 'developed' and rather emphasized their ideological identity. This alleviated their fear of being sent back to the indistinct camp of the developed countries by the developing countries. Similarly, the General Secretariat accepted the establishment of a 'Division on trade among countries with different economic and social systems' in 1967, the result of a working group that Eastern Bloc countries had succeeded in obtaining at the first UNCTAD and which gave them a special status within the organization.

These symbolic compensations did not, however, mean that their position in international organizations such as UNCTAD or UNIDO was taken for granted. Eastern Bloc countries had to adapt their discourse to political arenas structured not by an East-West divide but by a North-South divide. Accordingly, they reformulated their discourse to fit into the developmentalist frame of reference that prevailed in

---

[12] For an identification of these development projects at the time, see Klaus Billerbeck, *Die Auslandshilfe Des Ostblocks für die Entwicklungsländer: Analyse und Prognose* (Hamburg: Verlag Weltarchiv, 1960).
[13] Ibid.
[14] East German sources generally use the terms 'capitalist markets' or 'capitalist countries' and sometimes 'progressive capitalist states'.
[15] Stiftung Archiv für Parteien und Massenorganisation Bundesarchivs (SAPMO BArch) DE 1/54084: Bericht über die Ergebnisse des Auftretens des Stellvertreters des Leiters der RGW-Delegation auf der 2. UN-Konferenz für Handel und Entwicklung (UNCTAD) in New Delhi in der Zeit vom 1.-20.2.1968 und 12.-29.3.1968, 25.4. 1968.

these new arenas. In both UNCTAD and UNIDO, the 'socialist countries' worked on a 'presentation of self' that made the 'construction of socialism' congruent with the developmental narrative. The 'construction of socialism' combined the establishment of a new regime, economic planning, agricultural collectivization and the development of heavy industry and took place in Eastern Europe between 1948 and 1953 (and earlier in the 1930s in the Soviet Union). It coincided historically with the denigration of the term 'development' regarded as a disguised form of capitalist exploitation. When speaking at UNCTAD or UNIDO in the 1960s, however, the Eastern Bloc countries now presented this episode of their history as a possible path to development. In a statement to the Trade and Development Board, the executive body of UNCTAD, Eastern Bloc states declared in 1975 that 'the main efforts to accelerate development were incumbent upon the developing countries themselves, which should take all steps to mobilize their own resources. External sources of finance must be regarded as complementary to the efforts of the developing countries themselves.' They cited measures such as 'strengthening the State and co-operative sectors of the economy, controlling the activities of foreign capital, including those of transnational corporations, regulating the outflow of capital, broadening the planned sector of the economy and improving budgetary and tax legislation'. All those measures reminded of course the 'construction of socialism' but were cited here only because they 'could be conducive to economic and social progress and assist in removing obstacles to development'.[16]

Similarly, economic planning, which is at the heart of regimes in which private ownership of the means of production had been abolished, was regularly presented in a neutral way as a simple instrument of development. From the 1960s onwards, the UN organizations strongly encouraged the elaboration of national 'development plans', notably by creating a Committee for Development Planning, chaired by the economist Jan Tinbergen in 1967. The widespread notion of 'development planning' created a grey area which the governments of Eastern Europe tried to turn into a common ground between 'socialist' and 'developing' countries. State-planned economies also had trade implications that East European governments brought to the forefront again and again. They pragmatically presented economic planning as a factor of trade stability, while emphasizing the wide variations of markets which hit first the developing countries as exporters of raw material.[17] Within the Division for trade between countries with different economic and social systems, the discourse about Eastern Bloc economies had to be even more compliant with the developmentalist framework of UNCTAD. Its initial East-West dimension had been set aside in favour of the exclusive promotion of East-South trade.[18] Mainly staffed with international civil servants from the Eastern Bloc countries and from the developing countries, its work essentially consisted in

---

[16] General Assembly Official Records (GAOR), TD/B/ A/10015/Rev.1: *Report of the Trade and Development Board (10 March-2 October 1975)*, 1976, 137.

[17] "It is not a question of rigidly planning trade'. UNCTAD and the regulation of the international trade in the 1970s', in Michel Christian, Sandrine Kott, and Ondrej Matejka (ed.), *Planning in Cold War Europe. Competition, Cooperation, Circulations (1950s–1970s)* (Opladen: De Gruyter, 2018), 296–9.

[18] Michel Christian, 'UNCTAD', in *Den Kalten Krieg vermessen. Über Reichweite und Alternativen einer binären Ordnung*, ed. Frank Reichherzer, Emmanuel Droit, and Jan Hansen (De Gruyter: Oldenbourg, 2018), §22–4.

highlighting and publicizing the objective advantages of trade with Eastern European countries, without referring to any conflict between socialism and capitalism, or even to any ideological superiority of the former over the latter.

Defending the interests of the Eastern Bloc in international organizations

Eastern countries did use international organizations as a forum in their competition with Western countries, while adapting their discourse to a non-Cold War framework. Less well known is the fact that they also used these organizations to defend their own interests, mainly economic, against the countries of the West.

The economic development of Central Europe and Russia in the first half of the twentieth century was largely dependent on the trade with Western Europe. In this regard, the 'construction of socialism in one country' in the Soviet Union, and the subsequent building of the 'People's Republics' in Central Europe can be considered as attempts to develop economically in a more autonomous way. This did to a large extent reduce the importance of the economic ties with Western Europe, but Eastern Bloc countries nevertheless continued to be dependent on a number of strategic goods from Western Europe, as the Soviet Union had already been in the 1920s and 1930s. Against this background, the Cold War led to a gradual disruption in the trade with the West and was seen as a serious economic threat by Eastern Bloc states. First, the Marshall Plan, which worked as a free-trade organization, was focused on Western Europe and marginalized Eastern Europe[19], in contrast with the initial project of the Economic Commission for Europe led by Gunnar Myrdal, which aimed at establishing a pan-European cooperation based on the coordination of national plans and the rationalization of trade.[20] Then, from 1949 onwards, the Western Bloc states began to draw up lists of products under embargo, under the control of a Coordinating Committee for Multilateral Export Controls (COCOM), although it was possible to circumvent this system, as the lists and the rigour of the embargo were not the same from one country to another.[21] Finally, the creation in 1957 of a new free-trade area with a single external tariff, the European Economic Community (EEC), was seen in the East as a real economic threat. Its development was followed very closely in the GDR Foreign Office.[22] A 1962 report noted that 'the integration of the imperialist states has the effect of weighing on East-West trade and, apart from its political effects, it is also accompanied by negative economic effects for the socialist countries'.[23] This

---

[19] Kott, *Organiser le monde*, 59–64.
[20] Daniel Stinsky, 'A Bridge between East and West? Gunnar Myrdal and the Economic Commission for Europe, 1947–1957', in *Planning in the Cold War Europe. Competition, Cooperation, Circulations (1950s–1970s)*, ed. Michel Christian, Sandrine Kott, and Ondrej Matějka (Opladen: De Gruyter, 2018).
[21] Kott, *Organiser le monde*, 64–7.
[22] SAPMO-BArch DY 30/IV 2/6.10/196-197: Europäische Gemeinschaft, 1956–1962.
[23] SAPMO-BArch, DY 30/IV 2/6.10/197, 134–41: *Zu Problemen der Abstimmung einer gemeinsamen Haltung der sozialistischen Länder im RGW in bezug auf die westeuropäische Integration*, 22 May 1962, 138.

particularly concerned imports of 'modern machinery and equipment, certain semi-processed products and foodstuffs'. The 'co-ordination of the trade policies of the EEC countries vis-à-vis the countries of the socialist camp' was termed as 'discrimination'.[24]

The perception of that economic threat explains why Eastern Bloc countries were very supportive of the initiative of the first UNCTAD. They saw it primarily as a way of condemning trade discriminations and defending their own trade interests. Interestingly, the first document to be found when opening the 'UNCTAD 1963-5' file of the East German Foreign Ministry is a 'Summary of discrimination by type of problem'.[25] This concern was shared by other Eastern Bloc states, as evidenced by the discussions within the Council for Mutual Economic Assistance (CMEA). At a meeting of the CMEA's Standing Committee on Foreign Trade in June 1963, the delegations of the member countries jointly decided to support UNCTAD's transformation into an 'International Trade Organisation' with the specific aim of promoting trade 'independently of the different economic systems', in particular 'by mitigating the negative consequences of the economic integration of the highly developed capitalist countries'.[26] However, at a preparatory committee for the first UNCTAD in June 1963, only a minority of developing countries supported CMEA countries' proposal. A report by the East German Foreign Office deplored the fact that the issue of discrimination had been sidelined and that the conference was heading for a 'pure development conference'. Another report noted that developing countries were trying to use the 'World Trade Conference' – the reports never mention the term 'development' – 'exclusively in their own interest'.[27] In August 1963, the CMEA countries, at one of their co-ordination meetings, finally ended up accepting 'to take this inescapable fact into account' and drew up a 'co-ordinated programme on the question of the development of trade with the developing countries'[28] as a sign of goodwill. Only then was the creation of an international trade organization adopted as an agenda item at the first UNCTAD.[29]

This coordinated attempt by the Eastern Bloc states to push for their own interests in UNCTAD is little known and does not appear in its official history. Despite their failure and while supporting the demands of the developing countries, the Eastern Bloc countries nevertheless continued to pursue their initial line until in the 1980s, using UNCTAD to consistently criticize the EEC and its trade policy and to demand the inclusion of East-West trade in the debates. The developing countries, however, always opposed their demand, while the Western Bloc countries appealed to the Economic Commission for Europe, where negotiations had stalled since 1948.

---

[24] Ibid.
[25] SAPMO BArch DE1 49425: *Übersicht über die Zusammenfassung von Diskriminierungen nach Problemen.*
[26] SAPMO BArch DE1 49425: *Memorandum Vorläufige Vorstellungen über die Grundprinzipien einer Internationale Handelsorganisation (IHO)*, 10 September 1963.
[27] SAPMO-BArch DE1 49620: *Kurzinformation*, 15 August 1963, 2.
[28] SAPMO BArch DE1 49425: *Vorlage für das PB des ZK der SED zur „UN-Konferenz für Handel und Entwicklung' (Welthandelkonferenz)*, 7.
[29] SAPMO-BArch DE1 49620: *Information über die Ergebnisse der 3. Tagung des Vorbereitungskomitee der UN-Konferenz für Handel und Entwicklung (UNCTAD)*, 26 February 1964, 1-4.

Alongside with the issue of trade, Eastern Bloc states showed a marked interest in industrial development. Of course, they were not regarded as developing countries in that field and, from the end of the 1950s onwards, they were able to provide technical assistance on their own, delivering 'turnkey' industrial equipment to several countries, mainly in the Middle East.[30] However, from the 1970s at the latest, their technology policy shifted decisively from the development of endogenous technologies to the organized transfer of technologies from the West to the East. This transfer, which took advantage of the Détente, often took place on a bilateral basis,[31] but international organizations also played an unsuspected role in this process. Among them, UNIDO was of particular interest to the Eastern Bloc countries. In principle, these countries did not have priority in UNIDO's eyes, since they had the status of developed countries, except for Romania, which tried to impose its recognition as a 'socialist developing country'. In the economic thinking of UNIDO, however, it was important that the developing countries be a diversified and even differentiated group, so as to promote cooperation between developing countries independently of the industrialized countries of the West. This is how the Eastern Bloc countries ended up being included in the UNIDO regional division for the Middle East.

Eastern Bloc countries' main interest in participating lay in the fact that they could contribute to UNIDO's budget in their national, non-convertible currencies, while UNIDO in return provided them with equipment financed in dollars, in most cases through the United Nations Development Programme (UNDP), which provided more than three-quarters of UNIDO's budget.[32] However, non-convertible currencies could only be used in the countries where they had been issued. Eastern Bloc countries' governments then offered services (mainly trainings) or equipment to UNIDO, which paid them in their respective national currencies. This process was to the advantage of the Eastern Bloc countries, but it was slow and complex for UNIDO, which spent a lot of energy matching the 'supply' of the Eastern Bloc countries with the 'demand' of the developing countries. As the offers were not well identified by UNIDO officials, it proved to be necessary to visit the different countries[33] and even to establish 'National Committees' in which these issues were discussed over time.[34] UNIDO thus actually took over the functions usually performed by the market. The governments of the Eastern Bloc countries used UNIDO to overcome the rigidities of state trade, since in a planned economy without a convertible currency, a multilateral organization such as UNIDO made it possible to break out of the rigid bilateral trade structure. At the same time, UNIDO factually channelled goods and know-how to the Eastern Bloc countries, giving them access to technologies that may have been under embargo because of the COCOM.

The technical assistance offered by UNIDO was not used by all states to the same extent. Some made extensive use of it, such as Bulgaria, Poland, Hungary and especially

---

[30] Billerbeck, *Ostblocks für die Entwicklungsländer*.
[31] Ibid.
[32] *Annual Report of the Executive Director 1977*, mars 1978, 15.
[33] UNIDO Archives, ID/FI 321 CZE, ID/FI 321 BUL, ID/FI 321 HUN, ID/FI 321 POL.
[34] UNIDO Archives, ID/OR 340 GDR, ID/OR 340 HUN, ID/OR 340 BUL.

Table 8.1 Technical assistance project delivered by UNIDO between 1969 and 1980[35]

States	Number of projects	Economic sectors
Bulgaria	33	Packaging, food industry, research in instrument design, numerical control machine tools
Poland	28	Packaging, machines-outils, opto-electronic instruments, computerization of machine, computer-aided manufacturing technique
Hungary	44	Light industries (food, textile, leather, furniture), computer technique
Romania	71	Light industries (food, textile, plastic, packaging), use of computer in industry (metallurgy, petrochemicals) vehicle maintenance
Czechoslovakia	3	Numerical control machine tools, industrial ceramics

Romania, to develop sectors left behind because of the dominance of heavy industry, whether traditional light industries or advanced technologies (see Table 8.1). Others made minimal use of it, such as Czechoslovakia, or no use at all, such as the GDR and the Soviet Union. These differences reveal an interesting differentiation between those governments that accepted the occasional status of their country as recipient of international assistance and those that considered their country to be permanently developed and did not want to depart from their status.

In the 1970s, technological transfers particularly concerned two fields: computer-electronics and management techniques.[36] In Bulgaria, UNIDO supported the development of a national electronic and computer industry from the early 1970s until the 1980s. It obtained equipment and provided the Bulgarian government with consultants to train personnel locally and abroad in various projects, such as the creation of a 'Research Institute for Instrument Design',[37] the assistance programme in the field of automation,[38] the creation of a 'Demonstration Centre for Numerically Controlled Machines',[39] the creation of a 'Centre for Applied Informatics for Process Control'[40] and the creation of an 'Industrial Institute for Cybernetics and Robotics'.[41] These projects were financed by UNIDO with funds allocated by UNDP, as evidenced by the dollar value of the projects and correspondence with the UNDP Resident Representative in Geneva.[42]

---

[35] See UNIDO Archives, ID/OA 321 BUL 1 to 33, ID/OA 321 POL 1 to 28, ID/OA 321 HUN 1 to 44, ID OA 321 ROM 1 to 71 et ID/OA CZE 1 to 3.
[36] As evidenced in UNIDO annual reports, see for example *Annual Report of the Executive Director 1977*, mars 1978, 34–5.
[37] UNIDO Archives, ID/OA 321 BUL 14: *Research Institute for Instrument Design*, 1971.
[38] UNIDO Archives, ID/OA 321 BUL 12: *Assistance in Automation*, 1972.
[39] ID/OA 321 BUL 11: *Expert in MC Machine Tools Numerical Control Machine Tools Demonstrative Centre*,1972 et ID/OA 321 BUL 28: *Numerical Control Training Demonstration Centre*, 1976.
[40] UNIDO Archives, ID/OA 321 BUL 30: *Process Control Computer Application Centre*, 1976.
[41] UNIDO Archives, DP/BUL/81/002: *Strengthening of the Industrial Institute for Cybernetics and Robotics*, 1981–1985.
[42] Ibid.

The second field of technological transfers was the management training: taking advantage of the interest shown by Eastern European governments when they initiated reforms in their economic systems in the 1960s, the International Labour Office (ILO) and its 'Management Developing' division designed a series of programmes financed by the UNDP and including the training of personnel abroad (in Great Britain, West Germany, France or Japan) as well as the establishment of management training centres in each of the countries concerned. This was not a confidential programme: in Romania, the 'Centre for the Improvement of Managers' (Centrul pentru perfecționarea cadrelor de conducere din întreprinderi or CEPECA), supported jointly by the ILO and UNIDO,[43] trained more than 16,000 managers between 1967 and 1972. These transfers contributed to the creation of a common managerial culture in the West and the East.[44]

In a 'realist view', it would be tempting to conclude that governments just used the international organizations as tools to achieve specific goals. This conclusion, however, would overlook international organizations' ability to develop their own strategies and to influence states' policies in return. This is what UNIDO did when it supported the building of a Bulgarian computer technology sector. Supported by UNIDO and funded by the UNDP, institutes like the Bulgarian research Institute for instrument design set up twinning-schemes with other research institute in Egypt, Algeria, Jordan and Syria in the early 1980s. UNIDO's goal obviously was to use Bulgaria as a model for developing countries, particularly by offering training.[45] The same applied to management techniques: starting in 1973, the Romanian CEPECA trained a number of managers from developing countries, because according to ILO experts, 'the [were] in a better position to understand the problems faces by developing countries'.[46] In both cases, UNIDO, ILO and UNDP seemed to see the Eastern Bloc countries not primarily as 'socialist', but rather as newly developed countries and therefore better able to serve as models for developing countries. They were not manipulated but promoted transfers from West to East in order to accelerate transfers from North to South.

The involvement of Eastern Bloc states in the international organizations

International organizations were not simply facing member states, both of them struggling for discursive legitimacy or pursuing divergent goals. Eastern Bloc states, like other member states, were also directly involved in the functioning of the international organizations. This involvement consisted in participating in bilateral negotiations and in sending nationals as civil servants to work for these organizations.

[43] UNIDO Archives, OA 420 ROM(1): *Industrial Management Training and Development Centre, Parts A-B* (oct 1971-mai 1974).
[44] Sandrine Kott, 'The Social Engineering Project. Exportation of Capitalist Management Culture to Eastern Europe (1950–1980)', in *Planning in the Cold War Europe. Competition, Cooperation, Circulations (1950s–1970s)*, ed. Michel Christian, Sandrine Kott, and Ondrej Matějka (Opladen: De Gruyter, 2018).
[45] UNIDO Archives, ID 262/8 *Training Agreement NIPKIP*.
[46] Quoted in Kott, *The Social Engineering Project*, 137.

Because of their non-convertible currencies Eastern Bloc countries could not invest a large amount of capital or contribute to key targets such as the 0.7 per cent of GDP of each developed country to international development assistance. In their rhetoric, they were not bound to this commitment as they, unlike the colonial and imperialist countries, did not have any 'historical debt' to pay to developing countries. In reality, convertible currencies were too valuable to be used for development projects abroad. However, Eastern Bloc states did engage with UNCTAD and UNIDO in other ways such as 'bilateral negotiations', which had been initiated by both international organizations and were considered crucial. Following UNCTAD II in New Delhi in 1968, a system of 'trade consultations' was set up to facilitate the negotiations of bilateral agreements which would form the building blocks of the new world trade order to come. This strategy was well explained by an UNCTAD official in 1967, who, considering the growth of planning in many countries, wrote in a letter: 'The next logical step in my way of thinking is to extend this experience [of planning] to the sphere of international trade. In any such extension bilateral (or triangular, or multilateral) trade agreements would seem to serve in the field of international exchange presumably the same purpose as planning is now serving in the domestic field.'[47] After its General Conference in Lima in 1975 and the adoption of a 'Programme' and a 'Plan of Action' which set the goal of increasing the share of developing countries from 7 per cent to 25 per cent of world industrial production by the year 2000, the UNIDO Secretariat sought, on the same model as UNCTAD, to establish a system of consultations to advance this goal on the basis of bilateral agreements.[48]

The strategy of working on bilateral agreements according to a step-by-step approach so as to gradually build a multilateral framework was more appropriate for Eastern countries. It gave the initiative back to sovereign states and allowed them to negotiate on their own terms, unhampered by the shortage of convertible currency. This arrangement was closely aligned with the specific concept of assistance that Eastern Bloc states had been claiming since the 1950s, which was based not on financial aid but on so-called 'mutually beneficial bilateral trade agreements', possibly accompanied by 'technical assistance'. Throughout the 1970s and 1980s, Eastern Bloc governments frequently attended UNCTAD's trade consultations, which were held in the margins of the sessions of the Trade and Development Board, UNCTAD's executive body.[49] When this consultative system was evaluated in 1984, a report mentioned that more than 360 negotiations had been undertaken between Eastern and developing

---

[47] UNCTAD Archives, ARR 40/1929, 547, TD 810: Courrier de Patel à Rosario, 1.6.1967.
[48] Michel Christian, 'Der Nord-Süd Konflikt und die "neue internationale Arbeitsteilung" in den 1970er Jahren: UNIDO, UNCTAD und die Vorgeschichte unserer "Globalisierung"', in *Ungleichheiten diskutieren. Der Nord-Süd Konflikt in den internationalen Beziehungen nach 1945*, ed. Frank Reichherzer, Jürgen Dinkel, and Steffen Fiebrig (Oldenbourg: Degruyter, 2020), 173.
[49] UNCTAD Archives, ARR 40/1929, 546, TD 804: Trade and Development Board, 27 March 1969–22 November 1988.

countries since 1969.[50] The attendance of these consultations at UNIDO was also high. It may have been facilitated by the fact that UNIDO was based in Vienna, a city that seemed geographically but also culturally closer to Eastern Europe than Geneva where UNCTAD had its headquarters.

Another way of investing in international organizations was to have nationals among their staffs. The Eastern Bloc countries found themselves in a paradoxical situation. On several occasions, their representatives asked UNIDO to hire more of their nationals, including 'in higher positions'.[51] But despite this marked interest, it must be noted that they had little weight in the staff of the international organizations, with the exception of the Soviet Union, whose participation increased markedly in the 1960s and 1970s, as did that of other Western countries such as Great Britain and the FRG (see Table 8.2). On the other hand, the participation of Eastern European countries remained stable, more or less the same than countries such as Pakistan, Peru, Haiti, Austria and Brazil. It should be noted, however, that both UNCTAD and UNIDO were not autonomous UN agencies but 'subsidiary organizations'. This meant that the recruitment of their staff according to their geographical origin was decided not by their General Secretary but by the UN General Assembly and by its Economic and Social Council (ECOSOC).

In the UNCTAD Secretariat or in UNIDO, nationals from Eastern European countries had a specific kind of career compared to national from other countries. In

Table 8.2 Figures of UN personnel (including UNCAD's and UNIDO's) by national origins in 1963 and in 1977[52]

	1963	1977
USA	1781	1778
Soviet Union	163	476
FRG	7	106
Great Britain	385	851
Bulgaria	7	11
Hungary	11	13
Czechoslovakia	24	21
Poland	32	39
Romania	4	18
Yugoslavia	21	39
GDR	0	10

[50] UNCTAD Archives, TD/B/1061: *Consultative machinery for bilateral and multilateral consultations among countries having different economic and social systems*, 11 June 1985.
[51] UNIDO Archives, ID/OR 340 CZE: *Note for the File*, 21 April 1976.
[52] Figures found in *UN List of Staffs* for corresponding years.

the division for Trade with socialist countries, which operated in UNCTAD between 1966 and 1990,[53] nationals from the West (Finland and Austria) and the South (Algeria, Pakistan, Colombia) most often had ministerial or academic experience which they left behind to embark on a new career as international civil servants. They stayed years in office, often experiencing a gradual promotion within the same division. In contrast, Eastern European nationals were only seconded from their home institution, whether it be a ministry, a division of the Central Committee or a scientific institution. They spent three to seven years in the same position without promotion before returning to their home country. Only then did they take up a position of higher rank. This was illustrated by the Soviet researcher Ivan Ivanov, who worked for UNCTAD between 1967 and 1970 before becoming head of the Division for American and Canadian Studies of the Soviet Union Academy of Sciences in the 1970s. However, his contacts with UNCTAD were not broken as he produced two studies for UNCTAD in 1985 and 1988 and was even hired as a consultant in 1987.[54] Similarly, the Director of the Division of American and Canadian Studies of the Soviet Union Academy of Sciences was also a member of UNCTAD. Similarly, the director of the Division for Trade with Socialist Countries between 1971 and 1975, the Soviet citizen Nikolai Pankine, later became head of the Department for International Economic Organisations in the Ministry of Trade of the Soviet Union.[55] As in the previous case, the division he headed did not lose contact with him and turned to him to help draft a study in 1981. The same phenomenon can be observed at UNIDO. Employed in UNIDO's Metallurgical Industries Section between 1969 and 1972, the Bulgarian Christo Popov became Minister of Foreign Trade in the 1980s, a position in which he regularly worked with the UNIDO services, which he knew well[56].

The specificity of these careers can be explained for different reasons. The idea of a freely chosen international career did not have the same meaning in the West as in the East. There was no question of an individual choosing an international career on his or her own, leaving his or her home institution behind. Governments also seemed to maintain a regular rotation of functions, perhaps because of a shortage of specialists, but also because they feared that privileged relationships would be formed in places far from the central power and, moreover, located in Western countries. Another widespread fear of Eastern Bloc governments (which can be seen in cultural exchanges or sports competitions) was defection and the move to the West, which had to be prevented. This was the main function of the unofficial political police informers in the international organizations.[57] They certainly provided relevant information on the evolution of the work of the organization where they worked, but largely duplicating that of the traditional diplomatic reports. The authorities, on the other hand, seemed more interested in information on the individual behaviour of their nationals, their purchases, their outings and their possible reflections in private.

---

[53] That study includes 24 career paths in the TRADSOC division.
[54] UNCTAD Archives, ARR 40/1929, 550, TD 843/3: Memorandum, 11 March 1987.
[55] UNCTAD Archives, ARR 40/1929, 547, TD 806/3: Davydov à Pankin, 21 October 1987.
[56] ID BUL 131/1: Popov à Khane, 18 February 1985, 245, Popov à Judt, 5 September 1985, 201.
[57] As evidenced by an informant's file of the East German Staatssicherheit in UNCTAD (see BStU, 11045/91: Ingrid Koch, I thank Sandrine Kott who made that document available for me).

In spite of the control of the Eastern European states over their citizens, the latter nevertheless comply fully with their role as international officials. In the Division for Trade with socialist countries, there was never any mention of 'socialism' as a superior model of society to 'capitalism', or even of any competition between the two. Eastern Bloc nationals behaved as loyal civil servants and adopted the corresponding codes. English was used in all circumstances, even when the Russian-speaking division director addressed the CMEA headquarters in Moscow, and when his interlocutor – an East German employee of the CMEA – addressed him in Russian as 'comrade' ('tovaritch'), he responded in English by calling her 'Mrs'. Nationals from the Eastern Bloc countries thus had to appropriate codes and norms that were very different from their home institutions. As they moved from the national to the international stage, they had to learn to take on their different roles.

Conclusion

In a process that developed over time, UN organizations became relevant to Eastern Bloc countries for three main reasons. First, UN organizations became a forum those countries could use to stage the East-West conflict along new lines, presenting themselves as a socialist model of development to the developing countries. Second, they also were institutions where Eastern Bloc countries sought to defend their common practical interest as 'socialist countries'. The debates were not only about discourses but also about embargo lifting, development of East-West trade and transfer of technologies. Third, those countries sought to place their personnel in strategic positions within UN organizations. By doing so, they developed an original international culture over time, distinct from other countries.

9

Sandinista internationalism: The Nicaraguan revolution and the global Cold War

Mateo Jarquín

Introduction

Anastasio Somoza knew his fate had been sealed on 23 June 1979. He was safe in his hilltop bunker overlooking the Nicaraguan capital of Managua; the rebels were still weeks away. And yet the 54-year-old ruler – heir to a decades-old dynastic dictatorship – drafted his resignation letter anyway, to be signed and tendered at an appropriate later date.[1] Earlier that day, member countries at the Organization of American States (OAS) overwhelmingly voted in favour of a resolution calling on him to step down and transfer power to a provisional government – which was based at the time in neighbouring Costa Rica – led by the *Frente Sandinista de Liberación Nacional* (FSLN). Sandinista columns would march on Managua a month later, but this had been, to a significant extent, a 'diplomatic revolution'.[2]

Supranational organizations, made up entirely of non-socialist governments, played a decisive role in the first and only seizure of state power by the Latin American armed Left since the Cuban Revolution. This facet of the Sandinistas' victory raises questions about the nature of their revolutionary project. How did the FSLN's left-wing internationalism commingle with so-called 'liberal internationalism'? And how did the encounter between the two shape Nicaragua's revolutionary process?

This chapter explores multiple dimensions of Sandinista internationalism. Important displays of moderation notwithstanding, the Sandinista Front's upper echelon was strongly influenced by Marxism-Leninism. Local and regional circumstances made a transition to socialism unfeasible in the short- and medium run. But the nine *comandantes* of the FSLN National Directorate believed that, in the long run, alignment

---

[1] Somoza describes drafting his resignation letter in his memoir; see Anastasio Somoza and Jack Cox, *Nicaragua Betrayed* (Boston: Western Islands, 1981), 266.
[2] Diplomatic historian Matthew Connelly helped popularize the term in his study of Algeria's *Front de Libération Nationale* (FLN), which declared Algerian independence and won recognition from the international community long before it lacked the military means to control any of the territory they claimed. See Connelly, *A Diplomatic Revolution: Algeria's Fight for Independence and the Origins of the Post-Cold War Era* (London and New York: Oxford University Press, 2002).

with the Soviet bloc – and confrontation with the United States – was as desirable as it was inevitable. Moreover, for both strategic and ideological reasons they reasoned that it would be difficult to build socialism in Nicaragua without promoting revolutions in neighbouring countries such as El Salvador. Like other Cold War-era national liberation movements, the Sandinista leadership considered itself part of a 'global struggle of the peoples against imperialism'.[3] Shortly after Somoza's ouster, FSLN leader and co-founder Tomás Borge said as much: 'this revolution goes beyond our borders.'[4]

The Sandinista Revolution indeed did transcend Nicaragua, albeit not in the way Borge imagined. At every phase of the revolutionary process – insurrection, consolidation in power and loss of state control – engagement with the West and liberal international institutions proved critical. Formal and informal links with social-democratic parties in Western Europe and Latin America were of comparable importance to the understandings and mutual expectations they built with armed leftist organizations and communist parties.[5] In seizing state power and defending their project from the interventionist onslaught of the US Reagan administration, the Sandinistas cultivated support from the socialist camp by appealing to the imaginary of world revolution as well as the 'nationalist internationalism' of Third World solidarity.[6] The containment of the US-backed *Contras* would have been unimaginable without military advice and assistance from Cuba, the Soviet Union and other socialist partners. But the Revolution's survival also depended on appeals made within the confines of so-called liberal internationalism; the Nicaraguan government championed supranational political structures as avenues towards diplomatic and multilateral solutions, sought inclusion in the inter-American system – where the United States was hegemonic – and demanded Washington abide by the rules of the hemispheric order it helped write. This diplomatic theatre offered Sandinista Nicaragua something that the Soviet bloc could not provide and revolutionary Cuba had previously been denied at great cost: legitimacy in the eyes of regional governments.

By analysing its movements within the international arena, scholars can better understand a revolutionary project's defining themes and contradictions. Alejandro Bendaña – Secretary General of the Foreign Relations Ministry under the Sandinista Revolution – wrote in 1980 that 'the truism that a nation's foreign policy is the extension of its domestic policy applies to Nicaragua'.[7] It was also an extension of the

---

[3] Jaime Wheelock Román, interview with Mónica Baltodano, *Memorias de la Lucha Sandinista* (Managua: Fundación Rosa Luxemburgo, August 2018).

[4] Interior Minister Tomás Borge spoke in these terms in a speech at the Revolution's second anniversary celebrations on 19 July 1981. US State Department officials subsequently cited the statement as evidence that the Nicaraguan Revolution was an expansionist threat which required containment: The State Department actually titled one of its key reports to Congress 'Revolution beyond Our Borders: Sandinista Intervention in Central America,' September 1985, Digital National Security Archive (Proquest ID: 1679104736).

[5] For operating definitions of socialist and communist internationalism, see Talbot Imlay, *The Practice of Socialist Internationalism: European Socialists and International Politics, 1914–1960* (London and New York: Oxford University Press, 2018).

[6] Vijay Prashad describes Third Worldism as a form of 'nationalist internationalism', in *The Darker Nations: A People's History of the Third World* (New York: New Press, 2008).

[7] Alejandro Bendaña, 'The Foreign Policy of the Sandinista Revolution', in *Nicaragua in Revolution*, ed. Thomas W. Walker (New York: Praeger, 1982), 326.

Revolution's main dilemma, which saw the radical, ideological vision of the Sandinista National Directorate clash against the promises of liberalism and pragmatism they made to non-leftist members of the revolutionary coalition that triumphed in 1979. The question of the revolution's ultimate purpose and direction played out visibly in the revolutionary government's international relations. New archives in Latin America, Western Europe and the Eastern Bloc have fed scholarship that explains how Nicaragua fit within a global picture encompassing much more than the oft-studied domain of US foreign policy; new oral history interviews with FSLN commanders and diplomats, relied upon heavily in this essay, show how the Sandinistas themselves understood their position within the international arena.

The rise and fall of the Sandinista Revolution exposed the various menu options that revolutionary movements encountered in the Cold War international arena – as well as the associated price tags. Once in power, the FSLN could access decisive military assistance from the socialist camp to beat back counter-revolutionaries and their own international sponsors. But Nicaragua's position in a traditional US sphere of influence meant such aid was limited. Sandinista leaders therefore relied increasingly on backing from traditional American allies in Latin America and Western Europe who, for the most part, opposed President Ronald Reagan's support for anti-FSLN rebels known as the *Contra*. These shifts, in turn, saw Nicaraguan leaders make tactical concessions – particularly with regards to the liberalization of their political system – that accumulated over time and tended to become permanent features of their revolution. The Nicaraguan Revolution's twists and turns in the international arena help explain its unexpected final act: the Sandinistas ultimately defended their socialist project from US-backed military threats, only to be undone by Nicaraguan voters in liberal-democratic elections.

International origins of the Sandinista Revolution

Few students of the Latin American Left would dispute the importance of the Sandinista Front and their political project – the 'last social revolution of the twentieth century', as one historian recently put it.[8] Questions remain, nonetheless, about the nature and orientation of the Nicaraguan Revolution. Was it fundamentally a liberal, nationalist enterprise with redistributive characteristics, one easily distinguishable from the Cuban variant of 'Real Socialism?' Or was it primarily a popular, radical and socialist project?[9] Former participants and revolutionary leaders grapple with these questions

---

[8] Jeffrey Gould, interview in *Jacobin*, 19 July 2021.
[9] On the question of a transition to socialism in Nicaragua (or lackthereof), Argentine social scientist Carlos Vilas helped lead the debate in the 1980s; see 'Sobre la estrategia económica de la Revolución Sandinista', *Desarrollo Económico* 26, no. 101 (1986): 121–42 and 'El impacto de la transición revolucionaria en las clases populares: La clase obrera en la revolución Sandinista', *Cuadernos Políticos* 48 (1986): 92–114. For a more recent analysis, see Ileana Rodríguez, 'Transición o restauración: filosofías radicales y liberales. ¿Qué tipo de revolución era la Revolución Sandinista', in *La prosa de la contra-insurgencia: 'Lo político' durante la restauración neoliberal en Nicaragua* (Chapel Hill: University of North Carolina Press, 2019), 36–57.

even today.[10] A brief survey of the Sandinista Revolution's origins – especially one that emphasizes their overlap with the global Cold War – can help reconcile these competing perspectives.

In its earliest, embryonic form, the Sandinista National Liberation Front descended from the Nicaraguan Socialist Party (PSN) – the country's Moscow-line communist party. Carlos Fonseca, FSLN talisman from the movement's founding until his death in 1976, joined the PSN as a high school student in the mid-1950s. At the time, the Somoza family's ruling Liberal Party had successfully employed power-sharing agreements to co-opt or neutralize the opposition Conservative Party. In Nicaragua, as in many Latin American countries in this period, communist militancy was one of the few options available for young people who desired real change (some PSN militants, such as FSLN founder Tomás Borge, started off as disillusioned Conservatives).[11] The ultimate model of progress was the USSR; Henry Ruiz, who would later rise to the upper echelon of the Sandinista military command structure, recalled that as a young, PSN-sympathizing teenager he came to admire 'Laika, Sputnik, science, etc. – that whole world that the organized workers spoke so highly of'.[12] The programme, it followed, was the one recommended by Communist Party of the Soviet Union (CPSU): the conditions for a socialist transition in poor countries like Nicaragua were light years away, and therefore gradualism – rather than revolution – was recommended. Declassified documents from KGB archives suggest that Soviet officials may have viewed Fonseca and Borge as intelligence assets in the 1950s.[13]

The Cuban Revolution, however, changed everything for the would-be Sandinistas. The success of Fidel Castro's 19 July Movement in 1959 dramatically enhanced the appeal of armed insurrections in Latin America. In Nicaragua it also produced a concomitant disenchantment with the Nicaraguan Socialist Party, which Fonseca abandoned shortly thereafter. Though still committed to Marxism-Leninism as a tool for diagnosing his country's ills – poverty, inequality, dependence on the United States – a Caribbean example now replaced a Eurasian one. In the first half of the 1960s, Fonseca and other Nicaraguan radicals spent much of their time between Cuba and other countries – including neighbouring Honduras – dreaming up plans to emulate the Cuban experience and burning through potential names for their voluntarist revolutionary movement: *Movimiento Nueva Nicaragua* (MNN) and *Frente Interno de Resistencia* (FIR) were early contenders.[14] Victor Tirado López, a Mexican Communist Party militant who joined the Nicaraguans in these formative years, admits that nobody remembers the day or place when they settled on the final formula: *Frente Sandinista de Liberación Nacional*.[15]

---

[10] See proceedings from the conference *Nicaragua 1979 – 2019: The Sandinista Revolution after 40 Years*, held at Brown University, Providence, RI, 2–4 May 2019, https://watson.brown.edu/events/2019/conference-nicaragua-1979-2019-sandinista-revolution-after-40-years.

[11] On Fonseca's student years, see Matilde Zimmerman, *Sandinista: Carlos Fonseca and the Nicaraguan Revolution* (Durham, NC: Duke University Press, 2001), 37–49.

[12] Henry Ruíz, interview with Mónica Baltodano, *Memorias de la Lucha Sandinista,* August 2009.

[13] Christopher Andrew and Vasili Mitrokhin, *The World Was Going Our Way: The KGB and the Battle for the Third World* (New York: Basic Books, 2005), 41.

[14] Zimmerman, *Sandinista: Carlos Fonseca and the Nicaraguan Revolution*, 72.

[15] Victor Tirado López, interview with Mónica Baltodano, *Memorias de la Lucha Sandinista,* August 1999.

From the beginning, the FSLN cross-fertilized with revolutionary movements across the so-called Third World. The name bore the obvious inspiration of the *fronts de libération nationale* fighting in Algeria and Vietnam. But direct connections were also established. Sandinista cadres in the 1960s linked up with the secular, Marxist branches of the Palestine Liberation Organization, which provided access to training in Lebanon in exchange for Nicaraguan participation in some military operations.[16] Some, including Carlos Fonseca, went as far as North Korea for training. Cuba remained the hub, as well as the main source of inspiration, throughout the FSLN's adolescence. Throughout the 1960s, the heyday of Cuban efforts to export revolution in Latin America, Havana trained Sandinista cadres and provided weapons for each of their insurrectionary operations.[17]

However, attempts to emulate Ernesto 'Che' Guevara's *foco* strategies failed. Hugo Torres, another guerilla chief, recalls that 'the first shots at Río Coco y Bocay [an early incursion] were barely heard by anyone'.[18] Sandinista operatives – the vast majority of whom came from the cities – struggled to build an organic support base among the peasantry in the country's central highlands. After a crushing defeat by National Guard forces in 1967 at the mountain town Pancasán, the FSLN was viewed by the Somoza regime as a nuisance rather than a threat. By the early 1970s, Cuban officials continued to offer refuge for exiled Sandinistas but lost what little interest they previously had in promoting an insurrection in Nicaragua, a country that US policymakers saw as an island of stability in Cold War Latin America. The Soviet KGB, which had condemned the Pancasán operation for its prematurity and disorganization, hardly paid attention at all.[19]

These setbacks forced the Sandinistas to look inwards and outwards in new ways. Some leaders, such as Carlos Fonseca and Eduardo Contreras, revisited the historical experience of their namesake – Augusto César Sandino, who in the 1920s and early 1930s led a guerrilla resistance to US occupation. Of all the strategic and programmatic debates that divided the Sandinista movement in the 1970s, the most important was the question of building alliances with political movements and interest groups outside of the Nicaraguan Left. One faction – the so-called *Terceristas* – began courting notables from the Church, intelligentsia and even the business elite in 1977. Their plan was for a twelve-man bourgeois-elite support group – *el grupo de los doce* – to provide the political front to the armed struggle. The Terceristas therefore reconfigured the enemy and the objective in profound ways. The Somozas, rather than capitalism or US empire, were the target; their immediate overthrow, rather than the inauguration of a transition to socialism, was the main goal. In doing so, they prompted accusations of heresy from the more orthodox *Guerra Popular Propaganda* (GPP) faction, the only wing of the FSLN to preserve even limited contact with the Cubans. But as Tercerista commander

---

[16] Marshall Yurow, 'Evolving Relationships: Nicaragua, Israel, and the Palestinians', *Latin American Perspectives* 49, no. 3 (2019): 149–63.
[17] Gary Prevost, 'Cuba and Nicaragua: A Special Relationship?' *Latin American Perspectives* 17, no. 3 (1990): 121–3.
[18] Hugo Torres, interview with Mónica Baltodano, *Memorias de la Lucha Sandinista*, December 1999.
[19] Andrew and Mitrokhin, *The World Was Going Our Way*, 49–50.

Edén Pastora noted, the incipient construction of a popular front programme in 1977 allowed the Terceristas to connect with non-communist international partners, most notably Venezuelan President Carlos Andrés Pérez and Panamanian military leader Omar Torrijos.[20]

Their impact on the rise of the Sandinistas was tremendous. Pérez, as well as Costa Rican ex-President José Figueres (a foe of the Somoza family dating back to the 1940s), provided the cash necessary for the Terceristas to mount their first armed incursions against the Somoza family in the fall of 1977. Those operations failed, but when spontaneous popular rebellions erupted against Somocista repression in 1978 (something which also caused elite sectors to waver in their complacency with the regime), the voluntarist, popular-front approach put the Terceristas in a position to capitalize. The Costa Rican government began collaborating with Panama, Venezuela and the Sandinistas in the fall of 1978; at this point, Nicaragua's southern neighbour turned into a strategic rearguard for the anti-Somoza insurgents. And along with Mexico, these Latin American governments spearheaded the diplomatic isolation of the Somoza regime. As the Nicaraguan dictatorship descended into violent crisis, these international sponsors increasingly gave legitimacy to the armed solution offered by the Sandinista Front and their growing chorus of allies in civil society, the Church and business sector. Latin American diplomacy also counterbalanced efforts by the US government to seek a negotiated transition that would box out the armed Left by preserving some portion of the National Guard after Somoza's exit.[21]

These foreign actors had both unique and shared reasons for supporting Somoza's military overthrow. Costa Rica, for example, worried that Somoza might invade their territory in order to eliminate the FSLN. Mexico and Venezuela sought to exploit détente to gain regional influence.[22] But as Gerardo Sánchez Natera has explained, they also had a shared interest in moderating the Sandinistas in order to avoid a 'second Cuba' in Central America, an outcome which they felt might lead to greater instability; specifically, in the form of a direct US military invasion similar to the one which took place in the Dominican Republic in 1965.[23] Thus, they tended to reinforce the Terceristas' alliance with liberal parties and the private sector. They also participated directly in plans for a post-Somoza government, including the formulation of the Nicaraguan Revolution's three-pronged programme: political pluralism, mixed economy and non-alignment in international affairs.

Cuba threw its decisive weight behind the project in January 1979. Fidel Castro's involvement helped cement the alliance of disparate factions and further legitimized the Terceristas' broad front strategy. More importantly, they provided the firepower and

---

[20] Edén Pastora, interview with Mónica Baltodano, *Memorias de la Lucha Sandinista*, August 2001.
[21] For a wider discussion of Latin American sponsorship of the Revolution, see Gerardo Sánchez Nateras, 'The Sandinista Revolution and the Limits of the Cold War in Latin America: The Dilemma of Non-intervention during the Nicaraguan Crisis, 1977–78', *Cold War History* 18, no. 2 (2018): 111–29 and Mateo Jarquín, 'A Latin American Revolution: The Sandinistas, the Cold War, and Political Change in the Region, 1977–1990', PhD diss., Harvard University, 2019.
[22] Hal Brands, *Latin America's Cold War* (Cambridge, MA: Harvard University Press, 2012), 175–9.
[23] Sánchez Nateras, 'The Sandinista Revolution and the Limits of the Cold War in Latin America.'

expertise required to wage a conventional military struggle against Somoza's National Guard, which had just been denied military transfers from the US government for the first time. According to Tercerista commander Humberto Ortega, well over 1,000 leftists from across Latin America – including Costa Rica, El Salvador, Colombia, Panama, Argentina and Uruguay – joined the fight in 1979.[24] They answered the call to participate in a global struggle for revolution; in many cases they sought military experience and training in preparation for struggle in their own countries, as historian Victor Figueroa Clark notes of a dozens-strong Chilean contingent.[25]

Remarkably, Cuba's entrance to the fray did not produce an anti-communist backlash in Latin America. Countries increasingly withdrew diplomatic recognition from the Nicaraguan regime as they became convinced that Somoza would not negotiate a peaceful transition. With the exception of Alfredo Stroessner's Paraguay, even the continent's anti-communist dictatorships chose not to oppose the June 1979 OAS resolution calling for his ouster.[26] In order to consolidate this backing, the Sandinista-led Provisional Junta made formal commitments to the OAS: specifically, that it would hold legislative and presidential elections shortly after taking power.[27] Moreover, the Sandinista Front promised to co-govern with its allies, taking up a minority of cabinet posts and even appointing a former National Guardsman as Minister of Defence. These were the prices they paid for alliances with domestic political forces and Latin American countries, who backed their project despite US efforts to find a more agreeable alternative to the Sandinistas.[28]

Engagement in the international arena – the pursuit of both models and alliances – helped define Sandinismo over the decades. It also determined their road to power, which after the collapse of Somoza's National Guard left the Revolution with a looming contradiction: the tension between the National Directorate's long-term strategic plans, which were informed by their Marxist-Leninist inclinations, and the tactical promises of moderation they made to their liberal and centrist allies at home and abroad.

---

[24] See Humberto Ortega's memoir, for his estimates on the number of internationalist fighters who fell under Sandinista command during the insurrection; *Epopeya de la Insurreción* (Managua: Lea Grupo Editorial, 2004), 398.
[25] Victor Figueroa Clark, 'Nicaragua, Chile and the End of the Cold War in Latin America', in *The End of the Cold War and the Third World*, ed. Artemy Kalinovsky and Sergey Radchenko (London: Routledge, 2011), 195.
[26] 'OAS Votes for Ouster of Somoza', *The Washington Post*, 24 June 1979. Having seen their own resolution proposal shot down by a Latin American majority, the United States delegation – seeking to save face and avoid the impression of defeat – ultimately voted for the proposal advanced by the Latin American countries. Notably, several anti-communist dictatorships, including those of Argentina and Brazil, also voted in favour.
[27] In their letter on 12 July 1979, they attached their 'Plan del Gobierno de Reconstrucción Nacional Para Alcanzar la Paz', Sergio Ramírez Papers, Box 60, Folder 11. Specifically, the peace plan promised that the Sandinista army and the remaining sectors of the National Guard (who had agreed to the cease-fire) would join forces in maintaining order, and that the latter's ranks would be allowed to join the new national armed forces.
[28] For an account of US efforts to find a moderate 'third force' to replace Somoza, see Robert Pastor, *Not Condemned to Repetition: The United States and Nicaragua* (Boulder, CO: Westview Press, 2002).

Dualism in FSLN foreign policy

After a brief honeymoon period following Somoza's ouster, the broad revolutionary coalition unraveled and the Sandinista National Directorate – leveraging popular support and firm control over the military – took direct control. A decisive factor in the ensuing civil war was the Reagan administration's policy of destabilizing the FSLN government by training, funding and arming anti-Sandinista sectors (which came to be known as *Contras*). Other tools, including economic sanctions and sabotage operations, were employed in tandem. The scale of indirect US intervention against such a small and impoverished country was remarkable; perhaps even more notable was its ultimate failure to oust the FSLN. In withstanding a multi-layered, multi-front threat, Managua's revolutionary government aggressively took the fight to the international arena. As in the insurrectionary period, both socialist partners and traditional US allies played important roles.

Commander Luís Carrión, member of the National Directorate and key security official from his post as Vice-Minister of the Interior, described the FSLN's preparation for foreign intervention:

> We were convinced that the United States would inevitably try to destroy the Revolution, that this was in its imperialist nature. Very soon we felt the need to develop a defensive strategy with three legs. First, to support the guerillas of Central America – not only for reasons of solidarity but also defensive ones. Second, to establish an alliance with the Soviet Union, because we needed some form of umbrella to protect us from the 'monster'. And third, to create a strong army.[29]

The execution of this strategy exacerbated frictions with the Sandinista Front's erstwhile coalition partners. While the new government was quick to join the Non-Aligned Movement, FSLN delegations to Havana, Moscow and Sofia signalled an intention to lean to one side. Cuban advisers helped Nicaragua organize the largest standing army in Central America. And by assisting El Salvador's Farabundo Martí National Liberation Front, the leadership of which was headquartered in Managua, the Sandinistas reneged on explicit promises made to US President Jimmy Carter.[30] For the domestic partners who began breaking with the government in 1980, these actions confirmed suspicions that the FSLN was willing to use its relative strength to delay elections, nationalize the economy and generally take the revolution in a more radical direction.

In practice, Sandinista foreign policy balanced reliance on the socialist camp with crucial partnerships in Western Europe, Latin America and other parts of the Global

---

[29] Luis Carrión Cruz, '40 Años de la Revolución Nicaragüense: ¿Pudo haber sido de otra manera?' *Envío* 448 (July 2019).
[30] 'Memorandum of Conversation – Summary of the President's Meeting with Members of the Nicaraguan Junta,' Washington, 24 September 1979, *Foreign Relations of the United States: Volume XV*, 743–4.

South. Early on, most direct foreign aid and credit flowed from Latin American and Western countries (including the United States, up until early 1981).[31] Arab states also lent a helping hand; the Sandinistas, seeking broad voting support in the United Nations General Assembly, launched a flurry of diplomatic activity in the decolonized world. The organizational structure of revolution's foreign policy apparatus reflected a dual approach to foreign relations. As a rough rule, the FSLN's Department of International Relations took care of party-to-party relations with socialist countries and fraternal movements in Latin America. The formal foreign policy apparatus – the Foreign Relations and Foreign Commerce ministries – handled the United States, Latin America and Western Europe.

Support from the Soviet Union and Cuba – as well as other partners such as Libya, Algeria, Bulgaria and East Germany – was essential in the security sphere. Hundreds of Cuban advisers helped accomplish the difficult task of turning insurrectionary guerrilla columns into a professional military – the Sandinista Popular Army (EPS, by its Spanish acronym) – in the wake of the National Guard's total implosion. Though figures are difficult to come by, a significant number of non-Nicaraguan, internationalist combatants from Latin American countries were wounded and killed in the war.[32] Playing a more indirect but still significant role, Moscow and East European partners supplied military equipment and weapons estimated at hundreds of millions of dollars annually.[33] But there were important limits to their assistance. Soviet leaders were unwilling to risk a direct confrontation with the United States over the Nicaraguan Revolution; they rejected Sandinista requests to place MiG fighter jets in an airfield along Lake Nicaragua. This hesitancy to get involved in Nicaragua grew in parallel to Premier Mikhael Gorbachev's disillusionment with Sandinista mismanagement as well as his growing desire to 'withdraw' the Soviet Union more generally from the game of influence over the Third World.[34]

Socialist camp assistance was enough to help the EPS frustrate the Contra's main military objective, without destroying the insurgency altogether. Rebels managed to sustain a threat that undermined the government's popularity and drained its coffers. But they never attained the capacity to seize and hold a significant urban centre from which their political leadership might declare a provisional government. Still, the Contra's ranks continued to grow over the course of the decade. A virtual stalemate emerged; one which the Sandinista leadership doubted

---

[31] 'Nicaraguan Emergency Relief Assistance [Sources, Types, Amounts, and Descriptions of Relief Efforts]', U.S. Department of State Bureau of Inter-American Affairs, 19 October 1979, Digital National Security Archive (ProQuest ID: 1679047013).

[32] A particularly well-known case of internationalist combatants was that of the Simón Bolívar Brigade; see Jaime Ortega Reyna, '¿Revolución en la Revolución? La brigada Simón Bolívar en la Revolución Nicaragüense', *Tzintzun Revista de estudios históricos* 71 (2020): 149–71.

[33] United States Department of Defense, 'Soviet Bloc Military Equipment Supplied to Nicaragua (July 1979–December 1988)', 3. Non-classified report c. February 1989, https://www.brown.edu/Research/Understanding_the_Iran_Contra_Affair/documents/d-nic-4.pdf.

[34] Radoslav Yordanov, 'Outfoxing the Eagle: Soviet, East European and Cuban Involvement in Nicaragua in the 1980s', *Journal of Contemporary History* 55, no. 4 (2019): 871–92. On the 'Gorbachev withdrawal,' see Arne Westad, *The Global Cold War: Third World Interventions and the Making of Our Times* (London and New York: Oxford University Press, 2005), 364–95.

it could sustain, even as the 1986 Iran-Contra scandal also called their opponents' long-term capabilities into question.

Thankfully for Nicaragua's revolutionary government, Reagan's anti-Sandinista belligerence was the cause of much concern for US allies in Western Europe and Latin America. The former saw Central America as part of its efforts to save what little was left of détente from the 1970s. Social-democratic heads of state like Greece's Andreas Papandreou and Sweden's Olof Palme incurred the ire of American diplomats by offering military aid to the FSLN. Along with centre-left leaders in Spain, Austria, Italy and France, they argued that European aid to the Sandinistas was necessary in order to crowd out investment from Cuba and the Soviet Union; US hostility, in their view, had the opposite effect of pushing Nicaragua into the arms of the Eastern Bloc, increasing the risk of a direct East-West confrontation in the Central American powder keg.[35]

European diplomacy helped Latin American countries confront Reagan's Contra policy. Mexico and Venezuela were similarly interested in moderating the Sandinista government and reducing the risk of superpower intervention in their backyards.[36] They therefore led regional efforts to support Managua's government and were the first to denounce US-backed Contra attacks, calling instead for a multilateral, negotiated solution. To that end, they initiated – along with Panama and Colombia – the so-called Contadora Peace Process (named for the Panamanian island where the countries' foreign ministers first met), which called for the end of foreign intervention in Central America as a first step towards peace negotiations between its countries. As more South American countries transitioned from military dictatorships to democratic rule (some of which, including Argentina, had collaborated with US intervention in Central America), the Latin American consensus against the Contra programme grew. This collective effort to restrain US unilateralism represented a historically unique exercise in regional autonomy.[37]

Non-state actors also helped mitigate the consequences of the East-West conflict in Central America. The Socialist International – particularly leaders Willy Brandt, from West Germany, and Carlos Andrés Pérez, from Venezuela – helped articulate Latin American and European diplomatic initiatives. In parallel to the anti-nuclear movement which gained force in the 1980s, Central America solidarity movements in the United States and Western Europe helped limit public support for the Contra programme. The Sandinista government explicitly appealed to them by exploiting the 'David vs Goliath' narrative that US intervention had facilitated.[38] Finally, the Nicaraguan government made its presence felt in international institutions, perfecting the use of such bodies for the denunciation of US aggression. Most famously, they successfully sued the United States at the International Court of Justice (ICJ), which in 1986 ruled that the United States had violated international law by supporting the Contras and launching other

---

[35] Eline van Ommen, 'The Nicaraguan Revolution's Challenge to the Monroe Doctrine: Sandinistas and Western Europe, 1979-1990', *The Americas* 78 (2021): 639–66.
[36] Sánchez Nateras, 'The Sandinista Revolution and the Limits of the Cold War in Latin America'.
[37] Mateo Jarquín, 'The Nicaraguan Question: Contadora and the Latin American Response to U.S. Intervention', *The Americas*, 78, (2021): 581–608.
[38] Hector Perla, 'Heirs of Sandino: The Nicaraguan Revolution and the US-Nicaragua Solidarity Movement', *Latin American Perspectives* 36, no. 6 (2009): 80–100.

operations against Nicaragua. Few countries supported the US position in the suit, signalling Washington's isolation. More importantly, these Nicaraguan victories on the diplomatic front – including the Contadora Process, which affirmed the Sandinista government's 'right to exist' *a priori* – complicated the Reagan administration's efforts to attain congressional and diplomatic approval for its policies.[39]

The survival of the Sandinista government was made possible by dual, complementary foreign policies. Socialist countries provided essential tools but full alignment – of the Cuban sort – was not feasible. Long land borders shared with hostile US allies made military defence more difficult than on a Caribbean island. Countries like Austria and Spain could not send military advisers or helicopters to repel mountain guerrillas, but they could help prevent the Nicaraguan government from acquiring the pariah status that US foreign policy sought. As Somoza's overthrow had demonstrated, it would have been difficult to survive in an international environment which denied the government legitimacy (and legitimized its armed opponents instead). In the 1960s, most Latin American governments agreed with Washington that the Cuban Revolution posed a threat to hemispheric security, lacked legitimacy *a priori*, and that it should be expelled from the Organization of American States. In the 1980s, by contrast, Latin American diplomacy tended to run in the opposite direction, normalizing the existence of the Sandinista Revolution and rejecting certain US Cold War formulations. The Latin American Cold War had clearly changed in the interim.

Multilateral peace agreements and the end of the Revolution

By 1986, the Sandinista government was still standing, albeit on unstable ground. Two key realities constrained the Nicaraguan revolutionary process. First, four years of armed conflict had sapped the Sandinista Front's popular support and consumed enormous resources, derailing most reform programmes. 'By that point the human and economic fatigue in Nicaragua was brutal', Carrión recalls.[40] Second, the declining 'credibility of the communist global project as an alternative to liberal capitalism', as Silvio Pons put it, dimmed the prospects of continued external support for the war effort.[41] Julio López Campos, head of the FSLN's Department of International Relations, recalls a striking conversation with the Soviet leadership in 1985:

> ... Gorbachev urged [President Daniel] Ortega not to do anything that would further provoke North American hostility, not to skip stages, to maintain a mixed economy with room for the private sector, to maintain political pluralism ... What Gorbachev did not say was perhaps the most important message. He was on our side, but he did not commit to the war effort.[42]

---

[39] Cynthia Arnson, 'Contadora and the US Congress', in *Contadora and the Diplomacy of Peace in Central America* (New York, Abingdon and Oxfordshire: Routledge, 1987), 123–41.

[40] Carrión Cruz, '40 Años de la Revolución Nicaragüense: ¿Pudo haber sido de otra manera?'

[41] Silvio Pons, 'The History of Communism and the Global History of the Twentieth Century', in *The Cambridge History of Communism* (London and New York: Cambridge University Press, 2017), 20–3.

[42] Julio López Campos, 'Nicaragua y Afganistán: intereses globales y efectos colaterales', *Confidencial*, 30 August 2021.

As a military victory became less viable, the relative significance of socialist partners waned. Concomitantly, Latin American and European countries pushing a multilateral, negotiated solution rose to play a decisive role in the Nicaraguan Revolution's final stages.

While Contadora failed to produce a peace settlement in Nicaragua, it laid the groundwork for another, successful agreement negotiated at the Central American level. After definitively rejecting the Latin American peace process in 1986, Central America's presidents gathered in Guatemala to discuss their own multilateral solution. The August 1987 Esquipulas Accords mandated that Central American governments cease all efforts to support rebels in neighbouring countries. It also required them to stop hosting foreign bases on their soil. Taken together, these measures effectively prohibited CIA-led Contra operations in Honduras and Costa Rica; they also saw Central American neighbours reaffirm the *de facto* and *de jure* legitimacy of Nicaragua's revolutionary government. The plan, which drew heavily from the Contadora draft treaties' emphasis on the principle of non-intervention, was championed by civilian leaders in Costa Rica and Guatemala. But notably, the anti-communist military regimes of Honduras and El Salvador also signed. They, too, were wary of continued civil wars in their countries and stood to make potential gains from the agreement. After all, the treaty's provisions also required the FSLN to abandon support for Salvadoran guerrillas' effort to seize power with arms.[43]

In return for these non-aggression measures, the beleaguered government in Managua committed to making serious concessions with respect to its internal opponents. While the Guatemalan and Salvadoran governments made promises to hold talks with leftist guerrillas and eventually allow them to participate in elections, the Sandinista Front opened up a dialogue with opposition parties, brokered a cease-fire with US-backed Contra leaders, and eventually invited both to participate in a liberalized political system. These policies marked a departure from previous FSLN positions. Sandinista leaders, emphasizing the primacy of participatory forms of democracy (and, more generally, democratizing society along socioeconomic lines), had typically brushed aside the notion that representative elections should be a prerequisite for legitimacy in the international arena. 'Don't forget that in the United States', Tomás Borge told a North American journalist in 1983, 'there were eight years between the triumph of your revolution and your first elected President'. Borge and others explained that their revolutionary model valued political pluralism, so long as the Sandinista project's future was not called into question; those aligned with imperialist forces who would 'destroy the Revolution' would never be allowed to participate in the political system.[44] The reforms wrought in the wake of Esquipulas therefore led to much consternation within the Sandinista Front's General Assembly, where some wondered if it was truly worth diluting the revolutionary project through concessions that were 'contradictory to the revolutionary process'.[45]

[43] For a close account of the process, see the memoir of Guido Fernández, a close advisor of Costa Rican president Oscar Arias: *El desafío de la paz en Centroamérica* (San José: Editorial Costa Rica, 1989).
[44] Tomás Borge, interview in *Playboy*, 'Sandinistas: The Playboy Interview', September 1983.
[45] Presidencia de la República de Nicaragua, 'Resúmen de conclusiones de la coyuntura externa (Los resultados de Esquipulas II)', Managua, 29 July 1988, Archivo Nacional de Costa Rica, Fondo: Presidencia.

These trade-offs were a recurring theme in the Sandinista Revolution. As historian Eline van Ommen has written, 'the Sandinistas' campaign to challenge US hegemony in Central America through a pragmatic outreach to Western Europe was largely successful, but it came at a cost'. The same applied to Central American and Latin American efforts to counterbalance the Contra programme and help the Nicaraguan Revolution exist within the US-dominated inter-American system. Arguably, these actors placed more conditions on support to the Sandinistas than Cuba or the Warsaw Pact countries.[46] Indeed, the Soviet government – unwilling and unable to provide a long-term military alternative – consistently encouraged Nicaraguan participation in multilateral peace negotiations. Those agreements, Jaime Wheelock later explained, saw the Sandinistas implement democratizing reforms as tactical concessions. But because those tactical concessions were central to international dynamics that lent legitimacy to the regime and therefore shielded it from outside intervention, democracy became 'an essential component of the revolution'.[47] 'For the Nicaraguan Revolution to survive', van Ommen astutely notes, 'it had to evolve and give in to the demands of its critics'.[48]

Indeed, the only likely alternative to these painful concessions was violent overthrow. In signing Esquipulas, the Sandinista Front won legitimacy for itself and denied it to its armed opponents. As the government re-opened newspapers, freed political prisoners and reformed the electoral system, civilian opposition leaders slowly distanced themselves from the military wing of the Contra. The agreement also compromised the Contra's lifelines; Esquipulas fatally undermined the Reagan administration's efforts to secure renewed congressional support for continued military aid to the anti-Sandinista insurgents. By the time the 1990 elections rolled around, Costa Rica had expelled Contra leaders from its territories and Honduras had taken steps to do the same. The threat was not eliminated altogether; the government in Washington, now led by President George H.W. Bush, refused to unilaterally swear off support for armed counter-revolution in Nicaragua. But the chances of a direct US invasion, as well as the immediate danger posed by foreign-backed insurgents, were lower than ever. The Contadora countries, various European actors, the OAS and UN General Secretariat all supported Esquipulas and helped verify that its measures were being implemented; several signed on to observe the 1990 elections, ensuring confidence in the results on all sides.

Sandinista leaders went along with the agreement because they were convinced that their candidate, Commander Daniel Ortega, would win a fair contest, ensuring the Revolution's survival through peaceful means. Alas, this did not turn out to be the case. The opposition candidate – Violeta Chamorro de Barrios, a former member of the original 1979 Junta – defeated FSLN candidate Ortega 55 to 41 per cent. After a very brief internal debate, the FSLN leadership recognized the results, thereby becoming the first socialist revolutionary government to peacefully transfer power via elections after having seized it by armed force. This was not the outcome they had expected. They were

---

[46] See previously cited articles by Yordanov and Figueroa Clark.
[47] Jaime Wheelock, 'Revolution and Democratic Transition in Nicaragua, in *Democratic Transitions in Central America*, ed. Jorge Domínguez and Marc Lindenberg (Gainesville, FL: University of Florida Press, 1997), 74.
[48] Eline van Ommen, 'The Nicaraguan Revolution's Challenge to the Monroe Doctrine'.

not violently overthrown by US marines or their proxy counter-revolutionaries. And yet, the Revolution had still fallen. Sandinista leaders were left to console themselves with the hope that they might press their agenda through other, constitutional means in a new era. The Latin America of the 1990s, where most countries were governed by civilian liberal democracies, was a far cry from the Cold War world of anti-communist military dictatorships in which they had been forged.

Casting judgements about this transition is far from easy. Some Sandinista sympathizers inevitably saw the electoral result as the success of US intervention by other means. Though most of Washington, D.C. quickly forgot about Nicaragua, the Sandinistas' fall from power did feed into what historian Arne Westad calls America's 'delusion of victory' after the Cold War.[49] Indeed, the outcome obscured the constraints and difficulties that US policy had encountered. The United States enjoyed exceptional status throughout the Nicaraguan crisis – so much so that it consistently reserved the right to ignore the spirit and letter of the supranational, rules-based order it would pretend to lead and universalize in the 1990s – but, when confronted with adverse multipolar dynamics, was not uniquely influential enough to direct events in Central America – a traditionally American sphere of influence. And contrary to what Reagan hardliners had anticipated, the FSLN remained a powerful force in Nicaraguan politics in the 1990s and early 2000s. In 2006, Daniel Ortega even returned to the presidency. By then, the Sandinista Front was hardly recognizable from the movement which emerged in the 1960s or the organization that governed in the 1980s. The need to adapt to a new domestic and international context – neoliberalism and electoral democracy – saw the Sandinista Front, now hegemonized by the Ortega family, gradually transform into a Christian-conservative political machine that abandoned efforts to transform Nicaragua's socioeconomic structure. The ideological metamorphosis deepened as President Ortega and his wife, Vice President Rosario Murillo, worked to consolidate authoritarian rule and reverse the brief transition to democracy brought about, in part, by the Sandinista Revolution.[50] The twists and turns of the Sandinista movement in the twenty-first century era further underscore the need to study the contradictions this project faced during its earlier navigation of the global Cold War.

Conclusion

Like the Revolution itself, the Sandinistas' relationship with the world was many things at once. The dream of building one, two, three, many Vietnams, in natural partnership with established socialist governments and movements, fed both the FSLN imaginary and contributed to its rise to power in 1979. But the Nicaraguan revolutionary project was also framed by other concerns in international politics, from Latin American desires for regional sovereignty to European anxieties about waning détente. Both

---

[49] Odd Arne Westad, 'The Cold War and America's Delusion of Victory,' *The New York Times*, 28 August 2017.
[50] Gioconda Belli, 'How Nicaragua's Daniel Ortega Became a Tyrant', *Foreign Affairs*, 24 August 2018.

axes help explain the revolution's survival in a complicated Cold War environment. They also shed light on the revolution's hybrid tendencies, as well as its contradictory outcome in 1990.

The Nicaraguan case typified the unique constraints that Latin American leftists encountered when navigating the Cold War international arena.[51] Their region was squarely part of the US sphere of influence – full-fledged Soviet alignment was out of the question, especially after the Cuban Revolution and the 1962 Missile Crisis. But there were opportunities, too. Latin American elites of all ideological persuasions were wary of the long history of US intervention in the region. As the hemisphere's countries transformed, with growing numbers transitioning from military dictatorships towards civilian-led electoral democracies, so did the relationship with the United States; regional elites grew increasingly tired of the sort of pressure policies which had ultimately failed in Cuba. Their efforts to collectively manage US intervention in Nicaragua, as with other aspects of the Sandinista story, demonstrate the complexity of Cold War alliances. With that being said, the legitimacy won as a result did not come free to the Sandinistas, who had to modulate core features of their project in order to ride the tailwinds of these favourable international trends. The international history of the Sandinista Revolution therefore indicates contradictions facing the Latin American Left more widely in the twilight years of the Cold War. The collapse of this international system in the late 1980s provided opportunities for leftist participation in mainstream politics, but also new constraints and rules of the game that would define the projects of Venezuelan leader Hugo Chávez and a 'pink tide' of left-wing electoral movements a decade later.

Beyond Latin America, the Sandinistas also illustrate the risks and opportunities that national liberation movements more generally encountered within the global confrontation between capitalism and communism. As numerous recent histories of the Cold War in the Third World have noted, political actors in Asia, Africa and Latin America – including socialist movements – sometimes reaped benefits from the bipolar system.[52] Whether or not those benefits outweighed the costs varies widely by case. One thing, though, is certain: movements such as the Sandinista Front, far from being its passive subjects, were active belligerents in the Cold War – in all of its dimensions.

---

[51] See *Latin America and the Global Cold War*, ed. Thomas Field, Stella Krepp, and Vanni Pettina (Chapel Hill: University of North Carolina Press, 2020).

[52] See, for instance, the essays in *The Cold War in the Third World*, ed. Robert McMahon (London and New York: Oxford University Press, 2013).

10

The Socialist International and human rights

Michele Di Donato

Introduction

The past two decades have witnessed an explosion of historical research on human rights.¹ A sophisticated and diverse body of work has emerged, which has investigated the uneven rise of human rights to their current status of 'doxa of our time'.² Strictly connected to the transnational and global turns in historiography, the burgeoning interest in the history of human rights has rapidly resulted in cross-fertilization with different branches of international history, especially with regard to the twentieth century. In this context, scholars have also reflected on the relationship between different conceptions of human rights and some of the most influential political cultures of the twentieth century. We have excellent studies of human rights and communism, conservatism, anticolonial nationalism, neoliberalism – to mention just a few.³ These works show how human rights have been construed in alternative and often competing ways by different actors, as political and ideological battles played out in national and international political arenas. Surprisingly, however, the social democratic approach to human rights hasn't garnered the same level of attention. To date, we still lack

---

¹ For critical literature reviews see Stefan-Ludwig Hoffmann, 'Human Rights and History', *Past and Present* 232, no. 1 (2016): 279–310; Samuel Moyn, 'The End of Human Rights History', *Past and Present* 233, no. 1 (2016): 307–22; Lynn Hunt, 'The Long and the Short of the History of Human Rights', *Past and Present* 233, no. 1 (2016): 323–31. See also Silvia Salvatici, 'I diritti umani: storia e storiografia', *Storica* 23, no. 69 (2017): 7–40.

² Stefan-Ludwig Hoffmann, 'Introduction. Genealogies of Human Rights', in *Human Rights in the Twentieth Century*, ed. Stefan-Ludwig Hoffmann (Cambridge: Cambridge University Press, 2011), 1.

³ See Mark Philip Bradley, 'Human Rights and Communism', in *The Cambridge History of Communism*, vol. 3. *Endgames? Late Communism in Global Perspective, 1968 to the Present*, ed. Juliane Fürst, Silvio Pons and Mark Selden (Cambridge: Cambridge University Press, 2017), 151–77; Ned Richardson-Little, *The Human Rights Dictatorship: Socialism, Global Solidarity and Revolution in East Germany* (Cambridge: Cambridge University Press, 2020); Marco Duranti, *The Conservative Human Rights Revolution: European Identity, Transnational Politics, and the Origins of the European Convention* (New York: Oxford University Press, 2017); Steven LB Jensen, *The Making of International Human Rights: The 1960s, Decolonization and the Reconstruction of Global Values* (New York: Cambridge University Press, 2017); Samuel Moyn, *Not Enough: Human Rights in an Unequal World* (Cambridge, MA-London: The Belknap Press of Harvard University Press, 2018); Jessica Whyte, *The Morals of the Market: Human Rights and the Rise of Neoliberalism* (London: Verso, 2019).

comprehensive studies, and when social democratic positions are mentioned, it is often in relation to those of other political cultures, whose approach is considered to be more influential. This is all the more striking since the literature is unanimous in recognizing that human rights activism, in its various historical incarnations, was most often the prerogative of individuals who were, or had been, aligned with the democratic Left.[4] This is true also of some of the most prominent protagonists of the human rights renaissance of the 1960s and 1970s – starting with Peter Benenson, who had repeatedly stood unsuccessfully as a Labour Party candidate before leaving party politics and moving on to founding Amnesty International (AI) in 1961.[5]

This chapter aims at reflecting on the impact human rights discourses and activism had on the internationalist projects and practices of social democratic parties.[6] After proposing a survey of the literature, it will zoom in on the debate of the 1970s, a decade that represented a turning point for the social democratic engagement with this issue. The chapter will focus on the Socialist International (SI), the international organization of socialist parties, and especially on two facets of its engagement with the human rights issue: namely, the dialogue with the international bodies of the Liberal and Christian Democratic parties, and the experience of the working group the SI set up in 1977 with the goal of producing a declaration on social democracy and human rights.

Social democracy and human rights: In the picture, but out of focus

What is the place of social democrats in the history of human rights, and what is the place of human rights in the history of social democracy? Delving into the recent literature looking for answers to these questions can be a rather frustrating experience. While both research on human rights and on the international history of the social democratic movement can be considered part of a historiographical turn marked by the awareness of the importance of global and transnational dynamics, the two sub-fields seem to have scarcely interacted with one another. The index of Talbot Imlay's sweeping study of socialist internationalism, for instance, does not contain an entry for human rights.[7] The same goes for books covering transnational socialist cooperation during pivotal moments in the history of human rights, such as the post-Second World

---

[4] Mark Philip Bradley, *The World Reimagined: Americans and Human Rights in the Twentieth Century* (New York: Cambridge University Press, 2016), 222; Jan Eckel, *The Ambivalence of Good: Human Rights in International Politics since the 1940s* (Oxford: Oxford University Press, 2019), 22.

[5] James Loeffler, *Rooted Cosmopolitans: Jews and Human Rights in the Twentieth Century* (New Haven: Yale University Press, 2018), 202–29.

[6] In the chapter I will generally use the terms 'socialist' and 'social democratic' as synonyms to refer to democratic socialist parties that adhered to the Socialist International.

[7] Talbot C. Imlay, *The Practice of Socialist Internationalism: European Socialists and International Politics, 1914–1960* (Oxford: Oxford University Press, 2018). Imlay does however discuss more at length the socialist approach to human rights and decolonization in 'International Socialism and Decolonization during the 1950s: Competing Rights and the Postcolonial Order', *The American Historical Review* 118, no. 4 (2013): 1105–32.

War years or the 'breakthrough' decade of the 1970s.[8] This doesn't mean that the issue is completely absent from these studies, but it certainly is an indication of the fact that human rights do not seem to constitute a central theme in narratives of social democratic internationalism. The matter gets more attention in works that focus on socialist-communist relations during the Cold War, and especially on the controversies over dissent groups in the Soviet bloc. Human rights, however, figure in these studies as an aspect of broader political and ideological debates, and their use by the actors involved is very often instrumental. In short, they appear not as an autonomous discourse and practice, with the potential of influencing the social democratic political culture, but as one among many rhetorical devices used to fight a pre-existing socialist-communist Cold War.[9]

Turning to the literature on human rights, we find a paradox: while authors are generally keen to acknowledge the importance of the socialist movement to the affirmation of human rights both nationally and internationally, democratic socialists rarely take centre stage in their narratives. Socialist actors are in the picture, but most often they are out of focus. In his groundbreaking study, *The Last Utopia*, Samuel Moyn has put forward an essential argument that provides a first line of explanation for this phenomenon. Human rights, he argued, only emerged rather late, in the 1970s, as an ideology capable of catalysing utopian visions of a better world, and this happened because they displaced earlier ideals and internationalist practices – prominent among them, those of socialism. As the case of Amnesty International's Peter Benenson indicates, human rights activism should be seen as an explicit *alternative* to socialism.[10] In subsequent work, Moyn has linked this development to a broader ideological shift from ideals of equality to a more narrow focus on 'sufficient' standards of living, which matched the evolution in political economy from the welfare state to a new 'neoliberal' era. The shrinking place of social rights in the definition of what constituted 'human rights', he argues, paralleled the decline of the egalitarian visions of socialism in Western Europe, and of the global redistributive agenda put forward by anti-colonial nationalists.[11]

Other authors have challenged this chronology and proposed different images of the social democratic engagement with human rights. Steven Jensen focuses on the 1960s as a crucial turning point, and sees 'race and religion as the driving forces in the breakthrough of human rights law and politics'.[12] In his narrative, which hinges

---

[8] Ettore Costa, *The Labour Party, Denis Healey and the International Socialist Movement: Rebuilding the Socialist International during the Cold War, 1945-1951* (Cham: Palgrave Macmillan, 2018); Christian Salm, *Transnational Socialist Networks in the 1970s: European Community Development Aid and Southern Enlargement* (Basingstoke: Palgrave Macmillan, 2016). On human rights in the 1970s, see Jan Eckel and Samuel Moyn (eds.), *The Breakthrough: Human Rights in the 1970s* (Philadelphia: University of Pennsylvania Press, 2014).

[9] See Bent Boel, 'Transnationalisme social-démocrate et dissidents de l'Est pendant la guerre froide', *Vingtième siècle* 109, no. 1 (2011): 169–81; Valentine Lomellini, *Les Relations Dangereuses: French Socialists, Communists and the Human Rights Issue in the Soviet Bloc* (Brussels: Peter Lang, 2012).

[10] Samuel Moyn, *The Last Utopia: Human Rights in History* (Cambridge, MA and London: The Belknap Press of Harvard University Press, 2010).

[11] Moyn, *Not Enough*.

[12] Jensen, *The Making of International Human Rights*, 2. See also Roland Burke, *Decolonization and the Evolution of International Human Rights* (Philadelphia: University of Pennsylvania Press, 2010).

on the agency of Third World countries, social democrats appear only briefly and rather inconsequently for their anti-communist usage of the human rights theme. Socialist-communist competition is a leitmotif also in Ned Richardson-Little's work. In examining the competing definitions of human rights elaborated by the Western SPD (*Sozialdemokratische Partei Deutschlands*) and the SED (the Socialist Unity Party born out of the forced merger of the communist and socialist organizations in the Soviet zone of occupation), the study suggests that, rather than constituting an independent factor, the usage of this theme by the SPD evolved as a function of the party's strategy towards East Germany.[13]

Social democrats play second fiddle also in Marco Duranti's study of the origins of the 1950 European Convention on Human Rights (ECHR). The Convention, which still forms the basis for the work of the European Court of Human Rights, is seen by Duranti as the brainchild of a transnational coalition of conservative politicians and thinkers. Their influence was crucial in devising the European human rights system as a 'protection' for the 'West' against not only Fascism and Communism, but also the alleged tendency of democratic left-wing forces to impose on political minorities and implement social legislation that they deemed dangerous for individual liberties. As such, the study argues, the adoption of the ECHR and of its First Protocol, in 1952, 'signified a rejection of the expansive understanding of human rights enshrined in the Universal Declaration and the emergence of a transnational conservative countercurrent to domestic policies implemented in recent years at the level of the nation-state'.[14]

To find a narrative that spotlights the role of social democrats we have to get back to the pivotal 1970s. Jan Eckel's *The Ambivalence of Good* includes a thorough analysis of the human rights policies of two European social democratic governments, the Dutch one, led by Joop den Uyl (1973–7), and the British Labour cabinet, especially during the tenure of David Owen as Foreign Secretary (1977–9). Influenced by a *Zeitgeist* that saw human rights gain increasing centrality, and intending to channel the activism of the mushrooming grassroots movements, the two governments tried to devise a 'progressive' human rights policy that had to do both with the history of the respective countries, and especially their colonial past, and with the political-ideological inclinations of the ruling parties.[15]

What Eckel's study examines, however, is the agency of governments, rather than transnational social democratic politics. Socialist parties, it has been argued, can be seen as 'hybrid entities, incorporating aspects of both state and non-state actors'.[16] As such, they have often escaped the radars of a historiography that tends to privilege either the former or the latter. Social democrats certainly matter when they can directly influence governmental policies. Their role as a transnational actor, however, has probably been overlooked by scholars focusing on the 'global community' of international organizations.[17]

---

[13] Richardson-Little, *The Human Rights Dictatorship*.
[14] Duranti, *The Conservative Human Rights Revolution*, 218.
[15] Eckel, *The Ambivalence of Good*.
[16] Imlay, *The Practice of Socialist Internationalism*, 15.
[17] Akira Iriye, *Global Community: The Role of International Organizations in the Making of the Contemporary World* (Berkeley: University of California Press, 2002).

At the same time, the less-than-imposing presence of social democrats in this literature certainly speaks to historical and ideological factors that made the encounter between the socialist movement and the human rights issue delicate and tortuous. In an oft-cited essay on 'Labour and human rights', Eric Hobsbawm highlighted what he saw as a crucial paradox:

> More than any other force, the labour movement helped to unlock the politico-legal, individualist strait-jacket which confined human rights of the type of the French Declaration and the American Constitution. Compare the UN's Universal Declaration of Human Rights ... with the American Bill of Rights. If the UN Declaration includes economic, social and educational rights ... it is primarily due to the historical intervention of labour movements. At the same time labour movements demonstrated the limitations of a 'human rights' approach to politics.[18]

The sort of rights 'to a decent human life' that preoccupy labour movements, Hobsbawm argued, are harder to translate into law provisions than the classic political and civil rights of the individual. They are 'programmes for society and social action', hence 'everything depends on the strategies and mechanisms for achieving them'.[19] In the twentieth century, social democrats increasingly identified these 'strategies and mechanisms' with harnessing the power of the modern state to regulate the capitalist economy, promote social equality and advance democratization. This, however, put them at odds with interpretations of human rights as rights pertaining to the individual, outside of any notion of political community, and especially aimed at protecting people from the encroachments of state power on personal freedom.[20]

The 'Three Internationals' and human rights

The antinomies of human rights activism started becoming particularly evident from the 1970s, as social democrats tried to grapple with the increasing relevance of the theme. Historians have been debating whether the 1970s have represented a beginning for human rights history, or just a milestone among others. It is certain, however, that during the decade the issue gained an attention that was unheard of, thanks to a host of political developments – among them the insertion of human rights provisions in the Final Act of the 1975 Helsinki Conference on Security and Cooperation in Europe, the mobilization against the recently established dictatorships in Latin America, the activism of the US Congress, and the announcement of the Democratic US President, Jimmy Carter (1977–1981), that they would represent a cornerstone of US foreign policy.[21]

---

[18] Eric J. Hobsbawm, 'Labour and Human Rights', in Id., *Worlds of Labour: Further Studies in the History of Labour* (London: Weidenfeld and Nicholson, 1984), 312.
[19] Ibid., 312.
[20] See Mathieu Fulla and Marc Lazar (eds.), *European Socialists and the State in the Twentieth and Twenty-First Centuries* (Cham: Palgrave Macmillan, 2020).
[21] For a comprehensive view see Eckel and Moyn (eds.), *The Breakthrough*.

Many coeval sources indicate that the 1970s represented a turning point for social democrats too, when it came to the human rights issue. The Labour Minister for Overseas Development, Judith Hart, for instance, insisted on this point in her (numerous) statements on the subject. 'In the last two or three years there has been an explosion of UK interest in human rights in developing countries, largely as a result of its priority for President Carter and the US Congress', she noted in November 1978. What explained the change, for her, was not the level of human rights abuse, but rather the conscience of the public: 'developments in communication and technology have turned the world almost into a village. There is greater awareness of the consequences of our own past actions. To some extent guilt has spurred our new concern'.[22] To take another example, we can look at how, a few years later, the general secretary of the Socialist International, Bernt Carlsson, summed up to an American interlocutor what he saw as the novelties in the social democratic approach to 'promoting human rights on a universal basis':

> In the past ... our approach to this issue has been very one-sided, geared merely to the communist countries. The International had also earlier concentrated only on the civil rights aspects of human rights. We were now trying to widen the discussion on human rights to include also social and economic human rights.[23]

The turning point, for the Socialist International, coincided with the election of Willy Brandt, the former chancellor of West Germany and SPD leader, as president of the organization. His tenure would be characterized by an effort to revitalize the SI by overcoming its Eurocentrism and focusing its activities on global political challenges.[24] In his address to the Geneva Conference of the organization, in November 1976, the newly elected president proposed human rights as the focus of one of the three 'offensives' the Socialist International should promote (the other ones being dedicated to 'a secure peace' and 'new relations between North and South'). Brandt insisted on the interrelation between 'individual' and 'collective' rights, arguing that 'security of the material existence is the foundation of all other human rights'. At the same time, he explicitly called for cooperation with other organizations that were active on the issue, mentioning Amnesty International, churches, trade unions, as well as the 'international bodies of liberal and Christian democratic parties'.[25]

This final reference to collaboration with other political groupings was no coincidence. A few months earlier, the Christian Democratic World Union had begun building contacts with the Liberal International and Democratic and Republican

---

[22] Labour History Archives and Study Centre (LHASC), Manchester, Judith Hart Papers, HART/08/46, 'Human Rights in the United States and United Kingdom Foreign Policy'.
[23] International Institute of Social History, Amsterdam. Socialist International Archives (SIA), box 1023, Bernt Carlsson to Willy Brandt, 19 June 1981.
[24] See Willy Brandt, *Berliner Ausgabe: Über Europa hinaus: Dritte Welt und Sozialistische Internationale*, vol. VIII, ed. Bernd Rother and Wolfgang Schmidt (Bonn: Dietz, 2006).
[25] Willy Brandt, 'Future Tasks of the International', *Socialist Affairs*, January 1977, 5–8.

members of the US Congress with the goal of organizing a large international meeting on human rights protection.[26] Prominent among their partners was a Democratic congressman from Minnesota, Donald Fraser, the American politician 'most closely and consistently associated with the liberal international human rights agenda before Jimmy Carter made it central to US foreign policy'.[27] After a first encounter in Brussels in June 1976, the group agreed to meet again in New York, where representatives of the Socialist International would be invited as observers. The New York meeting was held on 4 December, at the presence of the outgoing secretary of the SI, Hans Janitschek, and of a small delegation of the Social Democrats, USA. The minutes indicate that 'the participants were reminded that the earlier Brussels meeting … had agreed that inter-party exchanges would concentrate on human rights of a political and civil nature'. It was also agreed that, in order to avoid 'charges of political bias', examples of violations would be drawn 'from countries on all points of the political spectrum'. The meeting was expected to be instrumental to the organization of a larger conference, which could 'provide for information-sharing and action co-ordination', and offer a forum for discussing 'new methods of action, including multi-party commissions of inquiry going to countries of alleged violations'.[28]

Quite evidently, socialists were not a driving force in this inter-party dialogue. They had not participated in the inception of the initiative, their status remained for the moment that of mere observers, and the definition of human rights the meeting was proposing was a political and civil one, which excluded the economic and social rights Willy Brandt had mentioned in his Geneva speech. In spite of this, the general opinion was that it was impossible for the SI to remain out of this dialogue. Some, such as Judith Hart of the British Labour Party, or the US social democrats, supported the 'Three Internationals' initiative quite enthusiastically.[29] Others were more prudent. An unsigned note of early 1977, now in the archives of the Socialist International, captures well this latter spirit:

> The question of human rights (individual and social) has always been of great concern to democratic socialists. Therefore we have to participate in the world-wide current debate on that matter. Abstaining from it would give the conservative forces the upper hand in using this issue for their own purposes. We enter into that debate also with the aim of helping to prevent that the topic of human rights will be played against the topic of détente.[30]

---

[26] Friedrich Ebert Stiftung, Bonn, Archiv der sozialen Demokratie (AdsD), SPD-PV, box 11492, 'Meeting on Cooperation among Democratic Political Parties on Human Rights. Brussels – 26–27 June 1976. Minutes'. See also SIA, box 861.
[27] Barbara J. Keys, *Reclaiming American Virtue: The Human Rights Revolution of the 1970s* (Cambridge, MA-London: Harvard University Press, 2014), 76.
[28] LHASC, LP, NEC Minutes, 19 January 1977, 'Draft minutes of the planning meeting for a conference of democratic party representatives on human rights'.
[29] See ibid., 'Conference on Human Rights. Letter from Judith Hart', 4 January 1977; Centre d'histoire de Sciences Po, Paris, Archives d'histoire contemporaine (CHSP, AHC), Fonds Daniel Mayer, 2 MA 10, 'Dossier Droits de l'homme, 17 avril 1977'.
[30] SIA, box 1023, unsigned and untitled note.

The preservation of East-West détente was in fact a crucial preoccupation for the SI. The 'opening to the East' represented the most important legacy of Willy Brandt's stints as foreign minister (1966–9) and chancellor (1969–74), and had earned him the Nobel Peace Prize. Entwined as they were with a broader shift in the Cold War attitude of the Western alliance, détente policies were seen by European socialists as their key foreign policy accomplishment, proving they could successfully adapt their traditional pacifist orientation to the needs of the modern era.[31] 'Offensive' interpretations of the promotion of human rights in the Eastern Bloc, such as the ones promoted by the emerging neoconservative movement in the United States, were seen as threats to these accomplishments and to the fragile East-West equilibrium.[32]

In the following months, two of Willy Brandt's closest associates – his former speechwriter, Klaus Harpprecht, and the SPD directorate member, Horst Ehmke – met with Donald Fraser to discuss the participation of the Socialist International in the interparty initiative.[33] The idea took shape of inviting the congressman to an official summit of the SI, the Bureau meeting to be held in Rome in June, in order to further discuss the conditions of an international dialogue on human rights. This perspective, combined with the ongoing discussion about the 'Three Internationals' initiative, stimulated the debate in other member parties of the Socialist International. This was the case especially with the French Socialist Party (PS), which, under the charismatic (and sometimes controversial) leadership of François Mitterrand, was by then trying to secure a more prominent role in international socialist politics.

In view of the Rome Bureau meeting, in which Mitterrand was to give an introductory speech, the international secretary of the PS asked the party's human rights 'expert', Daniel Mayer, to prepare reports both on the general issue of human rights protection, and on the question of the cooperation among the three internationals.[34] With a political upbringing under the wing of Léon Blum in the interwar years, a prominent role in the Resistance, and an independent stance on critical subjects such as the post-war German rearmament or the Algerian War, Mayer was a quintessential representative of the ethical tradition of the French 'republican' socialism. After breaking with the Socialist party over the latter's support of the Algerian war and of Charles de Gaulle's Fifth Republic, Mayer had become the president of the French *Ligue des droits de l'homme*, which he led from 1958 to 1975. He joined the re-founded Socialist party in the early 1970s, and in 1977 took the position as president of the International Federation for Human Rights.[35]

Mayer shared the general view on the need for the Socialist International to participate in the international dialogue over human rights. At the same time, however, he voiced several qualms about the 'Three Internationals' initiative. In addition to concerns over

---

[31] See Michele Di Donato, 'The Cold War and Socialist Identity. The Socialist International and the Italian "Communist Question" in the 1970s', *Contemporary European History* 24, no. 2 (2015): 193–211, here 194–7.

[32] On these approaches, see Keys, *Reclaiming American Virtue*.

[33] FES, AdsD, box 11067, Klaus Harpprecht to Willy Brandt, Egon Bahr and Horst Ehmke, 10 February 1977; Horst Ehmke to Hans-Eberhard Dingels, 16 March 1977.

[34] CHSP, AHC, 2 MA 10, Pontillon to Mayer, 12 April 1977 and 20 April 1977.

[35] See https://maitron.fr/spip.php?article50266, MAYER Daniel, Raphaël, by Martine Pradoux.

the prospected participants, or the fairly artificial quest for a left-right balance in the denunciation of abuses, he raised what he saw as a fundamental question: in its current conception, the planned inter-party meeting 'gave the impression of grouping the supporters of Western civilization' and thus risked alienating Third World parties. In a series of notes to the party leadership, he remarked:

> Currently, Third world representatives qualify [individual liberties] as formal. They give priority to economic problems. The Socialist International is making an effort in the direction of the Third world. To find ourselves with the other Internationals, and only on the plane that has been anticipated, risks to provide the conservative and liberal internationals with a guarantee or an alibi. The Socialist International would be the only one to suffer from this.[36]

The predicament of the Socialist International was quite evident. Shunning the human rights initiatives would have meant cutting off from one of the crucial debates of the day, especially as the new Carter administration was announcing its intention to make them a lynchpin of US foreign policy. At the same time, joining on the terms set by Christian democrats and liberals would have risked jeopardizing the other 'offensives' Brandt had announced, towards the Global South and for the preservation of peace and East-West détente, and diluting the specificity of the social democratic international views and programmes.

Defining social democratic human rights

The Socialist International's commitment to the international human rights dialogue was formalized at the Rome Bureau meeting of 2–3 June 1977, to which, with a fairly uncommon procedure, Donald Fraser was also invited. The congressman gave a speech in which he described the initiatives of the US Congress on the topic, confirmed the interest of the Democratic party in an international, inter-party initiative, and pleaded for the support of the Socialist International. The Bureau produced two decisions: a working group would be formed, charged with analysing the implications of the human rights issue, while the SI general secretary, Bernt Carlsson, would continue the exploratory talks with the other Internationals.[37] The chairmanship of the working group was confided to Daniel Mayer, who would work together with a Luxembourger and a Swiss representative, Robert Krieps and Andreas Blum.[38]

In spite of this commitment, the Socialist International continued to show a markedly defensive attitude to the issue. At the meeting of the Three Internationals held on 11 July, Carlsson dragged his feet, agreeing to pursue 'informal conversations', but warning that 'if human rights questions were badly handled, it may lead to some

---

[36] CHSP, AHC, 2 MA 10, 'Note à Robert Pontillon', 5 May 1977; 'Note pour François Mitterrand, Robert Pontillon, Michel Thauvin', 27 May 1977.
[37] SIA, box 294, 'Bureau Meeting in Rome. 2–3 June 1977'.
[38] CHSP, AHC, 2 MA 10, Brandt to Mayer, 8 June 1977.

political difficulties in the field of this engagement'.[39] Matters came to a head at the following enlarged meeting, in February 1978. Carlsson's initial request to 'define what is meant by human rights' received the usual response – discussions would be limited 'to "political" or "civil" rights, not economic and social rights' – and his insistence on the Socialist International's position that 'human rights are broad', pointed with a reference to Roosevelt's 'freedom from hunger', fell on deaf ears. Even more contentious was the discussion on human rights monitoring in Eastern Europe after the signing of the Helsinki agreements.[40] Carlsson remarked that the agreements had been 'a success in that they helped stabilise Europe' and argued that the activities of the interparty group should 'leave out the Warsaw Pact countries', for this would have 'big power implications involving détente and the SALT agreements'. To the objections of the other representatives, he replied bitterly referring to the concrete advances obtained by the détente policies promoted 'by both the Republican administration in the US and the Social democratic government in West Germany': 'We (this group meeting today) have yet to demonstrate that our group has produced any results'.[41]

Beset by these fundamental disagreements, the activities of the interparty group dragged on at an irregular pace without producing any noteworthy results. In their public interventions, socialist representatives often contrasted the progress that could be obtained with the 'small steps' of diplomacy with what they saw as the self-righteousness of the 'big words' of human rights rhetoric, especially as employed by conservatives who opposed East-West détente.[42] This view was reiterated also in contacts with the increasingly influential human rights NGOs, such as Amnesty International. Intervening on behalf of the Socialist International in an AI seminar of October 1977, Paavo Lipponen, of the Finnish social democratic party, expressed the organization's opposition to a 'perfectionist, maximalist approach', insisting instead on the 'merits of a pragmatic, gradualistic approach'. Human rights, he added, 'should not be seen in isolation from other major concerns. The maintenance of peace and the furthering of the process of détente is an absolutely necessary prerequisite to any progress in human rights.'[43]

This approach was also to characterize the report of the SI working party. Mayer, Krieps and Blum advanced at a painstakingly slow pace, producing a definitive draft only in the early months of 1980. Their text proposed a 'dynamic' interpretation of human rights: after the civil and political rights proclaimed by the 'various national

---

[39] SIA, box 898, 'Note on the informal meeting of the Christian Democratic World Union (SM Gebhardt), Liberal International (Richard Moore) and Socialist International (Bernt Carlsson) held in London on 11 July 1977'.
[40] See Nicolas Badalassi, *En finir avec la guerre froide: la France, l'Europe et le processus d'Helsinki, 1965–1975* (Rennes: Presses Universitaires de Rennes, 2014).
[41] SIA, box 898, 'Meeting on Human Rights of Democratic and Republican parties of the USA and the Socialist International, the Liberal International and the Christian Democratic World Union – February 3, 1978'.
[42] CHSP, AHC, 2 MA 10, 'SPD Mitteilung für die Presse, 28 April 1977. Willy Brandt, "Friedenpolitik und Menschenrechte", *Die Zeit*'.
[43] CHSP, AHC, 2 MA 10, 'Amnesty International. Seminar on "Torture and Human Rights". Strasbourg, 3–5 October 1977. Statement of Paavo Lipponen (Finland), Representative of the Socialist International'.

declarations' came the 'economic, social and cultural rights' of the 1948 Universal Declaration, as 'the achievement of one right opens up the prospect of claiming further rights, whether complementary or enabling the full exercise of the original right'. By virtue of their ideological orientation and of what, glossing over an often embarrassing history, the report defined as their 'concern with the liberation of peoples subjected to colonial regimes', socialist parties had a special role to play in advancing the recognition of new rights as well as in bringing about a more effective implementation of existing ones. The report paid special attention to the gap between internationally sanctioned rights and their effective enforcement, which it linked to social and cultural inequalities, underdevelopment and the legacy of colonial domination. The echo of the polemics with the other Internationals was also manifest in some passages:

> All too often human rights are invoked as propaganda agents or as a means of applying pressure in the power struggle ... between the major blocs. The excessively individualistic, essentially political and purely defensive concept of human rights upheld in conservative circles becomes an obstacle to progress and to the profound transformations needed to meet the aspirations of the underprivileged and the changing pattern of world economic relations.[44]

The worldwide recognition of human rights was seen as possible only in the context of an improvement of the material conditions of the less developed countries, for which a restructuring of international economic relations would be necessary. At the same time, the preservation of peace was considered an essential prerequisite, hence the interdependence between détente and human rights ('without human rights there can be no détente, and without détente there can be no human rights').[45]

It was, overall, a fairly tame and uninspiring document. 'There is little in this report to which one can openly object', commented Jenny Little of the British Labour Party. 'It starts from the best of intentions, but its analysis is wooly and its conclusions are vague.' Little suggested that much more needed to be said 'about the issue of race, and of immigration. ... The question of sexual equality is hardly touched on'.[46] In a letter to the SI secretariat, Arthur J. Faulkner, the spokesman for foreign affairs of the New Zealand Labour Party, also lamented the absence of women from the drafting committee. Moreover, he remarked that the fact that all the members of the committee were European had led to some distortions:

> The link that the documents seeks to establish between 'détente' and Human Rights is almost spurious and at the best doubtful. One can understand the European tendency to exaggerate the importance of European détente, but its connection with Human Rights or lack of them on a world scale as expressed in the document lacks conviction.[47]

[44] SIA, box 1023, 'The Socialist International and Human Rights'.
[45] Ibid.
[46] LHASC, NEC Minutes, 23 July 1980, 'Socialist International Report of Study Group on Human Rights – Office Note', Jenny Little, June 1980.
[47] SIA, box 1023, Faulkner to Carlsson, 13 May 1980.

Officially presented to the Oslo Bureau meeting of the SI on 12–13 June 1980, the report received several requests for revisions aimed at taking into account 'human rights in Eastern Europe, towards women, and in respect to the North-South conflict'.[48] An enlarged (but still all-European) study group was formed, which produced a thoroughly amended report. The new report met a destiny which is typical of this kind of documents: discussed in a further Bureau meeting and then submitted to the Madrid Congress of the SI, in November, it was officially endorsed and subsequently shelved without leaving significant traces.[49] The Socialist International's human rights 'offensive', announced by Willy Brandt in 1976, was ending in a stalemate.

Conclusion

In August 1981, Bernt Carlsson addressed the 14th International Council of Amnesty International. While praising AI's achievements and insisting on the potential for cooperation with the Socialist International, his speech also contained a frank assessment of the gulf that separated the human rights NGO from the socialist parties:

> The Socialist International shares Amnesty's concern for human rights. However, we approach these problems from a different perspective. We are a political organization and committed to policies of democracy and social change. Such a commitment would not be appropriate for an organization like Amnesty. ... The Socialist International has a fundamental commitment to an ideology – that of democratic socialism. ... The main focus of the activities of the Socialist International is designed to find ways of averting a nuclear catastrophe. We are committed to reducing the enormous tensions between the superpowers and their allies. ... The Socialist International will give support to forces like the liberation movements in Southern Africa and to the anti-dictatorship movements in Latin America. ... We recognize that Amnesty cannot involve itself in campaigns of political solidarity and we fully respect its independence on this. But we cannot be politically neutral ... We make no apologies for taking sides, and we support those fighting for social and economic justice because it is our belief that the denial of political freedom often grows out of inequalities bred by the colonial or neo-colonial systems. ... permanent hunger and starvation are the opposite to human rights.[50]

In trying to attune itself to the sudden popularity of the human rights theme, the Socialist International met with difficulties that proved to be insuperable. On the one

---

[48] SIA, box 962, 'Minutes of the Meeting of the Bureau of the Socialist International. Oslo, 12–13 June 1980'.
[49] SIA, box 1023, 'Report of the Enlarged Socialist International Study Group on Human Rights', 24 October 1980.
[50] SIA, box 859, 'Congress of Amnesty International. Montreal, Canada, 20–23 August 1981. Address by Bernt Carlsson, General secretary of the Socialist International'.

hand, there was the risk of losing political distinctiveness – epitomized by the dialogue with the other Internationals and the US representatives. Joining a human rights protection platform that focused exclusively on civil and political rights indeed 'gave the impression of grouping the supporters of Western civilization', as Daniel Mayer put it. The likelihood of the human rights theme being used in polemics against détente only added to the SI's unease. On the other hand, the post-political approach of the NGOs was hardly compatible with the way socialist parties interpreted reality and operated. The SI had a political understanding of problems: the predicament of individuals could only be comprehended as part of collective experiences and structural conditions. To change the latter, political action was needed – with all the attendant interlocutions and compromises. The mere denunciation of injustice was seen as naïve, self-righteous and generally ineffective.

The failure of the human rights offensive of the SI can also be seen as an indication of the discrepancy between a growing tendency to see social and political problems in global perspective, especially evident in the leadership of the organization, and the shortage of cultural and political instruments and categories to support this intuition. Willy Brandt's Socialist International did react to the 'shock of the global' of the 1970s, and tried to update its goals and approaches. Its 'three offensives', with their insistence on interdependence and on what Brandt called 'the survival of man and humanity', certainly contributed disseminating awareness about the common challenges humankind was facing in the last quarter of the twentieth century.[51] In this respect, the socialists' contribution to the 'making of a transnational world' has probably been overlooked by historiography.[52] At the same time, however, most socialist parties were also still wedded to a Cold War worldview, which foregrounded the superpowers and their relationships – their constant preoccupation with détente is certainly a case in point. In spite of the efforts to overcome Eurocentrism, the SI remained a predominantly European organization, and this conditioned the views of its members. Some themes that were to gain increasing relevance – in her comment on Mayer's report, Jenny Little aptly mentioned gender equality, race and immigration – remained largely off the socialists' radar. Lastly, and probably most importantly, the global solutions the socialists proposed – from the political restructuring of international economic relations to the continuation of East-West détente – were to be defeated in the space of a few years, as the world started grappling with the rise of market-oriented economic paradigms and with an apparent return to the Cold War among the superpowers.[53]

Politically sidelined, social democratic internationalism would find it increasingly difficult to assert itself as a credible alternative in the global arena of the late – and post-Cold War years. In the wake of old and new global challenges, it would ever more often come to face the unattractive alternative that manifested itself in the late 1970s: joining a broad 'Western' front, on the one hand, or choosing a vague 'humanitarian' perspective, on the other.

---

[51] Willy Brandt, 'Future Tasks of the International', 8.
[52] Akira Iriye (ed.), *Global Interdependence: The World after 1945* (Cambridge, MA and London: The Belknap Press of Harvard University Press, 2014).
[53] See, among others, Simon Reid-Henry, *Empire of Democracy: The Remaking of the West since the Cold War, 1971–2017* (New York: Simon & Schuster, 2019).

11

Solidarity struggles: Transnational feminisms and Cold War lefts in the Global South

Jocelyn Olcott

In early June 1976, 400 women arrived at the leafy campus of Wellesley College, an elite all-women's undergraduate institution outside Boston, for a conference on women and development, one of the three themes of the UN Decade for Women (1975–85). Sponsored by major US-based funding entities such as the Ford and Rockefeller foundations and the US Agency for International Development, the gathering displayed all the can-do feminist spirit of the 1970s, imagining that a 'global sisterhood' would allow women to forge alliances above the fray of partisan wrangling and geopolitical rivalries and to focus instead on 'women's issues' and the bread-and-butter matters of everyday life. Much like the International Women's Year conference, which many participants had attended in Mexico City the previous year, the Wellesley conference quickly erupted into a conflict over what constituted development and who had the authority to define it.

A small handful of scholars from the Global South, most of them based in the United States, sat through hours of presentations that seemed to misunderstand or misrepresent their histories and cultures, only to find that the programme left them no time to challenge these representations. The Kenyan anthropologist Achola Pala Okeyo underscored that the entire UN project – sustained by dozens of international aid agencies and focused on 'integrating women in development' – erased women's economic contributions, particularly in the critical realm of food cultivation and preparation. African women, Pala insisted, 'are well "integrated" into the dependent national economies'.[1] Several participants called for more research on US women's diverse experiences, rather than persistently scrutinizing women of the Global South using conceptual frameworks developed in Europe and North America. The Nigerian historian Bolanle Awe reflected later, 'One thing that became clear at the Conference on Women and Development in Wellesley, as well as the other activities that marked the International Women's Year in Mexico, is that many of our assumptions about the universality of female interests are questionable.'[2]

---

[1] Achola O. Pala, 'Definitions of Women and Development: An African Perspective', *Signs: Journal of Women in Culture and Society* 3, no. 1 (Autumn 1977): 12.

[2] Bolanle Awe, 'Reflections on the Conference on Women and Development: I', *Signs: Journal of Women in Culture and Society* 3, no. 1 (Autumn 1977): 12.

The Wellesley conference – despite, or perhaps because of, all the friction it generated – had important legacies for transnational feminism. As one trio of South-based participants reflected,

> This conference was successful precisely because it was a painful clash between well-meaning American women academicians who believed themselves to be ahead of American men, and freed from colonial and imperialist limitations on one hand, and on the other hand, overly optimistic third-world women who had believed that the impossible dialogue between developed/developing people could be restored by women, between women, and for women.[3]

One of the most immediate results of this conflict was the determination of many South-based intellectuals to claim control over knowledge production about their own societies. A group of African researchers wrote to the organizers, 'We wish to register here our deep objections to the language used in dialogue with us by some of the Conference convenors, which ranged from the patronizing to the insulting.' Rejecting the presumption that the conference organizers' wealth endowed them with the authority to set the agenda, they continued, 'We would like to remind the Convenors of this particular Conference that much of the wealth which allows for the funding of conferences such as this is derived from the exploitation of the regions from which we come.'[4] Six months after the frustrating Wellesley conference, having secured funding from the Swedish Agency for Research Cooperation with Developing Countries, a group of African researchers met in Lusaka, Zambia, to define a new agenda of 'socio-economic research priorities from an African perspective'.[5] The following year, this group founded AAWORD (Association of African Women for Research and Development).

For organizations such as AAWORD, the United Nations and other institutions of liberal internationalism provided the structure, legitimacy and occasionally funding that supported networks of activist intellectuals offering a critical assessment of capitalist modernization and emergent neoliberalism. The UN Decade for Women brought an explosion of civil society organizations and networks focused on improving women's status in various ways.[6] This chapter focuses on three of those

---

[3] Nawal El Saadawi, Fatima Mernissi and Mallica Vajrathon, 'Women and Development: The Wellesley Conference', *ISIS International Newsletter*, April 1977. All three authors were, by this point, prominent in transnational feminist circles.

[4] Quoted in 'The experience of the Association of African Women for Research and Development (AAWORD). A Workshop Report prepared for the High-level Meeting on the Review of Technical Cooperation among Developing Countries', *Development Dialogue*, no. 1–2 (1982): 108.

[5] 'AAWORD The Association of African Women for Research and Development', *Africa Development/ Afrique et Developpement* 6, no. 2 (1981): 147.

[6] On the IWY conference and its legacies, see Jocelyn Olcott, *International Women's Year: The Greatest Consciousness-Raising Event in History* (New York: Oxford University Press, 2017). See also Myra Marx Ferree and Aili Mari Tripp, *Global Feminism: Transnational Women's Activism, Organizing, and Human Rights* (New York: New York University Press, 2006); Valentine M. Moghadam, *Globalizing Women: Transnational Feminist Networks* (Baltimore: Johns Hopkins University Press, 2005).

networks, all based in the Global South and with a focus on political economy and on an effort to reorient feminist activism around an ethos of care rather than of rights: AAWORD, Development Alternatives for Women for a New Era (DAWN) and the Encuentros Feministas Latinoamericanos y del Caribe. These groups all had a high proportion of intellectuals and academics, although AAWORD was the most explicitly (and unambivalently) academic, while the Encuentros Feministas brought together academic feminists with burn-it-down activists and free-thinking creatives, and DAWN consisted principally of activist intellectuals who ran in policymaking circles.

These networks all interacted in important but complex ways both with the UN and its agencies and with militants and partisans of organized lefts. The three conferences of the UN Decade for Women – in Mexico City in 1975, Copenhagen in 1980 and Nairobi in 1985 – informed the timing, strategies and content of these networks' activities, and several UN entities, such as UNESCO and various commissions for economic development, offered spaces where network members and platforms could influence normative values around gender and political economy. Drawing on published materials and interviews by members of these networks, this chapter considers how they fashioned civil society internationalism around three important themes: the decolonization of knowledge production, the redefinition of concepts of feminism and the intersection of these two concerns to foster the emergent field of feminist economics as a critique of both Marxist and neoliberal approaches.

World changers: Redefining transnational civil society

Civil society activism had been powerfully redefined by feminist and anti-racist movements, and the transnational feminist networks that emerged in the wake of IWY conference distinguished their projects from those of the established NGOs that had existed since the late nineteenth century.[7] The political scientist Deborah Stienstra describes the explosion of organizations, many based in the Global South, that tried to analyse issues within a feminist framework – however they understood it – and, as the founder of one organization explained, they 'rejected rigid and heavy bureaucratic structures in favor of informal, nonhierarchical and open structures and ways of operating'.[8] This change marked a generational divide, reflecting the ethos of post-1968 social movements, and allowed the organizations to be more nimble and responsive to changing conditions. DAWN founder Devaki Jain recalled that, before 1975, 'what we called the conservative brand of NGOs' dominated at the UN's Commission on the Status of Women – organizations such as International Planned Parenthood Federation and the International League of Women Voters. 'We, the new ones after 1975, initially denounced them. I don't mean openly, but we just felt that they were the old, feudal

---

[7] Moghadam, *Globalizing Women*. See also Leila J. Rupp, *Worlds of Women: The Making of an International Women's Movement* (Princeton: Princeton University Press, 1997).

[8] Deborah Stienstra, *Women's Movements and International Organizations* (London: St. Martin's Press, 1994), 102 (citing ISIS International founder Marilee Karl).

people and we were the new, world-changers ... When we came on the scene and found them, we thought they were really weak.'[9]

The networks under consideration here insisted upon autonomy from states and political parties, distinguishing them from organizations, predominantly in communist and socialist countries, that openly received state support and whose members endeavoured to effect change within dominant parties or political structures. As Kristen Ghodsee has pointed out, the label of 'state feminism' emerged as a Cold War designation in the 1980s to discount efforts by activists and organizations that were dismissed as mere dupes of communist officials.[10] The distinction was often murky in practice, as governments (particularly the United States and the UK) channelled funding through various development and aid entities. The historian Mark Mazower points out that the CIA responded to Soviet support for 'front organizations' by routing funding through sixty different foundations to over one hundred nongovernmental organizations (NGOs). 'This shadow war of secret funding and Potemkin NGOs', he writes, 'raised the question whether a genuinely autonomous NGO was even possible in the Cold War.'[11]

Since these organizations lacked funding, the idea that they remained autonomous from state funding was often somewhat of a fiction but an important fiction nonetheless. The form of the transnational NGO allowed its members to mobilize around specific issues and to address their demands to entities such as the UN or the ILO to devise supranational norms and policies. Perhaps unsurprisingly, these networks struggled with the question of how to fund their activities. AAWORD was most assertive in insisting that the organization would refuse funding from 'governments and organizations whose policies were deemed to be in conflict with the objectives of AAWORD'.[12] DAWN and the Encuentro Feminista organizers have, over the years, been more willing to accept support from North-based private foundations.

The women who launched these networks were overwhelmingly urban intellectuals from middle-class or elite families who often had attended universities in imperial centres, returning to contribute to post-colonial state formation by working in academic and policymaking positions. There was some overlap among the three networks, with AAWORD founder Marie-Angelique Savané, for example, appearing on the roster of DAWN's founding members. Although they confer with supporters in the Global North, all three networks remain based in the Global South. As DAWN founder Devaki Jain explained to an interviewer, 'When you are struggling, politically located in your own political fabric, the incentives, the vibes, your priorities, your capacity to do is very different than when you are living in a country with a social security base, where your gas and water supply works, and every morning you read the Times of London.'[13] AAWORD is headquartered in Dakar but has chapters in

---

[9] Devaki Jain interview by Thomas Weiss, 19 March 2002 (New York: The United Nations Intellectual History Project, 2007), CD-ROM. In retrospect, Jain acknowledges how much their efforts built upon the foundation laid by these established NGOs.
[10] Kristen Ghodsee, *Second World, Second Sex: Socialist Women's Activism and Global Solidarity during the Cold War* (Durham: Duke University Press, 2018), chapter one.
[11] Mark Mazower, *Governing the World: The History of an Idea* (New York: Penguin, 2012).
[12] 'The experience ... AAWORD', 110.
[13] Devaki Jain interview.

fourteen African countries. Since the first meeting in Bogotá in 1981, the Encuentros Feministas have met every two or three years in cities throughout Latin America. The DAWN secretariat has moved from Bangalore to Rio de Janeiro to Barbados to Fiji to Nigeria to the Philippines to Thailand and back to Fiji.

All three networks advocated for a political economy oriented towards social, cultural and ecological well-being and sustainability rather than the developmentalist emphases on growth, productivity and efficiency. These were, of course, long-standing priorities of women's movements, dating back more than a century, but the UN Decade for Women spotlighted the gendered critiques of late twentieth-century development schemes, which were predicated upon the Fordist imaginary of a male-headed, heteronormative, nuclear family as the Danish economist Ester Boserup famously drew attention to the inappropriateness of this model.[14]

Despite important similarities, these networks had distinct profiles. AAWORD has focused principally on research per se, particularly on efforts to decolonize the research that provided the foundation for policymaking. AAWORD's organizers insisted that research not be a 'mere academic exercise' but rather 'directed towards solving pressing problems which affect the daily lives of our peoples'.[15] The first workshop in Dakar was organized around four working groups: rural development, urban development, women and the law, and psycho-cultural studies. Thus, AAWORD had two principal objectives: first, 'to promote multidimensional development, i.e. development in the service of political awareness as well as the economic, social, cultural and psychological fulfilment of the African people' and, second, 'to make governments, public authorities and research centres sensitive to the need for decolonizing research'.[16]

The Encuentros Feministas have been, since the first gathering in 1981 in Bogotá, as much consciousness-raising sessions as political meetings. If the AAWORD gatherings felt like a cross between an academic conference and a UN agency meeting, the Encuentros felt more like carnival. They have always included artistic performances and displays and have fostered vocal protests among participants, often around issues of insufficient inclusivity but also around strategies and priorities. While DAWN and AAWORD both established headquarters, leadership structures and consultative status with the UN's Department of Economic and Social Affairs, the Encuentros remain a more loosely defined collection of intellectuals and activists who organize a gathering every few years, moving among Latin American cities, with the flavour and agenda of any given Encuentro strongly informed by the local organizing committee. Still, the proceedings and published accounts demonstrate that participants see this as a movement and expect there to be some accumulation of knowledge and understanding from one meeting to the next. Like AAWORD, the Encuentros Feministas reflect their regional context. During the 1980s, participants spent considerable time discussing US

---

[14] Ester Boserup, *Woman's Role in Economic Development* (New York: St. Martin's Press, 1970). See also Günseli Berik, and Ebru Kongar, *The Routledge Handbook of Feminist Economics* (New York: Routledge, 2021); Lourdes Benería, Günseli Berik and Maria Floro, *Gender, Development, and Globalization: Economics As If All People Mattered* (New York: Routledge, 2016).

[15] 'The experience ... AAWORD', 110.

[16] 'The experience ... AAWORD', 112–13.

interventions in Central America, the abuses of military dictatorships in the Southern Cone and the effects of IMF- and World Bank-imposed structural adjustment programmes in the wake of the 1982 debt crisis.

A persistent debate at the Encuentros – more than at meetings of either AAWORD or DAWN – was about the extent to which feminists should work with the organized left, including political parties and other male-dominated entities such as labour unions. When a group of Venezuelan feminists proposed in 1979 to hold a regional conference in preparation for the UN's mid-Decade women's conference in Copenhagen in 1980, the proposal immediately foundered on disagreements about the relationship between these efforts and Latin America's militant but beleaguered organized left. From the outset, participants pointed to the burdens of *doble militancia* – the pull of activism in two or more movements – echoing concerns about the *doble jornada* – the double shift of paid and unpaid labours. Another persistent concern was that activists did not want the Encuentros to be dominated by academics and become yet another space for abstract debate or internecine conflicts of the sectarian left. Like the members of DAWN and AAWORD, the women who participated in the Encuentros wanted to go home afterwards and work for political change.

DAWN started in 1984 as a group of activist intellectuals meeting in the Bangalore living room of Indian economist Devaki Jain. Although it was the last of these three to constitute formally, DAWN founders hardly took time to catch their breath before seeking to capture the momentum gained in Mexico City. Devaki Jain and Eli Bhatt, the founder of the Self-Employed Women's Association (SEWA), wrote to fellow participants barely a month after the 1975 conference concluded, urging participants from the NGO tribune to send them materials so that they could begin planning an IWY Follow-Up Tribune to 'aim at the identification of basic lessons and issues emerging out of the [IWY] Tribune [and] strive for the acceptance of these ideas in our home countries'.[17] DAWN members often worked as advisers at the UN or within their home governments and gained an awareness that policymakers responded to pressure from civil society. Perhaps for this reason, DAWN leaned towards a decentred approach, in which change would be effected not through radical transformation but through the accretion of dispersed but significant changes in practice. They endeavoured to work at the level of governments and international organizations, transnational civil society networks and local grassroots organizations, pointing to examples such as SEWA, the Green-Belt Movement in Kenya, the Grameen Bank and Women's World Banking providing affordable credit, and the widespread translation and circulation of the Boston Women's Health Collective's classic text 'Our Bodies, Ourselves'.

If AAWORD was, first and foremost, a research organization that sought to inform policymaking and the Encuentros a 'happening' that sought to influence social movements, DAWN oriented itself more towards the intersection between policymaking and activism. At a 1985 gathering to finalize the proposals for the Nairobi

---

[17] 'Dear Sister' letter from Eli Bhatt, 12 August 1975; Betty Friedan Papers, Carton 107, file 1247; Schlesinger Library, Radcliffe Institute, Harvard University, Cambridge, Mass.

conference, organizers queried, 'To whom is this paper addressed? Feminist activists or policy makers? The consensus was that we are addressing conscious, feminist activists as it is they, by their pressure, who can change policy-makers.'[18] DAWN has always been the most geographically diverse of these three entities, due to the various relocations of its headquarters and the fact that its founding organizers hailed from throughout the global south.[19] This range of perspectives generated differences of opinions regarding priorities and strategies; repeated intentions to resolve differences respectfully indicate that this was not, in fact, always easy. The 1985 meeting included a resolution to reject 'personal aggrandizement' in favour of the 'cross-fertilizing potential' of dialogue and the 'humility to learn from the experiences of others'. Even within the report from this meeting, competing perspectives emerge – over issues such as decentralization, population measures and microcredit. The working group that was assigned to report on socialism came back with a report on 'visions', clearly ruffling feathers.

Ambivalent liberal internationalism: Boundary struggles at the United Nations

Although many of their members worked at times for the United Nations and its constituent agencies, all three of these networks had an ambivalent relationship with liberal internationalism, complaining frequently that UN agencies pushed a market-oriented developmentalist agenda. Even when the UN had stated positions on issues such as sex discrimination or gender violence, these often remained only paper commitments. Still, the UN Decade for Women, including instruments such as the 1979 Convention on the Elimination of All Forms of Discrimination against Women (CEDAW), created mechanisms and reporting structures that women's organizations could use to pressure their home governments, and UN agencies often had more resources than local governments and were, at least in principle, more responsive to women's concerns. These networks often planned their meetings around preparing for and participating in UN-sponsored meetings – often reading draft documents line by line to assess their implications for women's lives. AAWORD and DAWN, in particular, worked directly with UN agencies that supported and participated in their meetings. The Encuentros Feministas, which were more chaotic and anti-establishmentarian than AAWORD or DAWN, often structured their agendas around influencing UN policy but preferred to keep the UN itself at arm's length. A group of jurists attending the second Encuentro in Lima in 1983 pointed to the empty promises of the 1975 World Plan of Action and the CEDAW protocols, asserting that 'the international organisms with a mandate for human rights and women's equality are ineffective and obsolete and only signify costly bureaucracies that do nothing to help

---

[18] Tone Bleie and Raghnild Lund, *Proceedings from DAWN's Bergen Meeting*. Development Research and Action Programme (DERAP), Chr Michelson Institute (Bergen, Norway: 1985), 6.
[19] Gita Sen, and Caren Grown, *Development, Crises, and Alternative Visions: Third World Women's Perspectives* (New York: Monthly Review Press, 1987).

the unequal, discriminatory, and marginal situation currently endured by indigenous women, rural women, working women, housewives, elderly women, prostitutes and women in general'.[20]

These networks took root in a particular context for both civil society activism and the UN itself. The 1970s had witnessed a mushrooming of civil society organizations, including women's and feminist organizations, around the world.[21] The UN seemed just at the brink of overturning the geopolitical order.[22] The explosion of new nations emerging from colonial rule shifted the balance of power in the UN General Assembly, precipitating a host of policy changes, including the suspension of South Africa as punishment for its apartheid policies as well as support for the New International Economic Order. The momentum within the UN all seemed to be on the side of the nations of the Global South caucusing as the Group of 77. During the period from the mid-1970s into the early 1980s, the UN served as the staging ground for sweeping social and economic critique.

Thus, the UN Decade for Women took place amid what political theorist Nancy Fraser has described as a 'boundary struggle' over the divide between economy and society.[23] This moment seemed to allow considerable latitude in how activists could navigate ideological divides as this boundary-struggle moment left open the question of where to seek political solutions. These networks not only predicted the crisis of care that neoliberalism and structural adjustment policies would precipitate but also insisted on a holistic approach to the problem. They ordered à la carte from neoliberal and socialist menus, taking advantage of the space that was still, for the time being, held open by the Non-Aligned Movement. Support in the UN's General Assembly for the New International Economic Order emerged alongside the advent of neoliberalism in its Friedmanite instantiation. In this liminal moment, feminist intellectuals in the Global South drew ecumenically from elements of what, in retrospect, appear as sharply contradictory imaginaries of political economy.

In the mid-1970s, neoliberalism held out the promise of radical democratization through the cultivation of a dynamic civil society and decentralized politics. The neoliberal economic paradigms that took root in many societies at this point held out decentralization and local 'choice' with the promise of democratizing economies and devolving power to communities. For women who for decades had sought an entry point into decision-making processes that governed policies and resource distribution, these developments seemed to offer ways to circumvent the hermetic, nepotistic policymaking apparatuses that remained inaccessible. The push for decentralization often came with efforts to promote 'self-reliance' and 'autonomy' – a framing that

---

[20] Colectivo ISIS Internacional, 'Revista de las Mujeres', in *II Encuentro Feminista Latinoamericano y del Caribe* (Santiago, CL: ISIS Internacional, June 1984), 136.

[21] Akira Iriye, *Global Community: The Role of International Organizations in the Making of the Contemporary World* (Berkeley: University of California Press, 2002); Margaret E. Keck and Kathryn Sikkink, *Activists beyond Borders: Advocacy Networks in International Politics* (Ithaca, NY: Cornell University Press, 1998).

[22] See, for example, Glenda Sluga, *Internationalism in the Age of Nationalism* (Philadelphia: University of Pennsylvania Press, 2013), chapter four.

[23] Nancy Fraser, 'Behind Marx's Hidden Abode: For an Expanded Conception of Capitalism', *New Left Review* 86 (March–April 2014).

might be understood to naturalize market forces and sow distrust of state programmes or might be seen as a strategy for countering various forms of imperialism.

Furthermore, the embrace of core elements of neoliberalism – emphasis on choice, autonomy, decentralization and the cultivation of a robust civil society – hardly constituted an endorsement of the larger political economic project as these networks urged a reimagining of what constituted development and, by extension, an economy. First and foremost, they criticized how structural adjustment programmes eviscerated state-run social services, leaving women to take up the slack in areas such as health care, food security and even basic infrastructure failures. AAWORD and DAWN particularly advocated what they called 'Alternate Development' or 'Another Development' – a political economy that focused on the satisfaction of basic needs as defined within societies and using strategies in harmony with the environment. AAWORD members underscored that the pressure to shift agricultural land to commodities production and higher-yield processes had fostered food insecurity and desertification – both problems that contributed substantially to women's labour burdens. Such a model of development would require structural transformations but, they argued, 'immediate action is possible and necessary'. Their report from their 1982 meeting in Dakar continued:

> [T]he present world crisis is the result of a process of maldevelopment originating from a growth model geared to the use of resources for private profit and power. This kind of development fails to satisfy the material and spiritual needs of the majority of the world's peoples and it penetrates all political and economic systems, even if it does express itself in different forms and with varying intensity.[24]

AAWORD sought thoroughgoing structural changes in the political economy, clearly mapping out the connections among economic, social and cultural domination at the international, national and household levels. Pointing to 'the crises of capitalism as well as of existing socialist models of social progress [that] have deepened in the last decade', their 1982 Dakar Declaration calls for the 'elimination of patriarchal relations and the profound revalorization of the day-to-day work of household and family maintenance. The equal participation of men and women in domestic work and family and kinship relations implies a restructuring of the so-called working day in the wage labour sector.'[25] It goes on to offer an explicitly feminist analysis of the imbrication of patriarchy and political economy, citing the urgency of the looming social and environmental crises.

At the centre of these debates was the critical issue of whether entering the labour market was emancipatory for women. Developmentalists called for the 'mobilization of all natural and human resources' and saw women's incorporation into the labour

---

[24] Marie-Angélique Savané, Introduction to The Dakar Seminar on 'Another Development with Women', 21–25 June 1982, 5.

[25] 'The Dakar Declaration on Another Development with Women', *Development Dialogue*, no. 1–2 (1982): 14. Among the dozens of signatories were some of the most prominent figures in women's activism in the global south, including several of DAWN's founding members – figures such as Krishna Ahooja-Patel, Lourdes Arizpe, Fatima Mernissi and Marie-Angélique Savané.

market as a win all around – women would gain access to income and economies would become more 'productive' per the prevailing economic metrics.[26] Many feminists – particularly but not exclusively in wealthier countries – concentrated their efforts on improving labour conditions, pushing for pay equity, training and educational opportunities, and stronger laws to prevent sex discrimination. These Global South women's networks, however, recognized early on that the push to incorporate women into commodified labour would exacerbate the devaluation of the vast amounts of uncommodified labour performed overwhelmingly by women. Addressing this issue would require not a simple policy tweak or the introduction of a new labour-saving technology; it would require a wholesale reconsideration of what constituted an economy and whose well-being it served.

Decolonizing knowledge production

The UN has, since its inception, served as an important vehicle for collecting, analysing and disseminating data and research, and the UN Decade for Women drew attention to the relationship between knowledge production and policymaking priorities. Women activists attended closely to the ways in which the social conditions of knowledge production – who had access to the time and resources to perform research, which research questions were taken seriously, how methodological rigor was assessed – carried tangible implications for public policies. Several entities, such as ISIS International and WIN News, were created to disseminate more information about women's research and activism, but members of DAWN and AAWORD and the regular participants in the Encuentros Feministas called for a more fundamental reconsideration of the practices and assumptions undergirding research in universities, foundations, governments and international organizations.

AAWORD founder Marie-Angélique Savané insisted during the 1980 Copenhagen conference that it was a misconception that 'research is a luxury that Africans cannot afford'.[27] AAWORD's founders reported to a 1982 UN conference on technical cooperation that 'local research on women, particularly by local researchers, is considered an unimportant, irrelevant and useless imitation of Western women's liberation' and that most of this research was not even available in Africa, since it was produced for external consumption by foreign researchers and funding entities.[28] 'In its research policy, AAWORD is to promote the decolonization of research in Africa.'[29] In particular, AAWORD members insisted that African scholars should determine research agendas and that quantitative methods should not eclipse qualitative approaches. 'Historically, "research" on Africa was conducted by

---

[26] From a December 1979 meeting in Lusaka, Zambia, on the Integration of Women in Development, cited in Economic Commission for Africa (ECA) preparatory documents for 1980 UN women's conference in Copenhagen (E/CN.14/44, Add.1), 4 March 1980.
[27] Florence Howe, 'Women's Studies International at Copenhagen: From Idea to Network', *Women's Studies Quarterly* 9, no. 1 (1981): 10.
[28] 'The experience … AAWORD', 107.
[29] Ibid., 110.

merchants, missionaries, colonialists and anthropologists' and the authors were 'male and socialized within a society where patriarchal Victorian values predominated, they very often either underestimated, romanticized, or completely ignored the vital roles African women played in their societies. Distortions were not limited to accounts of African women but permeated almost all the records.'[30] That generation had been succeeded by a parade of modernizing development specialists, followed, most recently, by 'Western women academics' challenging male-dominated social science and launching the women and development agenda. Armed with a feminist analysis and a determination to tear down patriarchal structures, these researchers interpreted gender roles as artefacts of 'tradition' and 'the universal subordination of women ... as a conspiracy by men all over the world to exclude women from the benefits of modernization and development'.[31] Although the organizers did not want to overdetermine how AAWORD members would orient their research, they were quite certain that Africans did not need another study of population control or nutrition. As they explained in a 1981 article in *Africa Development*, 'It is important to note that while these two topics are solicited and supported by a steady supply of external funding, neither topic, particularly the former, is considered a priority locally.'[32]

Describing DAWN's origins, its founder Devaki Jain said the UN conferences allowed her to identify other researchers who shared her interests. Jain, who had studied SEWA and the ways that street vendors' organizing as a trade union had altered domestic relations, describes the opportunity to present on a panel with Ester Boserup at the Mexico City conference as a 'turning point' in confirming her suspicions that 'all the measuring is wrong, and that the measuring of women and their work had to be redone'.[33] But it also served as a turning point in building a transnational network of activist intellectuals who used the UN to extend their reach. After the IWY conference, Jain explained,

> no UN agency could do anything without inviting me or the [Institute of Social Studies Trust] because we became the post-Mexico informed focal point. That led us then, constantly, to look at the UN's agenda and to try to adapt for it. The very thing for which the UN is honored in fact happened. That is, the UN provided us with the international platform to universalize issues which we earlier thought were only country-specific.[34]

---

[30] Ibid., 103.
[31] Ibid., 106.
[32] 'AAWORD The Association of African Women for Research and Development', *Africa Development/ Afrique et Developpement* 6, no. 2 (1981): 147. Interesting to note, given that AAWORD's members were all intellectuals who were aware of the role of publishing in professional advancement, that all these pieces are signed by AAWORD without individual names. On the commitment of foundations, aid agencies and international organizations to population-control efforts, see Matthew Connelly, *Fatal Misconception: The Struggle to Control World Population* (Cambridge: Harvard University Press, 2008).
[33] Devaki Jain interview.
[34] Devaki Jain interview. The ISST was founded in New Delhi following the IWY conference with the purpose of 'bridging research and action' particularly with regard to women's issues (https://www.isstindia.org/pdf/ISST_25_yeras.pdf).

She realized that the time-use studies she performed in India might be interesting to compare with similar work in Brazil. After attending a conference women's labour-force participation in Latin America, they decided to connect with other researchers through the UN's Economic and Social Commission for Asia and the Pacific (ESCAP). She recalled, 'Then ILO said to me, "Would you please do that for us?" So you got into that kind of loop – interregional exchange of ideas, interregional research, and regional.'[35] She found that these networks allowed her to counter the discrimination she encountered in other settings. Citing the Wellesley conference in particular, she explained,

> We brown/black [women] from the South found that every time we went [to development seminars] we would be in some kind of a position where we were critiquing what was being said by our northern sisters and then huddling together and saying, 'Oh these women, they are neocolonists.' We were very troubled by racist and intellectual domination type of disturbances. So this I had experienced for three or four years between 1975 and 1980, when the Copenhagen conference was held. Then when we went to the UN conference in Copenhagen, the divide came out very sharply. ... It became very humiliating, because then the people would say, 'These Third World women – these Third World women, they'll come and disrupt this conference. These Third World Women, they are so political.' It was that kind of 'these Third World women' like you talk of 'these disturbing punks.' So that was also rather demeaning.[36]

The Encuentros Feministas offered a quite different and even more disruptive challenge to knowledge production. Every Encuentro included a diverse collection of artists, academics and activists, and understanding would come through these various avenues – creatively, haptically and intuitively as well as through the emergent interdiscipline of women's studies. The gatherings regularly include film festivals, exhibit spaces and workshop sessions on practices such as making self-portraits.[37] At her inaugural address to the 1983 Lima Encuentro, Roxana Carrillo acknowledged that many attendees remained conflicted about whether it made sense 'to talk about feminism in our continent when extreme poverty and threats to peace, the persistence of ignominious dictators and the voracity of the transnational [corporations] – to mention only a few factors – darken our outlook and our understanding'.[38] The region's challenges, she insisted, demanded the irreverence, defiance and openness that the Encuentros promised – a movement based on 'creativity, humor, doubts,

---

[35] Devaki Jain interview.
[36] Devaki Jain interview.
[37] For description of the diverse creative activity at the early EFLAC meetings, see *1er Encuentro Feminista Latinoamericano y del Caribe* (March 1982); Rita Arditti, 'Encuentro Feminista Latinoamericano y del Caribe: Latin American and Caribbean Feminists Meet', *Off Our Backs*, 30 November 1983; Colectivo ISIS Internacional, 'Revista de las Mujeres'; Fernanda Pompeu, 'No hay caso', *Brujas: las mujeres escriben*, April, 1984.
[38] Roxanna Carrillo, 'Discurso inaugural: Segundo Encuentro Feminista Latinoamericano y del Caribe', *Fem*, 1 December, 1983, 7.

solidarity and utopias'. The Chilean feminist Julieta Kirkwood, reflecting on this gathering, wrote,

> One of the most notable features of contemporary feminism is that sort of 'irresponsibility' towards the scientific paradigm and the concepts that are assumed in its language. That type of impudence in mixing everything, as if one had the certainty that the tablets with the commandments of knowledge, coming as they do from on high, would have been shattered in their fall to humanity, and that, consequently, 'we would have to make do with what we have.'[39]

Refashioning feminism: The roots of feminist economics

Feminism – as both a concept and a label – is a famously fraught issue, particularly in the Global South, where detractors still brand it an imperialist import designed to distract from more pressing concerns about poverty, sovereignty and racial inequities.[40] Encuentros Feministas organizers persistently warned against adhering to a too-dogmatic *feministómetro* that would purport to measure 'legitimate' feminism and insisted upon developing an understanding of feminism that reflected regional priorities. Veteran attendees sometimes lost patience 'explaining' feminism to newcomers, while the initiates dismissed as 'históricas' those whom they perceived as clinging to antiquated and narrow conceptions of feminism.

While the Encuentros Feministas were born of a full-throated endorsement of feminism – followed by endless disagreements of what that implied – both DAWN and AAWORD sidled up to feminism more cautiously and always with the disclaimer that they sought an alternative to Western or Northern feminism. As AAWORD founders asserted in a 1982 essay, 'While the fight against "male hegemony," that is, the view that holds men as the enemy, is presently almost exclusively limited to certain sectors of the Western feminist movement, it has alienated large sectors of Third World women to the point where, locally, feminism is construed as a Western plague to be strictly avoided.'[41] Nonetheless, AAWORD founders Marie-Angélique Savané and Zenebework Tadesse participated in a UNESCO meeting about the importance of creating interdisciplinary women's studies programmes to advance the teaching of human rights.[42] Although clearly less ambivalent than the AAWORD founders about adopting the label feminist, DAWN leaders echoed AAWORD's concerns, explaining, 'Feminists in the North have to learn not to impose their ethnocentric brand of it on their Third World sisters so as not to compromise their movements. They have to acknowledge the legitimacy of the brand of feminism brought out by each culture.'[43]

---

[39] Colectivo ISIS Internacional, 'Revista de las Mujeres ', 100.
[40] Moghadam, *Globalizing Women*, 78–9.
[41] 'The experience … AAWORD': 106.
[42] 'UNESCO Document by Twelve "Experts on Research and Teaching Related to Women," Paris, May 1980', *Women's Studies Newsletter* VIII, no. 4 (Fall/Winter 1980): 22–3.
[43] Bleie and Lund, *Proceedings*, 27.

This ambivalence about feminism often indexed concerns about imputed subjectivities of race and sexuality. The historian Amina Mama explains,

> The question of feminism has spawned a century of African debates over gender, feminism, women's movements, and the woman question. Even so, the term is poorly understood in public life. It is *still* an African common-place to attribute anything concerning women, rights, peace, and development to 'feminism,' or 'Beijing-people' in ways that situate it as a dangerous foreign interference, racialized white, and sexualized lesbian.[44]

DAWN founder Peggy Antrobus told an interviewer that, when she attended a 1984 event in Thailand titled 'Feminist Ideologies and Structures', she simply told people at home in Jamaica that she was attending a conference on 'national machinery' – the bureaucratic structures that had been set up to support the objectives of the UN Decade for Women. 'In Mexico City', Antrobus explained, 'all the feminists were white, North American women. ... When I started working, feminist meant a lesbian. I couldn't tell anyone that I was going to a feminist meeting because feminism was a bad word, bad associations, bad connotations; and I did not think of myself as a feminist.'[45]

Nonetheless, by the mid-1980s, as preparations were underway for the 1985 Nairobi meeting that would conclude the UN Decade for Women, all three of these networks claimed a feminist orientation to one degree or another. DAWN members stressed that a 'strong consensus' had emerged that 'particularly the feminist underpinnings ... need to be elaborated further ... to classify concepts like production, reproduction, the sexual division of labour and women's work, how it is perceived, why it is undervalued, how the nature of women's work is changing and how women view themselves'.[46] All of the sessions that DAWN organized for the Nairobi conference included feminism in the title. By 1985 pretty much all the leadership of DAWN and AAWORD self-identified as feminist, but they had redefined that label to more closely reflect their own epistemologies and priorities.

Their critique of knowledge production and engagement with feminism led all three of these networks, to one degree or another, to concentrate on issues that anchored what would come to be known as feminist economics. DAWN and AAWORD, in particular, offered analyses that would later be seen as the field's most significant contributions: degrowth, ecological sustainability, the looming crisis of care and thoroughgoing challenges to developmentalism and market fundamentalism.[47] The principal intervention of feminist economics – that all extant economic metrics, most especially GDP and the System of National Accounts ignore the largest economic

---

[44] Amina Mama, '"We Will Not Be Pacified": From Freedom Fighters to Feminists', *The European Journal of Women's Studies* 27, no. 4 (2020): 363.
[45] 'A Glimpse at DAWN's History: Interview with Peggy Antrobus' (29 January 2010), http://www.dawnnet.org/feminist-resources/archive/podcasts?page=3.
[46] Bleie and Lund, *Proceedings*, 4.
[47] Benería, Berik and Floro, *Gender, Development, and Globalization*; Berik and Kongar, *The Routledge Handbook of Feminist Economics*.

sector by omitting the vast amounts of time, labour and expertise required to sustain societies – was ineluctably evident in parts of the world with more robust subsistence economies. If the fiction of GDP were clear in places such as New Zealand and France, it was incontrovertible in places such as Zambia and Bolivia.

As the Indian trade unionist and International Labor Organization legal advisor Krishna Ahooja-Patel explained in 1979, '[I]f a total range of women's actual economic activities were to be taken into account, a different picture of social reality begins to emerge.' Time-budget studies and 'common sense observations' had demonstrated that

> across economic and social organisation and geographical regions, women work longer hours; in market and non-market activities; in industrialised countries and the urban sector of developing countries and more obviously in the rural areas of Asia, Africa and Latin America. It is the nature and type of their work and the global performance of work-hours which raises fundamental economic and social issues.[48]

Ahooja-Patel would reiterate this point three years later at the AAWORD conference that produced the 1982 Dakar Declaration. 'Fundamentally', she explained in her keynote address, 'most of women's activities appear to fall outside the definition of "gainful employment". They are confined to a pigeon-hole, labelled "non-market" or "non-monetized" activities. It is this differential between "work" and "creativity" that fundamentally affects women and erodes their economic and social status.'[49] The women of AAWORD offered an even more pointed critique. '"Modernization" and "development" have meant a few schools, a handful of industries and the ever-growing importance of cash crop production and other cash generating activities,' they explained to a UN agency meeting on technical cooperation in 1982. 'Each of these new institutions have increased women's work and simultaneously decreased the time and resources that the majority of women would have spent caring for their children and their own well-being.'[50]

Aftermaths: Legacies of solidarity struggles

A decade later, following the fourth UN Women's conference in Beijing, DAWN founder Peggy Antrobus reflected on the ways that the UN Decade for Women had created an infrastructure that brought together women of different views and backgrounds, particularly introducing women from the Global South in closer contact with various strands of feminism and exposing women from the Global North to the radical diversity of women's needs and experiences. Two decades after

---

[48] Krishna Ahooja-Patel, 'Women, Technology and Development Process', *Economic and Political Weekly* 14, no. 36 (8 September 1979): 1550.
[49] Krishna Ahooja-Patel, 'Another Development with Women', *Development Dialogue*, nos. 1–2 (1982): 20–1.
[50] 'The experience ... AAWORD', 101.

the controversial Wellesley conference, the assumptions that animated it – of a universal feminine experience, that women from the Global North would tutor their Southern sisters about development, that women did not already play a critical role in economies of the Global South – all seemed wildly inappropriate. But the process of recognizing the absurdity of these assumptions took place because of networks such as AAWORD, DAWN and the Encuentros Feministas. This process involved bringing feminist perspectives to bear on all issues – human rights, environmental degradation and economic justice – as well as those that had been considered 'women's issues' at the beginning of the decade – such as reproductive rights, domestic violence and equal opportunities. The 'infusion of feminism as a transformational politics' had fundamentally changed the strategies adopted by activists such as those who populated these networks, but their engagement also transformed feminism itself.[51]

The combination of the Third Worldist orientation of the UN during this period and the explosion of women-oriented civil society organizations fostered exchanges between feminists of all stripes from the Global North and women from the Global South whose political formation had often come through national liberation movements, Marxist political parties and anti-racism campaigns. These encounters remained frictive and combative, often highlighting differences more than commonalities, but those conflicts proved generative in the long run. After the Wellesley conference, organizers of international gatherings attended much more carefully to incorporating perspectives of the Global South and questioning the 'narrow classical concept of development, often equated with material and technical growth, divorced from human growth'.[52] The authors of this critique – Nawal El-Sawadi, Fatima Mernissi and Mallica Vajrathon – all worked within the UN during this period, as would many other members of these Global South networks. They also, along with other prominent network leaders such as Devaki Jain, Marie-Angélique Savané and Peggy Antrobus and renowned intellectuals such as Simone de Beauvoir, all contributed to the noted (and in some circles notorious) 1984 volume *Sisterhood Is Global*.[53] Networks such as AAWORD, DAWN and the Encuentros Feministas strategically navigated and leveraged the commitments of both liberal internationalism and 1970s feminism to advance a South-based transnational feminism grounded in anti-capitalist, anti-imperialist and anti-racist commitments in solidarity with but explicitly and insistently autonomous from the male-dominated political parties and militant movements that had consistently failed to create space for them.

---

[51] Peggy Antrobus, 'Bringing Grassroots Women's Needs to the International Arena', *Development* 39, no. 3 (September 1996): 64.
[52] Nawal El-Sawadi, Fatima Mernissi and Mallica Vajrathon, 'A Critical Look at the Wellesley Conference', *Quest: A Feminist Quarterly*, vol. IV, no. 2 (Winter 1978): 104.
[53] Robin Morgan, *Sisterhood Is Global: The International Women's Movement Anthology*, 1st ed. (Garden City, NY: Anchor Press/Doubleday, 1984).

Part Three

Grassroots internationalisms, informal networks and new mobilizations

12

The left and the international arena: The Rosenberg case

Phillip Deery

Introduction

Prior to the executions of Ethel and Julius Rosenberg in June 1953, a massive campaign to save the Rosenbergs was waged internationally. Transnational solidarity had been expressed before and would be again, but not with such raw passion as then. If it were simply directives from Moscow or even the customary communication between Anglophone communist parties, this solidarity might be less remarkable. Although communist parties in all countries played a significant, if belated, role in mobilizing support in each country, it was in fact a non-communist Left organization, the National Committee to Secure Justice in the Rosenberg Case (NCSJRC), formed on 10 October 1952, that spearheaded the protest movement and generated international solidarity. This chapter examines that committee: its genesis, the sources of its support, the extent of communist domination and its activation of international solidarity. The chapter is therefore a case study of 'grassroots internationalism' that emerged despite the hostile environment of the Cold War. Challenging the customary depiction of top-down control and asserting the agency of grassroots activism, it will argue that the various 'Save the Rosenbergs' committees, triggered by the NCSJRC, arose before, and largely independent from, official Communist Party involvement or Moscow's influence, instead communicating directly with New York. Such international solidarity by the Left failed in its ultimate objectives – clemency or a retrial – but revealed the scope and potential of global mobilization outside the Stalinist straitjacket in the early Cold War.

Charged with conspiracy to commit espionage, Julius and Ethel Rosenberg were arrested by the FBI in July and August 1950, put on trial in March 1951 and sentenced to death in April 1951.[1] They were the only American civilians, ever, to receive a death

---

[1] The literature on the Rosenberg case is vast, but the best-known secondary works are Walter and Miriam Schneir, *Invitation to an Inquest* (New York: Doubleday, 1965, republished 1973, 1983) and Ronald Radosh and Joyce Milton, *The Rosenberg File: A Search for the Truth* (New York: Holt, Rinehart & Winston, 1983). None of this literature deals specifically with the NCSJRC or uses the organization's records. For recent overviews, see Walter Schneir, *Final Verdict: What Really Happened in the Rosenberg Case* (New York: Melville House, 2010); Michael Meeropol, '"A Spy Who Turned His Family In": Revisiting David Greenglass and the Rosenberg Case', *American Communist History* 17, no. 2 (2018): 247–60.

sentence for spying. Although the actual charge, under the Espionage Act of 1917, was conspiracy to commit espionage, the widely held view, then and now, was that the Rosenbergs – or at least Julius – were 'atom bomb spies' who provided the Kremlin with *the* secret of the bomb and thereby committed, in J. Edgar Hoover's remarkable phrase, 'the crime of the century'. Defenders of the Rosenbergs maintained that their sentences resulted from a flagrant miscarriage of justice and that their deaths constituted legal murder. The widespread shock and outrage, and the elevation of this event into a *cause célèbre* of the Cold War, were primarily due to the efforts of the NCSJRC. The chapter will not revisit the well-trodden historiographical ground concerning the extent of the Rosenbergs' guilt, the judicial irregularities of their trial, the protracted appeals processes or the legacies of the case. What the chapter does demonstrate are the transatlantic and transpacific connections and crosscurrents that this committee reflected or stimulated in its quest to mobilize global opinion.

Genesis and early activity

Inspired by an article in the New York left weekly the *National Guardian*, entitled 'Is This the Dreyfus Case of Cold War America?', by their close reading of the trial transcript, and by their unequivocal moral objection to the death penalty, two New Yorkers, Emily and David Alman, formed the NCSJRC on 9 October 1951. It was tiny, they met in the Almans' apartment every Wednesday, and it was bereft of funds. But after the *Guardian* inserted an advertisement requesting 'enlistment' in the committee and a pledge of funds 'to bring the facts of the case to a wider audience', money and support began to trickle in and later escalated.

David Alman, the executive secretary of the NCSJRC, was a 32-year-old novelist. He had been a communist in his youth, but left the Communist Party of the United States of America (CPUSA) when the Nazi-Soviet pact was signed in 1939. His wife, Emily, a 29-year-old social worker, had never been a Party member, and became the committee's treasurer. The substantive chairman of the committee was Joseph Brainin, a publicist and veteran fund-raiser for several 'establishment' Jewish organizations. The infant NCSJRC leadership was disproportionately Jewish in composition and only Louis Harap, the editor of *Jewish Life*, was a communist. As Alman put it, 'We were not a Committee of Very Important Persons. We were unquestionably insular. All of us were Jewish, with bonds of common experience and history.'[2] The committee's assets consisted initially of $100, a borrowed old mimeograph machine and a single copy of the 2600-page trial record, which all had read. It had no office, no telephone and 'no certainty that our audience – the general public – would respond sympathetically.'[3]

The first major effort of the NCSJRC to mobilize opinion was a public meeting on 12 March 1952 at New York's Pythian Hall. Despite the mainstream press refusing to accept advertisements for the meeting, and the late cancellation of the first-booked

---

[2] Emily Arnow Alman and David Alman, *Exoneration: The Rosenberg-Sobell Case in the 21st Century* (Seattle: Green Elms Press, 2010), 22.
[3] Ibid., 161.

meeting hall, fifteen hundred New Yorkers paid their sixty cents admission fee to hear 'The Truth about the Rosenberg Case', as the meeting was billed in one press release.[4] The meeting lasted three and a half hours; was addressed by eight speakers, with further messages read out including a personal 'death house' letter from Ethel Rosenberg; and raised $5000. According to one report, the audience was 'moved to tears' during the address given by Helen Sobell – wife of Morton Sobell, imprisoned for thirty years for his complicity in espionage – and 'a rising salute' when she finished. As an FBI informant noted with understatement, '[the] audience seemed enthusiastic throughout the meeting'.[5] Finally, the meeting resolved to adopt an *Amicus Curiae* brief being prepared by the NCSJRC for submission to the Supreme Court, appealing for a review of the case, and called on the US Attorney General to consent to a new trial.[6]

The success of the Pythian Hall meeting energized the NCSJRC. After numerous rejections, it found an office, employed a full-time secretary, opened a bank account and issued further appeals. Hundreds of letters to 'Dear Friends' both within the United States and to Left sympathizers and progressive organizations in Europe, the UK, Australia and elsewhere. As we shall see, one of the consequences of this letter writing was transnational cooperation and solidarity. Not surprisingly, New Yorkers were the most responsive: informal networks and word-of-mouth meant that subsidiary committees were soon established across all boroughs. By the time the executive secretary reported to committee members on 30 April 1952, much had been accomplished. Scores of local committees were established not just in NYC but across the country, 35,000 signatures to the *Amicus Curiae* brief were obtained, and 400,000 pamphlets were distributed.[7] However, the national committee remained chronically short of funds. The $12,000 it borrowed to print a thousand copies of the court record meant it had no reserves for further legal fees, paid advertisements, financial support for the up-keep of the two Rosenberg children, printing new pamphlets or reprinting existing material. The overwhelming number of donations – the correspondence files of the NCSJRC bulge with letters from supporters attaching money – was small, often as little as one dollar. There was no 'Moscow Gold'. By mid-August 1952, after calling for $25,000 'to bring the truth to the public', less than $5000 was received.[8] In late November, 'we need not tell you how desperately we need your financial help'.[9] In

---

[4] William A. Reuben Papers, TAM.289, Box 12, Folder 47, Tamiment Library and Robert F. Wagner Labor Archives, New York University [hereafter Tamiment].
[5] FBI File No. 100-15241, FOIPA No. 1197746-000.
[6] The above is drawn from Cablegram, SAC [Special Agent in Charge] Scheidt, New York to Director, Washington, 13 March 1951, 1–3, and Report to Director and Assistant Attorney General, 17 March 1951, 1–4, FBI file; Leaflet, 'The Truth about the Rosenberg Case', FBI File; Letter, Alman to 'Dear Friend', 15 March 1952, Box 11, Folder 20, Committee to Secure Justice for Morton Sobell Records, 1946–1969, MSS 7, Wisconsin Historical Society Archives [hereafter Sobell Records]; *National Guardian*, 19 March 1953.
[7] David Alman, 'Progress in campaign to secure justice in the Rosenberg case', 30 April 1952, Sobell Records, Box 24, Folder 6. In the end, an astonishing 6 million leaflets and pamphlets were sent from the National Office alone. Emily Alman, 'The Lessons of the Rosenberg case', report to the National Officers, Rosenberg-Sobell Committees, 11 October 1953, Sobell Records, Box 21, Folder 3.
[8] Alman to 'Dear Friend', 15 August 1952, Sobell Records, Box 17, Folder 6.
[9] Alman to 'Dear Friend', 22 November 1952, ibid.

December, 'we are financially unable to operate. Please help us'.[10] By February 1953, the committee's funds were completely exhausted.[11] Only dedicated sympathizers, it seemed, were prepared to pay the ten dollars for the set of eight volumes (1800 pages) of the entire record of the Rosenbergs' trial, which the committee believed was the best means of persuading the public of the need for a new trial and thereby garnering more signatures for the *Amicus* petitions.[12]

A communist front?

Was the NCSJRC communist-inspired or a communist 'front' organization? This is an important question because of its historiographical depiction, its contemporaneous implications and its key role in this defining episode of Cold War espionage. For the purposes of this chapter, the question is crucial. If communist-inspired, then the worldwide protest movement can be seen as an international left campaign manipulated by Moscow in order to serve the foreign policy goals of the Soviet Union. This could still have represented a striking example of the 'left and the international arena' but if the role of Moscow were negligible and that of the local communist parties limited, then we must see this global Cold War protest movement in a different perspective, a perspective to which I will return later.

Certainly, mainstream and conservative opinion within the United States, and at least some of the literature, emphasized Communist Party manipulation or control of the NCSJRC, even in the early, struggling months of its existence. Three examples. In response to the Pythian Hall meeting, the normally liberal *New York Post* editorialized that the NCSJRC was 'a thinly-disguised Communist front'.[13] *Counterattack*, the weekly publication of American Business Consultants Inc., bluntly stated that the committee was a 'front set up by CP to direct agitation and propaganda'; that the Pythian Hall meeting was intended to 'whip up support for the Communist Party's campaign' on behalf of the Rosenbergs; and that the committee 'peddles inflammatory, divisive propaganda to further [the communists'] own ends'.[14] Investigators for the House Committee on Un-American Activities (HUAC) reported that 'in virtually every area' the Rosenberg campaign was 'initiated and conducted' by the CPUSA.[15] HUAC concluded that the NCSJRC (and every one of its forty-two local affiliates) was a subversive organization in thrall to the CPUSA and organized 'for the purposes of international communism', it was not communist-inspired.[16] And as

[10] Undated letter (December 1952), Alman to 'Dear Friend', Sobell Records, Box 19, Folder 4.
[11] Alman to 'Dear Friend', 12 February 1953, Sobell Records, Box 17, Folder 7.
[12] Alman to 'Dear Friend', 16 July 1952, Sobell Records, Box 17, Folder 6. As Alman acknowledged, 'We know that the price is high ... [but] if it helps reveal the truth and save lives, it may not be such a high price to pay.' Alman to 'Dear Friend', 22 July 1952, Sobell Records, Box 17, Folder 6.
[13] Cited in *National Guardian*, 26 March 1952.
[14] *Counterattack*, 28 March 1952 [1–2], in American Business Consultants, Inc Counterattack: Research Files, TAM.148, Box 28, Tamiment.
[15] Edmond Le Breton, 'Rosenberg Agitation Called Red Triumph', *Washington Post*, 27 August 1956, 19.
[16] Committee on Un-American Activities, *Trial by Treason: The National Committee to Secure Justice for the Rosenbergs and Morton Sobell* (Washington: House Committee on Un-American Activities, 1956); *Washington Post*, 27 August 1956, 118; *Guide to Subversive Organizations and Publications* (Washington: Committee on Un-American Activities, 1957), 60.

a typical communist 'front' organization, the NCSJRC engaged in clandestine, if not conspiratorial, activity.[17]

The evidence for CPUSA disinterest in if not outright opposition to the NCSJRC is extensive. All of the four 'cooperative' witnesses at the HUAC hearings into the NCSJRC in August 1955 testified that the CPUSA had not been instrumental in establishing the NCSJRC and that no funds collected were directed to the party. This did not deter HUAC from reaching the opposite conclusion in its report.[18] If we accept the authenticity of David Alman's recollection – and there is no reason to doubt it – the CPUSA was not only *un*involved but sought actively to undermine the committee and the clemency campaign. It sought first to abort it and then boycott it. This lasted for more than a year. Alman wrote in 2010:

> Shortly after the *National Guardian* carried news of the Committee's formation, emissaries from the CPUSA called on Committee members to urge that they disband, arguing that the Attorney General would label the Committee a Communist organization and that its challenge to the fairness of the trial would create the impression that the 'Communist' Committee was defending spies and traitors. This, in turn, would reflect badly on the CPUSA.[19]

It is probable that the party feared, at least until mid-1952, that Julius Rosenberg might confess, as KGB courier Harry Gold and atomic spy Klaus Fuchs had recently done. In that event, other Soviet agents in the United States would be named and the CPUSA would be implicated. Such an explicit identification with treason and espionage posed real dangers. Distancing was therefore essential. When the Rosenbergs refused to cooperate and maintained their innocence, the decision, subsequently, to defend a couple who had chosen martyrdom became far easier. As the high-ranking chairman of the CPUSA's Cultural Commission, Victor Jerome allegedly whispered to a trusted comrade, 'They're heroes. They're going to their death and not saying a word.'[20] It is little wonder, then, that Emily Alman – who herself was told by an emissary from the Party leadership that 'she was not to do the Rosenberg thing'[21] – was critical of the Party's 'secrecy and deviousness' in relation to the Rosenberg campaign.[22]

The NCSJRC, therefore, was neither conceived nor controlled by the CPUSA. Just as the committee was not controlled by the CPUSA, nor was the global protest movement controlled by the Kremlin. Indeed, it was only *after* European countries, notably France and Italy, began sprouting large-scale Rosenberg protests that the Communist Party leadership decided to participate.

---

[17] *Trial by Treason*; *Washington Post*, 27 August 1956.
[18] United States House of Representatives Committee on Un-American Activities, *Investigation of Communist Activities (The Committee to Secure Justice in the Rosenberg Case and Affiliates) Hearings*, 84th Congress, 1st Session, 2–5 August 1955, Parts I & II (Washington, DC, 1955).
[19] Alman and Alman, *Exoneration*, 181.
[20] Interview with John Gates, 14 June 1978, in Ronald Radosh and Joyce Milton, *The Rosenberg File: A Search for the Truth* (New York: Holt, Rinehart and Winston, 1983), 328.
[21] Cited in Radosh and Milton, *Rosenberg File*, 327.
[22] Alman and Alman, *Exoneration*, 210.

What emerges from the voluminous FBI files on the NCSJRC is the increasing number of *rank and file* communists who either in ignorance or defiance of the official party position cooperated with the NCSJRC. This became an issue, according to Alman, in late 1952, when both the NCSJRC and the communist-controlled American Labor Party held separate meetings in New York's Union Square. A sizable part of the audience listening initially to communist speakers deserted that meeting and crossed over to hear about the Rosenbergs. This minor incident is emblematic not only of the growing support for the Rosenbergs' cause but also of the *absence* of cooperation between the NCSJRC and the CPUSA – a feature overlooked when the American and international clemency campaigns are referred to.

From the beginning of 1953, it is more accurate to see the relationship between the CPUSA and the NCSJRC as one of convergence, not one of domination/subordination. To assume the committee's acquiescence to the party line – a distinguishing feature of the 'front' organization – is to deny its agency. The party's political shift to now supporting the cause (after initially boycotting it) did not mean organizational control. Undoubtedly the injection of the party's vast resources, networks, energy and propaganda apparatus in the first six months of 1953 extended the scope and reach of the clemency campaign. But, to repeat, the myriad activities undertaken by the various NCSJRCs were endorsed and assisted by the CPUSA, but not – and the internal committee records make this abundantly clear – instigated by it.

Countdown to execution

The final days of the Rosenbergs' lives were feverish ones for the NCSJRC. An astonishingly wide range of flyers, leaflets and brochures were produced and distributed in their hundreds of thousands.[23] As late as 15 June 1953, four days before the executions, David Alman was still writing 'The Rosenbergs can be saved'; meetings were still being held; petitions to the president were still being sent;[24] and supporters still believed that legal processes would rescue the Rosenbergs from the electric chair. Events now moved quickly. On 16 June a new motion filed with Justice William O. Douglas argued that the death penalty in this instance was applicable only under the Atomic Energy Act, not the Espionage Act and therefore grounds for a retrial existed. On 17 June Douglas granted an indefinite stay of execution pending argument on this point. Hopes soared. Those picketing the White House believed their vigil had become a victory celebration. But euphoria was quickly replaced by anxiety. Under pressure from the Department of Justice, Chief Justice Vinson reconvened the Supreme Court to hear arguments. In a highly controversial decision

---

[23] Copies of these are held in various boxes in the Sobell Records, the University of Wisconsin-Milwaukee Archives: UWM MSS 213, Box 7, Folder 4, and Tamiment: TAM.PE 036 ORGS Box 62.
[24] See Brainin to Eisenhower (with petition attached) 15 June 1953, Sobell Records, Box 5, Folder 11; for the scores of clemency petitions, see Sobell Records, Box 2, Folder 6.

on 19 June the Court, with Justices Black, Douglas and Frankfurter dissenting, vacated the stay of execution and denied a motion for further stay to consider a new petition for clemency filed by defence attorney Bloch.[25] Later that day, in defiance of a flood of international appeals and a spirited, cogent case presented in person by four ecclesiastic spokespeople (two Protestants, one Rabbi and one scholar) representative of 2300 clergymen, Eisenhower for the second time refused to exercise executive clemency. The execution time was advanced from 11 pm to avoid conflict with the Jewish Sabbath and by 8.16 pm on Friday 19 June, both the Rosenbergs were dead. Just hours before she was electrocuted Ethel wrote an emotionally charged letter to her 'Dearest sweethearts, my most precious children'. It concluded: 'Always remember that we were innocent and could not wrong our conscience. We press you close and kiss you with all our strength.'[26]

Of course, they were not innocent, and Dwight Eisenhower and Irving Kaufman and J. Edgar Hoover all knew this. Those dozens of deputations conducted, hundreds of meetings held, tens of thousands of petition signatures collected, and millions of flyers, letters and brochures distributed throughout the previous twenty months were all doomed. Why? Because the FBI had access to the top-secret intercepts of Soviet intelligence messages obtained by the Venona code-breaking operation, and these confirmed Julius's key role in an espionage ring. To prevent the Soviets realizing their codes had been compromised the intelligence was never used in court. However, Hoover shared it with Kaufman: 'Irving was in on everything', said Roy Cohn, a prosecuting attorney at the Rosenberg trial. 'He knew about the secret intercepts and that we couldn't use them.'[27] If so, it helps explain why 'Kaufman told me *before* the trial started that he was going to sentence Julius Rosenberg to death.'[28] Eisenhower, too, was informed. And this helps explain why *he* was so intransigent.

The international campaign – France

In the two-year period between the launching of legal appeals against the Rosenbergs' conviction and sentence, and the date of their execution, 19 June 1953, an international protest movement developed. What follows is a brief sketch suggesting the flavour of the French clemency campaign, and a more detailed analysis of the Australian campaign. Space prevents the discussion of activities undertaken in other countries (including Canada, Germany, Hungary, India, Ireland, Israel, Italy, Japan, Mexico, Poland, Scandinavia and South Africa), on which dedicated folders can be found in the records of the NCSJRC.

---

[25] For an overview of the Supreme Court's 'patently inadequate' performance, see Robert M. Lichtman, *The Supreme Court and McCarthy-Era Repression* (Urbana: University of Illinois Press, 2012), 58–63.
[26] Copy in Sobell Records, Box 48, Folder 5.
[27] Cited in Alan M. Dershowitz, 'Rosenbergs Were Guilty – and Framed', *Los Angeles Times*, 19 July 1995.
[28] Sidney Zion, *The Autobiography of Roy Cohn* (Secaucus, NJ: Lyle Stuart, 1998), 77. Emphasis in original.

Of the many European countries that witnessed widespread protests against the Rosenbergs' death sentence, France was the loudest and most sustained. According to the press attaché at the US embassy in Paris, the Rosenberg case swept France 'like a Kansas prairie fire'.[29] It dwarfed the efforts in all other countries outside the United States. The editor of a left newspaper, *Le Combat*, forged direct links with the NCSJRC in the United States and a French offshoot (Comité Français pour la Defense des Rosenbergs) was formed in late 1952.[30] The protest movement escalated and public opinion was mobilized. The overwhelming majority of the French press was opposed to the executions. This opposition extended far beyond the communist *L'Humanité* or the leftist *Libération*. The moderate *Le Monde* and *Le Figaro* and the conservative *L'Aurore* also gave sympathetic and regular coverage, sometimes front-page, to the Rosenbergs' case. *Le Figaro* interviewed fourteen prominent French intellectuals, all of whom protested the death sentence; some proclaiming the Rosenbergs' complete innocence.

The mainstream French press published letters and statements from the local Rosenberg Committee questioning judicial procedure of the trial, the unprecedented death sentence handed down in a civilian court for conspiracy to commit espionage and the stark contrast with the far more lenient sentence given to the British atomic spy, Klaus Fuchs, for a far more serious case of espionage. Among the French press, both moderate and radical, there was an unusual unanimity in their outright condemnation of the death sentence. Considerable publicity was given to the letter written to Eisenhower by the descendants of Alfred Dreyfus. The US embassy in Paris from late 1952 until the executions was inundated with many thousands of postcards, telegrams and petitions. The embassy was even picketed by French Catholic priests, emboldened by Pope Pius XII who in January 1953 publicly condemned the impending executions and called for clemency.

After President Eisenhower decided to deny clemency, a decision opposed by nearly all of the so-called (by the FBI) 'non-commie' Parisian press, the Rosenberg Committee escalated protests. On 19 February, for example, it organized a protest rally attended by 12,000 Parisians. The *New York Times* conceded that the Rosenberg case was the 'top issue' in France, which reflected the success of 'anti-American propaganda' even amongst die-hard anti-communists.[31] On the eve of the executions, in early June 1953, the protest movement had extended from Lyon to Strasbourg. High-level government officials, from the French Prime Minister (Edgar Faure), President of the National Assembly (Edouard Herriot) and the French President (Vincent Auriol); sections of the hierarchy of the Catholic and reformed Presbyterian church; and trade union leaders, lawyers, scientists and artists, all strongly recommended presidential

---

[29] Cited in John Neville, *The Press, the Rosenbergs, and the Cold War* (Westport: Praeger, 1995), 80. The following relies on Robert B. Glynn, 'L'Affaire Rosenberg in France', *Political Science Quarterly* 70, no. 4 (1955): 498–521; Lori Clune, *Executing the Rosenbergs: Death and Diplomacy in a Cold War World* (New York: Oxford University Press, 2016), 47, 52, 59, 105, 117; Neville, *The Press*, 80–1.

[30] Sobell Records, Box 10, Folder 15.

[31] *New York Times*, 22 February 1953, E4.

Figure 12.1 Demonstration at the Place de la Nation, Paris, to support Julius and Ethel Rosenberg. Photo by Dominique BERRETTY/Gamma-Rapho via Getty Images.

clemency. They may not have believed in the Rosenbergs' innocence but they did believe in justice and mercy.

In the days before the executions, dissent in France exploded. Petitions flooded into the Ambassador's office, a 'day of action' was declared and picketing of the US Embassy intensified. On one day, 18 June, more than 2000 petitions were received; up from 1500 petitions received over the previous three days. Paris led the world in the scale and intensity of the demonstrations. One, attended by 7000 people, approved a telegram to Eisenhower: 'the people of Paris, united as never before since liberation, beg you not to make an irreparable gesture'. In the hours before the executions, tens of thousands of Parisians assembled in the Place de la Concord. Passionate emotions erupted into violence, the police fired bullets into the rioting crowd, killing one, and arrested 400 before order was restored and the demonstrators were dispersed.

The international campaign – Australia

The strength and virulence of the pro-clemency movement in France were unparalleled. It was not matched in Australia. But the fact that a protest movement existed, and escalated, was indicative of the long reach of the fraternal handshake that embraced others on the Left. The Australian campaign to pressure the Truman and Eisenhower administrations to grant clemency to the Rosenbergs had distinctive features, but broadly echoed the American and European approaches: petitions, pickets, meetings, deputations and vigils. And as in England, France, Italy and the United States, the Communist Party of Australia (CPA) was certainly involved but was neither the originator nor the main perpetuator. Australian interest in the Rosenberg case surfaced before 'official' involvement commenced. When the CPA did, belatedly, throw its considerable resources and propaganda efforts into the campaign, the movement remained widely based and non-sectarian. By examining the activities of the Australian Rosenberg Committee, which were part of this spiralling international movement and exchange of ideas, we can discern cross-currents and patterns between Australia and other countries in what was truly a transnational Cold War global protest.

On 9 January 1952, the chairman of the NCSJRC, Joseph Brainin, wrote to the secretary of the left-leaning Democratic Rights Council (DRC) in Sydney, Harold Rich, appealing for help. This letter was to initiate a remarkable episode of international cooperation by two previously unconnected organizations on the Left. Brainin called on the DRC to communicate directly with President Truman and stage demonstrations in order that American officials in Australia become aware of local opinion. Brainin enclosed printed material to acquaint the DRC with detailed information about the case and pleaded: 'we beg of you … to organize actions on behalf of the Rosenbergs.'[32] Over the next two years the DRC did just that.

Numerous Save the Rosenbergs committees began to form across Australia. One was in the town of Glenelg, in South Australia. On 20 January 1952, thirteen members signed a letter urging Truman to lift the death sentence. 'Our reading of American reports', it stated, 'convince us that the trial was prejudiced'.[33] Often it was simply individuals, such as Joan Howard, who read 'various news reports' in the Melbourne press, felt 'compelled to raise a cry of protest'; she signed her letter 'Yours for the Christian way of life'.[34] A group of residents from the tiny NSW town of Nana Glen petitioned Truman 'urgently requesting [an] impartial review to avoid irreparable injustice'.[35] It is difficult to discern the hidden hand of the CPA, or even of the DRC, behind this correspondence. None of it appears orchestrated or standardized, and the timing and the tone suggest the writers were acting independently, spontaneously and viscerally to what they believed was a miscarriage of justice.

---

[32] Brainin to Rich, 9 January 1952, Sobell Records, Box 3, Folder 7.
[33] Duplicated copy of letter to Truman sent to the 'Rosenberg Clemency Committee' in New York, 20 January 1950; Sobell Records, Box 17, Folder 6.
[34] Howard to Truman, 7 July 1952, Sobell Records, Box 17, Folder 6.
[35] Ivan Shipman to Truman, 2 March 1952, Sobell Records, Box 17, Folder 6.

Well before the Communist Party took up the Rosenbergs' cause, other groups, unaffiliated to the party, expressed concern. One was the Australian Council of Civil Liberties. In September 1951, under the headline 'Is this Cold War America's Dreyfus Case?', it reprinted both the editorial from an August 1951 issue of the *National Guardian*, and a detailed report on the case by William A. Reuben.[36] The New York paper explicitly acknowledged the Australian support.[37] Another Australian organization that voiced early opposition to the death sentence was the Youth Section of the Jewish Council to Combat Fascism and Anti-Semitism. Also taking its cue from the *National Guardian*, it published a four-page leaflet in late 1951, *The Rosenberg Sentence – A Dreyfus Case?* It asked readers to 'remember the story' of Alfred Dreyfus, and drew parallels with the Rosenberg case: anti-Semitism, scanty evidence supplemented by 'propaganda and mass hysteria', and false conviction. It concluded: 'Will Julius and Ethel Rosenberg find their Zola?'[38]

Well over twelve months passed before the CPA, like its American counterpart, interested itself in the Rosenberg case. Such interest was stimulated, coordinated and mobilized by communist parties across both Western and Eastern Europe from November 1952; the CPA merely followed suit. In December 1952 the CPA's national paper *Tribune* publicized the Rosenberg case for the first time. 'Only days remain', it declared, 'for world protests to save these young parents from electrocution'. It likened the Rosenbergs' fate to that of Sacco and Vanzetti, two Italian anarchists executed in 1927, and invoked the urgency of Pablo Picasso's appeal: 'The hours, the minutes count.'[39]

Activists in Australia responded to Eisenhower's refusal to intervene in the Rosenberg case after the Second Circuit Court of Appeals granted a stay of execution on 5 January. In protest, the DRC in Melbourne organized a rally attended by 'more than 600 Melbourne citizens' on 12 January and a two-day continuous picket of the US Consulate in Bourke Street, where 'Free Rosenbergs' was painted in large letters on the footpath.[40] This picket was filmed by the Australian Security Intelligence Organisation (ASIO).[41] At least four different deputations met with US Consul Henry Stebbins. In Sydney on 9 January, approximately 10,000 people gathered outside the US Consulate in Wynyard Street, blocked traffic in George Street, distributed thousands of leaflets and hung a huge 'Save the Rosenbergs' banner from the eighth floor of a bank building. Again organized by the DRC, a small deputation – initially barred by a formidable contingent of police – was received by a Consular duty officer; he refused to talk to the deputation but agreed to transmit a written submission. A hastily written message was then handed to the officer. In hope as much as in self-delusion, *Tribune* declared that 'the Australian people had struck a mighty blow to secure justice for Julius and Ethel Rosenberg'.[42]

---

[36] *Australian News-Review*, September 1951, 8–9.
[37] 'Australia Rights Group Backs Fight to Save Rosenbergs', *National Guardian*, 3 October 1951, 5.
[38] H. Spitz, *The Rosenberg Sentence – A Dreyfus Case?* (Melbourne: Jewish Council to Combat Fascism and Anti-Semitism, Youth Section, 1951), 1, 4. Émile Zola wrote the famous open letter 'J'Accuse … !' and campaigned on Dreyfus' behalf.
[39] *Tribune*, 3 December 1952, 9.
[40] *Guardian*, 19 January 1953, 1, 3.
[41] The film is lodged at the National Archives of Australia (NAA): C5431/4, 32/1/299.2.
[42] *Tribune*, 14 January 1953, 1.

Save the Rosenbergs committees around the world, including in Australia, were both heartened and stimulated by the appeal of Pope Pius XII in February 1953 to President Eisenhower to intervene and commute the death penalty. Throughout the autumn of 1953, the campaign in Australia intensified. By 5 March, the US Embassy in Canberra had received twenty telegrams, twenty-one letters and four petitions. Subsequently, more direct approaches were pursued. The records of the New York-based NCSJRC contain copies of innumerable private letters, petitions, cables and protest resolutions sent directly from Australia to the United States.[43] One long letter was received in the New York office from Lilli Williams, the secretary of the Australian committee. Under various headings – newspaper publicity, public meetings, smaller meetings, deputations, demonstrations, picketing, cables sent to the US President, further cables and petitions – she provided a highly detailed report of the campaign. She thanked David Alman for the 'very helpful' news-sheets produced by the NCSJRC, which were passed on to other members of her committee, and concluded: 'We are all working as hard as we can to save the lives of these two young people ... as soon as there are any new developments in our campaign, we shall be in touch with you.'[44] Brainin's request to the Australian activist, Rev. Frank Hartley (DRC) – to 'please, keep us informed of your activities!' – underscores the reciprocal nature of this transnational solidarity.[45] And as the date of the executions drew closer, so the exchange of correspondence increased between the Save the Rosenbergs committee in Sydney and the national committee in New York.

At first glance, it may appear that transnational solidarity between the Australian and the American committee was a case of a fraternal relationship between two communist 'front' organizations. It is more complex than that. As we have seen, the clemency campaign in Australia commenced prior to CPA involvement and, whilst that involvement brought immense organizational energy, it was not communist inspired and remained a diverse, broad-based ecumenical movement.

With the Supreme Court's fourth and final rejection of an eleventh-hour appeal on behalf of the Rosenbergs – notwithstanding the dissenting opinions from Justices Black, Douglas and Frankfurter – the executions now seemed certain to proceed, barring executive mercy, at 11 pm on 18 June. In the early hours of 17 June, a vigil commenced in Wynyard Park, Sydney. It was to last nearly seventy hours.[46] An ASIO film of the event recorded speakers, individuals signing futile petitions under kerosene light, a display of a wreath of flowers and groups of people playing chess whilst awaiting the fateful hour.[47] A similar continuous vigil, often in driving rain, was held in Melbourne outside the US Consulate and over three days 10,000 leaflets were distributed. Moments after the executions, the pickets outside the US Consulate stood in silence for one minute. The next morning 180 protestors, wearing black armbands, held a commemorative service outside the Consulate.[48]

[43] Sobell Records, Box 3, Folder 3; Box 17, Folder 6.
[44] Williams to Alman, 6 May 1953, Sobell Records, Box 17, Folder 6.
[45] Brainin to Hartley, 8 May 1953, Sobell Records, Box 3, Folder 5.
[46] *Sydney Morning Herald*, 19 June 1953, 3.
[47] 'Pro-Clemency Vigil', NAA C5431/4, 32/1/200.2
[48] *Argus*, 22 June 1953, 6; *Sun*, 22 June 1953, 2.

After the Rosenbergs were electrocuted another vigil was held at Port Kembla on the NSW south coast: about sixty people gathered to observe two minutes' silence.[49] Larger memorial meetings were held in Sydney's Domain and Melbourne's Yarra Bank.[50] ASIO was not alone in producing a cinematic record. A short film, made by the Waterside Workers' Federation Film Unit, was entitled 'The Forever Living Julius and Ethel Rosenberg'. Appropriately, it was silent. The captions stated that the Rosenbergs 'died as a sacrifice to the waning powers of those who were afraid ... Our hope has turned to anger and hate for the Iron Heel.'[51] In the wake of their death, a plethora of poems was written. One began 'Dear Ethel, dear Julie,/Were we too late?/ These stupidly spent/burning tears/are not for you.'[52] More dispassionately, the Save the Rosenbergs Committee wrote to the NCSJRC pledging further support to the cause for the posthumous fight for innocence.[53]

To dismiss the clemency campaign in Australia as a communist 'front' initiative orchestrated by the CPA leadership for political purposes – as so frequently alleged – is misleading. Not only does this disparage the sincerity and agency of those dozen men and women from that little village of Nana Glen, or the heartfelt letter from a Parramatta grandmother to the orphaned sons,[54] it also overlooks the broad support the campaign received from Australia's most senior clergy from all denominations. These church leaders were nobody's dupes. And supporters such as the civil libertarian, Doris Blackburn MHR, and former Head of the Department of External Affairs, Dr John Burton, were too experienced, or canny, in the ways of politics to be subject to communist manipulation. It is unlikely they, and thousands of other independent thinking Australians, would at this time decide to hitch their wagon to a Party that, notwithstanding its continuing influence in several key trade unions, was so obviously adrift and isolated and beleaguered in the broader community. Undoubtedly the CPA invested the Save the Rosenbergs committees with networks, resources and publicity. But this does not diminish the sustained contribution that these committees made over a two-year period to an international movement on the Left. And this at a time when the domestic Cold War was at its chilliest and most dangerous.

Conclusion

Irrespective of the efficacy of its efforts (and, in the end, of course, these efforts were futile), the range of Rosenberg Committees – in Australia, America and across Europe – were a remarkable emblem of resistance. They drew deeply on the steadfast commitment, unflagging volunteer efforts and an almost zealous belief in the injustice

---

[49] *Tribune*, 24 June 1953, 6.
[50] *Tribune*, 24 June 1953, 3; *Guardian*, 25 June 1953, 5.
[51] NAA C5431/4, 32/1/204.2
[52] Untitled poem by Stan Segal, 20 June 1953, in *Guardian*, 2 July 1953, 7. See also 'Poems for Two Brave People', *Tribune*, 1 July 1953, 7.
[53] Sobell Records, Box 3, Folder 3.
[54] Bessie Millar to 'Dear Children', 29 June 1953 (copy sent to Manny Bloch, the children's guardian), Sobell Records, Box 3, Folder 5.

of Rosenbergs' sentence or, more naively, in their innocence. They resisted and then challenged the dominant hegemony that held that a fair trial had been conducted, that both Rosenbergs were guilty as charged and that, as traitors, they deserved to die. None of these charges were true, so the committees disputed these untruths.

Supporters of the Rosenbergs cannot be lumped together into one homogeneous group. There were up to five different groups of supporters, only one of them communist, each with their own priorities and objectives. The committees to which they belonged were therefore both diverse and ecumenical. The leaders' appeal to supporters to attend a meeting 'to go over our problems in relation to our many activities' and to 'plan our work together' was not uncommon. Nor was it an empty platitude, for '[a]s always, we turn to you for counsel, guidance and confirmation'.[55] Earlier, Joseph Brainin wrote: 'We need the advice of those friends who have been laboring with us for the past nine months.'[56] Later, Alman wrote: 'We want your advice [regarding a clemency delegation to Washington in January 1953]. What do you think? Let us know as soon as possible.'[57] This was not, therefore, an exclusive organization. It was open and democratic. And it did not operate conspiratorially, as alleged by HUAC.

It seems plausible to argue that, in certain important respects, members of these many Rosenberg Committees conformed to Antonio Gramsci's conception of 'organic intellectuals'.[58] Like such 'organic intellectuals', these grassroots committees emerged from but were still connected to the everyday life of the working classes, they were open and non-sectarian in outlook, non-elitist in organizational structure (and therefore contrary to Stalinist 'democratic centralism'), and they raised the consciousness of new social groups whose consent to counter-hegemonic ideas they won. Whilst such committees were not revolutionary forces for undermining existing social relations, as Gramsci envisaged, such organic intellectuals in the NCSJRCs confronted and undermined the anti-communist consensus by reaching into local communities in which they were grounded and from which grassroots support was mobilized. What Gramsci did not envisage, and what these committees achieved, was a significant measure of transnational solidarity amongst Left sympathizers. That the all-important New York NCSJRC, often through personal communication, could reach across the Atlantic and the Pacific and trigger the formation of these committees is a profound tribute to the potential of the Left and the international arena.

---

[55] Undated letter and dated letter (19 January 1953) from Aaron Schneider to 'Dear Friend'; letter from David Alman to 'Dear Friend', 9 September 1952, Sobell Records, Box 24, Folder 8; Box 26, Folder 13.
[56] Brainin to 'Dear Friend', 30 August 1952, Sobell Records, Box 19, Folder 4.
[57] Alman to 'Dear Friend', 15 January 1953, ibid.
[58] See Quinton Hoare and Geoffrey Nowell Smith (eds.), *Selections from the Prison Notebooks of Antonio Gramsci* (New York: International Publishers, 1971), 15–16, 332–5.

13

The networks of left-wing town planning in Mediterranean Europe (1960s–early 1980s)

Céline Vaz

In the mid-1970s, the eyes of the European left-wing were focused on the political changes taking place in the Iberian Peninsula. These international attraction and solidarity are well reflected in the words of Manuel Castells, who came to Portugal to visit the architect Nuno Portas, the Secretary of State for Housing in the Portuguese provisional government set up after the fall of the Salazarist regime (1926–74):

> I have known Nuno for some time [...]. The problems Nuno is trying to solve are the same as those faced by most progressive forces in Europe [...]. But we also need to talk "to the others", to those who are watching Portugal, to those who expect so much from the current experience [...]. We are not delivering here the statement of a minister, but the testimony and analysis of a comrade on a process in which he is no more a protagonist than the Portuguese people with whom his action is identified.[1]

A 'Latin urban Internationale': this is how the Catalan geographer and sociologist of the city Jordi Borja Sebastià described the urbanists and city experts who converged in Portugal in 1974–6, himself included.[2] This group of professionals specialized in shaping cities and reflecting on their problems and futures[3] came to observe and discuss the participatory urban planning operations then promoted by Portas.

Among these practitioners and academics were Italian, Catalan, Castilian, Portuguese architects-town planners, but also some engineers, geographers and

---

[1] Manuel Castells' introductory remarks to the interview with Nuno Portas in Lisbon on 23 June 1974 published in "La question du Logement au Portugal démocratique", *Espaces et Sociétés*, no. 13–14 (octobre 1974–janvier 1975): 200.
[2] Jordi Borja Sebastià, *Mis Universidades. Historia de un proceso de aprendizaje*, 65, additional thesis (302 p.) to Jordi Borja Sebastià, *Revolución urbana y derechos ciudadanos: Claves para interpretar las contradicciones de la ciudad actual*, thesis in geography under the supervision of Horacio Capel (Universidad de Barcelona, 2012), 536 p. For Spanish professionals, we will indicate both family names on the first occurrence and then only the first.
[3] As opposed to city managers as defined by Viviane Claude, *Faire la ville. Les métiers de l'urbanisme au XXe siècle* (Marseille: Parenthèses, 2006).

sociologists, in particular members of Marxist urban sociology, such as Henri Lefebvre and Manuel Castells. Several of them had founded or contributed to French review *Espaces et Sociétés*, created in 1970 and subtitled '*International critical review of planning, architecture and urbanization*'. What they had in common was their opposition to the dominant technocratic and functionalist conception of urbanism. On the contrary, they called for a more human urbanism, renewed thanks to the participation of inhabitants in the production of the city. Belonging to all the nuances of the Left, they formed a network of criticism and urban reform, if not an informal *Internationale* advocating an 'urban revolution' in Italy, France, Spain and Portugal from the 1960s to the early 1980s.[4]

These Mediterranean networks of left-wing town planning were part of wider networks of international exchange on urban issues, in Europe and beyond. The reflections of American authors such as Jane Jacobs and Christopher Alexander, for instance, had become well-known and accepted references in Mediterranean Europe by the end of the 1960s.[5] In fact, the internationalization of urban planning, and of urban knowledge in general, has been a feature of the discipline since its origins at the late nineteenth century.[6] The globalization of urban problems led to the view that only international cooperation could help solve them. Limiting the analysis to the more restricted space of Latin Mediterranean Europe, however, allows for a better detailed understanding of the conditions and actors of these circulations. Furthermore, as several testimonies attest, relations between city experts from these countries seem to have been particularly intense during the 1960s and 1970s. Beyond geographical or cultural proximity, similar political experiences and common urban problems can account for this.

Spain and Portugal shared the experience of decades of dictatorships – the Franco regime (1939–75) and the Salazar regime (1926–74), respectively – before engaging in a process of democratic transition from the mid-1970s onwards, which encouraged exchanges and solidarity, both official and clandestine. In Italy and France, both political authority and institutions were deeply challenged by the protest movements of the 1960s and 1970s. These movements contributed to the international spread of political ideas and experiences. In particular, they stimulated opposition to the dictatorships in the Iberian Peninsula by the underground left-wing parties, with the support of their French and Italian counterparts. Furthermore, all four countries were confronted with a situation of urban crisis, more or less acute, linked to the acceleration

---

[4] To borrow Henri Lefebvre's emblematic title, *La révolution urbaine* (Paris: Gallimard, 1970). The term 'reform' is considered here not as a political or ideological movement, but as a set of notions and methods aimed at setting and solving problems, as does Christian Topalov (ed.), *Laboratoires du nouveau siècle. La nébuleuse réformatrice et ses réseaux en France, 1880–1914* (Paris: Ed. EHESS, 1999).

[5] Jacobs criticized the undifferentiated application of functionalist urban planning and defended urban mix and density (*The Death and Life of Great American Cities* (New York: Random House, 1961)). Christopher Alexander was then one of the practitioners and theorists of 'advocacy planning', based on the participation of inhabitants in the definition of their living conditions.

[6] See Pierre-Yves Saunier, "Sketches from the Urban Internationale, 1910–50. Voluntary Societies, International Institutions and US Philanthropic Foundations", *International Journal of Urban and Regional Research*, 25, no. 2 (2001): 380–403.

of urbanization and the forms taken by urban growth from the 1950s onwards. In France, the planned urban production, symbolized by large public housing estates, generally met the housing needs, but state's excessive centralization, backwardness of the facilities, together with the ensuing social and spatial segregation came under criticism.[7] In Italy, Spain and Portugal, due to a lack of resources or political will, urban planning policies were insufficient or poorly implemented, resulting in a chaotic urban development, marked by a lack of infrastructure and facilities of all kinds. The shortcomings of housing policy or the concentration of construction aid to private developers, as in Spain and Italy, resulted in a serious social housing crisis, apparent in the multiplication of informal settlements, the overcrowding of buildings and the reinforcement of social and spatial segregation. Thus, from the end of the 1960s onwards, urban problems sparked social upheaval, all of them supported by left-wing organizations, such as rent strikes, housing occupations in Italy, struggles by neighbourhood associations to obtain facilities or to oppose speculation in Spain.[8] The urban question was then at the heart of political, professional and intellectual concerns in the countries of Mediterranean Europe.

This chapter aims to investigate the history of the Left's political families in the countries of Mediterranean Europe in the years 1960–70 but instead of starting from the political organizations, it intends to examine it by focusing on their common concern for the 'urban question'. This overview of Mediterranean networks of left-wing urban planners is based mainly on members' published testimonies or of those identified as such, personal interviews with Spanish urban planners and secondary sources.[9] I will sketch a portrait of the members of this '*Latin Urban Internationale*', presenting in particular their generational and professional characteristics. Secondly, this essay's goal is to identify the reasons for the internationalization of leftist thought on the city by examining the role of different kinds of organizations and institutions as well as the role that played by some 'transmitters' or 'intermediaries'.

---

[7] It became a field of action for municipal socialism and its communist equivalent: see Aude Chamouard, *Une autre histoire du socialisme: les politiques à l'épreuve du terrain* (Paris: CNRS Éditions, 2013); and Emmanuel Bellanger and Julian Mischi (dir.), *Les territoires du communisme. Élus locaux, politiques publiques et sociabilités militantes* (Paris: Armand Colin, 2013). However, tens of thousands of immigrants from North Africa and also Portugal could not get decent housing and lived in shanty towns. See Marie-Claude Blanc-Chaléard, *En finir avec les bidonvilles. Immigration et politique du logement dans la France des Trente Glorieuses* (Paris: Editions de la Sorbonne, 2016).

[8] On these urban struggles, see for Italy Martin Baumeister, Dieter Schott and Bruno Bonomo (eds.), *Urban Politics, Heritage, and Social Movements in Italy and West Germany in the 1970s* (Frankfurt: Campus Verlag, 2017), and for Spain Carme Molinero and Pere Ysàs (coords.), *Construint la ciutat democràtica: El moviment veïnal durant el tardà franquisme i al transició* (Barcelona: Icaria Editorial, 2010); Céline Vaz "Les mobilisations d'associations de quartier à Madrid à la fin du franquisme. L'exemple du secteur d'Orcasitas", I. dans Backouche et al.(dir.), *La ville est à nous ! Aménagement urbain et mobilisations sociales depuis le Moyen-Âge* (Paris: Éditions de la Sorbonne, 2018), 71–93.

[9] The health crisis linked to Covid reinforced the difficulties generally associated with transnational research and did not allow us to consult the primary sources – located in four countries where multilingualism sometimes exists, as in Spain – within the timeframe initially planned.

Sketching a group portrait of the *Latin Urban Internationale*

The active members of this *Internationale* had in common their young age – no more than thirty-five years old in 1968 – and the belief that political convictions and professional practice should go hand in hand.

a) Young left-wing professionals

Two generational groups should be distinguished.

The younger group, aged around twenty-five in 1968, also the larger, belonged to the generations who had developed a strong awareness of political issues at during the 1960s. As the sociologist Christian Topalov (1942-) pointed out: 'By the time we finished our studies, a little before '68 or immediately after, many of us had left the humanities faculties radicalized by the context of the time and the events of '68'.[10] The Catalan Jordi Borja (1941-), a refugee in France in 1962 where he studied geography and urban sociology, returned to Spain in the summer following the events known as May 68.[11] The Madrid architects Eduardo Leira Sánchez (1944), Félix Arias Goytre and Jesús Gago Dávila graduated in a context of unrest at the university that overlapped the French May 68. The former completed his degree at the Barcelona School of Architecture after being expelled from the Madrid School of Architecture for his clandestine actions within the Democratic Students' Union of the University of Madrid (SDEUM).[12]

But this international network of left-wing city specialists also included older personalities (around thirty-five years old in 1968), such as the Italian planners Francesco Indovina (1933-), Bernardo Secchi (1934-) or the Portuguese Nuno Portas (1934-) and the Spanish Eduardo Mangada Samaín (1932-), who both completed their studies in architecture in 1959. The latter served as link with some older personalities who were committed and concerned about what was happening abroad, but who had suffered greatly from their intellectual isolation under Iberian dictatorships after the Second World War. A case in point is Nuno Portas who began working in 1958 for the agency of the Portuguese Nuno Teotonio Pereira (1922–2016), who began to reflect on social housing problems in his early career stage.[13] On the other hand, this generation was particularly close to the younger one. The relations were established in the context of the massification of higher education. These young architects in their thirties combined their professional activity with teaching town planning in architecture schools in the 1960s. In parallel with his private professional activity,

---

[10] Interview by Louis Weber and Laurent Willemez, "Christian Topalov, chercheur et militant", *Savoir/Agir* 26, no. 4 (2013): 63–75.

[11] Jordi Borja, *Bandera Roja, 1968-1974. Del maig del 68 a l'inici de la transició* (Barcelona: Edicions, 2018), 62).

[12] Interview with Eduardo Leira on 21 June 2009 and J. M. Gómez Santander y A. Vélez, "Ordenación de las enseñanzas de la arquitectura durante el periodo 1960–1970", Antonio Fernández Alba, *Ideología y enseñanza de la arquitectura en la España contemporánea* (Madrid: Tucar Ediciones, 1975), 182.

[13] Interview with Nuno Portas published on 19 November 2013 in the periodical *Sapo*, https://ionline.sapo.pt/336509

Eduardo Mangada became assistant professor of town planning at the Madrid School of Architecture. It was the starting point of an enduring friendship and professional collaboration with Eduardo Leira and Jesús Gago.[14]

The professionals who endorsed critical approaches to urban issues were predominantly Left-Wing activists. In France, many of them belonged to the French Communist Party (PCF) despite the criticism it came under and the effervescence of the so-called 'Leftist' movements. Christian Topalov (1944–) became a militant through the Young Christian Students, and joined the Communist Party after the Prague events, at a time when, he points out, everyone was leaving.[15] According to Francis Godard (1948–), there was a sort of parallel between part of the so-called 'Marxist school of French urban sociology', including Topalov, François Ascher (1946–2009), Edmond Préteceille and himself, and a current within the PCF 'very attracted to the Italian Communist Party, Berlinguer in particular'.[16]

Across the Alps, urban planners were numerous in the ranks of the Italian Communist Party (PCI). The party administered several large cities after the war that were presented as areas for the implementation of innovative, if not socialist, urban policies. Giuseppe Campos Venuti (1926–2019), involved in the anti-fascist resistance during the war, who had specialized in urban planning after graduating from architecture school, became a Communist candidate for Bologna City Council in 1960 and was appointed Town Planning Councillor.[17] To the left of the PCI, the political movement *Manifesto* also had a strong appeal to intellectuals inside and outside Italy.[18] Francesco Indovina (1933–), a specialist in urban economics, who coordinated *Lo spreco edilizio* (1972), a book dedicated housing problems with great influence in Italy and the Iberian Peninsula, left socialist activism to join the *Manifesto* movement in the early 1970s.[19]

Under the Iberian dictatorships, interest in the city also went hand in hand with a commitment to the Left, often within the Communist Party, or in good relationships with it, as it appeared to be the most structured opposition organization, in spite of being clandestine. Young Spanish architects such as Jesús Gago and Eduardo Leira, who rallied against the regime as students on the university benches, 'naturally' joined the Spanish Communist Party (PCE), which was then identified as the 'party of anti-Francoism'.[20] The Portuguese Nuno Portas and Nuno Teotonio Pereira, both opponents of the Salazar regime, and who claimed to be 'progressive Catholics', had connections with the militants of the Portuguese Communist Party (PCP). They joined in some

---

[14] Interview with Jesús Gago on 20 and 26 May 2009.
[15] Weber, and Willemez, "Christian Topalov, chercheur et militant".
[16] Antonio Delfini and Janoé Vulbeau, "La sociologie urbaine et le marxisme des années 1970, entretien avec Francis Godard", *Espaces et sociétés* 176-7, nos. 1–2 (2019): 189–202, 192-3.
[17] Giuseppe Campos Venuti, *Un bolognese con accento trasteverino: autobiografia di un urbanista* (Bologna: Edizioni Pendragon, 2011).
[18] Founded as a newspaper by ICP activists who had been expelled because of their condemnation of the Soviet invasion of Czechoslovakia, it became a political organization and ran in the legislative elections of 1972.
[19] Laura Fregolent (dir.), *Economia, società, territorio. Riflettendo con Francesco Indovina* (Franco: Angeli Edizion, 2014).
[20] Interview with Jesús Gago on 20 and 26 May 2009. Carme Molinero and Pere Ysàs, «El partido del antifranquismo (1956–1977)», in Manuel Bueno et al., *Historia del PCE. I Congreso, 1920–1977. Vol. II* (Oviedo: FIM, 2004).

of their political actions and meetings, as Nuno Portas points out, 'it was a period of opposition that united us'.²¹ This could apply to other members of this critical *Internationale*, who were attached to their political independence even though their ideas or actions participated in the achievements of this left-wing town planning. The Catalan architect and urban planner Manuel de Solà-Morales (1939–2012) could be given as an example and also Mario Gaviria Labarta (1938–2018). Gaviria, who was trained in urban sociology by Henri Lefebvre in the early 1960s, described himself as a fellow traveller with the communists, but never joined the party, or any other.²²

b) Having an activist practice of town planning

For the members of this *Latin Urban Internationale*, being left-wing meant a professional activist practice in the field of urban issues. We must however distinguish between two very different ways of this committed practice, depending on whether the actors involved were urban researchers or professionals in the production of the city.

Representatives of French Marxist urban sociology such as Manuel Castells and Christian Topalov, all agree on the role of circumstances in their specialization in urban issues.²³ At the end of the 1960s, having just graduated, they responded to requests from the Ministry of Public Works, which made substantial budgets available to researchers in the Humanities to work on urbanization with the aim of rationalizing the modernization of France.²⁴ These calls for projects – such as 'Participation in urban power' – provided them with the opportunity to combine their political convictions with their professional activity by applying Marxist interpretative frameworks to the study of the urban phenomenon.²⁵ This led to the emergence of a critical urban sociology focusing on the analysis of capitalism in the growth of cities, the urban policies of the State and the social movements that challenged them.²⁶

For urban planners, mainly architects, the decision to enter this arena was rooted in a political motivation. In Spain, it was a conscious and positive choice for young, politicized architects in the 1960s, in line with their commitment to public interest. Urban planning was seen back then a way to be of service to society, but also a way

---

[21] Interview with Nuno Portas published in *Sapo*, 19 November 2013, https://ionline.sapo.pt/336509 (last accessed 30 August 2021), and José António Bandeirinha, "Nuno Teotónio Pereira 1950–1970. Arquitetura como prática política", *Estudo Prévio. Revista do Centro de Estudos de Arquitetura, Cidade e Território da Universidade Autónoma de Lisboa*, no. 10 (2016).

[22] Interview with Mario Gaviria on 22 July 2009.

[23] See Géraldine Pflieger, *De la ville aux réseaux. Dialogues avec Manuel Castells* (Lausanne: Presses polytechniques et universitaires romandes, 2006).

[24] Funding for 'urban research' increased more than fivefold between 1969 and 1976. See Christian Topalov, "Trente ans de sociologie urbaine. Un point de vue français", *Métropolitiques*, 16 October 2013, https://metropolitiques.eu/Trente-ans-de-sociologie-urbaine.html (last accessed 30 August 2021).

[25] For example Christian Topalov, *Les promoteurs immobiliers, contribution à l'analyse de la production capitaliste du logement en France* (Paris: Mouton, 1973); Manuel Castells and Francis Godard, *Monopolville. Analyse des rapports entre l'entreprise, l'État et l'urbain à partir d'une enquête sur la croissance industrielle et urbaine de la région de Dunkerque* (Paris: Mouton, 1974).

[26] Michel Amiot, *Contre l'État, les sociologues. Éléments pour une histoire de la sociologie urbaine en France (1900–1980)* (Paris: Éditions de l'école des hautes études en sciences sociales, 1986).

of not compromising themselves in a practice of architecture, especially housing construction, that they considered too mercantile, if not downright corrupt.[27] This position was shared by their foreign counterparts, particularly the group of young French architects.[28] As a result young architects set up their own town planning agencies. In 1968, for example, Eduardo Leira and friends from the Madrid School of Architecture founded a cooperative agency, named Centro de Estudios Territoriales y Ambientales (CETA), and reasserted its multidisciplinary character, after merging with members of the agency CINAM ESPAÑOLA, with a strong third-world commitment. Jesús Gago, who joined the firm the following year, clearly links this specialization to the political commitment of the members: 'when we left the school, we were sensitive to social and political aspects, and so we turned to town planning'.[29]

Whatever the path that led them to specialize in urban planning or urban studies, all of them had in common a practice based on their political commitments and militancy. Concretely, they led volunteer forms of expertise, such as supporting and assisting user groups, or advising Left-Wing parties, whether programmatic or theoretical.

In Barcelona, the '*Laboratorio de Urbanismo de Barcelona*' (LUB) created in 1969 around Solà Morales and a group of young graduates – Antonio Font Arellano (1944-) and Joan Busquets Grau (1946-) among them – played an active role in the mobilization against the '*Plan de la Ribera*', which aimed to reshape the coastal sector of the city. They supported the allegations of the neighbourhood associations and designed an alternative proposal for the redevelopment of the area in 1971.[30] This

Figure 13.1 A participatory urban planning experience in the Meseta de Orcasitas neighbourhood in Madrid, mid-1970s. Image courtesy of AV de Orcasitas-Archivo FRAVM.

---

[27] This comparative 'advantage' of public procurement, from an ethical point of view, beyond political contexts, is emphasized by Véronique Biau, "Stratégies de positionnement et trajectoires d'architectes", *Sociétés contemporaines*, no. 29 (1998/1): 19.
[28] Jean-Louis Violeau, *Les architectes et mai 68* (Paris: Éditions Recherches, 2005).
[29] Interview with Jesús Gago on 20 and 26 May 2009.
[30] Manuel de Solà Morales, J. Busquets, M. Domingo, A. Font and J.L. Gómez Ordóñez, *Barcelona: remodelación capitalista o desarrollo urbano en el sector de la Ribera Oriental* (Barcelona: Gustavo Gili, 1974).

'counterplan' (its process and content) became a point of reference in the struggle against the anti-social urban development actions promoted or supported by the Franco regime. Thus, their Madrid friends of the CETA agency fought alongside the inhabitants of the *Meseta de Orcasitas* shantytown to have them rehoused on the land from which they were to be evicted.

Together with the sociologist Manuel Castells, they played an important role in defining the Spanish Communist Party's project for the first democratic municipal elections in 1979. They published a diagnostic-programme for Madrid, the capital.[31] This programme echoed the proposals made by the sociologist Jordi Borja, close to Castells too, based on the strengthening of municipal power and its democratization through the implementation of new forms of popular participation.[32] On his return from Paris in 1968, he himself was involved in stimulating and coordinating mobilizations in the neighbourhoods on the outskirts of Barcelona – but also in the factories and at the university, within *'Bandera Roja'*. He was one of the founders of this self-organizing political movement. In 1974, when this movement joined the *Partit Socialista Unificat de Catalunya* (PSUC), linked to the PCE, Jordi Borja became one of the main architects of the PSUC's municipal reform programme.[33]

The socio-political commitment of the young Spanish city specialists, their modes of action and mobilization were very much inspired by the social and political movements of the Italian 'Autonomia'. This set of precedents in turn influenced Portuguese professionals who were thinking about how to improve the living conditions of the working classes. Thus, alongside texts published in France or in the Italian periodical *Il Manifesto*, Nuno Portas cites as references the researches of the Madrid-based CETA group.[34] Through what channels were these trans-Mediterranean interconnections which give substance to the idea of international networks of left-wing urban planners formed?

The vectors of the internationalization of the 'urban revolution' in Mediterranean Europe

This section is about the 'journey of ideas [...] the means of transport of ideas' which favoured the dissemination and proximity in time of critical reflections on the city and actions for the improvement of urban living conditions, within Mediterranean Europe, from the late 1960s.[35]

---

[31] Manuel Castells, Eduardo Leira, Ignacio Quintana et al., *Madrid por la democracia. La propuesta de los comunistas* (Madrid: Mayoría, 1977).

[32] Jordi Borja, Ricard Boix and Marçal Tarrag, *Por una política municipal democrática* (Barcelona: Editorial Avance, 1977).

[33] Borja, *Bandera Roja (1968-1974)*, 62 and Giaime Pala, "Una semilla de discordia. La entrada de Bandera Roja en el PSUC", *HMiC: Història moderna i contemporània*, no. 9 (2011).

[34] In particular the text 'Urbanismo y lucha de classes' wrote by Alfonso Iglesias García, Eduardo Leira Sánchez, Damián Quero Castanys, Augustín Rodriguez-Bachiller, Ignacio Solana Madariaga. See José Antonio Bandeirinha, *O Processo SAAL e a Arquitetura no 25 de Abril de 1974, op. cit.*, 95–6.

[35] Michel Trebitsch "Voyages autour de la Révolution. Les circulations de la pensée critique de 1956 à 1968", in Geneviève Dreyfus-Armand et al., *Les années 68. Le temps de la contestation* (Paris/Bruxelles: Éditions complexe, 2008), 69–87, 69.

a) An intersection of political, professional and academic relations

The testimonies attest to numerous and plural relationships between specialists in the city of the Left in Latin European countries. These relationships were most apparent among members of Communist parties or political organizations close to them. Hence the group of young Madrid architect-urbanists involved in the PCE established relations with critical French urbanists and sociologists, members of the PCF, such as Jean Lojkine (1939–) and Christian Topalov, whose works were references for the critique of Franco's urbanization. And, conversely, during the first democratic municipal elections in 1979 Topalov visited Spain and accompanied Jesús Gago in the meetings the latter organized in northern Madrid for the communist campaign.[36] He was in charge of the housing commission of the Communists, within the broader sector of the '*cadre de vie*' (living environment). The PCF was then engaged with the Socialists in the '*Programme commun*' (Common Programme) aimed at entering government and putting into practice the social transformation promoted by the Left.[37] Issues relating to housing, urban planning and, more broadly, the living environment played an important role in this transformation project, hence the PCF's concern to have experts on urban issues in its ranks and to encourage the exchange of experiences with countries facing the same problems.

The Spanish experience was of obvious interest on these issues. In the early 1970s, the PCE theorized the 'Alliance of the forces of work and culture' as a means to bring together all the mobilizations likely to weaken the regime and to achieve democratization, as an intermediate step towards socialism.[38] 'Intellectual' or 'professional' militants felt encouraged to seek points of convergence with the working classes.[39] The struggles led by neighbourhood associations materialized into a privileged field of application. The links between Communist Party activists specializing in urban issues in Mediterranean Europe bear witness to the place these parties gave to those issues in their political strategy. However, it is not always easy to identify whether these links were initiated by the parties themselves or rather in a greater proportion by these activists themselves. In the case of Spain, until the legalization of the PCE in 1977 and the return of the leadership from exile, the militants of the sectoral organizations, such as the group of communist architects, had almost total autonomy.[40]

Furthermore, it is worth highlighting the plurality of channels – political, but also professional and institutional – contributing to the establishment and consolidation of this network of left-wing urban planners, as well as their close interweaving. As Jordi Borja points out in relation to these years, the professional and political spheres intersected.[41]

---

[36] Interview with Jesús Gago on 20 and 26 May 2009.
[37] Weber, and Willemez, "Christian Topalov, chercheur et militant", 63–75.
[38] 'La crisis cultural en nuestros días', undated, Archivo Histórico del Partido Comunista de España (AHPCE), box 126 folder 1.9.2.
[39] Adriano Beltran's report on the intellectual professions movements, 1972, AHPCE, leaders section, article 2, pocket 3.1.
[40] Interview with Jesús Gago on 20 and 26 May 2009.
[41] Borja, "Mis universidades: Historia de un proceso de aprendizaje".

The *'Pequeños Congresos'* (1959–68) illustrate these relationships built around professional and intellectual issues. These informal meetings were initially organized to bring together architects from Madrid and Barcelona to discuss the achievements and challenges of contemporary architecture. They gradually opened up to other Spaniards, but also to the Portuguese, who organized them in 1967.[42] From the 1960s onwards, these meetings favoured contacts between architects from the Iberian Peninsula (including Portas, Mangada, de Solà Morales, Bohigas) and then with Italian colleagues, through the intermediary of the Catalans. The latter, particularly anxious to break with the cultural isolation that prevailed in the early years of Franco's dictatorship, re-established connections with Italian architects and urban planners from the late 1950s onwards.[43] For instance, the Madrid-based Eduardo Mangada met the Italian Bernardo Secchi in 1968 at one of these conferences in Barcelona.[44]

Thanks to these conferences, a first network of relationships was established between the intermediate generation of this critical urban *Internationale*, which the younger generation could join, and which led to collaborations or works in the 1970s. In 1976, urban architects from Madrid (Gago, Leira, Solana, Ferrán, Mangada) and the Italian Secchi collaborated with architects from Eastern Andalusia on the work *La crisis del modelo de crecimiento a partir del sector turístico inmobiliario*.[45] At any rate, if the circulations within this informal network of actors appear more salient during the 1970s, it seems essential to extend the study upstream, to the 1960s, in order to grasp the origin of these interconnections.

Institutional professional socialization – of an administrative or academic nature – was also an opportunity to foster this *Latin Urban Internationale*. In Spain and Portugal, until the end of the dictatorships, official positions allowed for travel outside the peninsula and contact with the most recent currents of town planning and research, even critical ones, while escaping the control of the political police. In the early 1960s, Nuno Teotonio Pereira encouraged Nuno Portas to join the *Laboratório Nacional de Engenharia Civil* (LNEC), Portugal's public civil engineering research centre, for this purpose.[46] There, Portas set up an interdisciplinary research section on social housing involving architects, engineers and sociologists, inspired in particular by the work of the French sociologist Chombart de Lauwe, a left-wing Catholic like himself, with whom he met and exchanged ideas.[47] This research post gave him the opportunity to

---

[42] Nuno Correia, *O Nome dos pequenos congressos. A primeira geração de encontros em Espanha (1959–1967) e o pequeno congresso de Portugal*, Tesina de Master Teoría e Historia de La Arquitectura (tutor Josep María Montaner), ETSAB, 2009/2010.

[43] The Italians also gained a better knowledge of the architectural and urban panorama of the peninsula, as shown by a special issue (n°15,1965) devoted to Spanish architecture by the Italian magazine *Zodiac*.

[44] 'Homenaje a Bernardo Secchi. Texto de la intervención de Eduardo Mangada', published on 2 July 2014, https://clubdebatesurbanos.org (last accessed 10 October 2021).

[45] Juan de Dios Mellado (ed.), *Crónica de un sueño: 1973–83. Memoria de la transición democrática en Málaga* (Málaga: C&T, D.L, 2005), 74. The members of the CETA agency, Gago at least, made a study on housing needs in the Lisbon metropolitan area in 1973. See the biographical presentation of Jesús Gago, 'Interviews: 20 visions', *Papers. Regió Metropolitana de Barcelona*, no. 43 (June 2005): 47.

[46] Bandeirinha, "Nuno Teotónio Pereira 1950–1970 …".

[47] Interview with Nuno Portas in the magazine *Urbanisme* on 1 February 2000, published in Thierry Paquot, *Conversations sur la ville et l'urbain* (Gollion: Infolio, 2008).

travel extensively in Europe and elsewhere to study forms of popular housing, which inspired the self-built housing operations implemented in Portugal after 1974.

Despite the critical stance they could take towards urban policies and even the regimes in place, left-wing specialists in the city worked in urban planners' offices or held university posts. In order to deal with the problems of urbanization, the authorities could not do without specialized expertise in urban planning or urban sociology, which were developing fields at the time.[48] This did not prevent the repression of the latter, for their involvement in political opposition, under the authoritarian regimes of the Iberian Peninsula.

b) The decisive role of few intermediaries

The personalities of this critical *Internationale* of urban issues were far from being all involved to the same degree. In line with other studies, it appears that the circulation of ideas and practices within it depended heavily on individuals who themselves circulated from one cultural world to another and acted as transmitters or intermediaries.[49]

In the case of Spain, the penetration of Marxist urban sociology and the ideas of Italian theorists appear to have been very much linked to the individual contacts established by young Spaniards who went to France or Italy – voluntarily or by force – to attend academic courses that did not exist in Spain at that time, or to complete their professional experience. In the 1960s, after reading economics at the London School of Economics, Mario Gaviria began to study sociology at the University of Strasbourg with Henri Lefebvre.[50] The Catalan Jordi Borja, involved in the opposition to Francoism, was forced to leave for Paris where he studied urban geography and sociology at the Sorbonne. During these formative years, they immersed themselves in the political panorama of the Left in France or Italy and established interpersonal links with activists. In Paris, Jordi Borja made friends with members of the Revolutionary Communist Youth (JCR), such as Alain Krivine, leaders of the UNEF – the main French student union which became increasingly left-wing after the Second World War, but above all with young communists, who were very much oriented towards the PCI, some of whom specialized in urban issues (Ascher, Topalov, Préteceille, Godard). Through these connections, he became interested in the Italian intellectual and trade union Left, and established contacts in Italy with the urban planners Paolo Ceccarelli, Francesco Indovina and Bernardo Secchi. Manuel Castells, whose profile was rather academic than political, became a world reference in urban sociology with his work on the urban contradictions of the capitalist mode of production. He was one of the facilitators of this *Latin urban internationale*. His career, however, placed him at the heart of a more global internationalization of critical thinking on the city in

---

[48] A 'paradox' highlighted for France by Amiot, *Contre l'État, les sociologues*; Pierre Lassave, *Les sociologues et la recherche urbaine en France* (Toulouse: Presses universitaires du Mirail, 1997); which we have verified in our work on Spain.

[49] Taoufik Souami, "Liens interpersonnels et circulation des idées en urbanisme. L'exemple des interventions de l'IAURIF au Caire et à Beyrouth", *Géocarrefour* 80, no. 3 (2005).

[50] As can be seen in other periods: Victor Karady, 'La migration internationale d'étudiants en Europe, 1890–1940', *Actes de la recherche en sciences sociales* (ARSS), n° 145, décembre 2002, 47–60.

the 1970s. Growing up in Catalonia, he had been forced to flee the Franco police and went into exile in France, where he went to university and turned to research on urban issues. During the 1970s, he made several research trips to Latin America and North America, but returned regularly to Spain and France.[51] Indeed the years of study were followed by frequent trips to strengthen and expand this network of critical thinking about the city.

Mediators proved essential to the circulation of ideas and practices by moving from one country to another, but above all by working in a concrete way towards the dissemination and influence of these. They ensure the 'social conditions of the internationalization of ideas'.[52] Back in Spain, Gaviria and Borja contributed to the circulation of urban sociology and Marxist urban thinking in Spain. From 1965 to 1966, the first were in charge of an 'Urban and Rural Sociology Seminar', which was very popular with architecture students. It was hosted by the *Centro de Enseñanza e Investigación Sociedad Anónima* (CEISA) in Madrid, a private teaching institute aimed at familiarizing students with fieldwork, which was finally closed in 1970 by Franco's authorities who found it too critical. From 1968 onwards, Jordi Borja taught urban sociology at the School of Architecture and later at the University of Barcelona and new Autonomous University of Barcelona. Alongside their teaching activities, these mediators originated editorial projects which both give substance to and make tangible – by attesting to ongoing intellectual exchanges – these intellectual and political networks of critical thought on the city. One striking example is the journal *Espaces et Sociétés*, founded in 1970, whose editorial board included Castells and Lefebvre, later joined by Topalov and Préteceille, among the founders of the journal, and whose first issues gave special attention to urban problems in Italy and Spain, with papers written by Gaviria and Borja.[53]

This network of trans-Mediterranean intellectual exchanges has also led to important translation work, a role that is often less visible, more underground, but nevertheless fundamental for the sharing and international discussion of ideas. The translation of *Le droit à la ville* in 1969, a year after its French publication, by Mario Gaviria, was not unrelated to the successful transfer of Lefebvre's thought into Spain.[54] In his prologue, Gaviria took care to make sense of Lefebvre's reflections in relation to the Spanish context and to use them as a basis for a critical reflection on the city in Spain. Leira, Solana and Gago also adopted this approach by translating two important books of Italian critical thought on the city, directed respectively by Paolo Ceccarelli (*Traffico urbano che fare?*, 1968) and Francesco Indovina (*Lo spreco edilizio*, 1971), in

---

[51] Pflieger, *De la ville aux réseaux. Dialogues avec Manuel Castells*.
[52] Pierre Bourdieu, "Les conditions sociales de la circulation internationale des idées", *Actes de la recherche en sciences sociales*, no. 145 (2002/5): 3–8.
[53] Marcos Pavia, "Le paternalisme urbain", n°2, 1971; Bandera Roja, "Les communistes et la lutte dans les quartiers en Espagne", n°8, 1973. Pseudonym or collective name ware used to avoid political reprisal of the Franco regime.
[54] Céline Vaz, "'Les Pyrénées séparent et relient la France et l'Espagne': Henri Lefebvre et la question urbaine espagnole à la fin du franquisme", *L'Homme & la Société* 185–6, nos. 3–4 (2012): 83–103.

the collection 'Ciencia urbanística'.[55] This collection was founded by the Catalan De Solà Morales to introduce Spanish students and professionals to the foreign intellectual panorama.

Conclusion

In many respects, the exchanges of ideas within this *Latin Urban Internationale* were asymmetrical.

Firstly, the status of the countries connected was not equivalent. France and Italy acted as reference poles, while Spain and Portugal were more like receiving ends. However, the evolution of these positions over time should not be underestimated. During the process of democratic transition and the first years of democracy, Spain and Portugal emerged as laboratories for thinking and acting on the city, as suggested by the attraction exerted beyond the Pyrenees by the town planning projects and local government reforms which took place in the Iberian Peninsula.

Moreover, the modes of circulation within this informal network of Left-Wing Mediterranean urban specialists were neither simultaneous nor symmetrical. For example, Lefebvre's urban thinking had a strong echo in Spain from the end of the 1960s, as the rapid translation of his works indicates, which does not seem to be the case in Portugal. This asymmetry in transfers, linked in part to the role of mediators in the selection of ideas that circulate, or the rather unstructured of the relationships, finally leads us to question the relevance of the notion of network to describe this *Latin Urban International*. Perhaps it would be better to speak of a 'nebula' or an 'invisible college' in this respect.[56]

This does not call into question the existence and importance of this 'network', which can be identified with the 'golden age' of left-wing town planning (or the left in town planning) in Latin Europe, from the mid-1960s to the early 1980s. This twenty-year period has resulted in the involvement of city professionals in leftist parties and their role in building leftist expertise and practices on urban issues – as briefly surveyed in the limited scope of this chapter, beyond national specific features. In the early 1980s, the new local urban masterplan of Madrid initiated by the first democratically elected municipality – a coalition of Communists and Socialists – is a tangible proof of this internationalized left-wing expertise. Its founders, the urban planners Leira, Gago, Arias, Mangada, etc., appointed the Portuguese Portas, the Catalan Solà de Morales and the Italians Campos Venuti and Secchi, official consultants to the masterplan.

---

[55] Paolo Ceccarelli et al., *La incógnitas del trafico urbano* (Barcelona: Gustavo Gili, 1971). Francesco Indovina (ed.), *El despilfarro inmobiliario* (Barcelona: Gustavo Gili, 1977).
[56] Metaphor used by Yves Winkin to highlight the personal (non-institutional) and intellectual character of the multidisciplinary network of researchers working on communication phenomena in the 1950s–80s, known as the Palo Alto School: Yves Winkin [presentation], *La nouvelle communication* (Paris: Seuil, 1981).

14

An 'Ecological Internationale'? Nuclear energy opponents in Western Europe, 1975-80

Andrew S. Tompkins

In March 1980, the French Interior Ministry was convinced that a spectre was once again haunting Europe: an 'Ecological Internationale' (*l'Internationale écologiste*), particularly the movement's anti-nuclear energy wing, had drawn together 'more than a thousand associations and anti-nuclear committees from around the world' and was 'coordinating their actions' to slow or stop nuclear programmes across the industrialized West. According to the police-spies who sought to exorcise this latest spectre of protest, the anti-nuclear movement's 'unstable' coalition of supporters ranged from trade unionists, leftists and anarchists to 'the credulous', 'the backward-looking' and 'youth ever ready to reject the society of their elders'. However, it also reached deep into the intelligentsia, the upper middle class and centrist parties, even appealing to some conservatives with its critique of modernity. The nuclear issue, it seemed, had led to an 'amalgam of protests' encompassing everything from concern about overpopulation and consumerism to advocacy for worker's self-management and a 'return to the land'. Activism rooted in myriad issues now targeted energy policy because of its centrality to production, consumption and pollution. In short, demonstrators seemed to regard nuclear power as the 'source of the ills of industrial society'.[1]

French authorities and their counterparts in West Germany had particular reason to be concerned, having watched anti-nuclear demonstrations grow from 1,000 participants in 1971 to 100,000 in 1979, with major protests in both countries regularly attracting 20,000-50,000 participants in the late 1970s.[2] Indeed, protest seemed to follow state and industry planners around, emerging nearly everywhere nuclear power facilities were proposed: from Fessenheim and Wyhl along the French-German border (where construction began, respectively, in 1971 on the French side and in 1975 on the German side) to Southern France (Creys-Malville, 1976) and Northern Germany

---

[1] Ministère de l'Intérieur (MdI), 'Le mouvement écologique: Internationalisation – Doctrine anti-énergétique – Amalgame des contestations', 1980, Pierrefitte-sur-Seine, Archives Nationales (AN), 19850718, art. 25.
[2] Andrew S. Tompkins, *Better Active than Radioactive! Anti-Nuclear Protest in 1970s France and West Germany* (Oxford: Oxford University Press, 2016), 15-16.

(Brokdorf, 1976 and Gorleben, 1980), nuclear energy opponents at different sites established translocal and transnational networks of protest. But if environmentalism seemed like a new *Internationale* in the (distorted) view of authorities, it was a curious one indeed, with a deeply ambivalent relationship to the traditions of the left and a variety of sometimes contradictory internationalist impulses.

For those directly concerned by the tangible impacts of environmental problems, protest was not a manifestation of coming world revolution so much as 'front porch politics' – or, in the view of their detractors, 'not in my backyard' attitudes.[3] Local activists who worried about safety risks and the rapid industrialization of their communities worked within 'citizens' initiatives' (*Bürgerinitiativen*) or 'local committees' (*comités locaux*) and framed their activism as 'apolitical' in nature. Many were reluctant to embrace extra-parliamentary activism, which they associated with students and the left. Their own internationalism was primarily provincial, linking disparate grassroots nodes via occasional contacts.

However, local activists alone could never have mobilized the hundreds of thousands who joined mass demonstrations throughout the 1970s. The bulk of antinuclear protesters consisted of supporters from outside the affected communities who opposed nuclear energy not out of their own 'direct concern' but based on broader principles. They brought with them different networks and ideals associated with pacifist, countercultural and radical left forms of internationalism. These overlapped to different degrees with local protest and could complement or compete with one another in ways that enhanced the reach of protest while also sometimes turning international solidarity itself into a balancing act. Anti-nuclear activists in the 1970s consistently exploited the possibilities that translocal and transnational connections created, even though most connections between protest sites remained loose and coordination at the national and especially international levels generally weak.[4] The anti-nuclear movement was thus a far cry from the Internationale of communist yore, or even from the NGOs that became so closely associated with environmentalism in the 1980s.[5]

This chapter will explore varieties of internationalism associated with antinuclear energy protests during the late 1970s, focusing on France and West Germany. The 1970s were in many respects a post-1968 decade, when impulses attributed to

---

[3] Michael Stewart Foley, 'No Nukes and Front Porch Politics: Environmental Protest Culture and Practice on the Second Cold War Home Front', in *Nuclear Threats, Nuclear Fear and the Cold War of the 1980s*, ed. Klimke et al. (Cambridge; Cambridge University Press, 2017), 186–205. See also Stephen Milder, *Greening Democracy: The Anti-Nuclear Movement and Political Environmentalism in West Germany and Beyond, 1968-1983* (Cambridge: Cambridge University Press, 2017).

[4] Andrew S. Tompkins, 'Grassroots Transnationalism(s): Franco-German Opposition to Nuclear Energy in the 1970s', *Contemporary European History* 25, no. 1 (2016): 117–42. National organizations such as Les Amis de la Terre in France or the Bundesverband Bürgerinitiativen Umweltschutz did exist, but they served primarily as networks of communication rather than command centres of protest. Dorothy Nelkin, and Michael Pollak, *The Atom Besieged. Extraparliamentary Dissent in France and Germany* (Cambridge, MA: MIT Press, 1981), 126–9.

[5] Frank Zelko, 'The Umweltmulti Arrives: Greenpeace and Grass Roots Environmentalism in West Germany', *Australian Journal of Politics and History* 61 (2015): 397–413.

the 'student movement' of that prior moment grew into something much broader.⁶ In this period of accelerating globalization, perceived by many as one of 'crisis' and impending change, contemporary social scientists used the term 'New Social Movements' (NSMs) to describe protest related to feminism, queer liberation, human rights, peace and environmentalism, all of which coexisted – and competed – with the organized left, including the hierarchical cadre groups of Maoist or Trotskyist inspiration that had (also) succeeded the student left and taken up its internationalist mantle.⁷ These different groups interacted within the anti-nuclear movement, which proved particularly strong and peculiarly interconnected in France and West Germany during the period in question. The close linkage between protest in these two countries had little to do with the institutions of the European Communities (which then included Euratom⁸) and far more to do with the timing and locations of nuclear power plant construction, especially along the two countries' shared border on the Rhine. However, French-German protest ties were not self-evident in light of both the living memory of war and critical contextual differences, including those related to left-wing traditions. Post-1945 France not only looked back on a distant Revolutionary past but had an active Communist Party that was integrated into the political establishment. In West Germany by contrast, National Socialism had disrupted many left-wing traditions and anti-communism was deeply ingrained in state and society. Activists in these two countries had ample opportunities to interact within post-war Western Europe, but exchange between them mostly took place outside the usual circuits linking francophone or germanophone countries and generally did not rely on English as a *lingua franca*. Ties between French and West German activists illustrated the complexity of internationalism in the 1970s because they were at once easily possible and relatively uncommon.⁹

This chapter examines the different forms of internationalism that manifested themselves in three cases of cross-border solidarity: the convergence of local and pacifist internationalisms in protests along the French-German border around 1975,

---

⁶ Martin Conway, 'The Rise and Fall of Western Europes Democratic Age, 1945–1973', *Contemporary European History* 13, no. 1 (2004): 67–88 (70). On 1968 as a moment and as a longer period, see Michelle Zancarini-Fournel, *Le moment 68: Une histoire contestée* (Paris: Seuil, 2008); Geneviève Dreyfus-Armand et al., *Les années 68: Le temps de la contestation* (Bruxelles: Éditions Complexe, 2000). On the breadth of contestation beyond the student milieu, see additionally Ludivine Bantigny, *1968: De grands soirs en petits matins* (Paris: Seuil, 2018).

⁷ Hartmut Rosa, 'Social Acceleration: Ethical and Political Consequences of a Desynchronized High-Speed Society', *Constellations* 10, no. 1 (2004): 3–33; Niall Ferguson, *The Shock of the Global: The 1970s in Perspective* (Cambridge: Belknap, 2010); Claus Offe, 'New Social Movements: Challenging the Boundaries of Institutional Politics', *Social Research* 52 (1985): 817–68. On perceptions of change and acceleration associated with nuclear energy, see Andrew S. Tompkins, 'Generating Post-Modernity: Nuclear Energy Opponents and the Future in the 1970s', *European Review of History/Revue européenne d'histoire* 28, no. 4 (2021): 507–30.

⁸ On anti-nuclear activists' attitudes towards Europe, see Andrew S. Tompkins, 'Towards a "Europe of Struggles"?: Three Visions of Europe in the Early Anti-Nuclear Energy Movement, 1975–79', in *The Environment and the European Public Sphere*, ed. Wenkel et al. (Cambridge: White Horse Press, 2020), 124–46.

⁹ They thus constitute an example of the 'improbable encounters' that Michelle Zancarini-Fournel and Xavier Vigna have described for the French domestic context in relation to May 1968 itself: 'Les rencontres improbables dans "les années 68"', *Vingtième Siècle* 101, no 1 (2009): 1–16.

the clash between left-wing and countercultural internationalisms at protests in Brokdorf and Malville in 1976–7 and parallel efforts by the radical left and non-violent activists around 1978–80 to link anti-nuclear protest in Gorleben with the struggle of farmers on the Larzac plateau in southern France against a military base. The text draws on police reports, activist media and protest ephemera from state and activist archives as well as oral history interviews conducted with former activists some thirty to thirty-five years after the period of activism in question.[10]

At the French-German border: Local and pacifist internationalisms

The first major anti-nuclear protests in France or West Germany took place along their shared border in the early 1970s. France began building the Fessenheim nuclear power station in 1971, the first of a new wave of power plants across the country (but ultimately the last built in Alsace). Early demonstrations there attracted hundreds of protesters from throughout the region, but only limited support from within the affected community and the nearby area itself. For subsequent protests, Alsatian environmentalists therefore worked to build sufficient local backing. On the German side of the border, nuclear energy opponents in Breisach registered a partial success in 1972 with a petition signed by almost 60,000 people, which led to a proposed site being moved further south. By 1974, plans were underway for a nuclear power station in Wyhl (West Germany) and a chemical factory in Marckolsheim (France) – the two only 10 km apart but separated by a national border. Environmentalists from throughout the region directed their energy towards opposing both projects, promising to jointly occupy each whenever construction began. They thus enacted a form of highly local internationalism that was compatible with existing regional identities in Alsace and South Baden.

In September 1974 activists made good on their promise to occupy the site in Marckolsheim, initiating an illegal occupation that would last until the French government cancelled the chemical company's building permit in late February 1975. In the meantime, nearby villages rotated responsibility for maintaining a presence on the site, and protesters built a wooden roundhouse to draw further supporters to it with concerts and events.[11] When construction crews rolled onto the planned nuclear site in Wyhl in mid-February 1975 (less than a week before the successful end of the protests in Marckolsheim), local activists thus had plenty of practice setting up and maintaining a site occupation. In Wyhl too, they camped in rotating village-based groups and built a wooden *Frendschafts Hüs* ('Friendship house' in the local dialect common on both sides of the border).[12] Anti-nuclear activists, including many from

---

[10] The author conducted approximately sixty life history interviews (usually lasting 90–120 minutes) with former activists, seeking a balance of male and female participants as well as members of different regions and movement factions.

[11] Solange Fernex, 'Non-violence Triumphant', *The Ecologist* 5, no. 10 (December 1975): 372–85.

[12] Bernd Nössler and Margret de Witt (eds.), *Kein Kernkraftwerk in Wyhl und auch sonst nirgends: Betroffene Bürger berichten* (Freiburg: Inform-Verlag, 1976): 148–9.

Freiburg and Strasbourg rather than the directly affected communities themselves, consciously contrasted this cooperation with the recent wartime past. In this manner, they linked the specific concerns of the affected communities with a larger story of French-German reconciliation 'from below' after the Second World War.[13] As similar protests took place in nearby Northern Switzerland, anti-nuclear activists christened the entire region *Dreyeckland* (the 'land of three corners') and claimed the pre-national sixteenth-century Peasant's War as a precedent for regional revolt. Though it would be years before the Wyhl project would finally be abandoned, the narrative of shared cross-border resistance fed a compelling 'legend' of internationalist protest that attracted attention throughout France, West Germany and in activist circles further afield.[14]

This borderland transnationalism was overlaid with other forms of internationalism, notably including peace activism, which naturally had particular resonance in the region after two World Wars. In 1971, the first anti-nuclear protest in Fessenheim was led by Esther Peter-Davis, a long-time pacifist who, together with two other Alsatian women, had authored a brochure about the dangers of nuclear energy based on French, West German, Swiss, American and British sources.[15] Esther was also the wife of Garry Davis, an American veteran of the Second World War who famously renounced his citizenship, declared himself to be the first 'Citizen of the World' and later issued official-looking 'world passports'. Esther worked closely with Jean-Jacques Rettig, a long-standing opponent of French nuclear tests and an advocate of non-violent protest.[16] As the Marckolsheim occupation began, they were joined by young non-violent activists involved in campaigns for conscientious objection from military service, which French as well as West German authorities often refused to recognize. Through the two site occupations, Alsatian anti-militarists established close ties with German non-violent action groups such as Gewaltfreie Aktion Freiburg (GAF). International and ecumenical religious groups and international pacifist such as the International Fellowship of Reconciliation and War Resisters' International provided additional foreign contacts.

Marie-Reine Haug was an anti-militarist activist from a town near Marckolsheim who participated in the environmental protests there and in Wyhl. Well before the mobilization in Marckolsheim began, she had already met Jean-Jacques Rettig and several opponents of the Fessenheim nuclear power station at IFOR-sponsored non-violent training seminars in Strasbourg. On the occupied site in Marckolsheim, Marie-Reine met her future partner, Raymond Schirmer, a conscientious objector and environmentalist, and both subsequently helped occupy the site in Wyhl. Despite plans by the local organizers to occupy each site jointly, Marie-Reine and Raymond

---

[13] Walter Moßmann, Interview with the author, Freiburg (1 April 2010).

[14] Padraic Kenney, 'Opposition Networks and Transnational Diffusion in the Revolutions of 1989', in *Transnational Moments of Change: Europe 1945, 1968, 1989*, ed. Horn and Kenney (Lanham, MD: Rowman & Littlefield, 2004), 207–23 (210–11).

[15] Esther Peter-Davis et al., *Fessenheim: Vie ou mort de l'Alsace*, Saales, CSFR, 1971; Alsace Panorama, 'Les femmes de Fessenheim', 1971, https://www.ina.fr/video/R18081202/les-femmes-de-fessenheim-video.html (last accessed 1 June 2021).

[16] Jean-Jacques Rettig, 'Eine persönliche Umweltgeschichte, Familiengeschichte und Regionalgeschichte im Elsass', 2013, http://www.bund-rvso.de/rettig-umweltgeschichte.html (last accessed 1 June 2021).

noted that not all the protesters from Marckolsheim made the short journey across the Rhine to join the occupation in Wyhl. The much-celebrated use of local dialect could be a hindrance as well as a help, since not even all residents of Alsace spoke it, and information had to be translated for French or German speakers from further afield.[17] Borderland internationalism made a compelling narrative, but it was insufficient by itself. Anti-nuclear protest within the region therefore derived much of its force from wider networks. Marie-Reine and Raymond helped bring anti-militarists to the region through events like the 1976 'International non-violent march for demilitarization' along the French-German border, which commemorated the bombing of Hiroshima with discussions of anti-nuclear energy protests in Alsace, Baden and elsewhere.[18] The next year, the countercultural environmentalist newspaper *La Gueule Ouverte* (*GO*) promoted the follow-up march along the French-German border as part of a series of environmentalist and anti-militarist protests taking place that summer in Malville, Naussac and on the Larzac plateau. In this manner, the highly local form of borderland transnationalism in and around Alsace linked up with peace-related internationalist networks.

In the directly affected rural areas where anti-nuclear protest took root, other forms of internationalism were not necessarily always equally welcome, especially within anti-communist West Germany. Marie-Reine was accustomed to communist groups in France, but she recalls that people in the affected mountain villages near Wyhl acted like 'they saw the devil when they saw the *Rote Fahne*', the party organ of the Kommunistische Partei Deutschlands/Aufbauorganisation (KPD/AO).[19] Cadre groups on the organized left based in Freiburg and other university towns supported anti-nuclear protests, but in Wyhl they were overwhelmingly treated as unwanted intruders. The Kommunistischer Bund Westdeutschland (KBW), the largest Maoist group in Freiburg, did itself no favours by insisting on internationalist references that did not resonate with the local community: the residents of small towns that saw nuclear energy as a harbinger of accelerated industrialization were uninterested in learning of how events in the Chinese village of Dadschai demonstrated that 'under socialism, it is possible to carry out a systematic and sensible industrialization' better than under capitalism.[20] And while pacifists made inroads with 'concerned citizens' by speaking a Christian-inflected language of non-violence, some radical left groups such as the pro-Albanian KPD/Marxisten-Leninisten found themselves excluded precisely for advocating – on principle rather than out of 'direct, existential necessity' – potentially violent protest strategy.[21]

---

[17] Marie-Reine Haug and Raymond Schirmer, Joint interview with the author, Rammersmatt (17 April 2010).
[18] 'Internationaler gewaltloser Marsch für Entmilitarisierung. Teilnehmer-Information' (brochure, 8 pp.), 4–10 August 1976, Hamburg, Archiv Aktiv, Internationaler Gewaltloser Marsch 1976–1980.
[19] Marie-Reine Haug and Raymond Schirmer, Interview.
[20] KBW, 'Kein Kernkraftwerk in Wyhl', 1975, Amsterdam, Internationaal Instituut voor Sociale Geschiedenis (IISG), Bro 4216-21.
[21] '"Mer setze uns durch, weil mer recht hen"', *Spiegel*, no. 14 (31 March 1975): 36–41; '" ... mehr Demokratie überhaupt": ein Bericht von den Bürgerinitiativen um Wyhl' (brochure, 68 pp.), January 1977, Amsterdam, IISG, Bro 2188/16.

Northern Germany and Southern France: Left-wing and countercultural internationalisms

If the organized left was marginal in Wyhl, this was not necessarily the case everywhere, particularly when it came to more dynamic groups like the Hamburg-based Kommunistischer Bund (KB) or its French sister organization, the Organisation Communiste des Travailleurs (OCT). Unlike some other Maoist groups, KB and OCT framed anti-nuclear protest not only as a mass movement with political potential but as a cause specifically for the internationalist left. Challenging the received wisdom of West Germany's largest trade union, KB argued that nuclear power destroyed more jobs than it created, allowing employers to replace human labour with capital- and energy-intensive machinery.[22] At the same time, nuclear energy was an anti-imperialist issue because of the competition among wealthy countries for both raw materials (uranium from Niger and Togo) and export markets (in Brazil and Iran) in the so-called 'Third World'.[23] KB and OCT also translated concern about nuclear risks into left-wing terms, emphasizing capitalist-imperialists' willingness to ride roughshod over safety considerations and to harm 'the life itself of workers and the masses [*masses populaires*]'.[24] Elements of the radical left felt drawn to environmental and anti-nuclear protest for reasons of principle, even though this placed them at odds with both the apoliticism of many local activists and the differently politicized visions of competing left-wing groups.

Solidarity with victims of police repression also drew the organized left into anti-nuclear protest. After the occupations in Marckolsheim and Wyhl, police did everything in their power to prevent activists from getting onto planned sites. When construction equipment was brought to the future site of Brokdorf nuclear power station (in northern Germany, about an hour's drive from Hamburg) on 26 October 1976, it arrived in the middle of the night under police escort, and private security companies quickly erected fencing to keep protesters out. At a first demonstration four days later, 825 police repelled the 5,000 or so (mostly local) demonstrators using not only water cannon and tear gas, but also horse-mounted officers, dogs and Chemical Mace.[25] The dramatic scenes repeated themselves at a second protest two weeks later, when nearly 2,000 officers used water cannon 'almost without interruption' against an estimated 25,000 demonstrators (from throughout the region), which the KB described in its journal *Arbeiterkampf* under the headline 'Brokdorf: The police state in action'.[26] KB mobilized its networks to support further Brokdorf protests in 1977 and it shared information with comrades abroad. OCT published news about West German demonstrations in its own journal, *l'étincelle*, alongside material about anti-nuclear

---

[22] KB, 'Atomenergie und Arbeitsplätze' (brochure, 2nd ed., 64 pp.), 1977, Hamburg, ak-Archiv.
[23] KB, 'Warum kämpfen wir gegen Atomkraftwerke?' (brochure, 2nd ed., 48 pp.), 1977, Hamburg, ak-Archiv, 19–30.
[24] Ibid., 19; OCT 'la lutte sur la "question du nucléaire"', *l'étincelle*, no. 27 (23 June 1977): 10–11.
[25] Landespolizei Schleswig-Holstein, 'Dokumentation über die Polizeieinsätze in Brokdorf (Band 1)', 1977, Schleswig, Landesarchiv Schleswig-Holstein, Abt. 621, Nr. 534, 37.
[26] Ibid., 132; KB, 'Brokdorf: Der Polizeistaat in Aktion', *Arbeiterkampf* 6, no. 93 (15 November 1976): 1.

protests in France, notably including an international demonstration planned for 31 July 1977 against the Fast Breeder Reactor (FBR) being built in Creys-Malville (a small town in southern France, between Lyon and Geneva).[27]

The FBR in Malville was considered a central element of France's nuclear programme because the technology generated (as a by-product) plutonium that could be used to power other, 'ordinary' nuclear reactors. Counterctural environmentalists from the surrounding region had organized a short-term site occupation in the summer of 1976 and held information sessions for the local population, who they felt should lead the struggle.[28] For hippies, neo-ruralists and others who subscribed to the idea that 'small is beautiful', decentralization was both a means and an end in itself.[29] Their ambitions for the 1977 protest were to replicate the good-natured, non-violent site occupation of the previous year, but this time on a larger scale, with greater resolve and within decentralized, participatory structures. According to Odile Wieder, a member of the coordinating committee in 1976 and 1977, 'Our goal was not to take power, it was – we were still a bit naive – we're going to organize a big demonstration in 1977, [...] and we're going to give power to people.' Part of this strategy involved placing local activists at the centre of a system that 'twinned' villages in the affected region with 'Comités Malville' elsewhere across France and abroad.[30]

The 1977 Malville demonstration was also promoted by other groups, with *l'étincelle* linking it to the Larzac (where OCT had long been involved) and *GO* building its itinerary for a 'summer of struggles' around Malville. *GO* even announced to its counterctural readership the goal of attracting 100,000 participants to Malville.[31] Like prior anti-nuclear protests, the Malville demonstration was thus not coordinated by a national organization, but by local and regional activists tapping into wider networks, which connected with like-minded factions abroad. Indeed, the irrelevance of national organizations like Les Amis de la Terre was illustrated by the reactions to comments by that organization's Paris-based leader, Brice Lalonde, that he would not attend the protest: local branches in Grenoble and Marseille insisted that Lalonde did not speak for them, and a satirical cartoon in *GO* downgraded plans for Malville to a new 'Objective: 99,999 (Brice Lalonde won't come)'.[32]

The decentralized and democratic coordination process was, however, quickly overwhelmed by a deluge of new participants. Instead of organizing accommodations and radio communications, 'working meetings turned into debates over violent versus non-violent strategy', inspired in no small part by developments in neighbouring West Germany.[33] Indeed, counterctural environmentalists, radical leftists and concerned

---

[27] See, for example, the jointly published OCT/KB, 'nucléaire: une possible prise de conscience ?', *l'étincelle/Arbeiterkampf* (1 May 1976).
[28] See Collectif d'enquête, *Aujourd'hui Malville, demain la France* (Claix: La Pensée Sauvage, 1978): 7–15.
[29] Several such interviewees mentioned having read E. F. Schumacher, *Small Is Beautiful: A Study of Economics as If People Mattered* (London: Blond and Briggs, 1973).
[30] Odile Wieder, Interview with the author, Annecy (29 April 2010).
[31] 'Malville: Objectif 100.000', *GO*, no. 159 (26 May 1977): 1.
[32] *Aujourd'hui Malville*, 43–5; *GO*, no. 167 (21 July 1977), 7.
[33] Odile Wieder, Interview.

citizens in both France and West Germany all mobilized for the Malville demonstration, billing it as the next step after Wyhl and Brokdorf. Organized groups like KB arranged buses to bring demonstrators from Hamburg and Frankfurt, and OCT members volunteered as stewards at the demonstration itself. However, most participants were 'non-organized' protesters, including countercultural environmentalists as well as autonomous protesters (the latter close to the radical left but disdainful of its hierarchical organizations). In the absence of a unified strategy and under intense pressure created by heavily armed police, this led to a clash of cultures in multiple dimensions: hippies and radicals had different visions for the protest, West German and French protesters responded differently to police, and autonomous protesters refused to submit to the authority of anyone (including local activists).[34] French riot police blocked the demonstration march several kilometres from the construction site, firing dangerous stun grenades into the crowd that killed one protester and maimed three other people (including one police officer). Transnational cooperation among authorities had also outpaced the internationalism of nuclear energy opponents: French authorities developed their policing strategy on the basis of information from West German colleagues about prior protests in Brokdorf.[35]

The demonstration in Malville also had an impact on West Germany, where a follow-up protest against a German FBR in Kalkar (near the Dutch border) was planned for two months later, on 24 September 1977. Local protesters from Malville, autonomous groups from Grenoble, Swiss non-violent activists, KB and OCT, and nuclear energy opponents in the Netherlands all mobilized for the demonstration, which police all but prevented from taking place: following unrelated violence by the Red Army Faction in early September, West German police conducted a nationwide dragnet on the day of the Kalkar protest, erecting roadblocks all across the country that prevented thousands of protesters from ever reaching the site – and hundreds of foreigners from even entering West Germany.[36] Of the forty-two buses that had reportedly left from Hamburg alone, only eleven reached the site (after journeys of up to nineteen hours and as many as ten police checks).[37]

For Günter Hopfenmüller, one of the KB's leading anti-nuclear organizers, the Kalkar protest illustrated how the West German state felt empowered 'to suspend a basic right [...] without pronouncing a ban on the demonstration [and] without changing the constitution'. When the KB printed glossy brochures with photos of the heavy-handed police action, they sold especially well in the neighbouring Netherlands, where Dutch activists opposed to a uranium enrichment facility in Almelo drew their own conclusions from Kalkar. Hopfenmüller described Almelo as 'a typical, well-to-do Dutch town where people have good jobs, earn well, and live in well-kept houses with manicured gardens', and thus a far cry from the Hamburg left-wing scene. It was therefore all the more surprising that local activists from the town approached the

---

[34] Bernard Dréano and Suzanne d'Hernies, Joint interview with the author, Paris (20 January 2010).
[35] MdI, 'Cas concret – Malville', 1977, Pierrefitte-sur-Seine, AN, 19850718, art. 25.
[36] Ermittlungsausschuss der Bürgerinitiativen gegen Kernenergie, 'Wir, das Volk ... ' Eine Dokumentation, Köln, Graphischer Betrieb Henke, 1977.
[37] KB, 'Kalkar am 24.9.' (brochure, 64 pp.), 1977, Amsterdam, IISG, Bro 537/10 fol, 6.

KB with a straightforward proposal: 'If one can't demonstrate in Germany, then one should at least demonstrate in the Netherlands'. On 4 March 1978, after the disastrous international demonstrations in Malville and Kalkar, tens of thousands of anti-nuclear activists converged on Almelo. According to estimates by West German police, some 30,000 people took part, nearly half of whom (14,000) travelled from West Germany.[38] After the demonstration, Almelo residents invited KB members to stay overnight in their bourgeois homes before returning to Hamburg. Hopfenmüller thus remembers this as a particularly vivid instance of internationalist solidarity reaching across boundaries of class as well as nation.[39]

Larzac-Gorleben: Complementary or competing internationalisms?

The anti-nuclear movement also benefited from cross-issue solidarities that brought other transnational ties with them, including with one of best-known causes in 1970s Western Europe: the struggle of local farmers on the Larzac plateau in southern France to prevent the expansion of a military base onto their farmlands. Their long and ultimately successful campaign (1971–81) profited from the same sort of dynamic that animated the anti-nuclear movement, namely the interaction between local farmers on the one hand and the radical left, pacifists and environmentalists on the other. The Larzac struggle became famous throughout France for, among other things, long, drawn-out tractor demonstrations that travelled from the affected region all the way to Paris in 1973 and again in 1978. The 103 directly affected farmers also hosted two enormous rallies on their own land in 1973 and 1974: the organizers' claim that 103,000 people came to the remote plateau in 1974 symbolically expressed the solidarity between local activists and outside supporters. Within France, the farmers demonstrated in solidarity with striking workers at the Lip watch factory in Besançon and opponents of a nuclear power station in Plogoff.

Internationalism and transnational networks were part of the Larzac struggle from the start. Religious pacifists associated with Lanza del Vasto, a European disciple of Gandhi, came to the plateau and encouraged the farmers to exploit the possibilities of non-violent action. Anti-imperialist groups on the radical left such as Gauche Ouvrière et Paysanne (a forerunner of OCT) helped set up Comités Larzac throughout France. Representatives from national liberation movements from Northern Ireland to Palestine were welcomed at the 1973 rally, and the 1974 event included a harvest in which food and funds were donated to the 'Third World'. The farmers later cultivated ties with Japanese peasants opposed to the expansion of Narita Airport near Tokyo as well as national liberation groups in the French colony of New Caledonia.[40]

---

[38] Bundesministerium des Innern (BMI), 'einsatz anlaeszlich der demonstration in almelo (nl) am 4.3.78' (telex), 4 March 1978, Koblenz, Bundesarchiv, B106/107375.
[39] Günter Hopfenmüller, Interview with the author, Hamburg (23 August 2010).
[40] See Robert Gildea and Andrew S Tompkins, 'The Transnational in the Local: The Larzac Plateau as a Site of Transnational Activism since 1970', *Journal of Contemporary History* 50, no. 3 (2015): 581–605.

The Larzac thus incarnated a form of local internationalism that was compatible with different social movements of the 1970s, and it became a site for experimentation with protest forms that environmental and anti-nuclear activists emulated. The rallies held on the plateau were in some ways a model for the site occupation in Marckolsheim, where Marie-Reine and others invited Lanza del Vasto to speak to the local community about the Larzac.[41] On the German side of the border, Freiburg-based journalists Freia Hoffmann and Walter Moßmann reported on both the Larzac and Wyhl struggles as part of a radio feature before subsequently becoming involved in Wyhl themselves.[42] Pacifists from GAF produced a special issue about the Larzac for the Wyhl squatters' newspaper, and KB regularly published articles in *Arbeiterkampf* based in part on information from OCT.[43] By the late 1970s, West German anti-nuclear activists had several channels through which to follow developments on the Larzac. When the Larzac farmers issued a call for volunteers to help with renovation and construction work in 1979, West German anti-nuclear activists jumped at the opportunity to act in solidarity. In August 1979, the farmers were 'drowned' in volunteers; so many were from West Germany that organizers asked for a German speaker to serve on the committee coordinating volunteer activities for the following year. When the exercise was repeated in 1980, it was estimated that fully half of the 700 volunteers came from West Germany, 'where publicity was incontestably better done than in France'.[44] While on the plateau, the Germans held events to publicize what was rapidly becoming the most important anti-nuclear protest in their home country: opposition to the nuclear waste treatment centre planned for Gorleben.

In February 1977, the state of Lower Saxony announced plans to build a nuclear reprocessing facility with an integrated waste disposal site in Gorleben, a remote location in the Wendland region along West Germany's border with East Germany. Designed from the start to be a world-leading facility, the Gorleben project was also a domestic necessity following a 1976 legal change that made the licensing of future nuclear power stations contingent on waste management plans.[45] By 1979, the government of Lower Saxony sought to quell the growing protests against Gorleben by holding a week of hearings in March at which pro- and anti-nuclear experts were invited to speak. In order to pile pressure on the government, Gorleben activists organized a tractor-led march to the state capital in Hanover, modelling their protest on the prior Larzac marches. The carefully paced procession allowed activists to build momentum over a period of weeks and establish contact with people all along the route. When the Harrisburg nuclear accident occurred on 28 March 1979 shortly before the march's

---

[41] 'Le Larzac rencontre l'Alsace à Marckolsheim' (flyer), 1974, Freiburg, Archiv der Sozialen Bewegungen in Baden, 24416.
[42] Freia Hoffmann and Walter Moßmann, 'Bürger werden Initiativ' (Südwestfunk broadcast script), 30 September and 7 October 1973, Amsterdam, IISG, Bro 1132-19.
[43] 'Bauern kämpfen gewaltfrei', *Was Wir Wollen* (September 1975); KB, '50.000 im Larzac', *Arbeiterkampf*, no. 111 (22 August 1977), 36.
[44] Comités Larzac, 'Bulletin de Liaison' (nos. 75 and 80), 17 March and 8 September 1980, Millau, AM, IZ64, 1980–1.
[45] Astrid M. Eckert, *West Germany and the Iron Curtain: Environment, Economy, and Culture in the Borderlands* (New York: Oxford University Press, 2019), 202.

arrival in Hanover, the demonstration presented a ready opportunity for as many as 100,000 people to express their concerns about nuclear power.[46]

Given the centrality of Gorleben to anti-nuclear struggle in West Germany and the inspiration many activists drew from the Larzac farmers, different groups sought to link the two struggles based on their own particular understandings of internationalist solidarity. By 1979, two distinct networks had forged ties between the Larzac plateau on the one hand and Gorleben supporters (in the Wendland region as well as in Hamburg) on the other. One was associated with Wolfgang Hertle, editor of the anarcho-pacifist monthly newspaper *Graswurzelrevolution*, and his friend Hervé Ott, a French conscientious objector who squatted a farm on the Larzac. Hertle wrote frequently about the Larzac in *Graswurzelrevolution*, presenting it as an example of creative, non-violent protest that might also be deployed in places like Gorleben. After Ott set up a non-violent training centre on the Larzac, Hertle proposed a similar centre in Gorleben and the two organized joint training programmes. In parallel, Volker Tonnätt and Heidi Burmeister, former leaders of a KB-friendly youth group, launched a separate Larzac support group in Hamburg that they described as 'non-non-violent', emphasizing anti-imperialist and anti-authoritarian dimensions of the Larzac struggle. Tonnätt and Burmeister maintained close contact with the coordinator of the Comités Larzac and publicized the struggle within left-wing publications such as *die tageszeitung* and *links*. They also organized events about Gorleben on the plateau and about the Larzac in Hamburg to foster solidarity between the two struggles.

The actions of these two distinct groups were in many ways complementary, helping to popularize the Larzac struggle among slightly different, partly overlapping milieus within the anti-nuclear movement in West Germany. They undertook similar activities, publishing full-length books as well as extensive articles and repeatedly inviting delegations from the Larzac to visit various sites in West Germany.[47] However, they also vied for authority within that movement. In late 1979 each group publicly criticized the other for selectively presenting the Larzac story to West German audiences and omitting information about non-violence or the left, respectively.[48] In effect, the non-violent and radical varieties of internationalism that might have mutually reinforced one another were instead placed in competition, as each group presented the Larzac as a model for its own preferred form of protest in Gorleben.

In spite of these tensions among outside supporters, local activists on the Larzac and in Gorleben visited one another several times. Pierre-Yves de Boissieu, a farmer from the Larzac who visited Gorleben, remembers that the purpose of such visits was to share experiences and not to present a model to follow: 'It's difficult to make suggestions. We explain how we work. You can't say "you must work like this" because the context elsewhere is different and because such-and-such a formula might not apply.'[49] During the first week of May 1980, farmers from the Larzac and Plogoff jointly

---

[46] KB, '100.000 in Hannover' (brochure, 48 pp.), 1979, Hamburg, ak-Archiv.
[47] See Heidi Burmeister and Volker Tonnätt, *Larzac: Zu kämpfen allein schon ist richtig* (Frankfurt: Jugend & Politik, 1981); Wolfgang Hertle, *Larzac, 1971–1981. Der gewaltfreie Widerstand gegen die Erweiterung eines Truppenübungsplatzes in Süd-Frankreich* (Kassel: Weber Zucht & Co., 1982).
[48] See *Informations-Dienst zur Verbreitung unterbliebener Nachrichten (ID)*, nos. 303 and 305 (1979).
[49] Pierre-Yves de Boissieu, Interview with the author, Nant (15 September 2010).

toured environmental protest sites in West Germany, arriving in Gorleben only days before one of the most spectacular anti-nuclear protests there began: the occupation of 'Drilling Site 1004', where geological tests were to be conducted for the future nuclear facility. Though plans for the occupation began well before the Larzac farmers' arrival, the visit represented not only an opportunity for exchange but, perhaps more importantly, a show of solidarity at a critical moment.

When anti-nuclear demonstrators occupied the site on 3 May 1980, they quickly set about transforming the terrain in this remote corner of West Germany into the 'Free Republic of Wendland' (RFW), building on a decade of protest experience in France, West Germany and beyond. Activists not only built a 'friendship house' (as in Marckolsheim and Wyhl) but also an entire 'anti-nuclear village', and they played up RFW's imitation statehood at every opportunity. Like Garry Davis in Alsace, RFW issued its own 'passports', which included a declaration that the bearer 'does not recognize as her/his own' any state which 'holds that internal and external security can only be achieved with weapons and uniforms'.[50] In cities like West Berlin, supporters set up 'embassies' and 'consulates' for RFW.[51] When squatters were evicted from the site by 8,000 West German police officers on 4 June 1980, RFW used its state broadcaster (i.e. pirate radio transmitter) to provide demonstrators with advice on passive resistance and to keep supporters elsewhere informed.[52] RFW represented a largely rhetorical form of internationalism that undermined the power of the nation-state by ridiculing it. At the same time, it gave the Gorleben struggle enduring importance for anti-nuclear protest in Germany and Western Europe by drawing on the impulses of ideologically diverse translocal and transnational protest networks.

Conclusion

The 'Ecological Internationale' referred to at the beginning of this chapter was never as united as French authorities or their West German counterparts imagined it to be. Indeed, it might well be argued that the opposition to nuclear energy owed its rapid expansion to the presence of multiple internationalisms within its orbit, each espousing solidarities with different scopes. The horizons of many local activists were primarily regional, though they also extended to other affected communities and opened up to a range of outside supporters. Countercultural environmentalists encouraged precisely the kind of decentralized, local action that prevailed within the anti-nuclear movement, and their presence changed the make-up of protest in rural communities especially. Pacifist networks and radical left organizations were more intrinsically focused on international developments and internationalist solidarities, helping to

---

[50] Dieter Halbach and Dieter Schaarschmidt, 'Widerstand wirkt!', *Oya*, no. 4 (September/October 2010): 19–23.

[51] BMI, 'Aktionen von Gegnern der Kernenergie' (report), 3 June 1980, Koblenz, Bundesarchiv, B106/107375.

[52] Günter Zint (ed.), *Republik Freies Wendland. Eine Dokumentation* (Frankfurt am Main: Zweitausendeins, 1980).

bring the wider world to places and protests that might otherwise have remained consciously provincial. However, despite overlapping and frequently complementary interests, non-violent and left-wing activists often competed with one another for hegemony among anti-nuclear protesters. With its emphasis on the personal concern of directly affected individuals, the anti-nuclear movement effectively fused the place-based nature of environmental protest with the 'politics in the first person' espoused by many so-called New Social Movements. It also foreshadowed the ways in which protest movements in the 1980s (from the revitalized peace movement to the decentralized, autonomous left) developed internationalist orientations and transnational networks on the basis of concern that was overwhelmingly understood as embodied, personal and local.

15

Analysing informal and indirect participation to transnational activist networks: The case of anti-authoritarian feminists in Berlin and Montreal

Emeline Fourment

This chapter focus on the transnational dimension of feminist anti-authoritarian activism in Berlin and Montreal. By 'anti-authoritarian' I mean anti-state, anti-capitalist and anti-hierarchical activists who have their own counter-cultural spaces (e.g. bars, cultural centres, squat houses or collective housing) and engage in various progressive social movements (e.g. the alter-globalization, migrant justice, housing rights or women's movements). At first glance, feminist anti-authoritarian activists do not appear to be particularly transnational. They value mainly local and community engagement, which they consider to be more authentic and concrete than involvement in transnational organizations and networks. Moreover, activists in Montreal and Berlin do not know each other as they rarely travel between the two cities. Yet, a comparison between these groups reveals that activists from Montreal and Berlin share similar ideas and practices.

First, activists in both cities reject any form of institutional political engagement, whether through traditional left-wing organizations such as political parties and trade unions or international NGOs and local non-profits organizations. They see such institutions as a means for an elite minority to take power from the majority: poor people, people of colour, women and other vulnerable groups in society. They therefore believe institutions cannot instigate social change as their activities necessarily reproduce capitalist, gendered and racialized power relations. Furthermore, anti-authoritarian feminists from Berlin and Montreal have simultaneously developed a number of shared practices, which cannot be explained by direct exchange of ideas by activists from Berlin in Montreal or vice versa. Though eschewing more formally structured organizations like the Socialist International, these activists belong to a loose and informal transnational network through which ideas and practices are transmitted. Focusing on the particular case of transformative justice practices, I aim to characterize that network. I propose a genealogy of diffusion processes to explain the simultaneous development of anti-authoritarian feminist practices in Berlin and Montreal.

The term 'transformative justice' refers to a set of practices designed as an alternative to criminal justice in conflict resolution. By establishing a dialogue between victims, perpetrators and the 'community'[1], it seeks to move away from the punitive paradigm of criminal justice. Moreover, it both offers victims recognition and perpetrators the possibility of rehabilitation. Considering state-controlled criminal justice systems inherently sexist and a form of 'class justice', anti-authoritarian feminists see transformative justice as a more equitable means of delivering justice. Since the early 2010s, both Montrealers and Berliners have used transformative justice in (relatively common) cases of sexual violence committed by one activist, usually a man, against another, usually a woman. In this way, they have simultaneously sought to assert their independence from the state while implementing a form of justice more compatible with their view of an emancipated society – that is, a society without class, gender or racial hierarchies. However, transformative justice practices are not endemic to anti-authoritarian communities, but rather used or promoted by a wide variety of social actors, institutions and NGOs.[2] It is then possible to trace the channels by which these practices came to be adopted by anti-authoritarian feminists. By reconstructing these channels, one may understand how anti-authoritarian feminists are embedded in transnational networks.

My analysis draws on two ethnographic studies of feminist anti-authoritarian activists, one conducted in Berlin over a period of fifteen months in 2015–16 and the other conducted over a period of seven months in 2017 among French-speaking activists in Montreal.[3] I present my research in four parts. In the first part, I introduce the present study in relation to the existing literature on transnational activism. In the second part, I examine the specific case of transformative justice practices within these communities. In the third part, I trace the origins of these shared practices to various diffusion processes enabled by old and new media and by activist travel. In the fourth part, I highlight the indirect role of academic, political, non-governmental and international institutions in the dissemination of activist practices.

---

[1] The 'community' can be people of the same social group, neighbourhood, city, state, etc. In institutionalized restorative justice processes, it can be represented by a professional mediator, a specialized police officer, a probation officer, a teacher, etc.
[2] Anthony Nocella, 'An Overview of the History and Theory of Transformative Justice', *Peace and Conflict Review* 6, no. 1 (2011).
[3] In addition to participant observation, I conducted biographical interviews with sixty-three activists (thirty-two in Berlin and thirty-one in Montreal) and collected biographical data on other activists online. I also examined numerous paper and digital documents produced by feminist anti-authoritarians. See my PhD Thesis: Emeline Fourment, 'Théories En Action. Appropriations Des Théories Féministes En Milieu Libertaire à Berlin et Montréal' (Thèse de doctorat en science politique, Paris, Institut d'Etudes Politiques de Paris, 2021).

From global to local targets: A general trend in social movements

The literature on social movements examines the transnationalization of protests, especially those that have taken place since the emergence of the alter-globalization movement in the late 1990s. At that time, this movement appeared to be novel, not so much because it led to simultaneous protests in different countries (something that had already happened in the 1960s) as because it targeted international institutions (e.g. the World Trade Organization in 1999 in Seattle, the G8 summit in 2001 in Genoa, the Summit of the Americas in 2001 in Quebec) and because it gathered activists from many countries in discussion forums for the duration of a counter-summit or of a World Social Forum.[4] Whilst various studies on these protests highlight the crucial impact of the internationalization of politics on the alter-globalization movement – thanks to international organizations and NGOs, increased international economic exchanges, the internet and low-cost air travel[5] – they also show that the transnational dimension of the alter-globalization movement does not diminish the importance of the local scale. According to Sidney Tarrow '[w]hat is new in our era is the increased number of people and groups whose relations place them beyond their local or national settings without detaching them from locality.'[6] These 'rooted cosmopolitans' are few in number, well-educated, accustomed to travel and strongly rooted in their local environment. Some of them are 'nesting pigeons', that is activists from immigrant communities who can be transnational activists because they are rooted both in their host and home countries.[7] Taking inspiration from critical geography, other researchers highlight the importance of the 'politics of scale' of a movement.[8] They show that activists articulate local and global scales of action and even create new scales of action. Here again, the transnationalization of activism does not imply the weakening of local activism.

These results can also be observed when looking at anti-authoritarian feminists in Berlin and Montreal. Both Berliners and Montrealers were part of the

---

[4] Donatella Della Porta, 'Making the Polis: Social Forums and Democracy in The Global Justice Movement', *Mobilization: An International Quarterly* 10, no. 1 (1 February 2005): 73–94; Donatella Della Porta et al. (eds.), *Globalization from below: Transnational Activists and Protest Networks* (Minneapolis: University of Minnesota Press, 2006).

[5] Sidney G. Tarrow, *The New Transnational Activism* (New York: Cambridge University Press, 2005), 36; Donatella Della Porta and Sidney G. Tarrow (eds.), *Transnational Protest and Global Activism* (Lanham, MD, Etats-Unis d'Amérique: Rowman & Littlefield, 2005); Margaret E. Keck and Kathryn Sikkink, *Activists beyond Borders: Advocacy Networks in International Politics* (Ithaca, London: Cornell university press, 1998).

[6] Tarrow, *The New Transnational Activism*, 42.

[7] Tarrow, *The New Transnational Activism*, 51–2.

[8] Pascale Dufour and Isabelle Giraud, 'Globalization and Political Change in the Women's Movement: The Politics of Scale and Political Empowerment in the World March of Women*', *Social Science Quarterly* 88, no. 5 (2007): 1152–73; Pascale Dufour and Renaud Goyer, 'Analyse de la transnationalisation de l'action collective: Proposition pour une géographie des solidarités transnationales', *Sociologie et sociétés* 41, no. 2 (2009): 111–34; Janet Conway, 'Geographies of Transnational Feminisms: The Politics of Place and Scale in the World March of Women', *Social Politics: International Studies in Gender, State & Society* 15, no. 2 (1 July 2008): 207–31.

alter-globalization movement, but the transnational scale was less important for the activities of the former than for the latter. In Berlin, anti-authoritarians have inherited a long tradition of activism – both alternative activism of the 1970s and 1980s[9] and that of the Autonomen movement in the 1980s and 1990s[10] – which is rooted in specific neighbourhoods, particularly in the *Kreuzberg* district. In this context, the alter-globalization mobilizations against the Genoa Summit (2001), the G8 meeting in Heiligendamm (2007) and the NATO Summit in Strasbourg (2009) were high points of mobilization, but were not central to (feminist) anti-authoritarian activities. The situation was quite different in Montreal. In this context, the alter-globalization mobilizations fostered the development of the anti-authoritarian (feminist) activism which had up to then been comparatively weak. At the same time anti-authoritarian activists became key players of the alter-globalization movement.[11]

Thus, transnational activism does not prove the existence of a 'global village', nor can it be analysed as a mechanical effect of the intensification of the globalization of state politics in the 1990s. This assertion is further supported by the place-based protests of the 2010s (e.g. the Arab Spring, the Indignados and Occupy Wall Street), whose main target was no longer transnational but national, and whose anchoring in a specific territory or neighbourhood was integral to those moments. Prefigurative practices, that is, practices which aim to anticipate the everyday life of an emancipated, equal and free, society, were also central.[12] These same developments can be observed in anti-authoritarian feminists in Berlin, and even more so in Montreal: when I met them in 2017, many Montrealers felt that counter-summit mobilizations and World Social Forums had become useless; according to them, only local action (e.g. activism against the gentrification of their neighbourhoods) could have a real impact on people's lives.

Although place-based movement is very territorialized, the similarities they share and their quasi-simultaneity (occurring in the early 2010s) in different countries are striking. It seems that transnational dynamics have remained important despite the refocusing on the local scale. Eduardo Romanos explains these similarities by tracing the spread of movements from Tahrir Square to the Puerta del Sol in Madrid to Occupy Wall Street.[13] He highlights two types of diffusion in these cases: indirect

---

[9] Sven Reichardt, *Authentizität und Gemeinschaft: Linksalternatives Leben in den siebziger und frühen achtziger Jahren* (Frankfurt-am-Main: Suhrkamp, 2014).

[10] George N. Katsiaficas, *The Subversion of Politics: European Autonomous Social Movements and the Decolonization of Everyday Life* (Atlantic Highlands, NJ: Humanities Press, 1997).

[11] Pascale Dufour, *Trois espaces de protestation: France, Canada, Québec* (Montréal: Presses de l'Université de Montréal, 2013), chap. 7; Francis Dupuis-Déri, 'Pistes Pour Une Histoire de l'anarchisme Au Québec', *Bulletin d'histoire Politique* 16, no. 2 (2008).

[12] Marcos Ancelovici, Pascale Dufour and Héloïse Nez, 'Introduction: From the Indignados to Occupy: Prospects for Comparison', in *Street Politics in the Age of Austerity: From the Indignados to Occupy*, ed. Marcos Ancelovici, Pascale Dufour and Héloïse Nez (Amsterdam: Amsterdam University Press, 2016).

[13] Eduardo Romanos, 'From Tahrir to Puerta Del Sol to Wall Street: The Transnational Diffusion of Social Movements in Comparative Perspective', *Revista Española de Investigaciones Sociológicas*, no. 154 (2016): 103–18.

diffusion (between Egypt and Spain) was enabled by old and new media which disseminated 'ideational elements' whilst direct diffusion (between Spain and the United States) was enabled by the presence of Spanish activists from the Puerta del Sol in Wall Street who shared 'behavioural innovations'. In this chapter, I argue that next to the diffusion enabled by old and new media or activist travels, academic, political non-governmental or international institutions can also play a role in such dissemination.

Transformative justice as a tool to tackle sexual violence within anti-authoritarian communities

Transformative justice is a form of restorative justice, an approach usually presented as an alternative to criminal justice and which encompasses a wide range of practices and actors critical of the idea of punishment. It seeks to establish dialogue between victims and the community, between perpetrators and the community and between victims and perpetrators. Thus, restorative justice aims to make the perpetrator aware of his wrongdoing, to repair damages, to prevent any recidivism and to reintegrate the perpetrator into the 'community' as soon as his relationship with the victim has been improved.[14] It also requires the perpetrator to acknowledge the transgression he is accused of, which is supposed to be facilitated by the absence of threat of punishment.

The term 'transformative justice' was first introduced in the 2000s by some proponents of 'restorative justice' practices critical of the adoption of restorative justice practices by several state justice systems, who integrated them within a punitive paradigm[15]. Restorative justice has been implemented on the national level in Western legal systems (with Canada as a precursor) as well as on the international level under the label of 'transitional justice': the expansion of international human rights and war crimes law in the 1990s led the UN Office of the High Commissioner for Human Rights (OHCHR)[16] and many NGOs to promote restorative justice in post-conflict situations.[17] Truth commissions, like those in South Africa (1996–2003) and Rwanda (1999 to present day), are then a central tool of these justice arrangements.[18] 'Transformative justice' therefore usually refers to practices advocated by activists in the prison abolition movement whereas proponents of 'restorative justice' are

---

[14] Sandrine Lefranc, 'Le mouvement pour la justice restauratrice: "an idea whose time has come"', *Droit et Société*, no. 63–4 (1 October 2006): 394.
[15] Mimi E. Kim, 'Transformative Justice and Restorative Justice: Gender-Based Violence and Alternative Visions of Justice in the United States', *International Review of Victimology* 27, no. 2 (2020): 162–72.
[16] The OHCHR presents itself as the 'lead entity within the United Nations system in the area of transitional justice'. The institution published its first report on transitional justice in 2004. It has also set standards for the implementation of transitional justice mechanisms. For more information, https://www.ohchr.org/EN/Issues/RuleOfLaw/Pages/TransitionalJustice.aspx
[17] Sandrine Lefranc, 'La professionnalisation d'un militantisme réformateur du droit: l'invention de la justice transitionnelle', *Droit et société* n° 73, no. 3 (2009): 561–89.
[18] Sandrine Lefranc, 'Politiques du pardon' (Paris: Presses universitaires de France, 2002).

typically institutional actors like police officers, probation officers and magistrates who work in accordance with the carceral system.[19] Advocates of transformative justice also tend to put a greater emphasis on community accountability as they frame transgressions mainly as the result of structural inequalities within the community. Thus, the primary aims of transformative justice are to achieve recognition for victims, to transform the transgressors' behaviour and to eliminate inequalities within the community.[20]

In both Berlin and Montreal, anti-authoritarian feminists use transformative justice for sexual violence committed within their community, most often by a man against a woman. Sexual violence is an ongoing problem in activist communities, especially when their activities involve a collective everyday life. Occupations, squats or collective housing spur proximity between activists. As sexual violence is mostly committed by acquaintances of the victim, this kind of activism increases the risk of assaults and rapes. Catherine Eschle has shown that sexual violence partly explains activists' withdrawal from Occupy Glasgow.[21] In Berlin, sexual violence has been a continual subject of anti-authoritarian discussions since the emergence of an internal feminist mobilization against such violence in the late 1980s. In Montreal, a similar feminist mobilization emerged during the 2012 student strike which, with 175,000 students on strike for seven months, is the longest and most sustained student strike in Quebec history. In both cities, anti-authoritarians refuse to take legal action because they consider state justice to be one of the causes of gender, class and racial inequalities. Furthermore, the conflicting relationship between anti-authoritarians and the police contributes to victims refraining from reporting. In Berlin, anti-authoritarians are under police surveillance. They fear that reporting sexual violence could lead to political repression such as search warrants against anti-authoritarian housing. In Montreal, the repression of the 2012 strike contributed to construct the police as an enemy.

Both in Montreal and Berlin, the first response to sexual violence has been the exclusion of perpetrators from the anti-authoritarian spaces. As exclusions have always been controversial and have even led to ruptures within activist communities, some feminists saw transformative justice as beneficial when they learned about it in the late 2000s and early 2010s. For these feminists, it was a solution both to address sexual violence and to avoid internal controversies. Transformative justice began to be part of anti-authoritarian discussion in 2013 in Montreal and around 2007 in Berlin. In Berlin, it renewed thoughts about *Täterarbeit* (work with the perpetrator) which appeared at the beginning of the 1990s in relation to initiatives in *Männer-radikale Therapie* (radical therapy for men) by which some activists sought to create a dialogue with the perpetrator to

---

[19] Kim, 'Transformative Justice and Restorative Justice', 169.
[20] Dragan Milovanovic, 'Justice-Rendering Schemas: A Typology for Forms of Justice and a Prolegomenon for Transformative Justice', *Journal of Theoretical and Philosophical Criminology* 3, no. 1 (2011): 18–19.
[21] Catherine Eschle, 'Troubling Stories of the End of Occupy: Feminist Narratives of Betrayal at Occupy Glasgow', *Social Movement Studies* 17, no. 5 (3 September 2018): 524–40.

Figure 15.1 Cover of the third issue of RAZZ, an anti-authoritarian newspaper from Hanover, June 1989; courtesy of author's personal archive.

raise awareness of his wrongdoings and to prevent recidivism. Thus, the receiving contexts of transformative justice are different in Berlin and Montreal which leads to different appropriations. Nevertheless, this contribution focuses more on the diffusion process than on practical appropriation of transformative justice.

A common narrative account of origins

In addition to sharing practices, activists in Berlin and Montreal share a common narrative account of the origins of transformative justice that differ from the accounts identified in researches on restorative justice. Whereas commonly held narrative accounts of the origins of restorative justice include the ancestral practices of the Maori in modern-day New Zealand, the Truth Commissions in Latin America and South Africa and the innovations of Canadian probation officer Marc Yantzi, who organized a mediation between perpetrators and victims of property damage in 1974,[22] anti-authoritarian feminists in both Montreal and Berlin claim that transformative justice was invented in the United States by women and queer people[23] of colour who confronted the overrepresentation of Black men in US prisons and domestic and sexual violence within the Black community. For instance, the Berlin-based collective RESPONS presents 'transformative justice' and 'community accountability' as 'People of Color Women*, Queer and Non-binary approaches':[24]

> Over the past twenty years, women and queer activists of colour in the US have repeatedly identified the need to create alternative and sustainable structures of safety and accountability beyond state institutions or state structures. This analysis and these claims fought for intersectionality and criticized social movements that had a limited understanding of violence – the movement against state violence on the one hand, and the movement against sexualised and relationship violence on the other[25].

In an anonymous zine, anti-authoritarian feminists in Montreal expose a similar account:

> Many black and queer feminist collectives have faced this problem: appealing to state justice or even the media renewed society's violence against them without solving anything about the violence in their communities. Transformative justice processes were partly born in such contexts.[26]

This narrative account of the origins of transformative justice seems to be based on the story of the creation of the network 'INCITE! Women of Color Against Violence' (now known as 'INCITE! Women, Trans and Gender Non-Conforming People of Color Against Violence'). This network of Black women has emerged in 2000 as a new player in the feminist anti-violence movement. It opposes both gender-based

---

[22] Lefranc, 'Le mouvement pour la justice restauratrice'; Lefranc, 'Politiques du pardon'.
[23] In this context 'queer' refers to people who are not heterosexual and/or who are transgender. It includes non-binary or genderqueer people, who are neither women nor men.
[24] RESPONS, *Was Tun Bei Sexualisierter Gewalt? Handbuch Für Die Transformative Arbeit Mit Gewaltausübenden Personen* (Münster: Unrast Verlag, 2018), 16.
[25] Ibid., 59.
[26] Anonymes, 'Premiers Pas Sur Une Corde Raide', 26 February 2014, 5–6, https://infokiosques.net/spip.php?article1138.

violence and 'state violence' (e.g. prisons and police brutality) from an intersectional perspective which takes both feminism and anti-racism into account.[27] INCITE! was followed by Generation FIVE, an organization that defends a similar approach but which is specialized in the issue of child victims of sexual violence. Several local organizations, such as CARA (Community against Rape and Abuse) in Seattle, were created afterwards.

These organizations and their supporters have produced numerous written documents which are available on the internet and read by anti-authoritarian feminists from Berlin and Montreal, which explains why one can find the same narrative account of the origins of transformative justice in both cities. One of these texts is a book entitled *The Revolution Starts at Home*, first published in 2011 by South End Press.[28] In Berlin, the book is mostly circulated online in PDF whilst in Montreal one can find hard copies in activists' personal libraries. Like many feminist books, *The Revolution Starts at Home* brings together testimonies, poems, thoughts on sexual violence and intimate relationships, social analyses and practical tips about transformative justice implementation. Its contributors are members of marginalized communities: people of colour as well as lesbian, gay, bisexual and transgender people, people with disabilities and those at the intersections of these communities. One contribution was written by CARA, and another is made up of excerpts from the 2005 INCITE! report. There is also an INCITE! fact sheet entitled 'How Do We Address Violence Within Our Communities?' At the end of the book, readers are invited to delve deeper into the subject with the help of an indicative bibliography. The recommended texts are the same as the one cited by anti-authoritarian feminists in Berlin and Montreal.

These other references are mainly zines, that is, self-published magazines made up of hand-bound printed pages. They contain different kinds of texts ranging from testimonies, to fictions and political argumentations, comic strips, drawings or collages. They can be easily reproduced with a photocopier or a printer which helps explain why they are such a widespread medium in anti-authoritarian feminist circles.[29] Many activists carefully preserve their zines in a dedicated box. In collective housing, zines are also available in shared spaces such as the kitchen, dining room or bathroom.

Zines are an important channel of diffusion for transformative justice practices. In both Berlin and Montreal, zines written or published online by Philly Pissed, a support group for sexual assault survivors in Philadelphia, are important references. Active in the 2000s, Philly Pissed promoted transformative justice. To this end, its members worked with the group Philly Stands Up, which took on transformative justice processes from 2004 to 2015.[30] Their website still provides zines such as Cindy Crabb's 'Learning Good Consent: On Healthy Relationships and Survivor Support',[31] which is widespread

---

[27] Kim, 'Transformative Justice and Restorative Justice'.
[28] Ching-In Chen, Jai Dulani, and Leah Lakshmi Piepzna-Samarasinha, *The Revolution Starts at Home: Confronting Intimate Violence within Activist Communities* (Chico, CA: AK Press, 2011).
[29] Red Chidgey, 'Reassess Your Weapons: The Making of Feminist Memory in Young Women's Zines', *Women's History Review* 22, no. 4 (2013): 658–72.
[30] Esteban Lance Kelly, 'Philly Stands Up: Inside the Politics and Poetics of Transformative Justice and Community Accountability in Sexual Assault Situations', *Social Justice* 37, no. 4 (122) (2011): 44–57.
[31] Cindy Crabb, 'Learning Good Consent', 2008, http://www.phillyspissed.net/sites/default/files/learning%20good%20consent2.pdf.

in both Berlin and Montreal and has been translated in French[32] and German[33]. Other popular zines are the ones entitled 'What to Do When? A Zine About Community Response to Sexual Assault' written and published by Philly Pissed.[34]

Some references are only circulated in Berlin or Montreal. The first zine established in Berlin was written by anarchists, probably from Detroit.[35] Berlin anti-authoritarian feminists also translated the text into German, which CARA had published in the book *The Revolution Starts at Home* under the title 'Taking Risks: Implementing Grassroots Community Accountability Strategies'.[36] Berliners also refer to several writings from the collective Generation FIVE. Activists in Montreal read Canadian texts like the feedback on transformative justice experiences published by A. J. Whiters in a zine entitled 'Transformative Justice and/as Harm',[37] as well as the writings of the Third Eye Collective, a group of Black women from Montreal that promote transformative justice[38].

Thus, anti-authoritarian feminists in both Berlin and Montreal received a Black feminist narrative account of origins primarily through texts. This ideational reception has probably been facilitated by many resonances between this narrative and anti-authoritarian feminist ideas. First of all, the feminist component of this narrative is important: the idea of rehabilitation of rape perpetrators has not reached a consensus within the feminist movement, which is primarily concerned with victims. Presenting transformative justice as a Black feminist creation also helps to legitimize it. It situates transformative justice on the side of intersectionality (which also originated with US Black feminists) when most anti-authoritarian feminists claim to be 'intersectional feminists' and reject what they call 'white feminism' (even though they are overwhelmingly white). Finally, this narrative presents transformative justice as a practice that opposes state justice, which resonates with the anti-authoritarian's anti-state beliefs.

Specific promoters

Nevertheless, ideas do not transmit themselves. Their reception depends on specific persons that promote them. Both in Montreal and in Berlin, transformative justice has been introduced by local activists with their own distinct life stories.

In Berlin, a group of seven members play a key role in the reception of transformative justice. Formed in 2009, they created the website trasnformativejustice.eu and made

---

[32] See the French version: https://infokiosques.net/lire.php?id_article=1121
[33] See the German version: https://konsenslernen.noblogs.org/files/2017/02/Konsens-lernen.pdf
[34] The three zines are available here: http://www.phillyspissed.net/taxonomy/term/3
[35] Anonyme, 'Thoughts about Community Support around Intimate Violence', env 2000, https://www.phillyspissed.net/sites/default/files/intviolzine-consecutive.pdf. It was first received in 2007 and translated into German in 2009.
[36] See the German version: https://www.transformativejustice.eu/wp-content/uploads/2017/04/Das-Risiko-wagen.pdf
[37] A.J. Whiters, 'Transformative Justice and/as Harm', 2015, https://stillmyrevolution.files.wordpress.com/2015/12/tj-zine-final-with-cover.pdf.
[38] See the group's website: https://thirdeyecollective.wordpress.com/

available *The Revolution Starts at Home* and the zines mentioned above. The website was very active from 2009 to 2012. During this time, the group translated several texts from English into German. In 2016, their website has been reactivated in order to communicate information about initiatives (especially text publications) launched by members of the groups. Some people of the website are also members of the collective RESPONS that have set up transformative justice processes since 2009.

Jane[39], a co-founder of transformativejustice.eu and RESPONS, is particularly important. Jane comes from the United States and has been living in Berlin since 2008. She graduated from the Humboldt University with a master's degree in gender studies in 2015. She wrote her master's thesis on transformative justice and has been writing a doctoral dissertation at UC-Santa Barbara since 2016, a participative research project which aims at developing a reflection on the implementation of transformative justice. The website transformativejustice.eu was reactivated in 2016 mainly to communicate about this research project. It has also presented the syllabus of a seminar on transformative justice given by Jane in 2016 at the Center for Transdisciplinary Gender Studies at the Humboldt University. The book *The Revolution Starts at Home* was a primary bibliographic reference of the seminar.

When looking at the participants in Jane's project, we note that they are committed to human rights and are particularly concerned about situations of armed conflict, namely in Palestine. A German-Palestinian lawyer specialized in international criminal law and human rights advocacy who has co-authored a book with Jane is a regular participant in the project. The lawyer's office is at the House of Democracy in Berlin, along with other organizations such as Amnesty International, and she is known for championing the Palestinian cause through her work. Another regular participant in the project is an African-American activist, journalist, midwife and human rights defender who worked in Palestine, Egypt and Chiapas. This woman has lived in Berlin since 2013. Situations of armed conflict may seem far away from the sexual violence that occurs in the Berlin anti-authoritarian community but they mirror the multiplicity of contexts in which transformative justice is currently developed: within this framework, the regulation of conflicts between communities and the regulation of relations between individuals are linked.

Jane's story reflects Tarrow's characterization of the 'rooted cosmopolitan': Jane plays an important role in the reception of transformative justice in Berlin because, though active in US and transnational research networks, she is firmly anchored in the local German activist community. Moreover, the reception of transformative justice in Berlin owes much to universities: academia enabled Jane to combine her education with political engagement, as when she could teach transformative justice principles at Humboldt University's Centre for Transdisciplinary Gender Studies. University funding, including three fellowships at the University of California at Santa Barbara for her PhD thesis, made it possible for her to finance her work. Jane's experience thus illustrates the important role played by academia in the diffusion of transformative justice.

---

[39] All names have been changed.

Jane has also received support from sources outside of academia. A salient example is the Rosa Luxemburg Foundation of the left-wing party *die Linke*, which awarded Jane grants when she was completing her master's degree. It is worth noting that Jane is not an exception in this regard: fellow anti-authoritarian activists have secured grants from the Foundation, whose scholarship department awards politically engaged, high-achieving students whose research supports the Foundation's socialist ideals.[40] The Rosa Luxemburg Foundation also funds anti-authoritarian events like workshops or festivals that promote 'a critical analysis of society and foster networks of emancipatory political, social and cultural initiatives'.[41] The Confederation of German Trade Unions' Hans Böckler Foundation and the Green Party's Heinrich Böll Foundation have been known to fund similar projects. These examples suggest that, despite their general scepticism of political institutions, anti-authoritarian activists' work often depends upon left-wing institutions for financial support.

A PhD student from the United States also plays a role in the Montreal reception of transformative justice. Maria lived in Montreal from 2009 to 2014. During this time, she wrote a McGill University-funded dissertation on transformative justice within Indigenous communities and directed an artistic project on Indigenous women's experiences of incarceration, also funded by McGill. In Montreal, Maria was mostly involved with anglophone activists. However, she was invited in January 2014 by francophone activists to lead a workshop on transformative justice at the Université de Québec à Montreal (UQÀM), the francophone university with the highest number of anti-authoritarian feminists as students. This event has been important for many francophone anti-authoritarian feminists. It has provided a forum for discussion about practices which they previously only knew about through readings.

Despite Maria's role in the reception of transformative justice, the anti-authoritarian feminists who invited her to give a workshop play an even greater role in the movement. These activists are all bilingual and active in both the francophone and anglophone anti-authoritarian communities. Some of them have created community-mediation trainings whilst others have gone back to school to become therapists; one activist whom I met in 2017 was considering becoming a doula. Despite their different backgrounds, they share the same goal of initiating collective 'healing' processes in the light of violence within communities. These feminists place great importance on both mental and physical health which they link to justice issues through the idea of collective 'healing'.

Of these anti-authoritarian feminists, Marie-Jo plays perhaps the most significant role in the anti-authoritarian community. She works as a social rights defender, and her unpaid activist work focuses on mental and physical health issues combining art and activism. Marie-Jo's biographical interview reveals the important part her aunt played in her politicization. Her aunt, who works in the international field of transitional justice – whether for NGOs, the Canadian government or the United Nations – is an expert in defending women's right, especially their justice rights for

---

[40] See the scholarship department of the Rosa Luxemburg Stiftung: https://www.rosalux.de/en/foundation/studienwerk
[41] See the aims of the Rosa Luxemburg Stiftung: https://www.rosalux.de/en/foundation/about-us

the violence they have suffered. Marie-Jo has discussed her aunt's work with her extensively since she was a child, and considered following in her footsteps. She ultimately preferred local activism which she felt was more useful. Nevertheless, she has continued to be close to her aunt and, following the 2012 student strike, founded a collective together with her and other feminists with the aim of promoting activist well-being to avoid burn-out and resolving interpersonal conflicts in order to build 'sustainable communities'. Marie-Jo sees transformative justice practices as an integral part of this 'sustainable community' project. As I have earlier asserted, situations of war and interpersonal violence can be understood through the same prism. They are seen as part of the same logic of escalating violence. During the interview, Marie-Jo evokes this idea:

> My aunt has always worked for women's rights in armed conflicts on issues of sexual violence. Like she was in Rwanda during the genocide. You know, I was very young, I was born in '85 – the genocide was in '90 [*sic*], so I was very small when I heard those horror stories. And I think this is a common thread of how I think about things, yeah, that's stories of women who were calling for justice. It was not like … it wasn't just horror stories. There were stories of how in a context of extreme violence, people had organised themselves so that children could continue to learn to read and write, and so that people could continue to feed their families. Then [my aunt] also worked in the Balkans, and I remember a story about people who had taken out, you know, boats, like five thousand soldiers, women who had taken out people so that they wouldn't fight in the war. And that's one of the threads of my understanding of violence, you know, I think that in difficult contexts, people make difficult choices. But I think when physical violence is used against human bodies, like everybody loses, you know, I think it doesn't matter which side you're on, like … it's, yeah, I think I learned a lot about that from my aunt, how intimate violence escalates in communities.[42]

In this context, preserving a community, whether national or anti-authoritarian, requires repairing but also preventing violence so that it no longer occurs. Prevention implies a community transformation which should be enabled by transformative justice. In practical terms, the group Marie-Jo co-founded organizes workshops and writes some texts. It also intervenes at political groups' request in various cases of conflict (in this context, sexual violence is understood as conflict). In addition to the activities of Marie-Jo's group, other transformative justice initiatives were launched by francophone anti-authoritarian feminists to meet the growing number of victims' requests of transformative justice from the end of 2013.

To sum up, academic institutions may have facilitated the reception of transformative justice in Montreal, but they did not play a primary role. The central players have been bilingual anti-authoritarian feminists that have learned about transformative justice through the anglophone activist community. Once again, the diffusion of

---

[42] Interview carried out by author on 11 August 2017.

transformative justice practices is due to activists rooted in two cultural and linguistic communities. Last but not least, in Marie Jo's aunt, we can see the indirect influence of international institutions that promote transitional justice.

Discussion and conclusion

This study of the reception of transformative justice aims at understanding how anti-authoritarian feminists are embedded in transnational dynamics. These feminists are neither active in transnational organizations nor engaged exclusively in international issues. They rather favour local activism in their neighbourhood or in their activist community. Nevertheless, anti-authoritarian feminist Montrealers and Berliners share common practices, including that of transformative justice, which are an effect of the transnationalization of their activism. Tracing the paths of the reception of transformative justice in Berlin and Montreal, I have provided evidence of an indirect ideational diffusion via a book and several zines. Like Romanos, I found that this ideational diffusion was facilitated by the internet. I have also highlighted the importance of certain activists who introduced these writings on transformative justice. These persons have common characteristics: they are both rooted in the anglophone North American world and in the German-speaking world (for Berlin) or the francophone world (for Montreal). This corroborates Tarrow's observations concerning the 'rooted cosmopolitan'.

We can also note that the profile of these activists is similar to the one found in sociological research on restorative justice[43]. First, they are academics, activists involved in advocacy and lawyers. The academics among them have an activist approach that is relatively marginalized in academia. I also found that promoters of transformative justice combine justice and health issues, leading some of them to choose health-related careers.

Furthermore, I have identified indirect influences of academic, political and international institutions (or organizations) on the reception of transformative justice, despite the anti-authoritarian feminist scepticism of any form of institution. The reception of transformative justice in Berlin owes much to US and German academics who consider transformative justice as a legitimate research object, as well as to political organizations like the German Rosa Luxemburg Foundation. Both in Berlin and Montreal, I have also noted a congruence between thoughts on armed conflicts and thoughts on sexual violence committed in peacetime. Through human rights activism, or even through family ties, a lawyer specialized in international criminal law, international organizations and NGOs has indirectly disseminated transitional justice ideas that they promote for post-conflict situations. The biography of Marie-Jo shows how indirect the influence of institutions can be, depending in this case on an

---

[43] Lefranc, 'Le mouvement pour la justice restauratrice'; Delphine Griveaud, and Sandrine Lefranc, 'La justice transitionnelle, un monde-carrefour', *Cultures Conflits* n° 119–20, no. 3 (2020): 39–65; Lefranc, 'La professionnalisation d'un militantisme réformateur du droit'.

aunt-niece relationship. It invites us to question the role of non-political relationships in the dissemination of political ideas and practices.

Finally, this contribution highlights the central position of the United States in the inception of activist ideas and practices, which has already been remarked upon in the context of the anti-Vietnam War movement of the 1960s and of the women's movement[44]. The way anti-authoritarian feminists are embedded in transnational dynamics reflects the United States' position as the Western world's leading power.

---

[44] Timothy Scott Brown, *West Germany and the Global Sixties: The Antiauthoritarian Revolt, 1962–1978* (New-York: Cambridge University Press, 2013); Jian Chen et al. (eds.), *The Routledge Handbook of the Global Sixties: Between Protest and Nation-Building* (London: Routledge, 2018).

Selected bibliography

This bibliography includes a small selection of secondary sources used in the chapters and identified by the authors as particularly relevant to the study of their topic. We hope it can serve as a handy introduction to the literature on significant aspects of the history of left-wing internationalisms. For a more comprehensive accounting of sources, we invite readers to refer to the footnotes in each chapter.

Introduction (Michele Di Donato and Mathieu Fulla)

Bensimon, Fabrice, Quentin Deluermoz and Jeanne Moisand, eds. *"Arise Ye Wretched of the Earth": The First International in a Global Perspective*. Leiden: Brill, 2018.
Byrne, Jeffrey James. *Mecca of Revolution: Algeria, Decolonization, and the Third World Order*. New York: Oxford University Press, 2016.
Delalande, Nicolas. *La lutte et l'entraide: L'âge des solidarités ouvrières*. Paris: Seuil, 2019.
Drachewych, Oleksa, and Ian McKay, eds. *Left Transnationalism: The Communist International and the National, Colonial, and Racial Questions*. Montreal & Kingston: McGill-Queen's University Press, 2019.
Eley, Geoff. *Forging Democracy: The History of the Left in Europe, 1850-2000*. Oxford: Oxford University Press, 2002.
Haupt, Georges. *La Deuxième Internationale 1884-1914: Étude critique des sources. Essai bibliographique*. Paris: Mouton, 1964.
Joll, James. *The Second International, 1889-1914*. London: Weidenfeld and Nicolson, 1968.
Kirschenbaum, Lisa A. *International Communism and the Spanish Civil War*. Cambridge: Cambridge University Press, 2015.
Laqua, Daniel. 'Democratic Politics and the League of Nations: The Labour and Socialist International as Protagonist of Interwar Internationalism'. *Contemporary European History* 24, no. 2 (2015), 175-92.
Mazower, Mark. *Governing the World: The History of an Idea, 1815 to the Present*. New York: Penguin, 2013.
Pons, Silvio. *The Global Revolution: A History of International Communism 1917-1991*. Oxford: Oxford University Press, 2014.
Pons, Silvio, ed. *Cambridge History of Communism*. Cambridge: Cambridge University Press, 2017.
Priestland, David. *The Red Flag: A History of Communism*. New York: Grove Press, 2009.
Renaud, Terence. *New Lefts: The Making of a Radical Tradition*. Princeton and Oxford: Princeton University Press, 2021.
Sassoon, Donald. *One Hundred Years of Socialism: The West European Left in the Twentieth Century*. London and New York: I.B. Tauris, 1996.
Sluga, Glenda, and Patricia Clavin, eds. *Internationalisms: A Twentieth-Century History*. Cambridge: Cambridge University Press, 2017.

Studer, Brigitte. *The Transnational World of the Cominternians*. Basingstoke: Palgrave Macmillan, 2015.
Van der Linden, Marcel. *Workers of the World: Essays toward a Global Labor History*. Leiden-Boston: Brill, 2008.
Van Kemseke, Peter. *Towards an Era of Development: The Globalization of Socialism and Christian Democracy, 1945–1965*. Leuven: Leuven University Press, 2006.

Chapter 1 (Kostis Karpozilos)

Dimou, Augusta. *Entangled Paths towards Modernity: Contextualizing Socialism and Nationalism in the Balkans*. Budapest and New York: Central European University Press, 2009.
Haupt, Georges. *Socialism and the Great War: The Collapse of the Second International*. Oxford: Oxford University Press, 1972.
Hillis, Faith. *Utopia's Discontents: Russian Émigrés and the Quest for Freedom, 1830s–1930s*. Oxford: Oxford University Press, 2021.
Khuri-Makdisi, Ilham. *The Eastern Mediterranean and the Making of Global Radicalism, 1860–1914*. Berkeley: University of California Press, 2013.
Leon, George B. *The Greek Socialist Movement and the First World War: The Road to Unity*. New York: Columbia University Press, 1976.
Potamianos, Nikos. 'Internationalism and the Emergence of Communist Politics in Greece, 1912–1924'. *Journal of Balkan and Near Eastern Studies* 20 (2018), 1–17.
Todorova, Maria. *The Lost World of Socialists at Europe's Margins: Imagining Utopia, 1870s–1920s*. New York and London: Bloomsbury Academic, 2020.

Chapter 2 (Nik. Brandal and Eirik Wig Sundvall)

Anderson, Gidske. *Halvard Lange – Portrett av en Nordmann*. Oslo: Gyldendal, 1981.
Bull, Trygve. *Mot Dag og Erling Falk*. Trondheim: J. W. Cappelens Forlag, 1987.
Lees, Lorraine M. 'De Witt Clinton Poole, the Foreign Nationalities Branch and Political Intelligence'. *Intelligence and National Security* 15, no. 4 (2008), 81–103.
Obenaus, Herbert, and Hans D. Schmid, eds. *Der Parteivorstand der SPD im Exil: Protokolle der Sopade 1933–1940*. Bonn: Verlag J.H.M Dietz Nachfolger, 1955.
Saunier, Pierre-Yves. *Transnational History*. Basingstoke: Palgrave Macmillan, 2013.
Troy, Thomas F. *Donovan and the CIA: A History of the Establishment of the Central Intelligence Agency*. Langley, VA: Central Intelligence Agency, 1981.

Chapter 3 (Yutaka Kanda)

Bose, Pradip. *Social Democracy in Practice: Socialist International, 1951–2001*. Delhi: Authorspress, 2005.
Braunthal, Julius. *History of the International, vol. 3, World Socialism, 1943–1968*. London: Victor Gollancz, 1980.
Costa, Ettore. *The Labour Party, Denis Healey and the International Socialist Movement: Rebuilding the Socialist International during the Cold War, 1945–1951*. Cham: Palgrave Macmillan, 2018.

Imlay, Talbot C. *The Practice of Socialist Internationalism: European Socialists and International Politics, 1914–1960*. Oxford: Oxford University Press, 2018.

Niclas-Tölle, Boris. *The Socialist Opposition in Nehruvian India, 1947–1964*. Frankfurt am Main: Peter Lang GmbH, 2015.

Rose, Saul. *Socialism in Southern Asia*. New York: Octagon Books, 1975.

Stockwin, J.A.A. *The Japanese Socialist Party and Neutralism: A Study of Political Party and Its Foreign Policy*. Melbourne: Melbourne University Press, 1968.

Chapter 4 (Silvio Pons)

Friedman, Jeremy. *Shadow Cold War: The Sino-Soviet Competition for the Third World*. Chapel Hill: University of North Carolina Press, 2015.

Kalter, Charles. *The Discovery of the Third World: Decolonization and the Rise of the New Left in France, 1950–1976*. Cambridge: Cambridge University Press, 2016.

Mazov, Sergey. *A Distant Front in the Cold War: The USSR in West Africa and the Congo 1956–1964*. Stanford, CA: Stanford University Press, 2010.

Pons, Silvio. *I comunisti italiani e gli altri. Visioni e legami internazionali nel mondo del Novecento*. Einaudi: Torino, 2021.

Rupprecht, Tobias. *Soviet Internationalism after Stalin. Interaction and Exchange between the USSR and Latin America during the Cold War*. Cambridge: Cambridge University Press, 2015.

Westad, Odd Arne. *The Global Cold War. Third World Interventions and the Making of Our Times*. Cambridge: Cambridge University Press, 2005.

Chapter 5 (Arianna Lissoni)

Lee, Christopher J. 'Introduction', in Alex La Guma, *A Soviet Journey, A Critical Annotated Edition*. London: Lexington Books, 2017, 1–60.

Lodge, Tom. *Red Road to Freedom: A History of the South African Communist Party, 1921–2021*. Auckland Park: Jacana Media, 2021.

Maloka, Eddy. *The South African Communist Party: Exile and After Apartheid*. Auckland Park: Jacana Media, 2013.

Shubin, Vladimir. *ANC: A View from Moscow*, 2nd ed. Auckland Park: Jacana Media, 2017.

Shubin, Vladimir, and Marina Traikova. 'There Is No Threat from the Eastern Bloc', in *The Road to Democracy in South Africa*, ed. South African Democracy Education Trust, vol. 3, part 2. Pretoria: Unisa Press, 2008, 985–1066.

Chapter 6 (Mathieu Fulla)

Devin, Guillaume. *L'Internationale socialiste: Histoire et sociologie du socialisme international*. Paris: Presses de Sciences Po, 1990.

Fulla, Mathieu, and Marc Lazar, eds. *European Socialists and the State in the Twentieth and Twenty-First Centuries*. London: Palgrave Macmillan, 2020.

Ogle, Vanessa. 'State Rights against Private Capital: The "New International Economic Order" and the Struggle over Aid, Trade, and Foreign Investment, 1962–1981'.

Humanity. An International Journal of Human Rights, Humanitarianism, and Development 5, no. 2 (Summer 2014), 211–34.
Rother, Bernd, and Klaus Larres, eds. *Willy Brandt and International Relations: Europe, the USA, and Latin America, 1974–1992*. London: Bloomsbury, 2019.
'The New International Economic Order: A Reintroduction'. Special issue co-ordinated by Nils Gilman. *Humanity. An International Journal of Human Rights, Humanitarianism, and Development* 6, no. 1 (Spring 2015).

Chapter 7 (Adeline Blaszkiewicz)

Blaszkiewicz-Maison, Adeline. '"Mieux vaudrait après tout se perdre avec Lénine que de se sauver avec Albert Thomas". Construire une voie révolutionnaire face au socialisme réformiste (1917–1924)'. *Le Mouvement social* 3, no. 270 (2020), 41–58.
Guérin, Denis. *Albert Thomas au BIT 1920–1932: De l'internationalisme à l'Europe*. Genève: Institut européen de l'Université de Genève, 1996.
Jean-Numa, Ducange, Razmig Keucheyan, and Roza Stéphanie, eds. *Histoire globale des socialismes*. Paris: Presses universitaires de France, 2021.
Lespinet-Moret, Isabelle, and Vincent Viet, eds. *L'Organisation internationale du travail: Origine, développement, avenir*. Rennes: Presses universitaires de Rennes, 2011.
Marcobelli, Elisa. *L'internationalisme à l'épreuve des crises: La IIe Internationale et les socialistes français, allemands et italiens, 1889–1915*. Nancy: Arbre bleu, 2019.
Maul, Daniel. *L'Organisation internationale du Travail: 100 ans de politique sociale à l'échelle mondiale*. Genève: Bureau international du Travail, 2019.

Chapter 8 (Michel Christian)

Bockman, Johanna. 'Socialist Globalization against Capitalist Neocolonialism: The Economic Ideas behind the New International Economic Order'. *Humanity: An International Journal of Human Rights, Humanitarianism, and Development* 6, no. 1 (2015).
Christian, Michel, Sandrine Kott, and Ondrej Matejka, eds. *Planning in Cold War Europe: Competition, Cooperation, Circulations (1950s–1970s)*. Opladen: De Gruyter, 2018.
Iriye, Akira. *Global Community: The Role of International Organizations in the Making of the Contemporary World*. Berkeley: University of California Press, 2002.
Kott, Sandrine. *Organiser le monde: Une autre histoire de la Guerre froide*. Paris: Seuil, 2021.
Lorenzini, Sara, 'Comecon and the South in the years of détente: A Study on East–South Economic Relations'. *European Review of History: Revue européenne d'histoire* 21, no. 2 (2014).

Chapter 9 (Mateo Jarquín)

Baltodano, Mónica, ed. *Memorias de la Lucha Sandinista*. Managua: Fundación Rosa Luxemburgo, Instituto de Historia de Nicaragua y Centroamerica, 2012.
Field, Thomas, Stella Krepp, and Vanni Pettina, eds. *Latin America and the Global Cold War*. Chapel Hill: University of North Carolina Press, 2020.

Harmer, Tanya, and Eline van Ommen, eds. *Internationalizing Revolution: The Nicaraguan Revolution and the World, 1977–1990*, special issue of *The Americas: A Quarterly Review of Latin American History* 78, no. 4 (2021).
Kalinovsky, Artemy, and Sergey Radchenko, eds. *The End of the Cold War and the Third World*. London: Routledge, 2011.
Pastor, Robert. *Not Condemned to Repetition: The United States and Nicaragua*. Boulder, CO: Westview Press, 2002.
Zimmerman, Matilde. *Sandinista: Carlos Fonseca and the Nicaraguan Revolution*. Durham, NC: Duke University Press, 2001.

Chapter 10 (Michele Di Donato)

Boel, Bent. 'Transnationalisme social-démocrate et dissidents de l'Est pendant la guerre froide'. *Vingtième siècle* 109, no. 1 (2011), 169–81.
Eckel, Jan. *The Ambivalence of Good: Human Rights in International Politics since the 1940s*. Oxford: Oxford University Press, 2019.
Hobsbawm, Eric J. 'Labour and Human Rights', in Eric J. Hobsbawm, *Worlds of Labour: Further Studies in the History of Labour*. London: Weidenfeld and Nicholson, 1984.
Moyn, Samuel. *The Last Utopia: Human Rights in History*. Cambridge, MA-London: The Belknap Press of Harvard University Press, 2010.
Salm, Christian. *Transnational Socialist Networks in the 1970s: European Community Development Aid and Southern Enlargement*. Basingstoke: Palgrave Macmillan, 2016.
Whyte, Jessica. *The Morals of the Market: Human Rights and the Rise of Neoliberalism*. London: Verso, 2019.

Chapter 11 (Jocelyn Olcott)

Benería, Lourdes, Günseli Berik and Maria Floro. *Gender, Development, and Globalization: Economics as If All People Mattered*. New York: Routledge, 2016.
Ferree, Myra Marx, and Aili Mari Tripp, eds. *Global Feminism: Transnational Women's Activism, Organizing, and Human Rights*. New York: New York University Press, 2006.
Ghodsee, Kristen. *Second World, Second Sex: Socialist Women's Activism and Global Solidarity during the Cold War*. Durham: Duke University Press, 2018.
Jain, Devaki. *Women, Development, and the UN: A Sixty-Year Quest for Equality and Justice*. Bloomington and Indianapolis: Indiana University Press, 2005.
Moghadam, Valentine M. *Globalizing Women: Transnational Feminist Networks*. Baltimore: Johns Hopkins University Press, 2005.
Olcott, Jocelyn. *International Women's Year: The Greatest Consciousness-Raising Event in History*. (New York: Oxford University Press, 2017).

Chapter 12 (Phillip Deery)

Alman, Emily Arnow, and David Alman. *Exoneration: The Rosenberg-Sobell Case in the 21st Century*. Seattle: Green Elms Press, 2010.

Clune, Lori. *Executing the Rosenbergs: Death and Diplomacy in a Cold War World*. New York: Oxford University Press, 2016.
Glynn, Robert B. 'L'Affaire Rosenberg in France'. *Political Science Quarterly* 70, no. 4 (1955), 498–521.
Neville, John. *The Press, the Rosenbergs, and the Cold War*. Westport: Praeger, 1995.
Radosh, Ronald, and Joyce Milton. *The Rosenberg File: A Search for the Truth*. New York: Holt, Rinehart & Winston, 1983.
Schneir, Walter, and Miriam Schneir. *Invitation to an Inquest*. New York: Doubleday, 1965, republished 1973, 1983.

Chapter 13 (Céline Vaz)

Baumeister, Martin, Dieter Schott and Bruno Bonomo, eds. *Urban Politics, Heritage, and Social Movements in Italy and West Germany in the 1970s*. Frankfurt: Campus Verlag, 2017.
Bourdieu, Pierre. 'Les conditions sociales de la circulation internationale des idées'. *Actes de la recherche en sciences sociales*, no 145 (December 2002), 3–8.
Lassave, Pierre. *Les sociologues et la recherche urbaine en France*. Toulouse: Presses universitaires du Mirail, 1997.
Lefebvre, Henri. *La révolution urbaine*. Paris: Gallimard, 1970.
Violeau, Jean-Louis. *Les architectes et mai 68*. Paris: Éditions Recherches, 2005.

Chapter 14 (Andrew S. Tompkins)

Augustine, Dolores L. *Taking on Technocracy: Nuclear Power in Germany, 1945 to the Present*. New York: Berghahn, 2018.
Kalmbach, Karena. *The Meanings of a Disaster: Chernobyl and Its Afterlives in Britain and France*. New York: Berghahn, 2020.
Milder, Stephen. *Greening Democracy: The Anti-Nuclear Movement and Political Environmentalism in West Germany and beyond, 1968–1983*. Cambridge: Cambridge University Press, 2017.
Tompkins, Andrew S. *Better Active than Radioactive! Anti-Nuclear Protest in 1970s France and West Germany*. Oxford: Oxford University Press, 2016.
Wenkel, Christian, Eric Bussière, Anahita Grisoni, and Hélène Miard-Delacroix, eds. *The Environment and the European Public Sphere: Perceptions, Actors, Policies*. Winwick: White Horse Press, 2020.

Chapter 15 (Emeline Fourment)

Donatella della Porta, Massimiliano Andretta, Lorenzo Mosca, and Herbert Reiter, eds. *Globalization from Below: Transnational Activists and Protest Networks*. Minneapolis: University of Minnesota Press, 2006.
Dufour, Pascale, and Isabelle Giraud. 'Globalization and Political Change in the Women's Movement: The Politics of Scale and Political Empowerment in the World March of Women'. *Social Science Quarterly* 88, no. 5 (2007), 1152–73.

Kim, Mimi E. 'Transformative Justice and Restorative Justice: Gender-Based Violence and Alternative Visions of Justice in the United States'. *International Review of Victimology* 27, no. 2 (2020), 162–72.

Lefranc, Sandrine. 'Le mouvement pour la justice restauratrice: "An idea whose time has come."' *Droit et Société*, no. 63–4 (October 2006).

Romanos, Eduardo. 'From Tahrir to Puerta Del Sol to Wall Street: The Transnational Diffusion of Social Movements in Comparative Perspective'. *Revista Española de Investigaciones Sociológicas*, no. 154 (2016), 103–18

Tarrow, Sidney G. *The New Transnational Activism*. New York: Cambridge University Press, 2005.

Index

AAWORD (Association of African Women for Research and Development) 174–9, 181–3, 185–8
Accion Democratica of Venezuela 106
Adler, Friedrich 41–3, 124–7
African National Congress (ANC) 81–2, 85, 90–5
Afro-Asian solidarity movements 16
Ahooja-Patel, Krishna 187
Algerian independence 73, 166
Algerian National Liberation Front 70
Alternative Economic Strategy of the British Labour Party (AES) 103, 110
Amnesty International (AI) 160–1, 164, 168, 170, 243
Andersen, Alsing 50
Andrés, Carlos 102, 148, 152
Anti-colonial movements 2, 11–13, 15–16, 54, 56–7, 61–2, 64, 73, 78, 83, 125, 161
Anti-communism 36, 48–9, 52–65, 79, 149, 154, 156, 162, 198, 204, 221, 224
Anti-imperialism 67, 74–5
Anti-nuclear energy 219–32
Anti-racism campaigns 16, 20, 188, 241
Antrobus, Peggy 186–8
Arbeidernes Ungdomsfylking (AUF) 41
Asian non-communist socialists 56–61
Asian Socialist Conference (ASC) 53–4, 57–61
Asian Socialist solidarity 61–4
Atomic bombing of Hiroshima and Nagasaki 93
Atomic Energy Act 196
Auriol, Vincent 198
Australian Council of Civil Liberties 201
Australian Security Intelligence Organisation (ASIO) 201–3

Awe, Bolanle 173
Ayala, Luis 107

Balkan Wars 25, 28, 31, 33–4
Bandung Conference 16, 74, 93
Bauer, Otto 27, 122–3
Beauvoir, Simone de 2, 188
Benaroya, Avraam 27, 29, 33, 35–6
Ben Bella, Ahmed 74, 77–8
Bendaña, Alejandro 144
Benenson, Peter 160–1
Bernstein, Rusty 90, 93–4
Bhatt, Eli 178
Blanc, Louis 7
Blum, Andreas 167–8
Blum, Léon 166
Bolshevism 3, 10–12, 36, 120–1
Borderland transnationalism 222–4
Borge, Tomás 144, 146, 154
Borja, Jordi 205, 208, 212–13, 215–16
Boserup, Ester 177, 183
Braatøy, Bjarne 18, 39–52
Brainin, Joseph 192, 200, 202, 204
Brandt, Willy 14, 97–8, 101–3, 105–7, 111, 152, 164–5, 171
Branting, Karl 122
Braunthal, Julius 50, 55, 59, 62
British Labour Party 50, 56, 63, 99, 103–4, 165, 169
Bryn, Dag 41, 49
Bulgarian Communist Party (BCP) 89–92
Burma, Communist Party 57
Bush, George H.W. 155

Cabet, Etienne 7
Cachalia, Molvi 93
Cahill, Damien 98
Cambridge Economic Policy Group (CEPG) 104
Camus, Albert 2

Capitalism 8, 11, 14, 19, 21, 62, 75, 88, 99–100, 109–12, 123, 134, 142, 147, 153, 157, 181, 210, 224
Carlsson, Bernt 164, 167–8, 170
Carozzi, Luigi 119
Carrillo, Roxana 184
Carrión, Luís 150, 153
Carter, Jimmy 150, 163–5, 167
Castells, Manuel 205–6, 210, 212, 215–16
Castro, Fidel 74, 146, 148
Central Intelligence Agency (CIA) 48–9, 154, 176
Centro de Enseñanza e Investigación Sociedad Anónima (CEISA) 216
Centro de Estudios Territoriales y Ambientales (CETA) 211–12
Chamorro de Barrios, Violeta 155
Chartism 7–8
Chinese Revolution 15, 69
Christian Democratic World Union 164
Churchill, Winston 44
Clark, Victor Figueroa 149
Cold War
   Asian anti-communism 53, 58, 61–5
   Australia 191–2, 194, 200–1, 203
   communist internationalism 3, 5, 13–15, 17, 19–21
   Eastern bloc countries 129–30, 134
   European communism 47, 52
   Global South 176
   human right controversies 161, 166, 171
   Italian communism 67–9, 72–6
   New International Economic Order 102, 111
   in Nicaragua 144–7, 153, 156–7
   South African communism 83–4, 92, 95–6
Cominform 14, 55–7, 59, 68
Comintern 4, 12–14, 40, 67, 85, 90
Committee of the International Socialist Conference (Comisco) 55–7
Communist internationalism 4, 12, 14–15, 17, 19, 68, 117, 121
Communist Party of Australia (CPA) 200–3
Communist Party of Great Britain (CPGB) 87, 89, 96

Communist Party of South Africa (CPSA) 81–2, 85, 90
Communist Party of the Soviet Union (CPSU) 85–8, 92, 95, 146
Communist Party of the United States of America (CPUSA) 192, 194–6
Confederation of the Socialist Parties of the European Community (CSPEC) 19, 98–100, 104, 106, 111
Contadora Peace Process 152–5
Contra 145, 152, 154–5
Contreras, Eduardo 147
Convention on the Elimination of All Forms of Discrimination against Women (CEDAW) 179
Coordinating Committee for Multilateral Export Controls (COCOM) 134, 136
Costa, Ettore 53
Council for Mutual Economic Assistance (CMEA) 135, 142
Countercultural internationalisms 228–32
Cripps, Francis 104
Cuban missile crisis 74
Cuban Revolution 15, 71, 143, 146, 153, 157

Dadoo, Yusuf M. 19, 81–4, 86–96
Decolonization 3, 13, 19, 53, 57, 65, 67–75, 83, 85, 94, 130–1, 175, 182
Democratic Party (USA) 99
Democratic Rights Council (DRC) 200–2
Democratic socialists or social democrats 41–2, 47–50, 53, 58, 107, 109, 121–2, 160–5
Den Uyl, Joop 106, 162
Destalinization 67, 78
Development Alternatives for Women for a New Era (DAWN) 175–9, 181–3, 185–8
Devin, Guillaume 98, 111
Dimitrov, Georgi 86, 89–92
DNA (Norwegian Labour Party) 40–1, 50
Donau, Willy 121
Dutch Labour Party (PvdA) 106

Economic and Social Commission for Asia and the Pacific (ESCAP) 184
Economic and Social Council (ECOSOC) 106, 140

Index

Ehmke, Horst 166
Eisenhower, Dwight 197–200, 202
Encuentros Feministas Latinoamericanos y del Caribe 175, 179, 184
Espionage Act 192, 196
Esquipulas Accords 154
Eurocommunism 15
European Convention on Human Rights (ECHR) 162
European Economic Community (EEC) 72, 111, 134–5

Farabundo Martí National Liberation Front 150
Faulkner, Arthur J. 169
Fauquet, Georges 119
Faure, Edgar 198
Faure, Paul 127
Federal Bureau of Investigation (FBI) 45–6, 191, 193, 196–8
Feminist economics 185–7
Figueres, José 148
Finnish labour movement 44
First World Congress of Peace in Moscow 92
First World War 2–3, 9–11, 18, 26, 115, 119
Fonseca, Carlos 146–7
Foreign Nationalities Branch (FNB) 46–7
Fourier, Charles 7
Frankfurt congress and Frankfurt Declaration of the Socialist International 1951 55–9
Fraser, Donald 165–7
French Communist Party (PCF) 70–1, 75, 79, 209, 213
French Revolution 7
French Section of the Workers' International (FSWI) 116, 120, 124, 127
French Socialist Party (PS) 19, 51, 98, 121, 166
Frente Interno de Resistencia (FIR) 146
Frente Sandinista de Liberación Nacional (FSLN) 20, 143–8, 150–6
Fuchs, Klaus 195, 198
Fuss, Henri 126

G77 100, 180
Gaitskell, Hugh 63
Gaulle, Charles de 71, 166
General Confederation of Labor (CGT, France) 127
General Jewish Labour Bund 28
Geneva Conference 164
German Social Democratic Party (SPD) 10, 41, 43, 48–51, 99, 162
German Social Democrats 121
Global left-feminist movement 16
Global North 20, 188
Global South 20, 150–1, 167, 173, 175–6, 179–80, 182, 185, 187–8
Globalization 4–5, 8–9, 17, 19, 52, 130, 206, 221, 233, 235–6
Godley, Wynne 104
Gold, Harry 195
Gonzalez, Felipe 99
Gorbachev, Mikhail 151, 153
Gorleben environmental protest 222, 228–31
Grameen Bank 178
Gramsci, Antonio 204
Greek socialism 25, 30–4, 36–7
Green-Belt Movement 178
Guerra Popular Propaganda (GPP) 147
Guevara, Ernesto 74, 147

Harpprecht, Klaus 166
Harrington, Michael 107
Hart, Judith 164–5
Havel, Václav 15
Hawke, Bob 98
Hedtoft, Hans 41, 44, 46–7, 49–50
Heine, Fritz 50–1
Helsinki Conference on Security and Cooperation 163
Herriot, Edouard 198
Hikmet, Nâzım 1–2
Hiroo, Wada 57
Holland, Stuart 103–4, 106–7
Hoover, J. Edgar 192
Human rights 159–71
Humphrys, Elizabeth 98
Hungarian Revolution (1956) 51–2, 83

Imlay, Talbot C. 5–6, 53, 101, 160
Independent Social Democratic Party of Germany 124

India, communist party 56–7
    Praja Socialist Party 64
Indonesia, communist party 58
Indovina, Francesco 208–9, 215–16
Informal transnational networks 39
Initiative for Political and Social Economy (IPSE) 103
International Association for Labor Legislation (IALL) 117
International Brigades 12
International Court of Justice (ICJ) 152
International Federation for Human Rights 166
International Federation of Trade Unions (IFTU) 124–7
Internationalism
    communist 17, 19
    Flora Tristan's perception 7
    ideological rifts 9
    last wave of historiography 4–6
    'Left' and 'left-wing' 6, 9, 16, 18
    liberal 179–82
    Marxian 8, 10
    and nationalization 11
    proletarian 84–6
    Sandinista 143
    social democratic 14, 171
    socialist 8, 20
International Labor Conference 116, 118, 125–5
International Labour Organisation (ILO) 13, 19–20, 115–28, 138, 176, 184, 187
International League of Women Voters 175
International Monetary Fund (IMF) 97–9, 105, 111–12, 178
International Socialist Congress 121
International solidarity 21, 65, 70, 83, 96, 191, 220
International Women's Year in Mexico 173
International Workers' Olympiads 122
International Working Men's Association (IWMA) 8
Iran-Contra scandal 152
Iranian Revolution 102
Italian communism 68–73
Italian Communist Party (PCI) 15, 19, 67, 70–5, 79, 209, 215
IWY conference 175, 178, 183

Jain, Devaki 175–6, 178, 183, 188
Janitschek, Hans 165
Japan Socialist Party (JSP) 54–60, 62–4
Jewish labour 27

Kalaw Bureau Meeting 64
Kaldor, Nicholas 104
Kaufman, Irving 197
Kemal, Mustafa 2
Khrushchev, Nikita 68–70, 78
Kirkwood, Julieta 185
Korean War 56, 58
Kreisky, Bruno 101, 105
Krieps, Robert 167–8

Laboratório Nacional de Engenharia Civil (LNEC) 214
Laboratorio de Urbanismo de Barcelona (LUB) 211
Labour and Socialist International (LSI) 11, 19, 41–4, 116, 121–6
Lange, Christian Lous 41
Lange, Halvard 41, 50
Larzac struggle 228–31
Laski, Harold 42
Latin American armed Left 143
Lauwe, Chombart de 214
League Against Imperialism 12
League for Industrial Democracy (LID) 45, 51
League of Nations 5, 10, 116, 119, 123
Lefebvre, Henri 206, 210, 215–17
Left-wing town planning 205–17
Leira Sánchez, Eduardo 208
Lemercier, Camille 119
Lenin, Vladimir 11, 82, 85, 92
Leroux, Pierre 7
Lewis, Su Lin 54
Lie, Haakon 41, 45, 50–1
Lie, Trygve 47
Lipponen, Paavo 168
Loeb, Edith 54
Lohia, Rammanohar 56–7, 62
London School of Economics (LSE) 42
Longo, Luigi 70–1, 78–9
López Campos, Julio 153
López, Victor Tirado 146
Lutuli, Albert 93

MacDonald, Ramsay 122
Mama, Amina 188
Man, Henri de 128
Mandela, Nelson 74, 82
Mangada, Eduardo 208–9, 214, 217
Manley, Michael 97–9, 104–6, 109–11
Marx, Karl 8, 33–4, 86, 123
Marxism-Leninism 85, 143, 146, 149
Mauroy, Pierre 98, 111
Maurseth, Per 39
May Day rallies 25, 116, 126
Mayer, Daniel 166–8, 171
Mazower, Mark 8, 176
Mazzini, Giuseppe 7
McNamara, Robert 102
Mexican Communist Party 146
Milhaud, Edgard 119–20, 123
Mitterrand, François 99, 166
Mollet, Guy 51, 63
Molotov-Ribbentrop pact 13, 192
Mosaburo, Suzuki 55–6
Movimiento Nueva Nicaragua (MNN) 146
Müller, Hermann 122

Natera, Gerardo Sánchez 148
National Committee for a Free Europe 48
National Committee to Secure Justice in the Rosenberg Case (NCSJRC) 191–8, 200, 202, 204
National Guard (Somoza) 147–9, 151
National Liberation Front. *See Frente Sandinista de Liberación Nacional* (FSLN)
National Revolutionary Movement of El Salvador 106
Nationalism 2, 10, 26, 28, 32–3, 37, 39, 57, 59–61, 71, 85, 159
Nazi Germany 43–4
Neoliberalism 20, 98–9, 130, 156, 161, 174–5, 180–1
Neuman, Franz 51
New International Economic Order (NIEO) 100–7, 110
New Zealand Labour Party 98, 169
NGOs 17, 168, 171, 175–6, 220, 233–5, 237, 244, 246
Nicaraguan Socialist Party (PSN) 146
Niclas-Tölle, Boris 54
Nkrumah, Kwame 74

Non-Aligned Movement 150, 180
Non-European United Front (NEUF) 90
North Atlantic Treaty Organization (NATO) 49, 132, 236
North-South conflict 18–19, 54, 99–100, 102, 105, 107, 109–11, 130, 132, 170
Norwegian Shipping and Trade Mission (Nortraship) 44–5
Norwegian Social Democratic Labour Party (NSA) 41–2
Norwegian Trades Union Congress (LO) 104
Nuclear energy opponents 219–32
Nyein, U Kyaw 62–3

OECD countries 97, 103, 107, 132
Office of Strategic Studies (OSS) 46–8
Office of War Information (OWI) 45–6
Okeyo, Achola Pala 173
Ollenhauer, Erich 41, 43, 47–51
Organization of American States (OAS) 143, 149, 155
Ortega, Humberto 149, 155–6
Ottoman Empire 18, 25–9, 32–3, 37
'Our Bodies, Ourselves' (Boston Women's Health Collective) 178
Out of Crisis Project 103–4, 106
Owen, Robert 123
Owen, David 162

Palestine Liberation Organization 147
Palme, Olof 98, 101, 109, 152
Papandreou, Andreas 98, 152
Paris Commune 9
Paris Peace Conference (1919) 116, 118
Partit Socialista Unificat de Catalunya (PSUC) 212
People's National Party of Jamaica 106
People's Republic of China, Chinese Civil War 55
Pérez, Carlos Andrés 102, 148, 152
Phillips, Morgan 50–1, 56, 61–2
Picasso, Pablo 2
Pollitt, Harry 89
Polycentrism 67–8, 71
Poole, De Witt Clinton 46–8
Pope Pius XII 198, 202
Portas, Nuno 205, 208–10, 212–14
Portugal, urban planning 205–18

Portuguese Communist Party (PCP) 209
Pottier, Eugène 9
Prague Spring (1968) 15, 79
Pronk, Jan 107
Putzrath, Heinz 49

Rakovsky, Kristian 26, 32
Rangoon meeting 59–61, 63
Reagan, Ronald 97, 103, 144, 152
Revolutionary Communist Youth (JCR) 215
Ribas, Fabra 121
Rich, Harold 200
Río Coco y Bocay 147
Rocard, Michel 111
Rogernomics 98
Roode, Jan de 119
Roosevelt, Franklin Delano 13, 168
Roques, Mario 121
Rosenberg case 191–204
Rosenberg, Julius And Ethel 192–3, 195–204. *See also* Rosenberg case
Ruiz, Henry 146
Russian Civil War 36
Russian Revolution 26, 35, 120

Saint-Simon, Henri de 7
Salazar regime 205–6, 209
SALT agreements 168
Sand, Ulf 104
Sandinista National Directorate 145, 150
Sandinista National Liberation Front 20, 146, 153
Sandinista Popular Army (EPS) 151
Sandinista Revolution 144–56
Sandino, Augusto César 147
Sartre, Jean-Paul 2, 74
Sauer, Arthur 42
Savané, Marie-Angélique 176, 182, 185, 188
Scandinavian labour movement 46–7
Schlicke, Alexander 121
Secchi, Bernardo 208, 214–15, 217
Second International 10, 27–8, 30, 115, 122, 124
Second World War 13, 18, 20, 39, 46, 54, 73, 89, 93, 107, 208, 215, 213
Seiichi, Katsumata 58

Self-Employed Women's Association (SEWA) 178, 183
Shaw, George Bernard 115, 123
Sino-Soviet conflict 67
Social Democratic youth movement in Norway (NSU) 40–1, 49
Socialist International (SI) 14, 19, 39
  human rights 164–71
  monetarism and the economic order 97–112
  non-European members 53–65
Socialist International Committee on Economic Policy (SICEP) 97, 103, 105–7, 109–10
Socialist Party of Senegal 106
Socialist Unity Party (SED, German Democratic Republic) 162
Socialist Workers' Federation of Salonica 25–6, 28–30
Socialist Workers' Party of Greece (SEKE) 26, 34–6
Socialist Youth International 41
Somoza, Anastasio 143–4, 146–50, 153
South African Communist Party (SACP) 19, 81–8, 90–2, 95–6
South African Indian Congress (SAIC) 81
South African Peace Council (SAPC) 93–4
South African Treason Trial of 1956–61 90
Soviet Union 2, 4–5, 12–14, 19, 64, 67–8, 74, 77–8
  Eastern Bloc countries 129, 133–4, 137, 140–1
  proletarian internationalism 83–91, 93, 96
  Sandinista internationalism 144, 146, 150–2
Spanish Communist Party (PCE) 209, 212–13
Spano, Velio 70
Special Operations Executive (SOE) 44
Stalin, Joseph 2, 12, 15, 62, 67–9, 72–3, 75, 95
Stebbins, Henry 201
Stienstra, Deborah 175
Stockholm congress 61
Stoltenberg, Thorvald 107
Stroessner, Alfredo 149
Suez Crisis 52
Swedish Social Democratic Party (SAP) 99

Tadesse, Zenebework 185
Terceristas (Nicaraguan Left) 147–8
Tetsu, Katayama 55
Thatcher, Margaret 99, 103
Thibert, Marguerite 120
Third World
  Italian communism 67–79
  South African communism 81–96
Thomas, Albert 13, 115, 117–22, 124, 127–8
Thompson, Douglas Chadwick 93
Three Internationals Initiative 166
Tixier, Adrien 119–20
Togliatti, Palmiro 67–8, 70–3, 75–9
Topalov, Christian 208
Torres, Hugo 147
Torrijos, Omar 148
Touré, Sékou 71
Transnational activist networks 233–47
Transnational feminisms 20, 173–4, 188
Transnational networks 3, 16, 21, 39–40
Treaty of Versailles 13, 117–18
Tristan, Flora 7
Truman, Harry 200
Tzara, Tristan 2

UN Charter of Economic Rights and Duties of States 106
UN conference on technical cooperation 182
UN Decade for Women 20, 173–5, 177–80, 186–7
UN General Assembly 180
UN Security Council 58
UN's Commission on the Status of Women 175
UNESCO 185
United Nations Conference for Trade and Development (UNCTAD) 105–7, 130–3, 135, 139–41

United Nations Development Programme (UNDP) 136–8
United Nations Industrial Development Organization (UNIDO) 130–3, 136–41
United States
  intelligence 5
  military actions 56, 58
  social democrats 165
  Displaced Persons Commission (US-DPC) 47–9
US-Japan Security Treaty 58

Vanden Abeele, Michel 105–6
Viple, Marius 119, 123–4
Volcker Shock (1979) 97

Warsaw Pact countries 155, 168
Waterside Workers' Federation Film Unit 203
Wellesley conference (1976) 173–4, 184
Western communism 68–9, 76, 78
Wijono 62
Wilson, Woodrow 11
Win, Kyaw Zaw 53
Winter War (Finland) 44
Women's World Banking 178
World Bank 102, 105, 112, 178
World communism 15
World Peace Council (WPC) 86, 92–4

Yalta memorandum (Togliatti) 77
Yata, Ali 70
Yona, Samuel 29
Young Turk Revolution 25
Youth Section of the Jewish Council to Combat Fascism and Anti-Semitism 201

Zionism 28

www.ingramcontent.com/pod-product-compliance
Lightning Source LLC
Chambersburg PA
CBHW062123300426
44115CB00012BA/1789